Jesus the Apocalyptic Prophet

Jesus the Apocalyptic Prophet

*Cecilia Wassén and
Tobias Hägerland*

t&tclark
LONDON • NEW YORK • OXFORD • NEW DELHI • SYDNEY

T&T CLARK
Bloomsbury Publishing Plc
50 Bedford Square, London, WC1B 3DP, UK
1385 Broadway, New York, NY 10018, USA

BLOOMSBURY, T&T CLARK and the T&T Clark logo are trademarks of Bloomsbury Publishing Plc

First published in Great Britain 2021

Copyright © Cecilia Wassén, Tobias Hägerland, 2021

This work is based on a translation by Cian J. Power of Cecilia Wassén and Tobias Hägerland (2016), *Den okände Jesus: Berättelsen om en profet som misslyckades*, Stockholm: Bokförlaget Langenskiöld. The authors have added material for the publication of the English edition.

Cecilia Wassén and Tobias Hägerland have asserted their right under the Copyright, Designs and Patents Act, 1988, to be identified as Authors of this work.

For legal purposes the Acknowledgements on p. xiii constitute an extension of this copyright page.

Cover design: Charlotte James
Cover image © Jesus´ sermon on the mount, graphic collage from engraving of Nazareene School, published in *The Holy Bible*, St.Vojtech Publishing, Trnava, Slovakia, 1937.
© Miriama Taneckova / Alamy Stock Photo

All rights reserved. No part of this publication may be reproduced or transmitted in any form or by any means, electronic or mechanical, including photocopying, recording, or any information storage or retrieval system, without prior permission in writing from the publishers.

Bloomsbury Publishing Plc does not have any control over, or responsibility for, any third-party websites referred to or in this book. All internet addresses given in this book were correct at the time of going to press. The author and publisher regret any inconvenience caused if addresses have changed or sites have ceased to exist, but can accept no responsibility for any such changes.

A catalogue record for this book is available from the British Library.

Library of Congress Cataloging-in-Publication Data
Names: Wassen, Cecilia, 1962– author. | Hägerland, Tobias, 1975– author. | Power, Cian, 1987– translator.
Title: Jesus the apocalyptic prophet / Cecilia Wassen, Tobias Hägerland ; translated by Cian J. Power.
Other titles: Den okände Jesus. English
Description: London ; New York : T&T Clark, 2021. | "An earlier version of this book is published in Swedish: Den okände Jesus: Berättelsen om en profet som misslyckades (The Unknown Jesus: The Story about a Prophet who Failed)." | Includes bibliographical references and index. | Summary: "This book is a reconstruction of the life of Jesus from his birth to his death, with a focus on understanding him in the context of his own time and place. Wassen and Hägerland consider Jesus as an apocalyptic prophetic figure within the context of first-century Judaism. They take a narrative approach, examining Jesus' life in order and draw together the threads of scholarly discussion on the history, archaeology and geography of first-century Galilee into a complete picture of Jesus' world suitable for a non-specialist audience. Together the chapters provide a deeply informed introduction to Jesus in his first-century context. The authors follow a scientific worldview for historical reconstruction, drawing readers' attention to the rhetorical aspects of the texts of the New Testament and problematising these elements. They embed the texts surrounding Jesus in the context of first-century Galilee with historical and archaeological reflections and discussion and, in particular, with penetrating insights from the Dead Sea Scrolls. Illustrated throughout with photographs taken by the authors specifically to offer insights into the world of Jesus and the New Testament writings"– Provided by publisher.
Identifiers: LCCN 2020031017 (print) | LCCN 2020031018 (ebook) | ISBN 9780567693815 (pb) | ISBN 9780567693822 (hb) | ISBN 9780567693808 (epdf) | ISBN 9780567693792 (epub)
Subjects: LCSH: Jesus Christ–Biography–History and criticism.
Classification: LCC BT301.9 .W3713 2021 (print) | LCC BT301.9 (ebook) | DDC 232.9/01—dc23
LC record available at https://lccn.loc.gov/2020031017
LC ebook record available at https://lccn.loc.gov/2020031018

ISBN: HB: 978-0-5676-9382-2
PB: 978-0-5676-9381-5
ePDF: 978-0-5676-9380-8
ePUB: 978-0-5676-9379-2

Typeset by RefineCatch Limited, Bungay, Suffolk
To find out more about our authors and books visit www.bloomsbury.com and sign up for our newsletters.

CONTENTS

Preface vi
List of abbreviations vii
Chronology xi
Acknowledgements xiii

Introduction 1

1 Jesus' birth and life in Galilee 5
2 Judaism in the time of Jesus 29
3 The Jesus of the Gospels and the Jesus of history 61
4 John the Baptist 85
5 The prophet leader 97
6 The kingdom 113
7 In conflict with Satan 129
8 Jesus and the laws 147
9 The anointed one 169
10 The final week 185
11 From a Jewish group to a multi-ethnic movement in the Roman Empire 211

Glossary of names and terms 233
Index 243

PREFACE

We would like to thank our colleagues and friends who encouraged us to write a book on the historical Jesus in the first place. An earlier version of this book has been published in Swedish: *Den okände Jesus: Berättelsen om en profet som misslyckades* (*The Unknown Jesus: The Story about a Prophet who Failed*), (2016) Stockholm: Bokförlaget Langenskiöld. We have received beneficial feedback from colleagues and scholars, which we have taken into account as we thoroughly revised the book for an English speaking audience.

We would like to thank the staff at Bloomsbury T & T Clark for accepting the manuscript and assisting us in the process of finalizing the manuscript, being professional in every way. In addition, we owe our gratitude to Dominic Mattos and Sarah Blake who have been involved in the project from start to finish and offered excellent advice along the way. We have also benefitted from the comments by the three anonymous reviewers, for which we are very grateful. Finally, great thanks to our translator Cian Power. He not only provided a great translation but also shared a good number of insightful ideas with us, which helped to improve the book.

LIST OF ABBREVIATIONS

Hebrew Bible
Gen.	Genesis
Exod.	Exodus
Lev.	Leviticus
Num.	Numbers
Deut.	Deuteronomy
Josh.	Joshua
Judg.	Judges
1 Sam.	1 Samuel
2 Sam.	2 Samuel
1 Kgs	1 Kings
2 Kgs	2 Kings
2 Chron.	2 Chronicles
Ps. (Pss.)	Psalms
Prov.	Proverbs
Eccl.	Ecclesiastes
Isa.	Isaiah
Jer.	Jeremiah
Ezek.	Ezekiel
Dan.	Daniel
Joel	Joel
Zeph.	Zephaniah
Zech.	Zechariah
Mal.	Malachi

Apocrypha or Deutero-Canonical Books

Tob.	Tobit
Sir.	Sirach (Ben Sira)
1 Macc.	1 Maccabees
2 Macc.	2 Maccabees

New Testament

Mt.	Matthew
Mk	Mark
Lk.	Luke
Jn	John
Acts	Acts of the Apostles
Rom.	Romans
1 Cor.	1 Corinthians
2 Cor.	2 Corinthians
Gal.	Galatians
Eph.	Ephesians
Phil.	Philippians
Col.	Colossians
1 Thess.	1 Thessalonians
1 Tim.	1 Timothy
Tit.	Titus
Heb.	Hebrews
Jas	James
1 Pet.	1 Peter
2 Pet.	2 Peter
Jude	Jude
Rev.	Revelation

Dead Sea Scrolls

D	Damascus Document
CD	medieval manuscripts of the Damascus Document

Qumran Cave 1

1QS	Community Rule
1QSa	Rule of the Congregation
1QSb	Blessings
1QH	Hodayot/Thanksgiving Psalms
1QM	War Scroll

Qumran Cave 4

4Q159	Ordinances
4Q174	Florilegium
4Q246	Apocryphon of Daniel
4Q252	Commentary on Genesis A
4Q265, 4QSD	Miscellaneous Rules
4Q266–273	Damascus Document
4Q285	Sefer ha-Milhamah/Rule of War
4QMMT, 4Q394–399	Miqsat Ma'aseh ha-Torah/Letter on Works
4Q400–407	Songs of the Sabbath Sacrifice
4Q521	Messianic Apocalypse

Qumran Cave 11

11Q11	Apocryphal Psalms
11Q13, 11QMelch	Melchizedek

Josephus

Ant.	*Antiquities of the Jews*
Apion	*Against Apion*
Life	*Life of Josephus*
War	*The Jewish War*

Miscellaneous Roman, Early Jewish and Christian Literature

1 Apol.	Justin Martyr, *1 Apology*
Did.	*Didache*
Gos. Thom.	*Gospel of Thomas*
Nat.	Pliny the Elder, *Natural History*

Smyrn.	Ignatius, *Letter to the Smyrnaeans*

Philo

Dec.	*De decalogo*
Hypoth.	*Hypothetica*
Leg. Gai.	*Legatio ad Gaium*
Omn. Prob. Lib.	*Quod omnis probus liber sit*
Spec. Leg.	*De specialibus legibus*

Pseudepigrapha

1 En.	*1 (Ethiopic) Enoch*
4 Ezra	*4 Ezra*
Jub.	*Jubilees*
Pss. Sol.	*Psalms of Solomon*
T. Benj.	*Testament of Benjamin*
T. Iss.	*Testament of Issachar*
T. Levi	*Testament of Levi*

Rabbinic Literature

m. Git.	Mishnah tractate Gittin
m. Pesahim	Mishnah tractate Pesahim
m. Rosh Hash.	Mishnah tractate Rosh Hashanah
m. Sanh.	Mishnah tractate Sanhedrin
m. Yoma	Mishnah tractate Yoma
b. Shabb.	Babylonian Talmud tractate Shabbat
t. Sanh.	Tosefta tractate Sanhedrin
t. Shabb.	Tosefta tractate Shabbat

CHRONOLOGY

Seleucid Rule of Palestine (200–140 BCE)
Antiochus III Megas (223–187 BCE)
Seleucus IV Philopater (187–175 BCE)
Antiochus IV Epiphanes (175–164 BCE)
Maccabean Revolt (168–165 BCE)
Judas Maccabee killed (161/160 BCE)
Jonathan Maccabee (Jewish leader 160/161–142) high priest from 152 BCE

Hasmonean Rule (140–63 BCE)
Simon Maccabee (142–135 BCE) high priest, ethnarch from 140 BCE
John Hyrcanus I (134–104 BCE) high priest and ethnarch
Aristobulus I (104–103 BCE) high priest and king
Alexander Jannaeus (103–76 BCE) high priest and king
Alexandra Salome (76–67 BCE) queen (Hyrcanus II high priest)
Hyrcanus II (67–66 BCE) high priest and king
Aristobulus II (66–63 BCE) high priest and king

Roman Rule (63 BCE–)
Pompey captures Jerusalem (63 BCE)
Hyrcanus II (63–40 BCE) high priest and ethnarch
Mattathias Antigonus (40–37 BCE) high priest and king
Herod the Great (37–4 BCE) king
Herod Archelaus (4 BCE–6 CE) rules Judea, Idumea and Samaria
Herod Antipas (4 BCE–39 CE) rules Galilee and Perea
Herod Philip (4 BCE–34 CE) rules area northeast of Galilee
Roman province of Judea ruled by prefects (6 CE–41 CE)
Pontius Pilate prefect of Judea (26–36 CE)
Caiaphas high priest (18–36 CE)
Agrippa I (39–41 CE) rules Galilee, (41–44 CE) king
Roman procurators (44–66 CE)
Jewish revolt against Rome (66–70 CE)
Fall of Jerusalem (70 CE)
Fall of Masada (73 CE)
Jewish revolts in the Diaspora: Egypt, Cyprus, and Cyrene (115–117 CE)
Bar Kokhba Revolt (132–135 CE)

Roman Emperors
Augustus (27 BCE–14 CE)
Tiberius (14–37 CE)
Caligula (37–41)
Claudius (41–54 CE)
Nero (54–68 CE)
Four emperors in a year (68–69 CE): Galba, Otho, Vitellius, Vespasian
Vespasian (69–79 CE)
Titus (79–81 CE)
Domitian (81–96 CE)
Nerva (96–98 CE)
Trajan (98–117 CE)
Hadrian (117–138 CE)

ACKNOWLEDGEMENTS

Primary sources

All scripture quotations are from the *New Revised Standard Version Bible* (NRSV), copyright © 1989 the Division of Christian Education of the National Council of the Churches of Christ in the United States of America. Used by permission. All rights reserved.

Dead Sea Scrolls

Citations of 1QS are based on:

Charlesworth, J. H., ed. (1994), *The Dead Sea Scrolls: Hebrew, Aramaic, and Greek Texts with English Translations, vol. 1: Rule of the Community and Related Documents*, Tübingen: Mohr Siebeck/ Louisville: Westminster John Knox Press.

Citations of the Damascus Document (CD) are from:

Charlesworth, J. H., ed. (1995), *The Dead Sea Scrolls: Hebrew, Aramaic, and Greek Texts with English Translations, vol. 2: Damascus Document, War Scroll and Related Documents*, Tübingen: Mohr Siebeck/ Louisville: Westminster John Knox Press.

Citations of the War Scroll (1QM) and Miscellaneous Rules (4Q265) are from:

Parry, D. W. and E. Tov, eds (2004), *The Dead Sea Scrolls Reader, vol. 1: Texts Concerned with Religious Law*, Leiden: Brill.

Citations of the Hodayot (1QH) are from:
Schuller, E. M. and C. A. Newsom, eds (2012), *The Hodayot (Thanksgiving Psalms): A Study Edition of 1QHa*, Atlanta: Society of Biblical Literature.

Josephus

Citation of *Ant.* 8.46-48 is from Josephus, *Jewish Antiquities, Volume III: Books 7–8* (1934), translated by R. Marcus, Loeb Classical Library 281, Cambridge, MA: Harvard University Press.

Citation of *War* 6.300-301 is from Josephus, *The Jewish War, Volume III: Books 5–7*, translated by H. St. J. Thackeray (1928), Loeb Classical Library 210, Cambridge, MA: Harvard University Press.

1 Enoch

Citations are from Black, M. ed. (1985), *The Book of Enoch or I Enoch: A New English Edition with Commentary and Textual Notes*, Leiden: Brill.

Psalms of Solomon

Citations are from R. B. Wright, ed. (2007), *Psalms of Solomon: A Critical Edition of the Greek* Text, New York: Bloomsbury T & T Clark.

Introduction

The Jesus of faith and the historical Jesus

'My God, my God, why have you forsaken me?' These are Jesus' last words, uttered while he hangs on the cross, according to the Gospel of Mark. By contrast, at the moment of his death in the Gospel of Luke, Jesus says: 'Father, into your hands I commend my spirit.' Since the two utterances contradict one another, he cannot possibly have said both. What did Jesus really say? Did he say one of these alternatives, or neither of them? As surprising as it may seem, most scholars consider Jesus' words on the cross to be literary inventions of the authors, written in order to provide fitting conclusions to their narratives of Jesus' earthly existence. The theological motifs behind these sayings will be explained later in the book (in ch. 10).

A fundamental principle in historical research into Jesus is that we must approach the Gospels from a critical perspective, just as we approach other ancient literature. Modern historiography, with its requirements for objectivity and fact checking, simply did not exist in antiquity. It was common, for example, for an author to ascribe to characters speeches that he himself composed. The active involvement of gods in human affairs formed part of the world-view of the time; prophets had the ability to discern omens about times to come; people could come back from the dead; and evil spirits caused diseases. The Gospels reflect an understanding of reality typical for the first century, in which supernatural events were possible and evil spirits were driven out through exorcism. Furthermore, the authors do not offer what might be called objective historical accounts. When John explains to his readers, or rather his audience, why he has written his story about Jesus, it becomes clear that his motivation is not to give a historically accurate account of Jesus' life:

> Now Jesus did many other signs in the presence of his disciples, which are not written in this book. But these are written so that you may come to believe that Jesus is the Messiah, the Son of God, and that through believing you may have life in his name.
>
> Jn 20.30-31

The Gospels thus represent ideologically motivated literature, written above all to arouse or strengthen the conviction that Jesus is the Christ, that is, the Messiah. In other words, we cannot read the Gospels as anything near detached accounts; instead, they constitute literary works which offer various portraits of Jesus rooted in each author's distinctive theology.

As is the common procedure of historical reconstruction, this attempt to reconstruct the life of the man from the first century known to us as Jesus will be based on what can be called a naturalistic world-view. This means that we will not assume the existence of angels, demons, spirits, gods or any other supernatural beings, nor will we ascribe any agency to them. Just as historians of the ancient Romans obviously disregard any involvement of the Roman gods and goddesses into human affairs, so do historians of biblical traditions exclude God, the Holy Spirit and Satan as active forces. Hence, we cannot take into account miraculous events in the stories about Jesus – such as that he walked on water or changed water to wine – that are impossible to reconcile with our naturalistic point of departure. Even so, it is not always easy to distinguish what constitutes historically reliable information from what does not, since the evangelists present all the details about Jesus and his age with equal conviction. Matthew tells, for example, of the dead coming out of their tombs and entering 'the holy city' when Jesus died (Mt. 27.53). In the same way, he relates that many women who had come to Jerusalem with Jesus from Galilee looked on from a distance while Jesus hung on the cross (Mt. 27.55). Historians will agree that the former clearly has the character of a legend, but how can we know whether or not the women were there when Jesus died? Here scholars make use of various methods, which we shall look at in greater detail below (ch. 3).

The Gospels were written towards the end of the first century, c. 65–100 CE, and thus a generation after Jesus' death. They were composed by Christ-believers, not by disciples of the historical Jesus (see ch. 3), and at a time when the movement had spread beyond Palestine and small groups of Christ-believers met regularly, for reasons that included holding services and worshipping the figure they saw as their saviour, the risen Jesus Christ. Naturally, the Gospel narratives reflect the view of Jesus that had emerged by the time they were written, and Jesus is therefore represented by the authors as more or less divine. Since we are interested in the historical Jesus, it will be important to scrutinize the authors' motives and environments, and to try to differentiate between traditions that may possibly go back to Jesus and those that arose at a later time. For example, Jesus can hardly have said, 'Is it not written in your law . . .' as he does when debating with other Jews in John (Jn 10.34), for it was his law too; he was, of course, Jewish himself. The phrase 'your law' reflects a time when, by contrast, most Christ-believers were gentiles. For them it was natural that Moses's law was the law of other people, not of Jesus himself.

One of the greatest challenges for us today in getting at the early history of Jesus is attempting to look beyond 2,000 years of Christian history. We need to go beyond the image that has emerged in the church of Jesus as the founder of Christianity. He was the founder of a movement, but that movement was Jewish through and through. Even if it is understandably impossible for us to forget about our own time and history, we can do our best to stop thinking of Jesus as Christian and instead to think of him as Jewish. Only then will we get closer to the historical man. Hence, we will make many comparisons in this book with how other Jews lived, thought and acted around the turn of the Common Era. We will also give some examples of how insights from psychological, sociological and anthropological research can help us to better understand Jesus and the people around him (see chs 5–7).

However meticulously the historian may work, an inherent feature of the enterprise is that we can never be completely certain that the results we arrive at are correct. Even if it were possible to prove that Jesus really did end his life with the words, 'My God, my God, why have you forsaken me?' scholars would still debate whether these words were an expression of deepest despair or of the confidence that comes through in the psalm that the words are taken from. Research into the historical Jesus is not simply concerned with determining which reports in the Gospels contain a kernel of historical truth; at least as important is interpreting the material in its historical context. This does not mean, however, that all interpretations are equally valid or that scholars cannot agree about anything at all. We, the authors of this book, have undertaken research for many years into the historical Jesus and Judaism of his time, using ancient texts in Hebrew, Aramaic and Greek. We have done this in dialogue with one another, with colleagues at our universities, and with countless scholars in other countries. The picture that we offer of the historical Jesus is therefore grounded in current and ongoing international research. Within the context of other scholars' work on the historical Jesus, our reconstruction of Jesus the man is consistent with a widely held understanding that sees him as an itinerant preacher and popular healer who believed in the coming of the kingdom associated with the final age. Nevertheless, scholars often disagree on various issues, including both the specific details and broader outlines of Jesus' ancient religious and social milieu, as well as his aims. Where we adopt a position that differs from the majority view, we inform the reader. In addition, from time to time we highlight debated issues that divide scholars.

No particular prior knowledge is needed to read this book. A number of issues surrounding the historical Jesus are relatively complicated, for example those having to do with how Jesus understood his own role, or with why he was executed. We therefore recommend reading the chapters in the order they appear in the book; it will then be easier to understand the more advanced reasoning of the final chapters. We begin by situating Jesus in his geographical, cultural and religious context and asking what we actually know about Jesus' background, birth and early life (chs 1–2). Afterwards we delve deeper into what sources we have for Jesus' life and into how we as historians can use that material (ch. 3). An important element in the picture we present of the historical Jesus is his identity as a prophet. In several chapters we focus on how Jesus himself was a disciple of the prophet John the Baptist (ch. 4) and how he formed a distinct prophetic movement in which proclaiming the kingdom of God occupied a central position alongside what were understood to be divine miracles (chs 5–7). These activities alone were enough to sow the seeds for conflicts between the Jesus movement and the surrounding society, conflicts which were exacerbated when Jesus found himself involved in debates about how the laws should be interpreted (ch. 8) and as it became clearer and clearer that he had definite opinions about his own significance (ch. 9). We devote one chapter to investigating why Jesus was executed and what we can know about his death (ch. 10). Lastly, although death marks the end of what we can say about the historical Jesus, we offer an account of what happened next: how the Jesus movement transformed into the Christ-believer movement, how within a short space of time a marginal group within Judaism became a multi-ethnic religious movement in the Roman Empire and how Jesus came to stand at the centre of a global religion (ch. 11).

A brief bibliography appears at the end of each chapter, listing books and articles that were particularly important to us in writing it. A glossary at the end of the book explains unusual terms and geographical and personal names, and this is followed by an index of ancient sources. This section is intended to be used as a resource during the reading of the book. Enjoy!

1

Jesus' birth and life in Galilee

Jesus' birth

What do we know about Jesus' birth? Almost nothing. Historical details include the name of Jesus' parents and the approximate date, at the end of Herod the Great's life (d. 4 BCE). What day of the year Jesus was born is not mentioned. The idea that Jesus was born on 25 December is a late Christian tradition linked to Saturnalia, the joyous Roman festival honouring the deity Saturn, which was celebrated at the end of December (Dec. 17–23). More specifically, 25 December was the festival of the birth the ancient Roman sun god Sol Invictus ('Unconquered Sun') and the official day of the winter solstice according to the Roman calendar. Christians appropriated the festival and applied it to the nativity of their Lord, Christ. Besides the indication of date and the name of Jesus' parents, no reliable historical information about Jesus' birth appears in the Gospels. Chronologically speaking, of course, his birth constitutes the event furthest removed in time from the Gospel authors. The earliest preserved account of Jesus' life is the Gospel of Mark, which was written *c.* 65–70 CE, thus roughly forty years after Jesus's death. Jesus was born at least thirty years earlier. Since the birth narratives occur only in Matthew and Luke, which may have been written in the 80s, they were written down nearly ninety years after Jesus' birth (6–4 BCE). We may assume that Jesus' origins first became important when Jesus came to be regarded as a divine figure, which happened gradually. In other words, at a much later date Christ-believers speculated about the miracles that must have taken place in connection with his birth, as with the births of other great men that were accompanied by signs, such as celestial events and extraordinary dreams. Here we may mention legends about Alexander the Great, whose mother Olympias, according to Plutarch, dreamt that a ball of fire entered her body when she conceived Alexander. The births of both Augustus and the mythical Mithras were preceded by celestial signs. In particular, a new star in the sky could signal the birth of a great man.

Matthew's and Luke's accounts of Jesus' birth are also radically different. Although both authors maintain that Mary was a virgin when she conceived and that Jesus was born in Bethlehem, the stories differ regarding practically everything else. It is clear that theological interests steer the evangelists, who want to stress the fact that Jesus was born of a virgin in David's city, Bethlehem (1 Sam. 16). Because they also know that Jesus was from Nazareth they offer varying solutions for how he could nevertheless have been born in Bethlehem. Matthew states that Herod the Great massacred the young boys of Bethlehem and that Jesus' family therefore fled to Egypt, later settling in Nazareth. The massacre is not mentioned in other historical sources; rather it was created by Matthew, who presents Jesus as a new Moses. For Moses, too, was hidden away from an evil ruler who killed all the young Israelite boys. It is evident that the well-known story of the Israelite people's sojourn in Egypt and their flight from that land – the exodus – underlies Matthew's tale of how Jesus fled to Egypt and later returned to Israel (Mt. 2.13–23). Here he wants to show that Jesus' own story in some way corresponds to the history of the people as a whole; Jesus becomes Israel personified. In Matthew's version, then, Jesus' family were living in Bethlehem and Mary gave birth to Jesus at home. According to Luke it was instead a census of 'all the world', that is, the Roman world, that brought Joseph and Mary from Nazareth to Bethlehem, where the inn was full and where Mary gave birth to her son in a stable. Whereas other censuses did take place in the empire, the census which is supposed to have taken place in the time of Herod the Great is otherwise unknown. In addition, the idea that throughout in the Roman Empire people had to make their way to the cities where their ancestors had lived, in Joseph's case around 1,000 years earlier, is, historically speaking, highly implausible and would seem to indicate a fictional account.

Neither Mark nor John addresses Jesus' birth and neither is aware that Jesus may have come into being through the Holy Spirit. In this context it is interesting to note that Paul, too, seems completely unaware of any virgin birth. Rather he states with certainty that Jesus 'was born of the seed [Greek *sperma*] of David according to the flesh' (Rom. 1.3). Paul further explains (Rom. 1.4) that Jesus 'was declared to be Son of God with power according to the spirit of holiness by resurrection from the dead.' In other words, he became Son of God at the resurrection. In Mark's account Jesus receives the title Son of God at baptism when a voice is heard from heaven: 'You are my Son, the Beloved; with you I am well pleased' (Mk 1.11). According to these authors, then, someone can be Son of God in various senses, not just biologically.

We may wonder how both Matthew and Luke can refer to Jesus' ancestors through Joseph and in addition claim that Jesus is Son of God through the Holy Spirit. Yet these apparently contradictory understandings were not problematic as divine paternity was a traditional way of expressing a close relationship between a ruler and the gods without thereby denying the existence of a human father. Traditionally Israel's and Judah's kings were seen as God's special agents, a connection between God and rulers that could be expressed as a father–son relationship. In Ps. 2, a hymn that may have been used in association with a royal enthronement ceremony, God says of the king: 'You are my son; today I have begotten you' (v. 7). The notion that the ruler was in some sense a son of God was a common one in the ancient world. In the Graeco-Roman world, for example, the king or emperor was the son of Zeus (or Jupiter). Likewise Alexander the Great was not only the son of Philip II, but also a son of Zeus-Ammon (according to Plutarch). Since the Roman emperors were declared divine at death their sons became sons of gods as well. Legends also existed about sexual liaisons between a male god and a human woman, and these may have inspired the early Christ-believers as they retold traditions about Jesus. Thus, the mythical hero Hercules was the son of a woman, Alcemene, and the high god Zeus. Suetonius relates that Augustus (Octavian) miraculously came into being when his mother Atia was impregnated by a snake, which in fact was the god Apollo, while she was sleeping in Apollo's temple. Additionally, he had a human father, Octavius. Ideas like these – the king as son of God, divine impregnations – evidently influenced Christ-believers when, long after Jesus' death, they came to interpret and give expression to Jesus' greatness.

After the narratives of Jesus' birth in Matthew and Luke, it is only Luke who mentions that Jesus attracted attention as a twelve-year-old when he was debating with the teachers in the temple during a pilgrimage to Jerusalem with his family. According to Luke, Jesus stayed behind when the rest of the company travelled home and it took the family a day to notice that their son had not come with them. When they eventually find him they are met by a boy who, unsympathetic to their concern, says: 'Why were you searching for me? Did you not know that I must be in my Father's house?' (Lk. 2.49). This is a charming legend which most likely lacks historical value. A hero figure showing himself to be unusually gifted at an early age is part of the common image of an ideal character. The narrative can be compared to how the Roman-Jewish history writer Flavius Josephus (37/38 to just after 100 CE) describes himself as a young man in his autobiography *The Life*. There he states that from when he was fourteen years old the senior priests and other leading men often sought him out to get his advice and guidance in legal matters, which similarly appears fictional.

Jesus' family

Jesus grew up in a small unremarkable village in Galilee of around 400 inhabitants. Coming from Nazareth was nothing to boast about, which John indicates when, on hearing about Jesus, Nathanael exclaims: 'Can anything good come out of Nazareth?' (Jn 1.45-46). The most important identity markers were a person's family and hometown, which is also evident in the standard designation of Jesus as 'Jesus of Nazareth', or in the reference to him as 'Jesus son of Joseph from Nazareth' (Jn 1.45). According to Luke, who also wrote Acts, Paul opens a speech in Jerusalem with the words 'I am a Jew, from Tarsus in Cilicia, a citizen of an important city' (Acts 21.39). In contrast to Paul, Jesus had no important city as his home, although it was very close to the town of Sepphoris. This town, as we will discuss further below, was expanding heavily at the time of Jesus. In spite of his menial background, there is a strong tradition that Jesus belonged to a royal lineage, that of David. Both Matthew and Luke ascribe Jesus with a genealogy that presumes that his father Joseph was of Davidic descent. Although the genealogies differ radically – even by the time we reach Jesus' paternal grandfather, who was either Jacob (Mt. 1.16) or Heli (Lk. 3.23) – they both maintain that the family derives from the House of David. The two genealogies show how important family identity was for an individual's status in antiquity and Jesus' heritage gave him great honour (Hanson and Oakman 2008: 48). As mentioned, Paul, who knew Jesus' family, also takes it as given that Jesus was descended from David (Rom. 1.3). Although one could suspect that the claim of a royal descent was a later invention made up by Christ-believers to support their claim of Jesus' messianic identity, there are several factors that speak against this according to John Meier (1991: 216–19). First, there was a widespread early tradition of a Davidic lineage (se also e.g. Mk 10.47; 12.35-37; Mt. 9.27; Acts 13.22-23); second, contemporary opponents could easily have disproved the claim, had it been false. In addition, the expectations of a Messiah were rather vague at this time, as we will demonstrate below, and a royal descent was not necessary for a person to fit a messianic role. But despite its allegedly noble lineage, Jesus' family belonged to the large proportion of the population that lived in very simple conditions. His family supported themselves through building work. Doubtless, there were some skilled craftsmen and artists of various kinds in the Roman Empire who were able to become wealthy by their craft, but the hometown of Nazareth speaks against Jesus' family having a large income. In ancient society there was a very small, extremely rich upper class, while a large proportion of the population had few resources. Unlike in the Western world of today, the middle class was not especially extensive. Consequently, at the outset Jesus' life was like the lives of the vast majority of people in antiquity. Everyday life consisted of hard labour for all the members of the family, which was absolutely necessary if a household was to survive.

Poverty is a relative term. From a modern, Western perspective, peasants and fishermen might be classed as fairly poor, especially in comparison with the wealthy elite, who were obviously well provided for with slaves and retainers who worked on their behalf. But the peasants and fishermen who belonged to Jesus' circle did not regard themselves as poor, as they could support themselves. Jesus says to the disciples, for example: 'You always have the poor with you' (Mk 14.7). From their perspective, 'the poor' were other people, such as beggars, not they themselves. Jesus was the eldest of several siblings. According to Mark he had four brothers and at least two sisters (Mk 6.3). Although later church theologians tried to interpret Jesus' brothers and sisters as his cousins or as Joseph's children from a previous marriage, there is nothing in the text that would indicate this. Based on the text alone, Mary seems to have had at least seven children who reached adulthood, but there may have been more since the number of sisters is not specified. Such a large number of children was typical for the time, as with most premodern societies before effective means of contraception were available and when women married young and bore children as long as they were fertile. It is estimated that on average families had between six and nine children. In addition to the surviving children it is possible that Mary and Joseph had lost one or more children, as infant mortality was high. The names of Jesus and his siblings are traditional Jewish names – James (Jacob), Joses (Joseph), Judas (Judah) and Simon (Simeon) – that testify to the fact that Jesus was raised in a normal Jewish home. 'Jesus' is the Greek for the Hebrew name Yeshua, which is a variant of Joshua, Yoshua, a common biblical name. Mary's name is Miriam in Hebrew and was the most common name among Jewish women at this time, which explains the prevalence of the name in the Gospels.

Jesus' mother tongue was Aramaic, a Semitic language closely related to Hebrew. The Jews had spoken this language since the end of the exile (from the end of the fifth century BCE on), when Palestine was part of the Persian Empire in which Aramaic was the official language. Jesus' Aramaic shows through a few times in the Gospels when Aramaic phrases turn up in the Greek text, for example 'Talitha cum' in Mk 5.41, which reads: 'He took her by the hand and said to her, "Talitha cum," which means, "Little girl, get up!"' The traditional Israelite language, Hebrew, was preserved by the reading aloud of the Torah and other ancient Hebrew scriptures in the synagogue, though translations of the scriptures into both Greek (the Septuagint) and Aramaic (the targums) were needed. In this period Jews primarily wrote new books in Aramaic and Greek, but also in Hebrew (among the Essenes at Qumran; see ch. 2). Ever since the conquests of Alexander the Great (356–323 BCE), Greek had been the common language of the Hellenistic world which the Romans inherited. Roman officials also used Latin, which can be seen in inscriptions on buildings in Palestine, but the language was not widely known in the land. It is unclear whether Jesus learned any Greek in his small village; perhaps, like many others, he knew a few polite phrases and possibly learned a little more through his work as a craftsman, which we turn to below.

Jesus' life before he met John the Baptist

After the events of Jesus' birth and childhood in the Gospels, Joseph disappears from view, a fact which none of the evangelists regard as meriting explanation. It is worth noting that Jesus is called 'son of Mary' (Mk 6.3) as an adult, which indicates that Joseph had been dead for a long time. He may have been considerably older than Mary. According to Roman custom it was usual for men to marry at a somewhat older age, around thirty, whilst women often married at puberty. Roman custom would certainly also have influenced Jews in Palestine, even though the ideal age for men to marry in Jewish texts is significantly lower. A text from the Dead Sea Scrolls (the Rule of the Congregation, 1QSa) prescribes marriage for men at twenty years but says nothing about the appropriate age for women. The Mishnah, the Jewish legal compilation dating from *c.* 200 CE, recommends that men should marry at eighteen and women at around thirteen, though various opinions are found among the rabbis. The few cases in which a woman's real age at marriage can be calculated in texts and inscriptions from Palestine, however, point to a broad range of ages, from thirteen to much older. Regardless of age, it was considered matter of course that a person should get married. And it was not primarily the individual's own choice that mattered; instead, marriage was a family affair above all. Through marriage, two families were joined together. Marriage between relatives, for example cousin marriage, was also common. In this way property was kept within the kin group. It would have been strange if Jesus, as the eldest son, had not married. But neither the Gospels nor Paul suggest that Jesus was married or had children. On the contrary, he seems to have been completely free both to move to Capernaum, where he stayed with Peter, and to travel around with his disciples. Jesus also preaches about the importance of not becoming tied down, and of leaving everything for the sake of the kingdom of God, even family (Mt. 10.37; Lk. 9.59-62; 14.25-26). Theoretically, it is possible that he was married at some point and later lost his wife in childbirth, although the lack of any such tradition in the earliest texts renders the suggestion highly speculative. Yet in later, so-called gnostic texts traditions do emerge about Jesus being especially close to Mary Magdalene.

In the *Gospel of Philip* and the *Gospel of Mary*, which are both from the second century, Mary of Magdala is the foremost disciple and the other disciples are angered by the fact that Jesus favours Mary over them. The author of the *Gospel of Philip* calls Mary 'Jesus' consort' and relates that Jesus kissed her often, a gesture which should probably not be taken as an expression of a romantic relationship but instead as a metaphor for the transfer of spiritual power. The author rejects belief in the virgin birth and the resurrection. The gnostic branch of the church came to be condemned as heretical, which led to its forbidden texts being hidden, among them the *Gospel of Philip*. The discovery of these in Nag Hammadi in Egypt in 1945 was of great significance for understanding the development of the early church, but they provide hardly any information relevant to reconstructing the historical Jesus. For example, here we find ideas such as that Jesus did not have a physical body, or that he borrowed the body of a human being for a while and later gave it up before the crucifixion. One exception, though, is the *Gospel of Thomas*, which contains early traditions, as we will describe below (ch. 3). In any case, it is worth noting that by the second century there was a branch of the early church in which Mary Magdalene was regarded as the foremost disciple. The small Coptic fragment which has been called 'The Gospel of Jesus' Wife', on the other hand, has proved to be a forgery.

When Karen King, a professor at Harvard University, presented the fragment in 2012, it was news across the world. In it Jesus refers to 'my wife' and even says that a woman may become a disciple. The fragment provoked wide-ranging discussions. Could Jesus have been married? If so, what would it mean for Catholic priests and others practising celibacy on the model of Jesus? The theory that Jesus was married to Mary Magdalene and had children with her gained widespread exposure through Dan Brown's novel of 2003, *The Da Vinci Code*. Was Brown – who had infuriated scholars with his speculative theories and lack of historical knowledge – about to receive support for this theory, which scholars had rejected out of hand? At an early stage, however, many scholars suspected that they were dealing with a modern forgery, although scientific analyses of both the papyrus and the ink had not shown this to be the case. Yet it was a journalist at *The Atlantic Monthly* who succeeded in establishing that the text of the fragment was written in modern times, after tracking down its anonymous owner and investigating his background. Now King, too, concedes that she was duped.

According to Mark, the earliest gospel, written just before the year 70, Jesus was a 'carpenter' (Mk 6.3). The Greek word *tekton*, however, has a broader meaning and includes craftsmen of various kinds, such as builders. It is unlikely that Jesus worked exclusively with wood and what is perhaps more probable is that he worked primarily with stone, the chief material for building, used for houses, walls, olive presses and so on. A few manuscripts of the Gospel of Mark read 'the son of a carpenter' instead, which Matthew, who used Mark's text in the 80s, also has (Mt. 13.55). In fact, both variants may be correct. Because sons often carried on their fathers' professions it is likely that Jesus learned the craft of his father. The fact that Jesus was known as 'the carpenter' offers a clue that he remained in Nazareth for quite some time. Luke states that Jesus commenced his public activity when he was about thirty (Lk. 3.23); perhaps he lived in Nazareth up to that point, practicing a standard profession.

Palestine during Jesus' time: Geography, politics and living conditions

Palestine consists of three main regions: Galilee in the north, Samaria in the centre, and Judaea in the south (see map). The territory is small with a maximum width of about 100 km. Despite its size it contains a rich variety of natural environments, including desert and barren mountains in the south, fertile plains along the coast, highlands with cultivable land in the central areas, and hilly, fertile terrain in the north where the Sea of Galilee, a large freshwater lake, is located. A distinction is usually made between the higher ranges of northern Galilee, 'Upper Galilee', and the lower, southern area, 'Lower Galilee'. During Jesus' lifetime the population of Galilee grew and settlement increased considerably. According to estimates the population doubled between the beginning of the first century BCE and the early part of the next century. The increase was mainly due to the movement of people from Judaea northwards. It was mostly a peaceful time, villages grew and new communities were established in previously undeveloped areas in valleys and along the lake. Two substantial cities were also built, Sepphoris, near Nazareth, and Tiberias, on the Sea of Galilee.

Galilee was ruled by Herod Antipas, son of Herod the Great who was a client king 37–4 BCE and whose family came from Idumean nobles. Herod the Great was of Idumean descent on his father's side (his mother was an Arab) and at this time identity was determined through patrilinear descent. The Idumeans were a neighbouring people who lived in an area south of Judea, which had been incorporated into the Jewish state during in the late second century BCE during the Hasmonean rule, that is before the Roman rule (from 63 BCE). By the time of Herod the Great, the Idumeans considered themselves Jews, but not all Jews accepted them as such according to Josephus (*Ant.* 14. 403), which was an obstacle for the king. Herod sought to strengthen his legitimacy by marrying the Hasmonean princess Mariamne in 37 BCE. He ruled the land with an iron fist and executed many enemies, both real and perceived. He appointed Mariamnes' brother Aristobulus as high priest at the beginning of his rule only to have him murdered shortly thereafter when he had become too popular to Herod's liking. He even had his wife Mariamne executed as well as her mother and much later also their two grown-up sons, because Herod believed they were conspiring against him. This allegedly led even Emperor Augustus to quip that it was better to be Herod's pig (Greek *hys*) than his son (*hyios*). The point is, of course, that Jews do not eat pork. Altogether Herod took ten wives, and Herod Antipas was the son he had with another wife, Malthace of Samaria.

Herod the Great commissioned huge building projects, including the extension and renovation of the temple in Jerusalem, which drew attention and admiration from far and wide. He also had numerous palaces and fortresses built, including in Jericho and at Masada, on a mountain with sheer cliff walls in the desert on the western shore of the Dead Sea. He founded a new city, Caesarea Maritima, in honour of Emperor Augustus, on the Mediterranean coast. This grand city had an enormous artificial harbour, a lighthouse, an aqueduct several kilometres in length, a theatre and a hippodrome. He even had a temple constructed there in honour of Augustus and Roma (the goddess of Rome), as he also did in Sebaste in Samaria and in Banias (Caesarea Philippi) in the north. According to Josephus the temple in Caesarea was adorned with gigantic statues of the emperor and the goddess (*War* 1.414). On Herod's death the kingdom was divided up amongst his heirs under the auspices of Rome. His son Archelaus became ruler of Judaea, Samaria and Idumaea. Interestingly, Herod the Great's sister Salome was given responsibility for a number of cities within Archelaus's territory. Herod Antipas became ruler of Galilee and Perea, an area east of the River Jordan (see map). A third son, Herod Philip, received the large territory east of Galilee. None of the sons acquired the title king, instead receiving the titles ethnarch (Archelaus) and tetrarch (Antipas and Philip). In light of the harshness of Herod the Great's reign, perhaps it should not strike us as strange that turbulent times followed his death. Uprisings in both Judaea and Galilee led to total anarchy, which forced Varus, the Roman legate in Syria, to intervene and send in his troops, who brutally quelled the rebellion. They burnt Sepphoris to the ground, turning its inhabitants into slaves, and crucified two thousand men, according to Josephus (*Ant.* 17. 289-296). Because of Archelaus's weak leadership he was deposed about ten years later (6 CE). After this Rome assumed control of Judaea with a series of prefects, the most well-known being Pontius Pilate (26–36 CE). Caesarea Maritima became the administrative centre of the Roman province of Judaea, which also contained Samaria in the north and Idumaea in the south.

As in the rest of the Roman Empire, the Roman overlords' primary concerns were maintaining peace within the empire, having strong borders and collecting taxes. Beyond this they did not get involved in internal governance more than was necessary. They also allowed the various peoples of the empire to continue with their religious practices and temple rituals – wary, of course, of incurring the wrath of foreign gods. The Roman prefects oversaw the judicial system and the collection of taxes for Rome, but there was a minimal military presence in the land: the Roman fortress in Jerusalem – the Antonia Fortress – as well as a few local outposts. The largest company of soldiers was in Caesarea, the seat of the prefect. Pilate's presence in Jerusalem at Passover when Jesus was executed can be attributed to the fact that he supervised security at the great pilgrimage festivals, when large crowds posed a constant risk of riots. The greater Roman force was stationed in Antioch, Syria and reinforcements could be summoned as needed, but it was native leaders, priests and aristocrats, who handled most of the administration. The most senior leader in Judaea, the high priest, was subordinate to the Roman prefect. The high priest was responsible for order in Judaea and had at his disposal a large temple guard which served as Jerusalem's police force. He also had the assistance of a governing council, the Sanhedrin. This was made up of senior priests and other prominent men, many of whom were from the aristocracy. Traditionally the high priests had significant power but Herod the Great made sure to limit their authority. He did away with the previous Hasmonaean high-priestly dynasty and appointed new high priests. The Romans were well aware that the office constituted an influential position of power. For that reason they kept charge of the high priest's official vestments, handing them over before the festivals and Yom Kippur, the Day of Atonement (*Ant.* 18.93–94). They also made sure to replace the high priest often so that no single high priest could acquire too much power, which explains the note in Jn 18.13 that Caiaphas was 'the high priest that year'. Caiaphas, though, was the high priest for eighteen years (18–36 CE), which means that he occupied the office during the whole of Pilate's time as prefect. Such a long term in office testifies to the fact that he cooperated effectively with the prefects. In addition, it suggests that Pilate strove for stability in Judaea.

A great deal of respect for Jewish manners and customs was required in governing the Jewish people, who had their own distinctive traditions that many were prepared to defend with their lives. Governing Jerusalem presented a particular challenge because the city, with its temple, was regarded as holy, but the Roman overlords did not always use a delicate touch. The Jewish historian Josephus tells of two riots that took place in Jerusalem during Pontius Pilate's prefecture and which indicate that on a couple of occasions Pilate misjudged the strong religious conviction of the residents of Jerusalem. In one instance, Pilate sent Roman troops into Jerusalem bearing Roman standards. These held deep religious symbolism inasmuch as in war the soldiers of a legion would offer sacrifices before them. Because the emperor's image was depicted on the standards, the Jews probably regarded these as 'idols', which aroused their anger, and many made their way to Caesarea to protest. After first threatening them, Pilate eventually yielded (*War* 2.169–74; *Ant.* 18.55–59). On another occasion Pilate used money from the temple treasury to build an aqueduct. Even though the aqueduct was much needed, the people were opposed to his taking money from the temple treasury that was to be used for offerings. This time, the protest turned violent. Pilate had soldiers dressed in civilian clothing infiltrate the crowd and, at a given signal, the soldiers attacked the unarmed protestors, killing many (*War* 2.175–77; *Ant.* 18.60–62). In general, though, there was little unrest in Judaea during Pilate's prefecture.

Unlike his brother Archelaus, Herod Antipas (4 BCE–39 CE), retained the Romans' trust and was able to hold on to power in his district, Galilee and Perea. Naturally his responsibilities involved getting rid of potential troublemakers and he had John the Baptist, among others, executed, an act, however, which aroused the ire of the people (see ch. 4). John's execution must have shaken Jesus, who came to view Herod Antipas as an enemy, calling him 'the fox' (Lk. 13.32). As a native, Herod Antipas undoubtedly understood the native culture well, but he also understood Roman culture because he had been educated for some time in Rome. He was therefore at home in both worlds. He followed in his father's footsteps, building two cities on the Roman model, Tiberias and Sepphoris. Tiberias, on the Sea of Galilee, was constructed in honour of Emperor Tiberius. According to Josephus, the city was built on a former graveyard, which made people disinclined to move there, as graves rendered a person ritually unclean. As mentioned, Sepphoris had been razed to the ground by the Roman troops in connection with the uprisings following Herod the Great's death, but Herod Antipas had the city rebuilt. These cities had roughly 8,000 to 12,000 inhabitants and formed Herod Antipas's administrative centre, with a military force, scribes and archives, tax-collectors, judges and banks. To begin with, Sepphoris was the capital city but later, around 20 CE, this status passed to Tiberias.

Josephus describes Sepphoris as the jewel of Galilee (*Ant.* 18.27). A visitor today can see the remains of paved roads, colonnaded sidewalks, shops, sewage systems and a theatre that held around 4,000 spectators. There are no archaeological remains, however, from the time of Jesus. In terms of ornamentation and splendour, Sepphoris was overshadowed by other cities like Caesarea and Scythopolis (Beth-Shean) where the vast majority of the population were gentiles. Scythopolis lies 27 km south of the Sea of Galilee and, despite its location west of the River Jordan, was part of the Decapolis ('ten cities'), not of Jewish territory. Here were found a temple to Dionysus, a theatre seating 5,000, Roman baths, public toilets and beautiful paved streets.

Thus, during Jesus' time two new cities were built in Galilee, which required a massive amount of labour. Sepphoris is only about 5 km away from Nazareth and it is possible that Jesus and his brothers worked there on various projects. Some scholars believe that Jesus may have become acquainted with Greek philosophy there, which enabled him to preach at a relatively sophisticated level. This is merely speculation. Even if Jesus did work in Sepphoris, we may assume that he spent all his time at work. Moreover, Sepphoris was a small Jewish city on the periphery of the Roman Empire, not a centre for learned men with a Greek philosophical education. Interestingly, neither Tiberias nor Sepphoris are mentioned in the Gospels, which suggests that Jesus was not interested in preaching in the cities of Galilee, preferring to wander the countryside from village to village.

In Samaria, between Galilee and Judaea, there was a large Samaritan population whose customs and practices were much like those of the Jews. What's more, they spoke the same language, Aramaic, and also considered the books of the Torah authoritative scripture. At the same time, they had their own version of these books (today called the Samaritan Pentateuch) that differed in wording to some extant from other versions. A major difference between the two groups, however, lay in their attitudes towards the temple in Jerusalem, which the Samaritans did not recognize. Instead, they had their own cultic site on Mount Gerizim, which lacked a temple, as an earlier Jewish king, John Hyrcanus, had destroyed theirs at the end of the second century BCE. A deep-seated conflict had existed for a long time between the groups, as the evangelist John points out in a fictive dialogue between Jesus and a Samaritan woman. When Jesus asks for water, the woman responds: 'How is it that you, a Jew, ask a drink of me, a woman of Samaria?', after which the narrator explains: 'Jews do not share things in common with Samaritans' (Jn 4.9). In the parable of the good Samaritan (Lk. 10.25-37) Jesus presents a member of this despised ethnic group as a moral example, which lends the parable its intended shock-value.

Palestine was far from being an isolated Jewish region. It formed part of the Roman Empire and was influenced by Roman customs, traditions and ideas. Popular opinion was divided on the issue of Roman influence and Roman rule. Some Jews, especially among the wealthy elite, were glad to be part of the wider world because it was ideal for trade and communication. By the time of Jesus, the Roman Empire encompassed practically the whole of the Mediterranean Sea and within the empire it was possible to travel around on good-quality roads, to communicate in Greek and to pay with a single currency. Yet other Jews suffered under Roman rule. Taxation was high and the Romans and their deputies had well-established means of administering and collecting taxes. There were various forms of taxation, such as the payment of a certain portion of cereals and other crops; a fixed tax for households, according to number of persons; fees for transporting goods (customs); tax on trade, for example at markets; and fees for fishing rights, etc. The episode in which Jesus calls Levi (Mk 2.14; 'Matthew' in Mt. 9.9) to follow him while he is sitting outside the tax office in Capernaum indicates that Levi dealt with the administration of fishing rights and collected taxes associated with fishing. Luke makes it clear that Levi was indeed a 'tax-collector' (Lk. 5.27). Tax-collectors were widely despised, both because they collaborated with the Romans and because they were known for being corrupt. For this reason they are often mentioned alongside 'sinners' in the Gospels (e.g. Lk. 5.30). We can suspect that a dismal reality lies behind John the Baptist's exhortation to tax-collectors not to take 'more than the amount prescribed', and to Roman soldiers not to extort money from the people (Lk. 3.13-14). Besides the taxes paid to Rome, a tenth of all crops, the tithe, was due to the priests who managed the sacrificial cult in the Jerusalem sanctuary and there was an annual temple tax of half a shekel for every adult male. Josephus, himself a priest from a wealthy family, complains of the heavy taxation of the people during Herod the Great's time and also mentions that officials could demand bribes (*Ant.* 17.306–308). However, it is difficult to determine the economic situation of a given historical period and scholars are deeply divided on the issue. Some point to an economically stable period of widespread prosperity, while others assert the opposite. Interestingly, economic differences between rich and poor at this time are visible not only in the cities but also in the villages of Galilee.

It was among people of modest means in a fairly poor society that Jesus went about his work, and he doubtless found a ready audience for his critique of social injustice and his hopeful message of aid for the poor and outcast. This concern for the poor is clearly evident, for example, in the statement, 'Blessed are you who are poor, for yours is the kingdom of God. Blessed are you who are hungry now, for you will be filled' (Lk. 6.21), as it also is in the promise that 'many who are first will be last, and the last will be first' (Mt. 19.30).

While the majority toiled to pay their taxes, there were groups of bandits who made their living from robbery and various kinds of theft instead. Jesus' parable of the good Samaritan describes an attack by just such bandits (Lk. 10.30-37). There were also political guerrilla groups, which Josephus calls Zealots, who violently targeted Romans and even other Jews regarded as traitors for collaborating with the Romans. These groups were often driven by a firm religious belief that they were fighting for the kingdom of God. Simon, one of Jesus' disciples, was called 'the zealot' according to Luke (6.15). The label may suggest, however, that he was very strict in observing the laws of Moses, rather than that he was a rebel. As mentioned above, Jesus' time was relatively peaceful, but according to Josephus incidents of unrest increased during the second half of the first century under the rule of incompetent prefects. This ultimately led to a major revolt in the year 66 which grew into a full-scale war with Rome, with disastrous consequences for the population. Under the leadership of the general Titus Jerusalem was destroyed in 70 CE, the temple was burnt and large stones from its precincts were pulled down and thrown over the temple wall. These can still be seen today. A large proportion of the population was massacred or taken into captivity.

Daily life and holidays

Trying to grasp how people in Galilee lived at the beginning of the Common Era presents challenges. For a person with access to modern medical care it is almost impossible to imagine what it was like to live in a premodern society, where a long life was far from given and where most people had no choice but to engage in hard physical labour to survive. With nothing corresponding to a publicly funded social safety net, people depended on their families and relatives for survival. Everyone had to help, whether young or old, male or female. Various essential tasks were extremely laborious and time consuming by our standards. For example, it took around two hours for someone to grind enough wheat into flour to provide a small family with bread for a day, though in many villages flour was produced on a larger scale by the use of millstones drawn in a circle by donkeys. Jesus himself uses a striking image involving a millstone in the warning, 'It would be better for you if a millstone were hung around your neck and you were thrown into the sea than for you to cause one of these little ones to stumble' (Lk. 17.2). Textiles were made at home, and it was the job of women to spin and weave the wool. Many small farms were almost self-sufficient, with animals, field crops, and fruit and olive trees. Olive cultivation was the largest industry in Galilee, but the region also produced ample quantities of wine, honey and wool from sheep. From goat's and sheep's milk, cheese and butter were made. Galilee was a fertile region and is described in lyrical terms by Josephus, who speaks of the rich soil and the great variety of fruits grown there, such as dates, figs, olives and grapes (*War* 3.42; 3.517–519). The farmers around Nazareth supplied the townspeople of Sepphoris with their produce, and it was here that the landowners lived who leased their fields to landless tenants. Many of Jesus' parables are taken from the day-to-day business of farming which was familiar to everyone, for example, how only a portion of what is sown yields a harvest (Mk 4.4-9). In a decidedly agrarian society, the regular cycles of nature and its rainy seasons were vital to survival and for smallholders a few bad years could lead to forfeiting a farm. It is no wonder that paradise is often described in images of abundant food and drink, usually as at a banquet, as in Jesus' words to the disciples: 'you may eat and drink at my table in my kingdom, and you will sit on thrones judging the twelve tribes of Israel' (Lk. 22.30).

There were many things that broke up the daily routine of hard labour. On the sabbath, Jews did not work (Gen. 2.2; Exod. 20.8). Instead, it was a day to spend time with others and to take part in discussions about the scriptures read at the synagogue. Days were thought to begin and end in the evening, so the sabbath began on Friday evening and continued until sunset on Saturday. Writers of the first century, including Josephus, Philo and Luke, take it for granted that Jews gathered in synagogues on the sabbath. Services at the synagogue were led by laymen while priests were responsible for the temple rituals. For example, in Mk 5.22 we hear of a certain Jairus who was a 'leader of the synagogue'. New Testament authors presume that anyone who wanted to could participate in discussions (Mk 6.1-5; Acts 13.15), and both Jesus and Paul are said to have taught in synagogues (Mk 1.21; Acts 13.15). Although there were synagogues both in Palestine (where Jesus taught in) and in the larger Roman Empire (where Paul taught in), they partly served different functions. The Greek word *synagoge* means 'gathering' and can refer to a building or to a particular group. In the diaspora there were associations of various kinds based on e.g. profession, ethnicity and cult. Jews formed their associations, or 'synagogues', in Roman cities in order to socialize with other Jews in different ways, including studying the Torah and having meals together (Runesson 2001: 467–70). Other immigrant groups formed similar associations whereby people belonging to the same ethnic community regularly came together. What distinguished the Jewish groups from other Graeco-Roman associations was their particular patron deity, the God of Israel. It was not necessary to have a special building in order to gather on the sabbath. People also met at home in larger residences on the sabbath, as the first Christ-believers outside Palestine did on Sundays. Synagogues in Palestine fulfilled a variety of functions as administrative centres and general public meeting places, and were not only used for religious services. Here people gathered to discuss various issues affecting the village or town.

Synagogues were very different from temples, which were holy buildings and served as centres for sacrificial cults. According to Luke (4.16) there was a synagogue in Nazareth, but no such remains have been discovered in archaeological excavations. Across the whole land, very few synagogue buildings at all – fewer than ten – have been found which date from the first century CE. The archaeological remains of such buildings testify to the fact that synagogues were built with consideration for discussion and interaction. In the synagogue at Gamla in the Golan Heights, north-west of the Sea of Galilee, there are rows of seats along the walls so that participants could see one another well (see fig. 1). The synagogue at Magdala likewise exhibits this architectural layout. In synagogues men, women and children gathered. The story of Jesus curing a woman in the synagogue on the sabbath (Lk. 13.10-17) shows that women were indeed present at these gatherings. There are no archaeological traces of different sections for men and women; rather everyone sat together.

In a story in Luke (Lk. 4.16-21), Jesus reads a passage aloud from the book of Isaiah which he then expounds. Was Jesus able to read? Previous scholarship supposed that Jewish boys learned to read and write at the synagogue and that as a result the literacy rate among Jews in general was higher than among other groups. This hypothesis has been reconsidered. Many scholars today rather believe that Jews knew the texts primarily through oral traditions learned at home and in the synagogue. Jewish boys most likely were not able to read or write at higher rates than others, meaning that at most 10 per cent of the population was literate. A farmer or

FIGURE 1 *The synagogue at Gamla, photo Anders Runesson.*

fisherman did not really need to be able to read. Knowledge was passed on by other means, through practical experience and oral communication. Writing in this period was a craft of its own, by which professional scribes made their living. We may observe that Paul, for one, who had some level of education, makes use of a scribe, a secretary, to whom he dictates (1 Cor. 16.21). Thus, it is very unclear whether Jesus was able to read or not, although Luke is eager to portray Jesus as a learned man (like Luke himself). Nevertheless, it is clear that Jesus knew the scriptures well and could refer to them (Mt. 22.32) and was literate in that sense. But whether he had gained this knowledge solely from memorization of a text or in fact had also read parts of the scriptures, is uncertain and the difference is not that great.

Major holidays provided a welcome break from the routine of work. Those willing and able made pilgrimages to Jerusalem and to the temple to celebrate the festivals with relatives and friends. These were festive occasions when pilgrims partook of meat and wine in large quantities (Sanders 1992: 128–29). The festivals followed the annual agricultural cycle and were originally tied to the various harvests. There were three major pilgrimage festivals. Passover in the spring fell at the time of the barley harvest and the festival came to be associated with the exodus, the flight from Egypt. This was the greatest of the pilgrimage festivals, when Jews from all over the Roman Empire made their way to Jerusalem, as did Jesus also. This is the reason he was there for the last week of his life. The Feast of Weeks (Pentecost), fifty days after Passover, marked the end of the grain harvests, when the giving of the Torah was celebrated. Tabernacles (Sukkot) was held at the time of the grape harvest in the autumn, when temporary leaf huts were erected for workers in the fields. Over time the tradition was associated with the Israelites' wanderings in the wilderness in Sinai.

Disease and life expectancy

As in other premodern societies, long before medical science was developed, serious diseases and sudden death presented a constant threat. Although there were medical experts who sought rational explanations for diseases, the general population regarded diseases as the work of evil spirits, whose attacks they tried to protect themselves from by, among other things, wearing amulets inscribed with special texts and by saying special prayers of protection. Magic, religion (if these can be distinguished) and medicine, including the use of herbs, were often combined in the fight against disease. In the Dead Sea Scrolls we find the names of a number of different evil spirits that caused disease. Among others, the female demon Lilith is named, who in later traditions is associated with the death of newborn infants. Diseases were treated with all manner of remedies of varying efficacy and occasionally with exorcism, which experts like Jesus were able to perform. In the Roman Empire malaria, termed the 'Roman fever', was a major problem. Because the disease is spread by mosquitoes, areas near standing water were badly affected, such as the northern and southern ends of the Sea of Galilee at its inlet and outlet of water, where there were extensive wetlands (*War* 4.456). The disease must also have been prevalent in the areas surrounding the Sea of Galilee, as it was as late as the beginning of the twentieth century. A population that has been exposed to malaria over a long period can develop immunity to the disease, but this in turn is associated with increased susceptibility to other diseases. Those who migrated to the new city of Tiberias, for instance, would have been afflicted with malaria, which may have been a contributing factor in why people did not move there, as Josephus states and as mentioned earlier. By contrast, the highlands were significantly less badly affected by malaria. This holds for Nazareth, which is located far from the lake in the Galilean hill country. Thus, when Jesus moved to the fishing village of Capernaum, he moved to an area where the locals suffered from malaria. High fever is symptomatic of the disease and it is probably this standard presentation of the condition that lies behind the story of Jesus curing Peter's mother-in-law of a fever in precisely Capernaum (Mk 1.30-31). In a few cases, those afflicted are febrile intermittently for short periods. Because the disease can take this course, it is not impossible that Jesus was able to temporarily 'cure' some people who had malaria. There may therefore be a grain of truth in Mark's account of Jesus healing Peter's mother-in-law: 'Now Simon's mother-in-law was in bed with a fever, and they told him about her at once. He came and took her by the hand and lifted her up. Then the fever left her, and she began to serve them.' John likewise associates Capernaum with febrile illness in the story of the Roman official's son who is cured by Jesus (Jn 4.52).

Malaria, which killed one in five, was of course just one of many diseases that afflicted the population. Other diseases, such as dysentery, typhoid, tuberculosis and plague, were also endemic. We get some insight into the average life expectancy of Galilean villagers of Jesus' time from an analysis of the tomb complex at the village of Meiron in Upper Galilee, which contains tombs dating from the second century BCE to the fourth century CE. About half of the 197 skeletons unearthed belonged to children and adolescents, 70 per cent of whom had died in the early years of life (Reed 2014). Infant mortality was extremely high. In cities, where people lived very close together, diseases spread very easily, ironically even at the Roman baths; since the water was not chlorinated, these were not especially sanitary. Traditional Jewish baths, which are small stepped pools carved into rock (see fig. 2), probably also contributed to the spread of disease as they lack drainage systems, indicating that they were not emptied particularly frequently.

Life in antiquity was precarious. A sudden, unpleasant death might befall a person at any time. Without any awareness of bacteria or the spread of infection, it is understandable that people assumed that evil forces were behind disease. As a healer, Jesus thus came into contact with many gravely

FIGURE 2 *Cecilia Wassén at a stepped pool in Jerusalem, photo Jutta Jokiranta.*

ill people and their desperate relatives. Undoubtedly he was also confronted with situations in which those who were ill died and relatives were in mourning, although we do not hear about these cases in the Gospels (in these, by contrast, he brings dead people back to life). Like others, Jesus associated diseases with evil spirits, which for their part, were supposed to be in the service of the overarching evil power. Casting out evil spirits was therefore a battle against the devil himself, as Jesus says to a woman who had been suffering from back pain, whom he cured according to Luke: 'Ought not this woman, a daughter of Abraham whom Satan bound for eighteen long years, be set free from this bondage on the Sabbath day?' (Lk. 13.16).

The centre at Capernaum

In Chapter 4, we shall see how Jesus' life gained new direction from his encounter with John the Baptist. After his time with John, Jesus returned to Galilee and settled in Capernaum, a fishing village on the north-western shore of the Sea of Galilee, which then became the centre of his activity (Mk 2.1; Mt. 4.13). Although the evangelists call Capernaum a city, extensive archaeological excavations have shown that it was in fact a fairly small community with around 600 to 1,500 inhabitants. There is no trace here of the paved streets with colonnades, the administrative buildings, the parade or the theatre that one might find in a major city. Nor were there any drains or aqueducts supplying running water to the houses. The city was not laid out like a Roman city with straight streets of pavestones, but had evolved gradually and was characterized by small winding streets and narrow alleys (Crossan and Reed 2001: 118–28). The building style was typical of Jewish villages in the region, where people lived very close together and not on the farmland outside the village.

Archaeologists have not uncovered a town square for shops or markets. Fish and vegetables were probably sold from stalls by the water instead. The scant finds of high-quality pottery and glass may indicate that few wealthy individuals lived in Capernaum. Nor have any stepped pools been found, although people would have been able to wash themselves in the lake nearby (Lev. 15.13). Stone vessels, on the other hand, were indeed found, which are characteristic of Jewish settlements. Scholars in general assume that these vessels were popular because they were considered insusceptible to ritual impurity in accordance with later rabbinic sources (Adler 2013; on ritual purity see below ch. 2). Yet in light of the absence of early literary evidence for this position a few scholars suggest there may have been other reasons for their popularity, such as practical reasons, or as markers of Jewish identity (Miller 2015: 153–83; Wassén 2019). The simple houses often comprised one or two rooms with a courtyard enclosed by a wall. As in other villages, these habitations were often extended with the addition of further rooms and storage when relatives and their families joined the household. Most of the household's domestic activities were done outdoors, in the courtyard or on the roof. The roof was flat and consisted of clay supported by wooden beams. This is the kind of architecture described in Mark when he relates that some villagers of Capernaum came to Jesus bearing a lame man on a mat. Because of the crowd, they could not get near him and had to 'remove the roof' and 'dig through' it before they could lower him down (Mk 2.4). In Luke the same event is described in different terms; they let the man down 'through the tiles' of the roof (Lk. 5.19), which surely reflects Luke's surroundings but does not fit with buildings in Capernaum. A visitor to Capernaum today can see the purported site of Peter's house. According to the Franciscan archaeologists who excavated the site, there was a house church built there in the fourth century, which a century later was extended into an octagonal church. Christian graffiti in the house church shows that the place was a destination for pilgrims.

Many villagers subsisted by fishing, for which the north-western part of the lake with its gently-inclining shores was ideal. Hot springs nearby that drew fish in the winter meant that fishing could continue all year. There was also year-round fishing further to the north at Bethsaida (meaning 'house of fishing') where the River Jordan flows into the lake. Fish were plentiful in the lake, but as a rule fishermen did not grow wealthy from their trade because they had to pay high fees for fishing rights. Nevertheless, there was a big difference in income between those who owned the equipment, that is, the boats and nets of various kinds, and the hired labourers. Simon Peter and his brother Andrew, who lived in Capernaum (Mk 1.29), were fishermen. In the scene presented in Mark, they were fishing when Jesus saw them:

> As Jesus passed along the Sea of Galilee, he saw Simon and his brother Andrew casting a net into the lake – for they were fishermen. And Jesus said to them, 'Follow me and I will make you fish for people.' And immediately they left their nets and followed him.
>
> Mk 1.16-18

Throwing circular cast nets into shallow water was a simple fishing technique that did not require a boat or additional men. Mark continues:

> As he went a little farther, he saw James son of Zebedee and his brother John, who were in their boat mending the nets. Immediately he called them; and they left their father Zebedee in the boat with the hired men, and followed him.
>
> Mk 1.19-20

Although the action of this story is clearly quite simplistic, Mark gives some idea of how fishing worked and of the disciples' background. Evidently the sons of Zebedee came from a fairly well-off family, as their father owned his boat and could hire labourers. The scholar John Kloppenborg has attempted to calculate the income level of fishermen in the time of Jesus and concludes that they belonged to a social class that lived above subsistence, but were not part of the upper class (Kloppenborg 2018).

Incredibly, a boat from the first century CE has survived, having been preserved in the clayey bottom of the lake, and hence we know something about these simple boats, which were equipped with sails and oars (see fig. 3). Unlike in modern fishing techniques, nets were not dropped very deep. Instead, fishermen stayed near land where they could catch fish and draw them in with nets while standing on the shore. A boat was needed to set the net out some distance from shore. Later, the fishermen could draw in the net from the shoreline, bringing in the catch. This is the image that Jesus uses when he describes the last judgement:

> Again, the kingdom of heaven is like a net that was thrown into the sea and caught fish of every kind; when it was full, they drew it ashore, sat down, and put the good into baskets but threw out the bad. So it will be at the end of the age. The angels will come out and separate the evil from the righteous and throw them into the furnace of fire, where there will be weeping and gnashing of teeth.
>
> Mt. 13.47-50

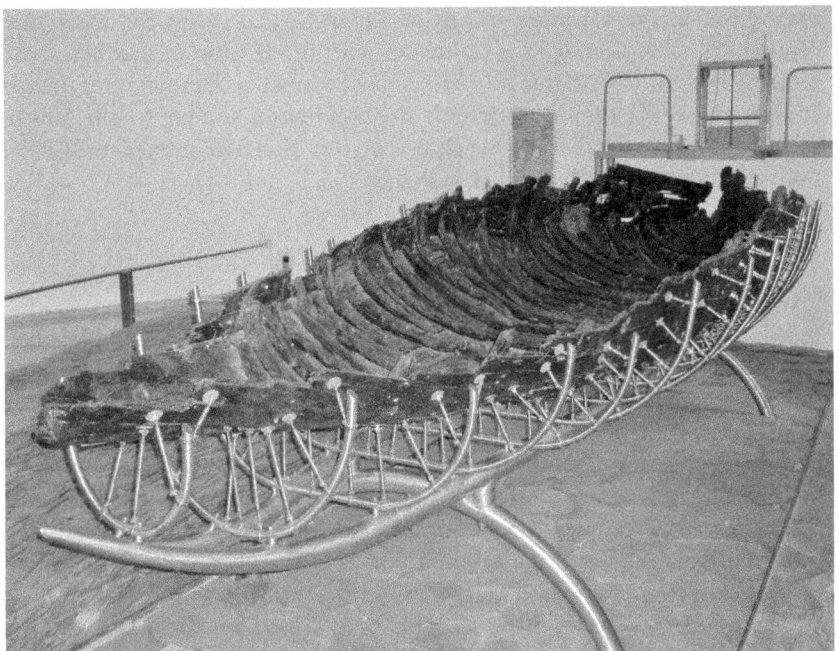

FIGURE 3 *Ancient boat from Galilee, photo Cecilia Wassén..*

Several of the miracle stories involve fish (the feedings of the multitudes in Mk 6.30-44; 8.1-10; the risen Jesus eating fish in Lk. 24.42; the miraculous catch in Jn 21.1-14), which reflects an environment in which fishing was part of everyday life.

In the Gospels, we find references to a synagogue in Capernaum (Mk 1.21; Lk. 7.5; Jn 6.59), and there is no reason to doubt this information. But scholars debate whether the remains of a first-century synagogue have in fact been found (Mattila 2015). There is a monumental synagogue building in white limestone, which scholars have dated variously to the third, fifth or sixth century CE. Interestingly enough, underneath it are some remains of a pavement and an outer wall made of the local stone, black basalt. One theory identifies at least part of these structures as belonging to a first-century synagogue (Runesson 2007). If so, the first synagogue would have been much smaller than the later monumental one, but still substantially larger than an ordinary house. Other scholars disagree, including Jodi Magness, who instead argues that the basalt remains are part of the foundations of the later synagogue (Magness 2001).

According to Luke, the officer whose servant Jesus cured donated money for the building of the synagogue in Capernaum (Lk. 7.5). Although it may seem unlikely that a Roman officer would have sponsored the building of a synagogue in a small village, it is not impossible. In comparison, an inscription in the Galilean village of Kefar Othnay from the early third century CE is dedicated to a centurion who funded the mosaic floor of a meeting hall for Christians. If Luke's note is correct, it demonstrates that the system of benefaction was current in Capernaum similar to the Roman society in general whereby wealthy patrons donated money to various public buildings, temples and synagogues.

Summary

In this chapter we have looked at what daily life in Galilee might have been like in antiquity and we have given some account of its geography and of the prevailing political situation. We noted that the accounts of Jesus' birth in Matthew and Luke differ substantially and reflect late traditions with little historical value for determining Jesus' origins. Both of these Gospel authors attempt to tie Jesus to the Davidic lineage through Joseph while claiming divine paternity through divine conception. By contrast, neither Paul nor the other Gospels mention any virgin birth. Historically speaking, Jesus was most likely both born and raised in Nazareth. This small village in the Galilean hills was fairly close to Sepphoris, which was being rebuilt, and where Jesus and his brothers may have carried out construction work.

Life for common people was hard and most people spent their days performing manual labour to feed the family and keep the tax-collectors at bay. Nevertheless, Jews refrained from working on the sabbath, getting one weekly day of rest. On the sabbath many Jews listened to and discussed authoritative texts from the Torah and other scriptures. Some Jewish villages such as Magdala possessed public buildings for these and other gatherings, but others did not. In contrast to the Jerusalem temple, the synagogue was run by lay people and services did not involve any sacrifices, which was otherwise the usual way of maintaining a good relationship with the gods in antiquity.

Infant mortality was high and diseases of various kinds were common, particularly in crowded cities and close to standing water. At a time when there were few effective medical remedies for illnesses and little to no knowledge about the transmission of contagious diseases, evil spirits were blamed for all these ills. A popular healer such as Jesus would have been very busy.

Whereas Herod the Great had ruled the whole area of Palestine as a client king of the Romans, following his death in 4 BCE the country was divided into several administrative regions governed by his sons. Archelaus, who ruled over the province of Judaea, was removed in 6 CE after his unsatisfactory handling of an uprising. From this time on the Roman state ruled the province directly through prefects. Herod Antipas, by contrast, was successful – from the Roman point of view – in governing Galilee and Perea and remained in power. We saw that the Roman government had no qualms about brutally quelling rebellions and it is therefore not surprising that, in proclaiming their bold messages, popular preachers like John the Baptist and Jesus were risking their lives. The Roman prefect and his government worked closely with the priestly authorities in Jerusalem. They shared the same ultimate goal: peace and stability in the land. In the next section we will focus more closely on Judaism in Palestine so that we may understand Jesus' message and the controversies he was involved in, in light of the currents in religious life and thought of the first century.

Bibliography

Adler, Y. (2013), 'Purity in the Roman Period', in *The Oxford Encyclopedia of the Bible and Archaeology*, vol. 2, 240–9, New York: Oxford University Press.

Crossan, J. D. and J. L. Reed (2001), *Excavating Jesus: Beneath the Stones, Behind the Texts*, New York: Harper One.

Duling, D. G. (2003), *The New Testament: History, Literature, and Social Context*, 4th edn, London: Wadsworth.

Fiensy, D. A. and J. R. Strange, eds (2014–15), *Galilee in the Late Second Temple and Mishnaic Periods*, 2 vols., Minneapolis: Fortress Press.

Fredriksen, P. (1999), *Jesus of Nazareth, King of the Jews: A Jewish Life and the Emergence of Christianity*, New York: Vintage Books.

Freyne, S. (2004), *Jesus A Jewish Galilean: A New Reading of the Jesus-story*, London: T&T Clark.

Hanson, K. C. and D. E. Oakman (2008), *Palestine in the Time of Jesus: Social Structures and Social Conflicts*, 2nd edn, Minneapolis: Fortress.

Ilan, T. (1996), *Jewish Women in Greco-Roman Palestine*, Peabody: Hendrickson.

Kloppenborg, J. (2018), 'Jesus, Fishermen and Tax Collectors: Papyrology and the Construction of the Ancient Economy of Roman Palestine', *Ephemerides Theologicae Lovanienses*, 94 (4): 571–99.

Magness, J. (2001), 'The question of the Synagogue: The Problem of Typology', in A. J. Avery-Peck and J. Neusner (eds), *Judaism in Late Antiquity, Part 3, Where We Stand: Issues and Debates in Ancient Judaism*, vol. 4. *The Special Problems of the Synagogue*, 1–48, Leiden: Brill.

Mattila, Sh. L. (2015), 'Capernaum, Village of Nahum, From the Hellenistic to Byzantine Times', in D. A. Fiensy and J. R. Strange, (eds), vol. 2, *Galilee in the Late Second Temple and Mishnaic Periods*, 217–57, Minneapolis: Fortress.

Miller, S. S. (2015), *At the Intersection of Texts and Material Finds: Stepped Pools, Stone Vessels, and Ritual Purity among the Jews of Roman Galilee*, Göttingen: Vandenhoeck & Ruprecht.

Reed, J. L. (2000), *Archaeology and the Galilean Jesus: A Re-examination of the Evidence*, Harrisburg, PA: Trinity Press.

Reed, J. L. (2014), 'Mortality, Morbidity, and Economics in Jesus' Galilee', in D. A. Fiensy and J. R. Strange (eds), vol. 1, *Galilee in the Late Second Temple and Mishnaic Periods*, 242–52, Minneapolis: Fortress Press.

Runesson, A. (2001), *The Origins of the Synagogue: A Socio-Historical Study*, Stockholm: Almqvist & Wiksell.

Runesson, A. (2007), 'Architecture, Conflict, and Identity Formation: Jews and Christians in Capernaum From the First to the Sixth Century', in J. Zangenberg, et al. (eds), *Religion, Ethnicity, and Identity in Ancient Galilee: A Region in Transition*, 231–57, Wissenschaftliche Untersuchungen zum Neuen Testament 210, Tübingen: Mohr Siebeck.

Runesson, A. (2014), 'Saving the Lost Sheep of the House of Israel: Purity, Forgiveness, and Synagogues in the Gospel of Matthew', *Melilah Manchester Journal of Jewish Studies*, 11: 8–24.

Sanders, E. P. (1992), *Judaism: Practice and Belief 63 BCE-66 CE*, London: SCM Press.

Wassén, C. (2019), 'Stepped Pools and Stone Vessels: Rethinking Jewish Purity Practices in Palestine', *Biblical Archaeological Review*, July/August/September/October: 53–8.

2

Judaism in the time of Jesus

Religion – A way of life

In modern descriptions of ancient society, the term 'religion' is something of an anachronism. What we today call 'religion' was fully integrated into society and not a distinct part of life. Nor was there a Greek term corresponding to our 'religion'. It was common knowledge that gods controlled major events in the world and guarded cities as well as human beings, and this fact about how reality was constituted seemed quite natural. Thus, belief in the god or gods was not much of an issue. People knew that the gods were extremely powerful and that they should honour the gods and live according to their will, which was made known in laws and traditions.

Jews believed, as did others, that humanity's relation to the deity was defined by submission and obedience. But they differed from other ethnic groups in worshipping only one god, the god of Israel. It was natural that the Jewish people should live by their own traditions, just as other peoples lived by theirs. The Pentateuch tells of how God gave his laws to the people through Moses. Yet it was perhaps not chiefly the fact that the commandments were in the Scriptures that led that people to live by them. It was mostly a matter of living by manners and customs one had learnt since childhood, that is to say, the cultural system into which a person had been socialized. For example, abstaining from pork and shellfish was probably not primarily driven by the fact that according to Lev. 11 these were prohibited foods. Rather it was because not eating these animals seemed self-evident to Jews, presumably as not eating bats did, which was also forbidden (Exod. 11.19). Not working on the sabbath, which lasted from Friday evening to Saturday evening, was likewise a given. Practically all Jews in Palestine followed certain customs and manners that were distinctive of their identity. Hence, almost no pig bones, for example, are found in areas inhabited by Jews, in contrast to communities in Palestine with other occupants. At the same time, it is a formidable task to reconstruct early Judaism out of various and often diverse textual and archaeological sources. We should recall that, as in all historical reconstructions, we are dealing with degrees of plausibility and few certainties.

What, then, may we say about shared beliefs and traditions that appear to have been especially characteristic of Judaism in the time of Jesus? Overall, Jews supported the temple and its priests through the tithe and the temple tax, abstained from work on the sabbath, practised various purity rules, had special dietary regulations, and circumcised newborn boys on the eighth day. They worshipped just one god, Yahweh, who was known for being a jealous god (Exod. 20.5; 34.14). Even so, they had no doubt that lesser deities and other supernatural beings existed (Ps. 86.8; 1 Cor. 8.5). As we will explain below, angels and demons were a given part of the universe of the ancient people. Jews were known for not working on the sabbath and for abstaining from pork also in the diaspora. As pork was a delicacy to the Romans, people were amazed by their disgust at it. The Jewish philosopher Philo of Alexandria relates, for example, that he took part in a delegation which travelled to the emperor Caligula in Rome to protest against a pogrom in Alexandria (38 CE), and that the emperor seemed more interested in why Jews did not eat pork than in the massacre (*Leg. Gai.*). Jews believed that their god had chosen the Jewish people from among all others and had entered into a covenant, or contract, with them (Exod 19-24, 34). The covenant stated that God would protect and lead the people, who in turn promised to live by God's will as expressed in the Torah, with various punishments or rewards as possible consequences. This fundamental conception implied that in principle the laws of Moses only applied to the Jewish people, although civil laws, such as the prohibition of killing, applied to all humanity. Additionally there were some further prohibitions, including against consuming blood, that applied to others as well (see ch. 11).

While more or less all Jews followed their customs and manners without further thought, the priests and members of various religious groups were engaged in debates about how to interpret certain Mosaic laws, debates that Jesus also took part in. As we shall see, Judaism was extremely diverse with various factions that held differing opinions on how best to live by laws like the sabbath commandment and the purity prescriptions. How the temple service should be managed was a particularly divisive issue. Since there was just one temple – in contrast to the many Graeco-Roman temples to the numerous gods worshipped within the Roman Empire – there was just one group of priests who got to make decisions about the Jerusalem temple. Even so, other groups held firm views on how the priests should behave, without being able to influence the situation to any extent. In the Dead Sea Scrolls, this frustration is apparent among the group who left the scrolls behind in the caves at Qumran by the Dead Sea and who are usually identified as Essenes. These were especially critical of how the temple was run and accused the temple priests of serious corruption. It is clear that Jesus, too, was troubled by some aspects of the temple services, as he physically assaulted the sellers and money-changers who worked there (Mk 11.15-17; see ch. 10). Still, the temple was extremely important for all

Jews because God was present there in some special way. It was the house of God.

In addition, Jews shared a knowledge of legends about Israel's history as described in the Scriptures, legends they respected greatly. Although most people were unable to read, as children they became familiar with tales about the patriarchs Abraham, Isaac and Jacob and his twelve sons, about the matriarchs Sarah, Rebecca, Rachel and Leah, and about kings and prophets from Israel's past. They were also proud of the heroes of old. Jesus refers to these occasionally, as when he is arguing, against the Sadducees, that there is a resurrection after death:

> And as for the dead being raised, have you not read in the book of Moses, in the story about the bush, how God said to him, 'I am the God of Abraham, the God of Isaac, and the God of Jacob'? He is God not of the dead, but of the living; you are quite wrong.
>
> Mk 12.26

Most of the Scriptures had been around for several centuries by the time Jesus was growing up. The traditional stories from the Torah were read aloud in synagogues, and Jews were in general thoroughly well-versed in their history. The narratives about the patriarchs and Moses were very popular, being retold again and again. In the course of time, new material was added and a great deal was changed. Many Jews were also engaged in actively interpreting the traditional material in light of their own particular theology and setting. In addition, some Jews claimed to have received divinely inspired interpretations of the Scriptures, while others asserted that they had the ability to present new revelations from God. This engagement with scriptural traditions and claims of divine inspiration resulted in extensive literary production among Jews during the centuries around the turn of the Common Era. This literature, which was never included in the corpus that would become the Hebrew Bible, is collectively known as pseudepigrapha, meaning 'false title', because the authors did not use their own names but instead attributed their works to heroes of the past like Abraham or Moses. As these texts were not included in the canon they were largely forgotten about and are not widely known today. In Jesus' time, though, several of them were well known, including the book of *Jubilees* and the books of Enoch. First Enoch, for instance, contains elaborate speculations about the myth of the angels who lay with human women (Gen. 6.1-5) and is even cited in the New Testament (Jude 14–15), which testifies to its popularity. Besides these, there are the Apocrypha, which are books that are included in many Christian Bibles, often in a separate section to the Old and New Testaments. All together this rich Jewish literature bears witness to the fact that Jews kept their ancient traditions alive, while these also inspired new tales and legends of a religious nature.

Jesus the Jew

Was Jesus the founder of Christianity, as we sometimes hear? Yes and no. Jesus worked within Judaism and did not establish a new religion. The movement that he started did in time separate from Judaism, but that occurred much later. Even as late as the fifth century, bishops were warning their congregants not to visit the synagogue on the sabbath. It should go without saying that Jesus was born and died a Jew, but since the Jesus movement developed into a global Christian religion, this fact has often been neglected. In an effort to correct this ignorance, Geza Vermes made strong point about Jesus' Jewish identity in his book from 1973 labelled *Jesus the Jew*. This fact still needs to be stressed.

We can point to various situations that show that Jesus acted in accordance with the same traditions as his countrymen and shared their Jewish worldview. Like other Jews, Jesus went to the synagogue on the sabbath (Mk 1.21-28). He made a pilgrimage to Jerusalem together with other Galileans at Passover. He assumed that sacrificing an animal was necessary when someone recovered from a serious skin disease ('leprosy'; Mk 1.40-45; cf. Lev. 13), and he showed great respect for the temple as God's special abode (Mt. 23.21). In line with traditional Jewish theology, he preached about a merciful God who forgave sins (Mt. 6.12; Lk. 11.4; cf. Pss. 86.15; 116.5) and took for granted that the Jewish scriptures were authoritative (Mk 2.25-26; Lk. 22.43). His main message was about the coming kingdom of God – a time when God would rule over humanity in some tangible way (see ch. 6) – which is a concept that can only be understood with reference to the contemporary Jewish world-view.

That Jesus' speech and behaviour should fit with his Jewish context is a basic criterion for determining whether a given tradition about Jesus in the Gospels may be at all historical, as we discuss in Chapter 3. At the same time, Jesus was someone who set himself apart in his society and protested against certain social norms through his words and actions, much like other founders of new movements. Part of the role of such vibrant, fearless individuals is to criticize the prevailing system and demand change, as Siddhartha Gautama (the Buddha) and Mohandas ('Mahatma') Gandhi did. What Jesus took issue with, however, was not the Jewish laws, as Christians later would, but with rulers who took advantage of their position of power and with the strong who oppressed the weak. His call for people to live by God's commandments and look after their neighbours (see, for example, Lk. 10.25-37 on the good Samaritan) recalls the speeches in the Prophets about social justice and obedience to God. His announcement of the coming kingdom of God was radical and subversive in nature – family was unimportant (Mk 3.31-35; 10.28-31), the first would be last (Mk 10.17-27, 42-44), the temple would fall and the Son of Man would come on the clouds of heaven (Mk 13). It was this radical, uncompromising element in his message that made the authorities nervous and ultimately led to his execution. But the message was Jewish through and through.

The sanctuary

The Jerusalem sanctuary plays a central role in the Gospel narratives. According to Luke, it was here that Zechariah, the father of John the Baptist, received a revelation. Jesus acted violently in the temple when he drove out the sellers and money-changers, but he would have preached there too (Mk 11.15-17; 12.35). What kind of institution was it and why was it holy?

The temple in Jerusalem had been the central religious institution in Palestine for centuries. The first temple was destroyed in 587/586 BCE by Babylonian forces, to be rebuilt at the end of the same century when that empire was conquered by the Persians. The Jerusalem sanctuary of Jesus' time was a magnificent building; Herod the Great had had it enlarged and richly adorned with marble and gold, and it was known far and wide (see fig. 4). The temple and its forecourts constituted the largest religious structure in the Roman Empire outside Egypt. The spontaneous remark made by one of the disciples as they leave the sanctuary during Jesus' final week – 'Look, Teacher, what large stones and what large buildings!' (Mk 13.1) – conveys the sense of amazement that would have been typical of how a visitor of ancient times reacted on seeing the structure. Jesus' prediction that 'not one stone will be left here upon another; all will be thrown down' (Mk 13.2) must have been hard to imagine. Herod's ambitious renovation and expansion of the sanctuary was only completed in the 60s CE, when, according to Josephus, 18,000 workers lost their employment (*Ant.* 20.219). Jesus must therefore have seen scaffolding at various locations around the temple when he visited. Even though the Romans burned down the buildings in 70 CE and hurled large stone blocks over the wall, not everything was actually destroyed (despite Jesus' prophecy). The foundations of the area, with its walls and the vaults that support the platform on which the temple stood, can still be seen today. This is the site of the Dome of the Rock and the Al-Aqsa Mosque and the area constitutes Islam's third holiest place. A visitor today will get a sense of the great size of the site, which, with an area of approximately 144,000 m^2, is comparable to about twenty soccer fields. Herod also had an enormous basilica built, a stoa, inside the great southern entrance (see fig. 5). The stairs leading up to this entrance have survived to modern times. The stoa was where visitors could buy animals and grain for offerings and exchange money for the currency valid in the temple, the Tyrian shekel, to pay the annual temple tax.

Visitors in antiquity were not just met with magnificent splendour, but also with loud sounds and strong smells. We can imagine what an absolute throng of people and animals it was. There must have been a great din in the

FIGURE 4 *A model of the Jerusalem sanctuary, photo Cecilia Wassén.*

FIGURE 5 *A reconstructed ancient stoa in Athens, photo Cecilia Wassén.*

sanctuary as the babble from the crowd and the calls of various animals combined with strains of trumpets, choral singing and noise from ongoing building projects. The experience must have been overwhelming for visitors like the group accompanying Jesus, who had come from small villages in Galilee. Of course, there was also a downside to a population centre of this kind that attracted great crowds of people at the holidays. Scholars estimate that Jerusalem had a resident population of between sixty and seventy thousand people, which doubled or tripled during the holidays. This meant that many thousand lambs had to be slaughtered for the festival of Passover. At these times human odours mingled with the smells of animals, smoke from sacrifices, incense and blood. It is no great stretch of the imagination to think that visitors would have been beset by flies and foul odours on hot days in the outer court, which was protected from strong winds by high walls, though in the past people were more accustomed to these kinds of things than we are today. It is probably not an exaggeration to suppose that the priests, who day in and day out handled the raw flesh and body parts of animals in a hot climate in an age before refrigeration, caught bacterial infections. Problems like this are touched upon in the Mishnah, but contemporary literature is marked by great respect and reverence for the holy place.

The architecture of the temple, with its various courts (see Plan 1), reflected different degrees of holiness, with corresponding restrictions on access. The vast outer court was open to all, even gentiles. Only one group, menstruating women, was prohibited from entering it according to Josephus (*Apion* 2.102–105). This large court was a public area where people could catch up on the day's news and gossip or even make their ideas known before a large audience. It was also an international hub where Jews from all over the Roman Empire gathered for the major festivals. It is little wonder that Jesus preached in the sanctuary when he was in Jerusalem (Mk 12.35) – it was like speaking to the whole world. According to Mark, he taught in the temple for several days in his final week: 'Day after day I was with you in the temple teaching, and you did not arrest me' (Mk 14.49). The sanctuary was also a natural place to pray alongside others, as many visitors did in connection with sacrificial worship. After Jesus' death, many of his followers – those who were from Jerusalem and others who moved there – regularly gathered in the sanctuary to preach and pray (Acts 2.46–3.1). Evidently they tended to keep to Solomon's Porch, in the eastern section of the nine-metre high columned hallways that surrounded the court on three sides (Jn 1.23; Acts 3.11).

The temple was the house of God and strict purity rules applied for access to the holy precincts within the outer court. Purity in this context was not about hygiene, but about the ritual status of a person as pure or impure. There were different kinds of impurities. For instance, a person became impure through sexual intercourse (Lev. 15.18) and menstruation (Lev. 15.19); even touching a menstruating woman or her bed resulted in impurity

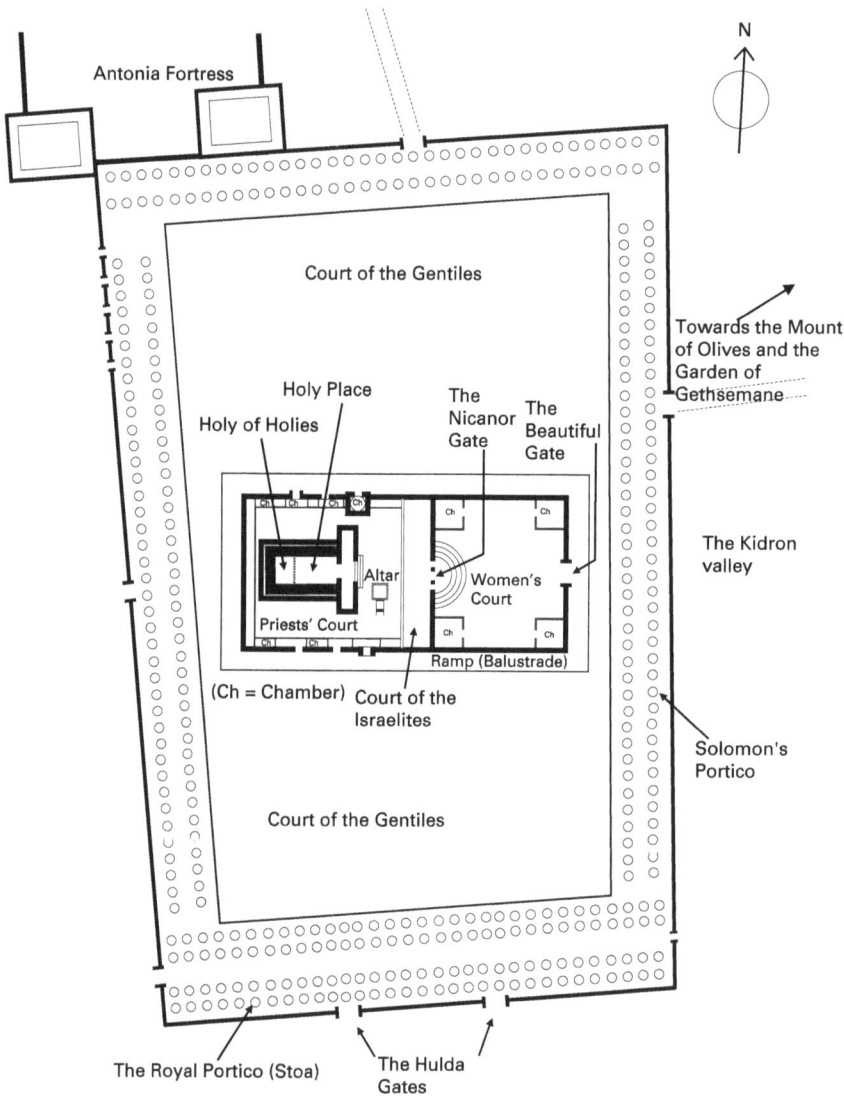

PLAN 1 *The Jerusalem temple in the time of Jesus.* © Dieter Mitternacht.

(Lev. 15.19-24). Discharges from the vagina or penis rendered someone impure (Lev. 15), as did contact with dead bodies (Num. 19) and giving birth (Lev. 12). Impurity was thus a normal part of daily life and not something that needed to be avoided. Quite the opposite – couples had sex, women gave birth and people buried their deceased family members, actions that resulted in impurity. People purified themselves by entering a stepped pool (later called a *mikveh*) or natural bodies of water, like lakes, seas or rivers, and waiting for a certain period of time (see Lev. 15). Additionally, if someone had been in contact with a dead body, he or she would be sprinkled with special water (Num. 19.14-22). For purification of severe cases of impurity, like scale disease (often called 'leprosy'), a sacrifice was also needed (Lev. 14). In Jerusalem many stepped pools have been discovered in excavations south of the sanctuary. Only ritually pure Jewish men and women were allowed to enter the women's court and inside this was the 'court of the Israelites', to which all Jewish men had access. Women only entered this court to hand their offerings to the priests. Around the temple building itself was the court of the priests, which only priests could enter (see plan of the temple). Offerings were burned there on a large sacrificial altar.

Gentiles were strictly prohibited from entering the women's court and violation carried the death penalty. An inscription in Greek warning gentile visitors of this has been found. In a dramatic account Luke describes how Paul was arrested on false accusations of bringing gentiles ('Greeks') into the holy area, which almost led to him being lynched (Acts 21.27-36). Historically speaking, it is difficult to know what happened. In any event, Paul was arrested by the Romans and eventually taken to Rome, where he was most likely executed in Nero's crazed massacre of Christ-believers in the city in 64 CE. The story demonstrates beyond all doubt the sacred status of the temple site and the importance of obeying God's rules in his house.

The sacrificial cult

As we touched upon in Chapter 1, the synagogue was a completely different kind of institution from the temple. In the synagogue people gathered to read and discuss the Scriptures, especially the Torah, and to pray. Worship at the temple, by contrast, consisted of a sacrificial cult in which parts of animals and various produce were offered up and portions of flesh were burned upon the great altar outside the temple building itself, in the court of the priests. Some of the blood was sprinkled on the altar. The sacrificial cult was the basic means of religious expression for Jews, as it was for the other peoples of antiquity. In the modern Western world, it may be hard to imagine that sacrifices in the form of animal parts and agricultural produce could be tokens of divine worship. But sacrifices held a deep symbolism for the offerers and were the normal way of communicating with the god or gods in Graeco-Roman society, as they had been for millennia in the Near East. There were temples throughout the Roman Empire where animal parts were offered to the gods and where other offerings, like grain, were made. Today we may regard it as strange that slaughter should be part of the sacred rites surrounding the very act of making an offering. But unlike in modern Western societies, ancient people were accustomed to slaughtering or helping with the slaughter and butchering of animals. It was part of everyday life. Lester Grabbe points to the importance of sacrificial offerings in the ancient world by highlighting that the central metaphor of Jesus' death is that of a sacrifice (Grabbe 2010: 41).

The sacrificial cult in Jerusalem was comprised, among other things, of the daily morning and evening sacrifices (Exod. 29.38-42), which from the time of Herod the Great, were offered for the well-being of Rome and the emperor (*War* 2.197, 409–10). Other offerings included the sabbath sacrifices, sacrifices at the beginning of every month, and sacrifices for the festivals (Num. 28–29). The priests who administered the sacrificial cult belonged to special priestly lineages of which the men automatically became priests. The Levites made up the temple staff, who were lower in rank than the actual priests and whose duties included performing various tasks other than ministering at the altar, like singing. The priests and Levites lived throughout the land and were grouped into twenty-four divisions that served at the sanctuary for two separate weeks a year on a rolling schedule, as well as at the major festivals. Luke is well aware of how the sanctuary operated and begins his story about Jesus by describing how Zechariah was serving at the temple (Lk. 1.5-25). Luke knows that various duties were assigned to the priests by lot and this is how his focal character, Zechariah, could be tasked 'to enter the sanctuary of the Lord and offer incense' (1.9). It was there, according to Luke, that he had a vision of the angel Gabriel who told him that he would have a son. In the story Zechariah was alone in the temple, which fits well with common practice, as the temple building itself was often empty of people. Nearly all rituals took place outdoors, in the court of the priests with its great altar, but priests would go into the outer room of the temple to light incense and present the showbread (Lev. 24.5-9). The innermost room, which was called 'the most holy place', was entered only once a year, on the Day of Atonement (Yom Kippur), by the high priest. It was holier than other areas because God's presence, often expressed as his 'glory', dwelt there (Exod. 29.43-46). The concentrated holiness of God also made this a dangerous place (cf. Exod. 19.9-25). According to the Mishnah, in the evening after the ceremonies the high priest, together with friends, would celebrate his having come away from the temple unscathed (m. Yoma 7.4).

Ordinary people, that is, anyone who was not a priest, participated in the cult by giving sacrificial animals and offerings in the form of produce and wine at the pilgrimage festivals and on other occasions. Sacrifices, as gifts for God, could be brought for various reasons, most commonly to express gratitude, to honour God or to entreat for atonement. In the latter instance, a so-called sin offering (Lev. 1–7) was made. After someone acquired certain types of impurity, for example after childbirth, offerings were required as part of the purification rituals. Thus, Luke relates that Mary and Joseph travelled to Jerusalem after Jesus' birth 'for their purification', and he describes how 'they offered a sacrifice according to what is stated in the law of the Lord, "a pair of turtle-doves or two young pigeons"' (Lk. 2.22-24). The reference is to Lev. 12, which states that a woman should bring an offering forty days after the birth of a boy and eighty days after the birth of a girl.

The Wisdom of Jesus Ben Sirach (Ben Sira) from the second century BCE expresses a mixture of reverence, respect and pride towards the temple cult, sentiments that many pilgrims and visitors surely shared. The author lyrically describes how the high priest carried out the sacrifice at the altar before the priests and the people (Sir. 50.11-21). It is worth pointing out that the priests ('the sons of Aaron') and the people fall to the ground in order to pay homage to their god, a gesture expressing great respect.

> When he put on his glorious robe
> and clothed himself in perfect splendour,
> when he went up to the holy altar,
> he made the court of the sanctuary glorious.
> When he received the portions from the hands of the priests,
> as he stood by the hearth of the altar
> with a garland of brothers around him,
> he was like a young cedar on Lebanon
> surrounded by the trunks of palm trees.
> All the sons of Aaron in their splendour
> held the Lord's offering in their hands
> before the whole congregation of Israel.
> Finishing the service at the altars,
> and arranging the offering to the Most High, the Almighty,
> he held out his hand for the cup
> and poured a drink-offering of the blood of the grape;
> he poured it out at the foot of the altar,
> a pleasing odour to the Most High, the king of all.
> Then the sons of Aaron shouted;
> they blew their trumpets of hammered metal;
> they sounded a mighty fanfare
> as a reminder before the Most High.
> Then all the people together quickly
> fell to the ground on their faces
> to worship their Lord,
> the Almighty, God Most High.

In certain sacrifices, the so-called burnt offerings, the entire animal was burned. This was the case for the daily sacrifice, which consisted of a lamb as well as flour, olive oil and wine, and was presented in the morning and evening (Exod. 29.40). Usually only portions of the animal were burned – the fat, kidneys and liver – and the priests ate the rest. A person could also make an offering of well-being in the form of a sheep, a goat, or a bull or cow (Lev. 3.1). The priests, after butchering it, then received a portion, but most of the meat was returned to the giver, who later ate it at a ceremonial meal with family and friends. Good meat was a luxury that ordinary people could not indulge in very often, so sacrificial meals were festive occasions for those taking part. The sacrificial act itself was thus only one part of the ceremonies.

The Passover lamb was a special sacrifice. Laymen slaughtered the animals themselves in one of the courts of the temple, most likely the women's court, with the blood being collected in bowls and poured out at the foot of the altar. The Mishnah describes how the priests stood in long rows to pass the bowls of blood up to the altar (m. Pesahim 5.5; Sanders 1992, 136–8). In the evening, the lamb was roasted over a fire at a feast for family and friends (Exod. 12.8-9). It is strange that meat is not mentioned in any of the narratives of Jesus' last supper, when he uttered special words over the bread and wine. According to three of the Gospels, the last meal was a Passover meal, but John implies that it took place the day before instead, on the day of preparation. If he is correct, which is possible (see ch. 10), this provides an explanation for why only the wine and bread are mentioned.

Priests and parties

The priests supported themselves in part from gifts made to the temple. In most cases this income in kind was not sufficient for their subsistence, so they typically had other occupations, for instance, as scribes, teachers and judges. This meant that priests, unlike the great majority of people, had the opportunity to learn to read and write and to engage in intellectual pursuits like writing books and teaching (Grabbe 2010: 43–6). Priests were also experts in the laws of Moses and were capable of interpreting them (*Ant.* 4.304; *Apion* 2.165) Josephus, who belonged to the priestly upper class, demonstrates a clear expertise in matters of Scripture and Jewish traditions. Priests held positions of leadership among the Essenes. The large library at Qumran bears witness to the high level of education among the sect's members, in terms both of the interpretation of Scripture and of the scribal arts, which can partly be explained with reference to their priestly background. Priests had an extremely important place in society, representing different socio-economic classes and occupying various positions of authority. They were also to be found within the parties described by Josephus.

There were three Jewish parties that Josephus terms 'philosophies' or 'schools' for the benefit of his Roman readers: Pharisees, Sadducees and Essenes (*War* 2.119–166; *Ant.* 13.171–173; 18.12–22; *Life* 10–11). On one occasion Josephus mentions guerrilla movements as a fourth 'philosophy', but these did not constitute a unified organization (*War* 2.118–119). In this period philosophy (Greek *philosophia*, literally, 'love of wisdom') was not simply concerned with theoretical speculation at the general level, but just as much with the right way to live. Graeco-Roman philosophies had in common that they emphasized inner value over outer, stressed the importance of mastering irrational emotions and practised a simple way of life. Hence philosophers enjoyed the fellowship of like-minded people who advocated a certain lifestyle and teaching. In this context it is important to remember that most people at this time did not belong to any particular party.

The name Pharisees comes from the Hebrew *perushim*, which means 'separatists', but it is uncertain what specifically the term refers to; perhaps to the fact that they separated themselves from various sources of impurity to a greater degree than others did. The name Sadducees may be connected to Zadok, who was the high priest in the time of David. It is unclear whether there is a Hebrew word behind the Greek name Essenes. Perhaps it refers to the Hebrew 'doers' (*'osim*) as in the 'doers of the law', that is, those who observe the law. The Sadducees were a small party whose adherents mainly came from the wealthy aristocracy (*Ant.* 18.17). In Acts 4.1; 5.17, this party is associated with the high priest, confirming Josephus's statement that it attracted its members from the elite of society. Josephus describes the Essenes in detail, but devotes very little time to the Pharisees, and even less to the Sadducees. He compares the various schools' views on life after death. His picture of three Jewish parties is meant to show that Judaism had its own philosophical schools, just as the Greeks and Romans had theirs. The Pharisees believed in resurrection and in a last judgement, something that the Sadducees rejected (*War* 2.165; *Ant.* 18.14). Their different positions on this issue are confirmed in the New Testament. In a memorable story about Paul's trial in Jerusalem, Paul used this disagreement to his advantage, according to Luke:

> When Paul noticed that some were Sadducees and others were Pharisees, he called out in the council, 'Brothers, I am a Pharisee, a son of Pharisees. I am on trial concerning the hope of the resurrection of the dead.' When he said this, a dissension began between the Pharisees and the Sadducees, and the assembly was divided.
>
> Acts 23.6-7

Luke explains to his readers that 'the Sadducees say that there is no resurrection, or angel, or spirit; but the Pharisees acknowledge all three' (Acts 23.8). In this context, it is interesting to note that Paul the Pharisee was convinced that the resurrection would happen, during his lifetime even (1 Thess. 4.16-17). Luke's claim that the Sadducees did not believe in angels is remarkable given that the existence of angels is taken for granted in the world-view of the Hebrew Bible. Presumably angels were thought to be associated with belief in the resurrection, since a common conception was that at the resurrection people would become like angels, a view espoused by Jesus (Lk. 20.32). In that case, Luke means that the Sadducees did not believe in the resurrection of the dead in any form. Instead, they probably held to the traditional view that at death everyone, regardless of how they had conducted their lives, went to the realm of the dead, Sheol. It was a state between life and death, whose inhabitants led a shadowy existence (see Isa. 14.9-11).

The Pharisees

Josephus estimates that there were six thousand Pharisees in Palestine (*War* 17.42). Though we cannot completely rely on his figures, this indicates that it was a large party. The Pharisees have long had a bad reputation in the Christian church because they are described negatively in the Gospels, where they assume the role of stereotypical opponents who are constantly challenging Jesus and who are always losing. Within Jewish tradition, on the other hand, the Pharisees are seen as role models who laid the foundation for the nascent rabbinic movement. The negative picture of the Pharisees was not challenged within the Christian church until modern times. But where does the critical attitude of the Gospels come from and why are the Pharisees the chief opponents? What do we know about them historically?

Our extant sources for information on the Pharisees are the Gospels, the Acts of the Apostles, Josephus and early rabbinic literature, that is, the Mishnah and the Tosefta. Besides these we have letters from the 50s CE from a Pharisee, namely Paul, who, as an unusually zealous individual (as he himself says in Gal. 1.14), was hardly a typical member of that group. Nevertheless, through Paul we certainly gain some insights into Pharisaic views on the Torah and its ritual laws and ethics, as well as into common methods of interpreting Scripture. Despite this wealth of sources, it is difficult to pin-point exactly what characterized the historical Pharisees and their teachings. For one thing, the Gospels have a strongly negative view of the Pharisees on numerous counts, in contrast to rabbinic literature, which gives a uniformly positive image. But since the Mishnah and the Tosefta were written in the third century, they reflect a much later perspective, even if certain traditions they attribute to the Pharisees are early. Josephus is generally critical of the party, but nevertheless maintains that it was popular among the masses. Paul ultimately changed course from persecuting Christ-believers to becoming a prominent figure as a missionary for that movement. From Acts we know of other Pharisees who joined the Christ-believer movement (Acts 15.5). Below we focus on the Gospels and Josephus as the sources that provide the most information from the first century CE about the Pharisees, albeit from completely different standpoints.

The Pharisees appear at various points in Josephus's tales from Jewish history. They show up in the second century BCE as a political party striving against the Sadducees for influence with the ruling Hasmonaeans. They took part in an uprising against the tyrannical rule of Alexander Jannaeus (103–76 BCE), which ended in a massacre when he had thousands of his opponents executed, among them Pharisees. Yet their fortunes changed when his widow, Queen Alexandra, succeeded to the throne and the Pharisees gained a great deal of influence as her advisers (*War* 1.112). After 63 BCE, however, when the Romans assumed control and particularly after Herod the Great became a client king in the early 30s BCE, there was no room for powerful Jewish parties of a political bent. The Pharisees do reappear later, though, along with the Sadducees, in the domestic Jewish council in Jerusalem, the Sanhedrin. This council served as a court, as well as making decisions on local issues. According to the Gospels, Jesus was condemned by this body (Mt. 26.57-68; Mk 14.53-65). Josephus also mentions that the Pharisees favoured more lenient punishments than the other parties. This may have been a contributing factor in their being so popular among the people, given that it was those from the lower class who were most likely to be subject to punishments of various kinds. The fact that they were popular among ordinary people was not a good thing in Josephus's opinion, since he believed that the ideal configuration for a society involved power being wielded by an aristocratic elite (Mason 2007: 10).

The Pharisees were not a uniform party. They were divided into two schools following two important teachers, Hillel and Shammai. The latter often adopted a stricter stance than the former. Josephus states that the Pharisees were regarded as experts in legal matters (*War* 1.110; 2.162; *Life* 191), and this fits well with the stories in the Gospels which focus precisely on interpretations of laws. Like Jesus they instructed the general public on how to live by the laws, in both ritual matters, like the sabbath, and ethical ones. The laws ascribed to Pharisees in the Mishnah are mainly concerned with rules for the sabbath and festivals, the tithe, and purity rules pertaining to meals eaten at home. Among other things, they advocated eating meals in the home in relative ritual purity, which was made possible by the ritual washing of hands (see ch. 8). Their efforts to eat meals in relative purity and to instruct others about doing so indicate that they were looking for a realm of influence in society other than the sanctuary, where the priests were in charge. There is good evidence that ordinary people looked up to the Pharisees as examples of model behaviour. Jesus may well have had some disputes with the Pharisees about legal issues and way of life. If an individual or group assumes the role of a positive example, they also expose themselves to criticism for not living up to the ideal they preach, a criticism purportedly made by Jesus.

In the Gospels, the Pharisees often make an appearance to criticize or ensnare Jesus on issues of legal interpretation, among others. In Matthew, the polemic between Jesus and the Pharisees is at its most acrimonious. As we shall discuss in Chapter 3, one source that Matthew makes use of is the text of Mark, which he modifies as he writes his own gospel. In several instances Matthew alters the text of Mark so that the Pharisees become

Jesus' chief opponents. For example, whereas Mark relates that 'the scribes' – that is, professional scribes known for their knowledge of the Scriptures – came from Jerusalem to Galilee and accused Jesus of being possessed by a demon (Mk 3.22), in Matthew's version these are 'Pharisees' instead (Mt. 12.24). While the chief priests, the scribes and the elders are the indirect targets of criticism in Mark's parables of the tenants in the vineyard (Mk 11.27–12.12), the parable in Matthew's version (Mt. 21.45) is about the chief priests and the Pharisees. The harshest criticism of the Pharisees is to be found in Mt. 23. Here Jesus repeatedly curses the scribes and the Pharisees, calling them hypocrites. Among other things, he says, 'Woe to you, scribes and Pharisees, hypocrites! For you lock people out of the kingdom of heaven. For you do not go in yourselves, and when others are going in, you stop them' (Mt. 23.13). It is a surprise, then, to say the least, when Jesus says in Matthew 23.2-3 – and only in Matthew – that the teachings of the Pharisees are correct: 'The scribes and the Pharisees sit on Moses' seat; therefore, do whatever they teach you and follow it; but do not do as they do, for they do not practise what they teach.' It thus seems that the Gospel reflects Matthew's own views on the Pharisees rather than Jesus'. On the one hand Matthew seems to admire the Pharisees' interpretation of the law, while on the other his fierce attacks on them indicate that in the evangelist's historical context Christ-believers and Pharisees were in conflict. Certain disputes plausibly go back to the historical Jesus, including those about sabbath rules and the washing of hands (see ch. 8), but Matthew exaggerates the hostility between the groups. A tendency to show the Pharisees in a negative light is also seen in Mark. According to Mark, the Pharisees wanted rid of Jesus from the very beginning of his activity (Mk 3.6), and confronts Jesus in order 'to test him' (Mk 8.11-12; 10.2) but they do not feature in the Passion narrative (their last appearance is in 12.13-17) and seem not to have been involved in either his arrest or execution. Luke on the other hand presents a mixed view on the Pharisees' interaction with Jesus. While the Pharisees are criticized in stereotypical fashion for loving money and being self-righteous (16.14-15), they are also said to warn Jesus about Herod Antipas whom they believe is seeking to kill Jesus (13.31). Moreover, only in Luke's Gospel is Jesus invited to banquets hosted by a Pharisee, which happens no less than three times (Lk. 7.36-50; 11.37-54; 14.1-24). This portrayal lessens the negative image of the Pharisees at least to some extent. Overall, we must take the evangelists' negative descriptions of the Pharisees with a pinch of salt. They largely reflect a conflict between Christ-believers and Pharisees that dates from several decades after Jesus' death.

One reason why the Pharisees appear so often in the Gospel narratives, whereas the Sadducees are only mentioned very rarely and the Essenes never are, may simply be that the Pharisees showed an interest in Jesus' teaching and wanted to debate with him. What is more, they were competing for the same audience. As we shall see, Jesus and the Pharisees did not differ greatly in their teachings. Unlike the Pharisees, the Essenes were not an outward-looking group and had no interest in disputing with Jesus. They formed a strict sect who separated themselves from others to varying degrees. Although in the main the Pharisees come across as stricter than Jesus in interpreting the law, for the sake of comparison it is interesting to observe that, from the Essenes' point of view, the Pharisees were considered to be far too lax in their interpretations, as becomes apparent in the Dead Sea Scrolls.

The Essenes, Qumran and the Dead Sea Scrolls

Up until the end of the 1940s there were two main sources of information about the Essenes, Philo (*Omn. Prob. Lib.* 75–91) and Josephus (*War* 2.119–61; *Ant.* 18.18–22). Both of them proudly describe the sect as representatives of the Jewish people, embodying the ideals of piety and self-control. According to these authors, there were Essene men living throughout the land, who had established communes where they held property in common and practised an ascetic and celibate lifestyle devoted to study, work and prayer. Josephus also mentions that there was a branch of the Essenes who married and had families instead. In addition, the Roman general and geographer Pliny the Elder briefly mentions the Essenes, writing that they lived some distance to the west of the Dead Sea and had palm trees for company rather than women (*Nat.* 53). Scholars would like to connect this description with Qumran, on the north-western shore of the Dead Sea, where by chance a large library was discovered one winter's day in 1947.

There are various versions of the tale of this discovery, which has assumed somewhat legendary proportions. A common version is as follows: Three Bedouin boys from the Ta'amireh clan were pasturing their sheep up in the hills by the Dead Sea. One of the teenagers was taking the opportunity to explore some of the countless natural caves that are found in the region, possibly in the hope of finding hidden treasure or alternatively because he was looking for a lost sheep. The latter seems unlikely given the small opening high up on a cliff face. When he threw small stones down to hear how deep the hole was, he was surprised to hear echoing. He realized they had found something exciting. When the boy climbed down, he found many jars with lids. Some were empty, some contained seeds, but one contained seven old parchment scrolls. The boys were very disappointed as they had been hoping for 'real treasure'. They took the scrolls to the clan and so began the story of what would come to be called the greatest archaeological discovery of the century, dubbed 'the Dead Sea Scrolls'.

These were unsettled times and a war was soon to break out when Israel declared independence in 1948. When scholars finally got to examine some of the scrolls from Cave 1, they were able to establish that they were around two thousand years old, which also meant that they were valuable. The hunt for more scrolls began, with archaeologists on one side and Bedouins on the other. The Bedouins were the big winners because they discovered Cave 4, among others, which contained over fifteen thousand fragments. They quickly emptied the cave, carrying the fragments away haphazardly in bags and boxes. Thanks to contributions from several universities, the state of Jordan (the West Bank belonged to Jordan from 1948 to 1967) was able purchase the fragments. The task of publishing the texts was given to a biblical and archaeological school and research centre in East Jerusalem, École biblique et archéologique française. The school invited several internationally renowned scholars to work with the fragments, which came to be called the world's largest puzzle.

In total an enormous library of up to nine hundred manuscripts, written between the third century BCE and the beginning of the first century CE, was found in eleven caves. Scholars early on identified the group behind the scrolls with the Essenes. Most of the material is very fragmentary and only a fraction of the manuscripts are in the form of long scrolls. The majority are written in Hebrew, followed by Aramaic, but there were also some texts from the Septuagint, the Greek translation of the Hebrew Bible. Interestingly, the texts are almost exclusively religious in nature. They comprise three different categories: 1) Manuscripts of books of the Hebrew Bible (all books are represented except for the book of Esther); 2) non-canonical books, that is, Jewish religious literature which was not incorporated into the Hebrew Bible; 3) texts composed within a particular religious movement that exhibit similar terminology and theology. The latter bear witness to a group who separated themselves from others and had a high estimation of their role. They regarded themselves as a chosen portion of the people of Israel who alone had gained knowledge of God's will. They are, in short, a sect. Equally the library provides an insight into ideas and theological reflections indicative of religious beliefs common among Jews.

With this great textual discovery, scholarly interest turned to the ruins at Qumran, called Khirbet Qumran (see fig. 6). The Dominican priest and archaeologist Roland de Vaux of the École biblique led an excavation of the site in the 1950s. Besides an extensive building complex with large halls, an impressive watchtower, a long wall and ten baths for purification, the excavators also found a sizeable cemetery containing around 1,200 graves. In light of the texts from the caves and the archaeological finds, de Vaux identified Khirbet Qumran as a centre for the sect. He dated the buildings to the 130s BCE, but this dating has since been revised by the archaeologist Jodi Magness to between 100 and 50 BCE.

According to the traditional theory, the sect was formed in the 150s BCE by priests who had lost power in the aftermath of the Maccabaean liberation of the land from Seleucid rule. The Seleucid Empire was made up of the Syrian provinces of the Hellenistic empire forged by Alexander the Great and broken up after his death. Today many scholars date the origins of the movement somewhat later, toward the end of the second century BCE, which fits better with the archaeological remains (Collins 2010: 88–121). The group, which settled at Qumran and elsewhere, was formed under the

FIGURE 6 *The ruin at Qumran, photo Cecilia Wassén.*

leadership of a man who is called the Teacher of Righteousness. We do not know much about him beyond that he was a priest and that he was in conflict with a high priest who is referred to as the Wicked Priest.

The contents of the Dead Sea Scrolls

The descriptions of the Essenes in Josephus, Philo and Pliny give the impression that most Essenes were unmarried men. The sect's own texts from Qumran paint another picture. These texts take marriage and families for granted and they contain many laws concerning marriage contracts, sexual relations and purity rules for both men and women. Rather than constituting a sect of celibates, the movement was made up of both families and unmarried men who lived all across the land. Qumran was probably an assembly centre where members from various locations could gather for meetings and festivals, while a fairly large group of perhaps 100–150 resided there permanently. Remains of bones from the cemetery indicate that the majority of the residents were men, but that there were women living there too. The sect's books of rules show that the group was organized hierarchically according to an order of precedence observed at communal meals. Some groups held property in common, whilst others retained private property but made contributions of a certain proportion of their income. Members had to follow not only the laws of Moses but also the group's internal regulations. If members violated the regulations, they received smaller portions of food for different periods as a punishment and were excluded from certain festival meals. In the *Community Rule* (1QS), for example, we read that anyone who fell asleep during a meeting where 'the Many' were gathered was punished with food rationing for thirty days, whilst someone who insulted another member could be punished with exclusion from communal meals and subjected to food rationing for a year. However, if someone rebelled against the leadership he could be excluded from the sect. Similarly, in the *Damascus Document*, which is primarily addressed to married members, a member who is disparaging of a female leader (a group who are called 'the Mothers') is punished by receiving less food for ten days.

Why did so many people seek out a life of subordination and strict discipline? In what way did they benefit? Undoubtedly the sect offered an ideal setting for those who wanted to devote their lives to serving God. The rule texts reflect an existence filled with prayer, praising and study of the Scriptures:

> They shall eat (in) unity, say benedictions (in) unity, and give counsel (in) unity. And in every place where there are ten men (belonging to) the Council of the Community, there must not be lacking among them a man (who is) a priest. And each member shall sit according to his rank before him, and in thus they shall be asked for their counsel concerning every matter. When the table has been prepared for eating, or the new wine for drinking, the priest shall be the first to stretch out his hand, in order to bless the first (produce of) the bread and the new wine. And where there are ten (members) there must not be lacking there a man who studies the Torah day and night continually, each man relieving another. The Many shall spend the third part of every night of the year in unity, reading the Book, studying judgment, and saying benedictions in unity.
>
> 1QS 6.2–8

Other factors besides strong religious belief may have also come into play for those who sought out the sect. In a time when poor people might have to sell themselves or their children into slavery, it is easy to imagine that, for some, membership in the sect presented itself as a means of survival. The strong sense of community that the sect fostered among its members must have contributed to its popularity as well. Through communal meals and rituals strong bonds were formed and these were also supported by a robust ideology according to which this group and no other had come to know God's wisdom and was guided by the Holy Spirit. Fellowship within the group is underlined in the name *hayachad*, 'the Community', that the members themselves used. Both Josephus and Philo testify to a strong friendship among the members. Philo describes them in this way: 'To the elder men too is given the respect and care which real children give to their parents, and they receive from countless hands and minds a full and generous maintenance for their latter years.' (*Omn. Prob. Lib.* 87; cf. *War* 2.119).

The sect's names for themselves, such as the 'Children of Light', 'the Holy Ones' and 'the perfect ones' indicate that they viewed themselves as being on the side of God and his angels against a world of darkness. Believing that salvation, or deliverance, was only possible within their own group must have given the members a certain degree of satisfaction. They were engaged in a battle with the 'Children of Darkness' or 'Children of Deceit', that is, the rest of humanity, who were governed by Satan, or 'the Angel of Darkness':

> In a spring of light emanates the nature of truth and from a well of darkness emerges the nature of deceit. In the hand of the Prince of Lights (is) the dominion of all the Children of Righteousness; in the ways of light they walk. But in the hand of the Angel of Darkness (is) the dominion of the Children of Deceit; and in the ways of darkness they walk. By the Angel of Darkness comes the aberration of all the Children of Righteousness; and all their sins, their iniquities, their guilt, and their iniquitous works (are caused) by his dominion, according to God's mysteries, until his end.
>
> 1QS 3.19-23

By living in close proximity to God, the members were also able to live perfectly, as the preacher behind the *Damascus Document* says:

> And now, O sons, hearken to me and I will uncover your eyes so you may see and understand the works of God and choose that which he wants and despise that which he hates: to walk perfectly in all his ways and not to stray in the thoughts of a guilty inclination and licentious eyes.
>
> CD 2.14-16

The members of the Qumran sect firmly believed that all other Jews had turned from the right way and that God had entered into a covenant with the sect, 'a new covenant'. The notion of covenant was of course extremely important for the first Christ-believers, too, who interpreted Jesus' death as the foundation of a new covenant (Gal. 4.22-30; Lk. 22.20; Heb. 9.15-22). Like the Christ-believers, the sect held that salvation was only possible within the new covenant. In the Dead Sea Scrolls, the new covenant is concerned with living rightly by God's law:

> Out of those who held fast to God's ordinances, who remained of them, God established his covenant with Israel forever, revealing to them hidden things in which all Israel had strayed: his holy sabbaths, the glorious appointed times, his righteous testimonies, his true ways, and the desires of his will, which a person shall do and live by them. (These) he opened

before them and they dug a well of abundant water. But those who scorn them will not live.

CD 3.12–17

Overall the texts voice a strong belief that the group's members, through their unique knowledge, have the ability to live perfectly in accordance with God's laws. Nevertheless, we also find acknowledgement that humans are completely dependent on God. A psalm in 1QS explains that everything comes from God: 'For my way (belongs) to Adam. The human cannot establish his righteousness; for to God (alone) belongs the judgment and from him is the perfection of the Way' (1QS 11.10–11). Likewise, the *Thanksgiving Psalms* (or *Hodayot*) convey humanity's inability to live perfectly and emphasize the need for forgiveness and guidance:

I know that no one can be righteous apart from you, and so I entreat you with the spirit that you have placed in me that you make your kindness to your servant complete [for]ever, cleansing me by your holy spirit and drawing me nearer by your good favor, according to your great kindness [wh]ich you have shown to me.

1QH 8.29–30

The sect lived in the belief that the present age was coming to an end. In the *Letter on Works* (4QMMT C 21), the writer of the letter explains to the recipient that 'these are the latter days'. Many of the texts from Qumran articulate an apocalyptic hope for the imminent righting of wrongs. Although understandings of how this would occur differ greatly, the belief that it would indeed occur was very strong. The Qumran movement shared this belief with many other Jewish groups, among them Jesus and his followers. In modern usage 'apocalypse' has become associated with disasters and the end of the world, but the Greek word originally meant that something is 'uncovered', that is, revealed. In a religious setting, an apocalyptic expectation meant something entirely positive since this kind of vision for the future always involved decisive deliverance for the faithful. God would imminently intervene in history, destroying the wicked and rewarding the good. In the *Damascus Document*, the punishment for sinners is described: 'All those who despise the ordinances and statutes, the evil ones will be repaid their due when God visits the land' (CD [MS B] 19.5–6). The reward for the faithful is described as follows: '(These men) will be joyous and happy, and their heart will take courage, and they will overcome all the sons of the world. And God will atone for them, and they will see his salvation, for they took refuge in his holy name' (CD [MS B] 20.33–34).

Overall the Dead Sea Scrolls reflect common religious beliefs that were widespread at the time and thus they provide us with a window onto ancient Judaism. Many of the texts exhibit a clear interest in angels, entities that became increasingly important in this period in Jewish speculations about the heavenly world and about God's plan for humanity. Several of the scrolls express a belief that the members of the group had a special communion with these beings. Thus the fragmentary *Songs of the Sabbath Sacrifice* describe in vague and mystical terms a heavenly temple, or possibly seven temples, where the angels praise God and where even the building's interior joins in the song of praise. Through the songs the worshippers could participate in the heavenly service and praise God along with the angels. In a hymn in the *Community Rule*, this communion is made explicit: 'With the sons of heaven he has joined together their assembly for the Council of the Community. (Their) assembly (is) a House of Holiness for the eternal plant' (1QS 11.8). In addition, according to the Rule of the Congregation ritually impure members and people with disabilities were excluded from special meetings, 'for holy angels [(are) in] their [Coun]cil' (1QSa 2.8–9). The same firm belief in a genuine communion with the angels is also seen in a letter of Paul's in which he urges women to cover their hair when they pray or prophesy 'because of the angels' (1 Cor. 11.10). As we shall see below, angels played an important role both in the present age and in apocalyptic speculations about the future.

Angels and demons

God was never alone in his heaven, according to the traditional Israelite understanding; he was always surrounded by angels. They are sometimes called 'sons of God' and even 'gods' (*elohim*) in the plural, and underlying such usage is an ancient tradition from a time when these beings were regarded as lesser deities. This idea comes across in Ps. 82, where 'the gods' are members of God's council: 'God has taken his place in the divine council; in the midst of the gods he holds judgement'; and 'I say, "You are gods, children of the Most High, all of you"' (cf. Deut. 32.8; Ps. 29). The common title Lord of hosts (Yahweh Sebaoth) refers to God as the military commander of armies of angels. The great number of angels is an indication of God's might, as in Daniel's vision of God as judge: 'A thousand thousand served him, and ten thousand times ten thousand stood attending him' (Dan. 7.10). Here God occupies the role of king, with the angels as his subjects. Another common image used in descriptions of the heavenly realm is the temple in which angels have the role of priests serving God. It was thought that worship in the earthly temple was in harmony with heavenly worship and followed the same cosmic calendar as that used by the angels.

In modern images, angels are often presented as benign, gentle figures who protect human beings, sometimes depicted in the form of cherubs, delightful beings resembling babies. This is a far cry from their portrayal in Jewish texts, where angels are always awe-inspiring and often extremely masculine. For example, Joshua sees an angel wielding a drawn sword, who is said to be 'commander of the army of the LORD'. The correct response is to fall to the ground in reverence (Josh. 5.14). Similarly Daniel is terror-stricken when he lays eyes on an angel, in a scene narrated in the first person: 'My strength left me, and my complexion grew deathly pale, and I retained no strength. Then I heard the sound of his words; and when I heard the sound of his words, I fell into a trance, face to the ground' (Dan. 10.8-9). Encounters with angels often inspire dread as they involve drawing near to another, holy world, God's world, an experience that makes human beings realize how small and imperfect they are. When Isaiah sees God on his throne in the temple surrounded by seraphs, a type of being resembling an animal, he cries out in dismay, 'Woe is me! I am lost, for I am a man of unclean lips, and I live among a people of unclean lips' (Isa. 6.5). Angels were powerful beings. Accordingly, in Jesus' sermons angels appear as judges who cast the wicked into the blazing furnace (Mt. 13.49). Sometimes, however, they may pose as human beings, hiding their true nature from those they meet (Gen. 19.1-11; Tob. 5.4). They can also serve as heavenly guides for visionaries and as interpreters of human visions, typical roles for angels in apocalyptic literature (Dan. 7.16; 8.16; Rev. 7.13-17).

Angels played an important role in Jewish conceptions of how God interacted with humanity. Angel in Hebrew means 'messenger', a term that indicates one of their primary functions, that of conveying a divine message to human beings. This is also a motif in the Gospels, where angels play a prominent role, in, for example, the birth narratives and the narratives of the resurrection. In the latter, the women encounter angels in or outside the tomb. While Mark describes 'a young man dressed in a white robe' in the tomb who tells the women what has happened, Matthew's account is more dramatic: 'Suddenly there was a great earthquake; for an angel of the Lord, descending from heaven, came and rolled back the stone and sat on it. His appearance was like lightning, and his clothing white as snow' (Mt. 28.2-3). In the birth narrative in Luke, an angel delivers messages to Zechariah and Mary. He introduces himself with the words: 'I am Gabriel. I stand in the presence of God, and I have been sent to speak to you and to bring you this good news' (Lk. 1.19). These descriptions of angels illustrate well the development that occurred in the last centuries before the Common Era when interest grew in the role and nature of angels. There was speculation about angelic hierarchies, and the highest angels, the archangels, were given names, such as Gabriel. In the book of Daniel from the 160s BCE, the archangel Michael appears (Dan. 10), while Raphael shows up in Tobit (Tob. 3.17). In the *Songs of the Sabbath Sacrifice* from Qumran, Melchizedek is the highest angel instead. Different angels were assigned different tasks, like being the guardians of particular countries (Dan. 10.13) and people (Mt. 18.10; Rev. 2.1, 8, 12, 18). They were also in charge of various natural phenomena such as wind, rain, lightning, snow and the like and they were closely associated with the stars. Anyone who has been in an area remote from human settlement on a clear night can imagine how magnificent the night sky must have been for people of ancient times before artificial light, or light pollution, almost obscured the stars from view. Faced with this majestic starry sky, a human being could feel quite small, as the writer of Ps. 8.3-4 conveys:

> When I look at your heavens, the work of your fingers, the moon and the stars that you have established; what are human beings that you are mindful of them, mortals that you care for them?

It is no wonder that these brilliant suns were thought of as angels. The link between stars and angels is evident in, for example, Deut. 4.19, where the people are warned not to worship the celestial host: 'When you look up to the heavens and see the sun, the moon, and the stars, all the host of heaven, do not be led astray and bow down to them and serve them.'

Just as God had his loyal subjects, the evil power, Satan or Belial ('worthlessness'), likewise had his minions who terrorized human beings with disease and adversity. These too were called angels, but also demons or evil spirits. In prayers from Qumran, angels are called upon as powerful protection against attacks from demons. Angels also frequently feature in descriptions of the end times. One common belief was that the good and evil forces would meet in a final war, at which point the evil side would be destroyed once and for all and God would establish his kingdom. The *War Scroll* from Cave 1 at Qumran is a combat manual for a cosmic war involving both human armies and good and evil angels. The war lasts forty years and follows a predetermined plan, meaning that the outcome is decided. The ending is already described in the first column: 'in his [Belial's] anger he shall set out to destroy and eliminate the strength of [. . .] a time of salvation for the People of God, and a time of domination for all the men of His forces, and eternal annihilation for all the forces of Belial' (1QM 1.4-5). As stated in this passage, the world has to endure Belial's anger before God destroys him. The last days were marked by the evil side being in ascendance and by the world suffering every kind of disaster and misery imaginable. It was as if Satan was making one last show of force before his dominion would finally be eradicated. The adversities of the end times are sometimes referred to in the literature of the period as 'birth pangs', a figurative expression for how suffering would be replaced with joy when God saved his people. Apocalyptic expectations dictated that the worse the situation became for a group, the surer they could be that the end was nigh. Jesus' sermon in Mk 13 is about just such 'birth pangs' (13.8), sufferings in the form of war and famine that were to precede the deliverance attending the coming of the Son of Man in the clouds (13.26). In these future events, a salvation figure often, though not always, has a decisive role to play, like the Son of Man in Mk 13.26. Sometimes that role fell to a messiah figure, but it could fall to others too. The rich literature of Judaism, both biblical and extrabiblical, contains a broad spectrum of ideas about salvation figures of the end times, which we shall now familiarize ourselves with.

Salvation figures

The early Christ-believers were convinced that Jesus was the Christ. Mark, for example, begins his Gospel with: 'The beginning of the good news of Jesus Christ, the Son of God.' The Greek word *christos* (Christ) is a translation of the Hebrew word *mashiach*, that is, Messiah. Why did the Christ-believers regard Jesus as the Messiah? Where does the idea of a Messiah come from and how does Jesus actually fit into those expectations?

The word *mashiach* means 'anointed one' and in the Hebrew Bible it is applied to kings, priests and prophets, who were smeared with oil at their inauguration (Lev. 4.3; 1 Sam. 24.6; Ps. 105.15). In these texts, the term does not per se refer to some future eschatological saviour figure. Yet after the Babylonian exile, under Persian and later Greek rule (from the 530s BCE on), hopes grew for a new anointed king who would liberate the land. Fertile ground for visions of the future was provided by promises in the Scriptures of a royal liberator who would reign over a powerful kingdom. In the seventh century, Isaiah describes the coming of a prince of peace whose dominion 'shall grow continually' and in whose time 'there shall be endless peace for the throne of David and his kingdom' (Isa. 9.7, cf. Zech. 9). Isaiah 11 describes the future king as a wise judge, upon whom 'the spirit of the LORD shall rest' and who establishes justice in the land. Jeremiah, prophesying at the time of the Babylonian invasion, promised both the future restoration of the land and a new, strong king: 'The days are surely coming, says the LORD, when I will raise up for David a righteous Branch, and he shall reign as king and deal wisely, and shall execute justice and righteousness in the land' (Jer. 23.5). Another influential text was Nathan's promise to David that his heir would be a son to God, and that the Davidic line would never cease: 'I will establish the throne of his kingdom for ever. I will be a father to him, and he shall be a son to me' (2 Sam. 7.13b-14; cf. Ps. 89.30). In being called a son of God (also in Pss. 2.7; 89.27), the king is presented as God's adopted son, his agent, without any implication that he was a divine incarnation. Unlike in the Gospels, the Messiah is rarely called the son of God. But there is a figure who is called the son of God in in the fragmentary 4Q246 (*Apocryphon of Daniel*) from Qumran: "He will be called the Son of God, they will call him the son of the Most High" (4Q246 ii 1). Unfortunately the fragmentary nature of the manuscript makes it hard to know for certain whether the title is used in a positive sense with reference to a redeemer figure, or negatively with regard to a king who (wrongly) is venerated in this way. Nevertheless, John Collins makes a strong case for why the passage most likely refers to a future royal, messianic figure (see Collins and Collins 2008: 65–74).

Despite the promises, Judah had no king in the postexilic period until royal titles were assumed by the Hasmonaean leaders, starting with Judah Aristobulus I (104–103 BCE). Nevertheless, these rulers were not especially popular and, as mentioned above, under Alexander Jannaeus (103–76 BCE) a bitter civil war erupted. In short, the Jewish rulers who were not of David's line did not fulfil the messianic expectations. Instead, many hoped that a new David, an anointed king, would come forth. This Messiah was tied up with hopes of an ever more wondrous future and he would usher in a completely new era. The *Psalms of Solomon* from the first century BCE describe a future son of David, who is called 'the Messiah' (*christos*) and who would expel all the gentiles from Jerusalem and reign over, not only Judah, but all realms (*Pss. Sol.* 17). In the Dead Sea Scrolls a firm messianic expectation is also evident, but here we are not dealing with one Messiah, but rather two, a royal Messiah and a priestly one. The fact that the members of the Qumran movement were waiting for two messianic leaders is not especially strange, since the governance of the land was traditionally divided up between the king and the high priest. In Zechariah, which was written soon after the return from Babylon, messianic hopes are pinned on two individuals, the high priest and the governor and, what is more, Davidic descendant Zerubbabel, who are called 'the two anointed ones'. One of them is the high priest and the other is the governor Zerubbabel, who is a Davidic descendant (Zech. 4.14). When the two Messiah figures occur together in the texts from Qumran, the priest has a leading role. Both appear at a banquet described in the *Rule of the Congregation* (1QSa 2.11–22). At that time 'the priest' will bless the bread and wine before 'the Messiah of Israel' pronounces blessings over the bread. In certain texts, the royal Davidic Messiah has an important role to play in God's ultimate victory over his enemies. In a possible fragment of the *War Scroll*, 4Q285, the Prince of the Congregation (the Messiah) leads the forces into battle against the eschatological enemies the Kittim, often a reference to the Romans (cf. 1QM 5.1). The time that will follow is described as a paradise, when the ground will yield rich fruit, when disease will be no more and when humans will live alongside angels. With allusions to Isa. 11, 1QSb (*Blessings*) expresses blessings for the Prince of the Congregation, which include the hope that he will vanquish the nations and establish an everlasting dominion. The 'Prince of all the congregation' as he is called in the *Damascus Document (CD)* 7.20–21, will wipe out the enemies.

In addition, within the Qumran movement a third individual was anticipated at the end times, a prophet, an anticipation that built on God's promise to Moses about a future prophet like him (Deut. 18.15-18; see 1QS 9.11; 4Q174). A text known as the *Messianic Apocalypse* (4Q521) may be about this prophet. In the document we read that heaven and earth will listen to his (God's) Messiah and that the Lord (probably through him) will cure diseases, raise the dead and preach good news to the poor. The text uses quotations from Ps. 146.7-8 and Isa. 61.1, which is particularly interesting because references to the very same texts are found in Jesus' answer to the question posed to him by John the Baptist (Mt. 11.4-5; Lk. 7.22-23). The question is whether Jesus is 'the one who is to come' or whether they are to wait for another. Jesus says, 'Go and tell John what you hear and see: the blind receive their sight, the lame walk, the lepers are cleansed, the deaf hear, the dead are raised, and the poor have good news brought to them' (Mt. 11.4-5). Despite the fact that the same scriptural passages are used in Matthew and Luke, it is unclear whether there is any allusion here to the awaited prophet. Rather, the parallels show that certain texts from the Hebrew Bible grew to be important as prophecies of the end times, but that they could also be interpreted in various ways. In the Gospel of John, however, people do explicitly wonder whether Jesus is 'the prophet' or 'the Messiah' (Jn 7.40-41). Luke, too, alludes to the prophet. Twice he quotes Deut. 18.15, concerning a prophet like Moses, in a manner suggestive of Jesus (Acts 3.22-23; 7.37). Although Jesus was chiefly presented as the promised Davidic Messiah, or Christ, he could also be associated with other figures of the end times. The Christ-believers wrote with the benefit of hindsight – from their perspective Jesus was the only saviour figure God used as his agent in the end times, and therefore prophecies about different figures could be interpreted as applying to Jesus. This was also true in the case of future figures of a heavenly nature.

In Melchizedek (11Q13), a text from Qumran, Melchizedek is the one who will wipe out the enemy and Belial. Melchizedek is the legendary priest king of Salem (later Jerusalem) who blesses Abraham in Gen. 14.17-20. He is also mentioned in Ps. 110.4, where the Lord proclaims: 'You are a priest for ever according to the order of Melchizedek.' These texts formed the basis of later speculations about him. According to the *Songs of the Sabbath Sacrifice*, Melchizedek is the name of the highest angel. The Melchizedek figure in 11QMelch (11Q13) stands out as remarkably godlike. He is said to be accompanied by hosts and biblical texts such as Ps. 2.1, originally about God, are applied to him. His elevated status is reminiscent of the Angel of Light in 1QS, the opposite of the Angel of Darkness. Later the author of the Letter to the Hebrews makes use of speculations surrounding Melchizedek when he presents Jesus as a heavenly high priest like Melchizedek: 'where Jesus, a forerunner on our behalf, has entered, having become a high priest for ever according to the order of Melchizedek' (Heb. 6.20).

Another heavenly figure with divine characteristics is the 'one like a human being' or literally 'a son of man', in Dan. 7, who can be interpreted as the highest angel and is of great importance in the Gospels. He is explicitly presented as a being close to God, who is described here as a very old man. After seeing four beasts representing different evil empires, Daniel beholds this son of man coming to save the people:

> As I watched in the night visions, I saw one like a human being coming with the clouds of heaven. And he came to the Ancient One and was presented before him. To him was given dominion and glory and kingship, that all peoples, nations, and languages should serve him. His dominion

is an everlasting dominion that shall not pass away, and his kingship is one that shall never be destroyed.

Dan. 7.13-14

Jesus was himself influenced by Daniel's prophecies and talked of a future son of man who would come on the clouds of heaven and save his people (Mk 13.26–27). The question is, Who was he talking about in this case? Was Jesus talking about himself and about God exalting him at the coming of the kingdom, or was he talking about a saviour figure that God would send in the future? As far as later Christ-believers were concerned, Jesus' statements regarding the son of man were of course about his own second coming. We will return to this issue in Chapter 9 when we discuss Jesus' understanding of himself. Then we will also consider ideas surrounding the human-like figure in Daniel that appear in the pseudepigraphical books, *1 Enoch* and *4 Ezra*.

In light of the messianic expectations of various kinds that were circulating in early Judaism, clearly it must have been difficult for Jesus' disciples to claim, after his death, that Jesus was the Christ – be it the Davidic king or some other Messiah figure – who had come to liberate his people and restore the land. For, to an outsider, everything seemed to be just as it had been before Jesus died. The Romans ruled the land, the sick were still sick and there was not an angel in sight. Complete liberation was thus postponed until the future; all the promises would be fulfilled on Jesus' return, *parousia* ('arrival' in Greek), which the early Christ-believers eagerly awaited. But they also maintained that something had changed, that his death was part of God's plan and that it held meaning for all humanity. The evangelists wanted to convince readers that God worked through his special agent, Jesus, who was the Messiah.

Summary

Like other peoples in the ancient world, Jews had their own set of specific traditions and rules by which they lived. And like others, they pointed to a divine origin for their laws. According to the Torah, Moses had received the laws from God, and Jews largely accepted this as fact. Some customs were particularly important for Jewish identity since they differed from the common Roman norms. These included abstaining from work on the sabbath, circumcising boys on the eighth day, and observing particular dietary laws such as the prohibition against eating pork and shellfish. Jews were also distinctive in worshipping only one god, whom they considered supreme above all other, lesser deities, that is, angels and the gods of other peoples. In contrast to the Roman world where gods had temples in every city, Jews in general only recognized the temple in Jerusalem as the abode of their god. Here the priests offered sacrifices on a daily basis. Jesus was one of the large number of pilgrims who gathered in Jerusalem at the great pilgrimage festivals and took part in the celebrations in the sanctuary. Aside from at the sanctuary, Jews everywhere gathered on the sabbath at homes and at special places for gathering, synagogues, to read and discuss the Scriptures and to pray. It is notable that many of Jesus' healings and debates take place in synagogues in Galilee.

Although most Jews, Jesus included, accepted the laws as divinely ordained and agreed on their importance, there were differing views on how to observe them properly. In the time of Jesus, different parties had different viewpoints on matters such as how best to observe the sabbath laws and how to run the Jerusalem temple. Among the parties that Josephus describes, Jesus appears to have been engaged in debates mostly with the Pharisees, a group who, according to the Gospels, challenged Jesus' actions and teaching. Although it is likely that Jesus disagreed with them on various points, the negative portrayal of them in the Gospels, apart from indicating an obvious favourable bias towards Jesus, rather reflects the milieu in which these works were composed. The party that was popular among the priests and the elite, the Sadducees, only rarely appears in the Gospels, and the Essenes, who in various ways separated themselves from others, are never mentioned. Hence, the Pharisees at least appear to have been interested in Jesus' teaching.

We know a great deal about Judaism around the turn of the Common Era from the writings of the Jewish historian Josephus, but also from Jewish literature that did not make it into the canon. The huge library found at Qumran by the Dead Sea in the mid-twentieth century is a treasure trove that not only tells us about a specific, strict sect – likely the Essenes – but also provides information about the world of ideas circulating at the time. Many Jewish books from this period testify to the popularity of apocalyptic ideas, according to which the people were living in an evil age that was dominated by Satan and his forces. Soon, however, after a period of terrible tribulations, God, through his angels and often a saviour figure, would decisively transform the world, punishing or annihilating the wicked and establishing his kingdom. Ideas about exactly what this kingdom would look like differ widely, ranging from altogether utopian expectations to more realistic ideas of hopes for freedom from foreign rule. In this period we also find increasing reflection on the role of good and bad angels, or evil spirits, as well as saviour figures. Hope in the coming of the Messiah, the anointed one, as an ideal king who would defeat foreign forces, was prevalent, but expectations concerning other end-time figures appear as well, such as the prophet like Moses, or an archangel, such as Melchizedek, or the enigmatic 'one like a human being' in Daniel 7. For the New Testament writers Jesus fulfilled all the promises relating to God's deliverance through a saviour and they could therefore apply diverse messianic expectations to him. Still, the title 'Messiah', Christ, became the common designation for Jesus in the early Jesus movement. Given that Jesus was executed and the expected paradise did not materialize, Jesus' followers deferred many of the traditional expectations associated with God's kingdom to a later time when they hoped their Messiah would return. But what do scholars do when they want to push past the images of a saviour figure and uncover the person who gave rise to the stories that built up around him? We shall take a look at this next.

Bibliography

Collins, A. Y. and J. J. Collins (2008), *King and Messiah as Son of God: Divine, Human, and Angelic Figures in Biblical and Related Literature*, Grand Rapids: Eerdmans.
Collins, J. J. (2010), *Beyond the Qumran Community: The Sectarian Movement of the Dead Sea Scrolls*, Grand Rapids: Eerdmans.
Collins, J. J. (2016), *The Apocalyptic Imagination: An Introduction to Jewish Apocalyptic Literature*, 3rd edn, Grand Rapids: Eerdmans.
Grabbe, L. (2010), *An Introduction to Second Temple Judaism: History and Religion of the Jews in the Time of Nehemiah, the Maccabees, Hillel, and Jesus*, London: T&T Clark.
Mason, S. (2007), 'Josephus's Pharisees: The Narratives', in J. Neusner and B. D. Chilton (eds), *In Quest of the Historical Pharisees*, 3–40, Waco: Baylor University Press.
Neusner, J. and B. D. Chilton, eds (2007), *In Quest of the Historical Pharisees*, Waco: Baylor University Press.
Sanders, E. P. (1992), *Judaism: Practice and Belief 63 BCE-66 CE*, London: SCM Press.
Uro, R. (2016), *Ritual and Christian Beginnings: A Socio-Cognitive Analysis*, Oxford: Oxford University Press.
VanderKam J. and P. Flint (2002), *The Meaning of the Dead Sea Scrolls: Their Significance for Understanding the Bible, Judaism, Jesus, and Christianity*, New York: HarperSanFransisco.
Vermes, G. (1973), *Jesus the Jew: A Historian's Reading of the Gospels*, London: Collins.
Zetterholm, M., ed. (2007), *The Messiah in Early Judaism and Christianity*, Minneapolis: Fortress.

3

The Jesus of the Gospels and the Jesus of history

At this stage we should take some time to consider how historians are able to arrive at a credible picture of the historical Jesus. The Gospels are religious writings that were composed by people of strong faith, in an era when factual accuracy was not always a top priority for those who claimed to be retelling the past. The information given by the Gospels cannot simply be accepted as historically reliable by current standards. We have already seen that most aspects of the stories about Jesus' background and birth are doubtful from a historian's point of view, whereas what we read about how Jesus spoke of the kingdom of God is grounded in actual events. What reasoning can we use to judge the level of accuracy in various parts of the Gospels? That is the question that we shall answer in this chapter.

The stories about Jesus

What we know about the historical Jesus is based on written texts. Archaeological discoveries afford often invaluable insights into how Jewish society looked in the past and therefore contribute indirectly to what we know about Jesus. But to be able to find out about him as an individual, we have to turn to written documents. Of the sources we have, the most important are the so-called canonical gospels, the four narratives of Jesus' life, written in Greek, that are part of the New Testament. In particular, the first three Gospels, which are usually called the Synoptic Gospels – the Gospels of Matthew, Mark and Luke – can be used to reconstruct a picture of the historical Jesus, whereas the historical value of the Gospel of John is more debatable. We will come back to why this is the case later on in the chapter.

The Gospels contain two types of material: narrative material, that is, episodes depicting various events in the life of Jesus or deeds that he is said to have done; and sayings material, that is, short utterances and longer speeches attributed to Jesus. All four Gospels describe Jesus' final days and the events leading up to his execution in a level of detail that a modern reader may easily regard as out of proportion compared to how the rest of his life is described. Matthew's and Luke's Gospels also contain relatively detailed accounts of events surrounding Jesus' birth. All of these features – a combination of actions and words, a focus on the protagonist's death as well as a description of his or her origins and birth – are typical of ancient biographies written in Greek and Latin. Scholars today, especially after the publication of Richard Burridge's (1992) important work on this topic, are therefore generally of the opinion that the Gospels are ancient biographies of some sort. As such, they contain a great deal of interesting information about Jesus, but, as with all records, they must be treated critically as sources: Can we trust what these documents assert?

When investigating the historical reliability of a source, historians have to consider the extent to which that source is contemporaneous with the events it purports to relate. A text that was written soon after a particular event has a good chance of giving a relatively accurate picture of the incident. The longer the time that has passed between the actual event and the text describing it, the greater the likelihood is that the memory of what happened has had time to be reshaped and adapted in line with subsequent experiences and reassessments. Thus, an earlier source is to be preferred to a later one. This principle cannot be applied mechanically, nor should it be understood to imply that early sources offer a picture of the past that is somehow neutral or unbiased. However, this principle is useful as a rule of thumb. To what extent, then, can we say that the Gospels are contemporaneous with Jesus' life?

The question is not an easy one to answer. The dating of the Gospels is, in fact, uncertain, for three reasons. First, since we do not have access to the original manuscripts of the Gospels – or of any other New Testament texts, for that matter – we depend on reconstructions of the original wording based on more than five thousand handwritten copies from various periods. The very oldest textual fragments have been dated to the first half of the second century CE. A few of the more complete manuscripts are from the fourth century, whilst the vast majority are significantly later. Secondly, we cannot be certain that any of the Gospels were authored by known individuals. It is unlikely that they were written by Jesus' disciples, who were uneducated and so could not possibly have composed literary works in Greek, or by other eyewitnesses. In even the oldest manuscripts, the Gospels have the superscriptions 'According to Matthew', 'According to Mark', 'According to Luke', and 'According to John'. It is by no means impossible that the superscriptions were present from the beginning, but these were not uncommon names in antiquity and we cannot determine which individuals they refer to. Third, the nature of the Gospels as biographical narratives makes is difficult to draw conclusions about dating from their content. All of the Gospels must of course post-date Jesus' death, probably in 33 CE, but scarcely anyone believes that they were written in the years immediately following. Many factors suggest that Mark's is the oldest surviving gospel. According to an early Christian tradition, the Gospel of Mark was written shortly after the death of the apostle Peter in the latter half of the 60s CE, which may very well be correct. The authors of both Matthew and Luke seem to have used Mark as a template, so these two gospels must have been written later, but just how much later is hard to ascertain. The 80s or 90s would not be an unreasonable guess. The Gospel of John may also have been written in the 90s. The ending of John touches on the problems that arose when the first generation of Jesus' disciples was dying off, and this fits well with early Christian tradition, which assigns the origin of the Gospel to the end of the first century.

Thus, the four canonical gospels came into being sometime between the possible dates for Jesus' death (in the 30s CE) and the dates of the oldest surviving textual fragments (around 150 CE at the latest), more precisely in the range 65–100 CE. This means that the sources are later than the events they depict by between thirty-five and seventy years. Compared to the dating of many other ancient works of biography and history in relation to the events told in them, this is not a particularly long period, but the Gospels can nevertheless hardly be regarded as 'contemporary'. As we will see shortly, this does not render them useless as historical sources, but the time gap poses a challenge that any serious historian cannot simply neglect.

Non-canonical Gospels

Nevertheless, the canonical gospels are relatively early sources when compared to the non-canonical, or apocryphal, gospels. These are texts generally dating from the second century at the earliest, and often even later, which elaborate upon some element from the canonical gospels with details that are sometimes quite fanciful. The list includes the *Infancy Gospel of Thomas* and the *Protoevangelium of James*, which supplement the meagre information that the canonical gospels provide about Jesus' family background and upbringing; the *Gospel of Peter*, which contains a particularly vivid account of Jesus' death and resurrection; and a series of 'gospels' claiming to record what Jesus revealed to chosen disciples after his resurrection, such as the *Gospel of Philip* and the *Gospel of Mary*. Several of these texts are valuable sources of knowledge about different varieties of Christianity from the third and fourth centuries in particular, but they provide hardly any information about the historical Jesus. The single possible exception is the *Gospel of Thomas*, which was found along with several other non-canonical texts at Nag Hammadi in Egypt in 1945.

Unlike the canonical gospels, but like most other non-canonical gospels, the *Gospel of Thomas* is not a biography devoted to the life of Jesus. The text begins by stating that it contains the words that were spoken by 'the living Jesus', and consists of 114 sayings that for the most part begin with the formula 'Jesus said'. Absent is any framing narrative about Jesus' activity and death. Consequently Jesus is portrayed neither as a miracle-worker nor as a suffering saviour figure, but rather purely as teacher of wisdom. Roughly two-thirds of the sayings are among those found in the canonical gospels, where they usually have a somewhat different formulation. We may compare, for example, the following well-known saying of Jesus from the Gospel of Matthew with its counterpart in the *Gospel of Thomas*:

> Give therefore to the emperor the things that are the emperor's, and to God the things that are God's
>
> Mt. 22.21

> Give to the emperor the things that are the emperor's, give to God the things that are God's, and what is mine, give that to me.
>
> *Gos. Thom.* 100.2 translation Tobias Hägerland

The manuscript found at Nag Hammadi is written in Coptic and can be dated to around 340, but it is clear that the text was initially composed in Greek. Indeed, the Greek originals of a few of the sayings of Jesus in the *Gospel of Thomas* had already been recovered at the beginning of the twentieth century. Some scholars, such as Stephen Patterson, have argued that the first Greek version was written as early as the first century, independently of the canonical gospels, which would make the *Gospel of Thomas* a very important source (Patterson 1993: 18–73). More recent investigations by Simon Gathercole and Mark Goodacre have shown that this cannot be correct. The author or authors of the *Gospel of Thomas* must have been familiar with the canonical gospels, and what is most likely is that the *Gospel of Thomas* was composed sometime in the middle of the second century (Gathercole 2012; Goodacre 2012). This does not rule out the possibility that some of the sayings of Jesus in the *Gospel of Thomas* may in fact have been preserved in a form closer to the original than in the canonical gospels. However, it is unlikely that the *Gospel of Thomas* presents a more accurate overall picture of Jesus. Notably, the *Gospel of Thomas* lacks the firm rooting in Jewish identity that is readily apparent in the canonical gospels. For example, Jesus relativizes the value of circumcision in the *Gospel of Thomas* (*Gos. Thom.* 53), which is, historically speaking, completely implausible.

Why so little about Jesus?

Thus, among texts written by Christians, the canonical gospels nonetheless represent our most important sources, but what about other, external documents? Are there any early non-Christian texts that can supplement or indeed correct the information about Jesus in the canonical gospels? No, in fact there aren't. The references to Christ, or 'Chrestus', found in Pliny the Younger (d. *c.*112), Tacitus (d. *c.*118), Suetonius (d. 130s?) and Lucian (d. *c.* 200) are early testimonies about Christ-believers in the Roman Empire, but they do not supply any knowledge about the historical Jesus. More interesting are two references in Josephus's work *Antiquities of the Jews* (*Ant.*). On one occasion Josephus mentions Jesus in passing, when he relates that a certain James was sentenced to death by stoning and identifies him as the 'brother of Jesus who is called Christ' (*Ant.* 20.200). Later in the *Antiquities of the Jews* we find a more detailed passage about Jesus. Among scholars it is known as the *Testimonium Flavianum* (loosely 'the testimony of Flavius Josephus'). In translation from Greek it reads as follows:

> About this time appeared Jesus, a wise man, if indeed it is appropriate to call him a man. For he was a doer of wondrous deeds, a teacher of such people as receive the truth with pleasure. He won over both many Jews and many of Greek origin. He is the one who was Christ. When Pilate had condemned him to be crucified on the basis of an accusation by the most prominent men among us, those who had in the first place come to love him did not give up. For he had appeared to them on the third day, restored to life, in accordance with the prophets of God, who had prophesied these and myriads of other marvellous things about him. And up to now, the tribe of the Christians, so called after him, has not disappeared.
>
> *Ant.* 18.63–64 translation Tobias Hägerland

At first glance this text seems to broadly confirm the narratives about Jesus in the canonical gospels. But scholars disagree about the value of this text as a historical source. One theory, advocated in recent times by Ken Olson, holds that the entire passage about Jesus is the later addition of some Christian scribe and thus has nothing to do with Josephus (Olson 1999). This would explain why the passage contains a seemingly transparent confession of faith in Jesus as the Christ/Messiah and why early Christian writers do not seem to have been aware that Josephus refers to Jesus in such detail. Other scholars, among whom are Geza Vermes and John Meier, argue that the framework of the passage comes from Josephus and that it started out as a neutral – or even dismissive – report about Jesus. A later Christian scribe is then supposed to have 'improved' the text with insertions – that Jesus was more than human, that he was the Christ/Messiah, and that he rose from the dead (Vermes 1987; Meier 1991: 56–88). A third theory, advocated by among others Alice Whealey and T. C. Schmidt, holds that it is plausible after all to assume that Josephus wrote the whole passage and that it has been altered only marginally or not at all by scribes of later generations (Whealey 2003). For the phrases in the text that have commonly been interpreted as Christian confessions can be understood in other ways. The qualification 'if indeed it is appropriate to call him a man' is similar to the way Josephus writes about other prophets and hence is not necessarily an indication that the author saw Jesus as divine in the sense Christian tradition did. The assertion 'He is the one who was Christ' may be a way of identifying Jesus as 'the so-called Christ' rather than an expression of the author's own belief. As demonstrated by Schmidt, the seeming confession of the resurrection through the phrase 'he had appeared to them on the third day, restored to life' may be more appropriately translated as a more detached statement, 'it seemed to them that he had been restored to life on the third day' (Schmidt 2018). It does not seem improbable, then, that the passage was in fact written by Josephus and thus constitutes evidence that a distillation of the gospel story was known outside Christ-believing circles at the end of the first century. What is improbable, however, is that the *Testimonium Flavianum* is based on information independent of the Christ-believers' traditions. Josephus's statement that Jesus' followers were of both Jewish and Greek (i.e. gentile) origin conflicts with the otherwise unambiguous picture of Jesus as the leader of a movement wholly internal to Judaism. It is more likely that the groups of Christ-believers in Rome in Josephus's own time were made up of both Jews and gentiles, and that Josephus therefore assumes that Jesus himself founded a movement of this kind. His reference to Jesus as 'a wise man' likewise indicates that Josephus was influenced by the portrayal of Jesus as a wisdom teacher in some Christian texts. Elsewhere Josephus uses the phrase 'a wise man' to describe Solomon and Daniel, two of the Hebrew Bible's most learned personages. That the historical Jesus fits into the mould of a man of learning is less likely. Rather, as we shall see later (ch. 5), Jesus was a so-called popular prophet, and the fact that Josephus does not characterize him as such confirms that he does not have access to information about Jesus beyond what Roman Christ-believers provided him with.

Contemporary non-Christian sources are thus essentially silent about Jesus, but we should not overstate the significance of this fact. We might be tempted to conclude that Jesus could be a completely fabricated figure, since the only real information we have about him comes from groups who saw in him the awaited Messiah and for whom the story of Jesus' life, death and resurrection had a decisive existential meaning. Such a conclusion, however, would be unfounded. As we will see later, the fundamental story of Jesus contains too many elements that are inconvenient from a Christ-believer's point of view for it to be explicable as outright myth or fiction. The reason why Jesus is scarcely mentioned by first-century Roman and Jewish historians is not that he never existed, but rather that during his lifetime he appeared to be fairly unimportant. To be sure, there is reason to trust reports in the Gospels that Jesus attracted large crowds of followers and that he got into conflicts with the religious and political establishment both in Galilee and in Jerusalem. The fact that he was executed for treason suggests that Jesus was regarded as a potential instigator of rebellion. But in the wider context none of these details need have attracted much attention – Flavius Josephus mentions a number of prophets and Messiah figures who achieved notoriety among the uneducated Jewish classes in the middle of the first century and who later suffered a brutal fate at the hands of the Roman authorities. In the first decades following Jesus' death, the Christ-believer movement was probably regarded as a marginal phenomenon, as but one insignificant sect in a long line of Jewish dissident groups, which would soon disappear and be replaced by something new.

Paul and oral tradition

The starting point, therefore, for even today's historians is the Christ-believers' own texts, the Gospels. As we have pointed out, these texts are relatively late in comparison with the events they describe, but their value as historical sources increases with the realization that the Gospels contain traditions that are significantly older.

In the year 56/57 CE a letter was written by the missionary Paul, a founder of congregations who himself had never met Jesus, to the Christ-believing community in Corinth, in present-day Greece. The letter contains a series of instructions and admonitions regarding various aspects of the congregation, and Paul invokes other authorities several times, above all the Hebrew Bible, but also traditions about what Jesus purportedly said and did during his earthly life.

While making an argument in the letter about marriage and divorce, Paul mentions a 'command' that is from 'the Lord' that states that divorce and remarriage is forbidden (1 Cor. 7.10-11). By 'the Lord' he means Jesus. In a subsequent discussion of the right of apostles and missionaries to maintenance, Paul writes that 'the Lord commanded that those who proclaim the gospel should get their living by the gospel' (1 Cor. 9.14). Both of these rules seem to refer to sayings of Jesus that are recorded in the Gospels. However, it is not as though Paul and the Christ-believers he is writing to had access to these sayings in some written text. Rather they knew them through oral tradition. On a couple of occasions, Paul explicitly mentions that he is passing on such a tradition. The most interesting case is the brief account of Jesus' last supper:

> I received from the Lord what I also handed on to you, that the Lord Jesus on the night when he was betrayed took a loaf of bread, and when he had given thanks, he broke it and said, 'This is my body that is for you. Do this in remembrance of me.' In the same way he took the cup also, after supper, saying, 'This cup is the new covenant in my blood. Do this, as often as you drink it, in remembrance of me.'
>
> 1 Cor. 11.23–25

The Greek words translated as 'I received' and 'I handed on' here were used in antiquity to express how an authoritative, usually oral, tradition was committed to memory and taught to others. Thus, what Paul is claiming here is that on a previous visit to Corinth – probably his year-and-a-half long stay in the city in the very early 50s – he taught the story of Jesus' last supper, which we also find in the Synoptic Gospels of several years later. Paul reports that the story was told to him by others, perhaps as early as his joining the Christ-believer movement in the mid-30s. All of a sudden we are not very far removed in time from the historical Jesus.

Research into the Synoptic Gospels has demonstrated that in all likelihood the oral tradition went far beyond the sayings of Jesus and stories about him that Paul happens to refer to in his letters. At the beginning of the twentieth century, German scholars associated with the method of form criticism, most notably Martin Dibelius and Rudolf Bultmann, discovered that the Gospels are in reality collections of independent episodes about Jesus and his sayings, and that these short units have only loosely been joined together into a continuous narrative. It seems plausible that before these various episodes were written down they circulated as just such oral traditions (Dibelius 1919; Bultmann 1921). More recent studies by Burton Mack, Vernon Robbins and others have pushed these insights further by highlighting the similarities between several episodes in the Gospels and a type of short mnemonic narrative, so-called '*chreiai*', which were often used in ancient times to preserve and teach traditions about the words and deeds of philosophers and other famous men (Mack and Robbins 1989). Many of the episodes about Jesus that we find in the Gospels probably had a long prehistory as traditions told orally. Nothing precludes the possibility that in the very beginning these were in fact recounted by eyewitnesses who had themselves seen and heard Jesus act and speak.

Now, this does not mean that the Gospels are altogether undistorted eyewitness accounts of Jesus, an inference sometimes too hastily drawn from Richard Bauckham's valuable work on the role of eyewitnesses in early Christ-believing communities (Bauckham 2017). Naturally, the oral traditions may have changed considerably in the decades that passed between the death of Jesus and when the Gospel of Mark was written down. Just the fact that Jesus and his disciples spoke Aramaic, a Semitic language closely related to Hebrew, means that the Greek sayings of Jesus in the Gospels do not represent precisely what Jesus actually said. We do not know when or how the Aramaic traditions were translated into Greek, but the translation appears to have taken place relatively early considering that Paul – who had mastered both languages – seems have become acquainted with the traditions in Greek. What is more, it is important to realize that our modern desire to reproduce a quotation in exactly the form that it was first uttered was not known in antiquity. When schoolboys (and, in rare cases, schoolgirls) in the first century learned traditions in the form of *chreiai*, they were also taught to 'improve' the sayings by reformulating them so that the important points came across with the greatest possible clarity. Thus, what was paramount was not word-for-word adherence to the original, but rather the endeavour to bring out the essential meaning of the tradition. When it came to narrative material, an even greater degree of freedom could be exercised. Evidently the evangelists thought likewise – as, surely, did the anonymous individuals who transmitted the traditions before them – when they altered details in the stories and sometimes even in the sayings of Jesus. For the aim in recalling Jesus' words, repeating them and ultimately writing them down was not simply to preserve the memory of the past, but also to give the words some meaning in the present. For that reason they came to be adapted for new situations and conditions. We may consider how the prohibition on divorce, for example, is formulated in several ways and with varying shades of meaning in the different texts. In Paul's writings and in the Gospel of Mark, both women and men are forbidden from divorcing and remarrying, which was otherwise possible in the Roman world (1 Cor. 7.10-11; Mk 10.11-12). By contrast, Matthew and Luke presuppose a more thoroughly Jewish background in which it is, of course, only the man who can initiate a divorce – Matthew contains an additional 'exception clause' allowing a man to divorce on the ground of 'unchastity' (Mt. 5.32; 19.7; cf. Lk. 16.18). But which of these variants of the same saying of Jesus comes closest to what he actually said? And can we really be sure that the prohibition of divorce comes from the historical Jesus?

The Gospels – Similar and different

To be able to answer these questions, we first of all have to ascertain whether and in what way the various sources are dependent on one another. Even in the early church, theologians noticed that the Synoptic Gospels exhibit major points of similarity, both in overall outline and in specific details. The similarities are especially apparent when the Synoptics are compared with the Gospel of John. For example, John presents a picture in which Jesus' activity lasts two to three years and involves several trips between Galilee and Jerusalem, whereas the Synoptics seem to depict just one year of activity and a single, decisive journey to Jerusalem.

The similarities between the Synoptics are even more striking at a greater level of detail. Scholars have calculated that 90 per cent of the events and of the sayings of Jesus recounted in the Gospel of Mark are also found in Matthew. Over 50 per cent of this same material is also found in Luke. In addition, in many instances the wording is almost identical. Below is an example, using translations from the NRSV. At times where the translation creates an impression of similarities or differences that are not present in the Greek base text, we give the Greek of the relevant phrases in brackets (See Table 1).

Although the man who became Jesus' disciple has different names and the three versions diverge linguistically at some points, the episode is narrated in such a similar way that it cannot be coincidental. The Synoptics

TABLE 1

Mt. 9.9-10	Mk 2.14-15	Lk. 5.27-29
As Jesus was walking along [*paragon*], he saw [*eiden*] a man called Matthew sitting at the tax booth [*kathemenon epi to telonion*]; and he said to him [*kai legei auto*], 'Follow me [*akolouthei moi*].'	As he was walking along [*paragon*], he saw [*eiden*] Levi son of Alphaeus sitting at the tax booth [*kathemenon epi to telonion*], and he said to him [*kai legei auto*], 'Follow me [*akolouthei moi*].'	After this he went out [*exelthen*] and saw [*etheasato*] a tax-collector named Levi, sitting at the tax booth [*kathemenon epi to telonion*]; and he said to him [*kai eipen auto*], 'Follow me [*akolouthei moi*].'
And he got up and followed him [*kai anastas ekolouthesen auto*].	And he got up and followed him [*kai anastas ekolouthesen auto*].	And he got up, left everything, and followed him [*anastas ekolouthei auto*].
And as he sat at dinner in the house [*en te oikia*], many tax-collectors and sinners [*polloi telonai kai hamartoloi*] came and were sitting with him and his disciples [*synanekeinto to Iesou kai tois mathetais autou*].	And as he sat at dinner in Levi's house [*en te oikia autou*], many tax-collectors and sinners [*polloi telonai kai hamartoloi*] were also sitting with Jesus and his disciples [*synanekeinto to Iesou kai tois mathetais autou*] – for there were many who followed him.	Then Levi gave a great banquet for him in his house [*en te oikia autou*]; and there was a large crowd of tax-collectors and others [*ochlos polys telonon kai allon*] sitting at the table with them [*esan met' auton katakeimenoi*].

must have made use either of one another or of common sources. Hence, we are not looking at three independent accounts of Jesus' words and deeds. At this point we realize that our sources are not as valuable as they may at first have seemed. For the purpose of historical reconstruction, two sources must be independent in order to be able to reinforce one another, and this is not the case with the gospels. More often than not a given episode about Jesus or saying of his is present in all of the Synoptic Gospels, but in actual fact these authors made use of one another rather than working from distinct eyewitness traditions.

Most modern scholars agree that the Gospel of Mark is the oldest of the three Synoptics. Could the reverse not be true? Could not Mark have made use of Matthew or Luke? To begin with, the Gospel of Mark is shorter than the other two and lacks important material like the Beatitudes (Mt. 5.3-12; Lk. 6.20-23) and the Lord's Prayer (Mt. 6.9-13; Lk. 11.2-4). It is hard to understand why Mark would have omitted traditions such as these if he had had access to either of the other Synoptic Gospels. A more understandable situation is if Matthew and Luke omitted the small number of episodes that are unique to Mark. The stories of Jesus healing a deaf man (Mk 7.32-36) and a blind man in Bethsaida (8.22-26), for example, do not appear in either Matthew or Luke. These episodes may have been regarded as inappropriate since in them Jesus cures with the use of saliva. On the whole, the presentation of Jesus in Matthew and Luke is more systematized, and this too speaks against Mark's being dependent upon them. One good example is the episode in which Jesus encounters disbelief and resistance in his hometown of Nazareth. Jesus 'could do no deed of power there', states Mark (Mk 6.5), whereas Matthew writes 'he did not do many deeds of power there' (Mt. 13.58). Matthew has probably changed the wording so as to avoid the image of Jesus wanting to work wonders but being unable. We may also consider the fact that, according to Luke, Jesus dies with a confident 'Father, into your hands I commend my spirit' (Lk. 23.46; cf. Ps. 31.6), but in Mark (and in Matthew) he instead cries out, 'My God, my God, why have you forsaken me?' (Mk 15.34; Mt. 27.46; cf. Ps. 22.2), which might imply that Jesus did indeed experience a sense of being abandoned by God on the cross. Here, too, Mark's version must be the more original.

If the Gospel of Mark was written first, then it remains for us to determine the relationship between Matthew and Luke. On this issue there is greater disagreement among scholars. In the mid-twentieth century, Austin Farrer proposed a fairly simple solution: Luke used Mark and Matthew as sources when he wrote his own gospel (Farrer 1955). There are many reasons to believe that Luke was indeed the last of the Synoptic Gospels to be written. Luke's Greek is of a higher standard than the language of Mark and Matthew, and in many places we can see that Luke has improved upon the wording of the other two. For example, the Sea of Galilee, properly a freshwater lake, is called a 'lake' (Greek *limne*) in Luke and not a 'sea' (*thalassa*), as it is referred to, somewhat misleadingly, in Mark and Matthew. According to the adherents of Farrer's hypothesis, supposing that Luke used the two other Synoptics explains why the Gospel is at times closer to Mark, but at other times agrees more with Matthew. For Luke and Matthew have a great deal of material in common that is found nowhere in the Gospel of Mark. We have already pointed out that the Beatitudes and the Lord's Prayer are absent from Mark. In total, the material in question common to Matthew and Luke comprises roughly two hundred verses, most of which are sayings of Jesus (e.g. much of the content of the Sermon on the Mount in Mt. 5–7, or the Sermon on the Plain in Lk. 6) and, to a lesser extent, narrative episodes (e.g. the account of Jesus' temptation in the wilderness, Mt. 4.1–11; Lk. 4.1–13). Could all of this be material added by Matthew to what was already found in Mark? If so, at a later stage Luke might have adopted this material from Matthew.

In recent times an increasing number of scholars have been persuaded by Farrer's hypothesis and have argued in support of it. Above all, Mark

Goodacre has provided strong arguments in favour of this hypothesis in several well-received publications (e.g. Goodacre 2002). Nevertheless we have reason to doubt the idea that Luke did indeed use the Gospel of Matthew. One important objection is that Matthew displays a very well-organized structure and that it is hard to explain why this structure is not taken up in Luke in any way. Matthew, uniquely, has separated most of Jesus' teaching from the narrative episodes and has gathered it into five cohesive speeches, or 'discourses'. The most extensive discourse is the Sermon on the Mount (Mt. 5–7). In Matthew we also find the Mission Discourse (Mt. 10), the Parabolic Discourse (Mt. 13), the Discourse on the Church (Mt. 18) and the Olivet Discourse (Mt. 24–25). Much of the content of these discourses is precisely material not found in Mark's Gospel but present in Luke. Yet in Luke this teaching does not form large blocks, as in Matthew, but is rather interspersed throughout the wider narrative at several points, in a way that seems more haphazard. To most scholars it seems highly unlikely that a capable author like Luke would have broken up the neat structure of the Gospel of Matthew in such a way.

Another objection to Luke's being dependent on Matthew may be even more evident. In the first chapter, we touched upon the fact that the stories about Jesus' background, birth and upbringing are very different in Matthew and Luke. The difference lies not only in that Matthew tells the story from Joseph's perspective, while Luke views the events through Mary's eyes. In addition, Matthew includes a series of episodes not referred to in Luke: the visit of the Magi from the East, the flight to Egypt, and the massacre of the infants in Bethlehem (Mt. 2.1-18). For his part, Luke has an account of the shepherds near Bethlehem, something not included in the Gospel of Matthew (Lk. 2.8-20). On some points Matthew and Luke seem to directly contradict one another. One thing is for certain: Luke can hardly have been using Matthew's Gospel when he was composing his story of Jesus' birth and childhood. Only when Jesus, in adulthood, gets baptized by John the Baptist do similarities begin to appear between Matthew's and Luke's narratives, which is also the point at which the Gospel of Mark begins its story of Jesus. This should lead us to the conclusion that Matthew and Luke independently used some version of Mark, each without making use of the other. As argued most extensively by Delbert Burkett, they most likely had access to an earlier, now lost edition of Mark's Gospel, which is usually given the name 'Proto-Mark' in biblical scholarship (Burkett 2004).

The two-source hypothesis

How, then, should we explain the material common to Matthew and Luke that lacks parallels in Mark, for example the Lord's Prayer and the episode of Jesus' temptation by Satan? The most common explanation since the 1830s is the two-source hypothesis. According to this hypothesis, which is advocated by John Kloppenborg, Burkett and other present-day scholars, Matthew and Luke had access to an additional text that no longer exists (Kloppenborg 1999; Burkett 2009). This hypothetical document is known as 'Q' (from *Quelle,* 'source', the name given, rather unimaginatively, by German scholars). Thus, Matthew and Luke took material from the Gospel of Mark and from Q, combined that material in different ways and added material of their own as well.

A fairly common objection to the two-source hypothesis is that it presumes the existence of a text that no one has been able to produce. Should such guesswork really count as academic research? As a matter of fact, it is not uncommon for scholars to hypothesize the existence of objects that no one has been able to observe. In the 1840s, around the time that the two-source hypothesis was gaining a foothold among biblical scholars, astronomers were starting to realize that our solar system must contain additional celestial objects beyond Uranus, the farthest known planet at the time. Uranus's path around the sun was not entirely regular, and it seemed as if something else was affecting it. By the end of the century, Neptune had been observed for the first time. Yet the mystery of Uranus's orbit had still not been satisfactorily solved. For several years the search continued for what people were calling 'Planet X'. It was only in 1930 that an American astronomer succeeded in observing and photographing 'Planet X', or Pluto, as it came to be called. The existence of Pluto was no longer a hypothesis, but a fact.

Biblical scholars have not been as fortunate as astronomers when it comes to locating the unknown object Q. There is, of course, a chance that a copy of Q has survived in some place with a desert climate and may one day be found, but the chance is extremely small. Scholars who accept the two-source hypothesis instead have to try to reconstruct Q using Matthew and Luke. As we mentioned above, the material that these two gospels have in common, and which is not taken from the Gospel of Mark, consists mainly of sayings of Jesus, without any narrative to link them together. Q seems to have contained a relatively large amount of material about John the Baptist and his prophetic pronouncements (e.g. Mt. 3.7-10 = Lk. 3.7-9; Mt. 11.7-11 = Lk. 7.24-28). A great deal of space in this gospel was devoted to Jesus' ethical teaching, including the core of the Sermon on the Mount/ Sermon on the Plain. The Mission Discourses in Mt. 10 and Lk. 10 likewise seem to be based on Q. There were some parables in Q, such as the parable of the lost sheep (Mt. 18.12-13 = Lk. 15.4-7). Two narrative episodes were also part of Q: the stories of the temptation of Jesus (Mt. 4.1-11 = Lk. 4.1-13) and of the healing of the centurion's servant (Mt. 8.5-13 = Lk. 7.1-10). Many of the sayings of Jesus in Q are concerned with the imminent coming of the Son of Man for judgement as well as vindication (e.g. Mt. 24.42-44 = Lk. 12.39-40; Mt. 8.11-12 = Lk. 13.28-29). Some scholars, notably Kloppenborg, have supposed that the different theological attitudes evident in the material are due to the fact that Q was composed in several stages (Kloppenborg 1999). This may, of course, be true, but it is almost impossible to identify different editorial 'strata' in a text that no longer exists. What we can be more certain of is that Q did not contain anything corresponding to the account of the suffering, death and resurrection of Jesus found in the Gospel of Mark.

The conclusion must therefore be that the Synoptic Gospels do not constitute three independent sources, but two – Mark and Q – with the second of these, moreover, having to be reconstructed on the basis of other texts. In a few exceptional cases, as already mentioned, we have additional evidence for traditions about Jesus from Paul's letters. Paul drew exclusively on oral traditions and neither Mark nor Q is likely to be directly dependent on Paul's letters. The Gospel of John is another matter. For one thing, it is unclear whether John represents a tradition all of its own or whether it too is dependent on Mark for some portions. What is more, the statements attributed to Jesus in John's Gospel are so radically different in nature from all the other source material that they cannot possibly go back to the historical Jesus. John's Jesus is entirely preoccupied with expounding his identity as the Son of God, his mission as the saviour of the world and his relationship to the Father, whereas Mark, Q and the meagre evidence in Paul paint a picture of a prophet whose primary focus is on debating the Torah and its interpretation, in light of apocalyptic ideas.

Let us return to Jesus' prohibition of divorce. There is no trace of it in John, which is not surprising considering what has just been said about the tendentious nature of this particular gospel. The prohibition is, however, cited once each by Paul, Mark and Luke, and twice by Matthew:

> To the married I give this command – not I but the Lord – that the wife should not separate from her husband (but if she does separate, let her remain unmarried or else be reconciled to her husband), and that the husband should not divorce his wife.
>
> 1 Cor. 7.10-11

> [Jesus] said to them, 'Whoever divorces his wife and marries another commits adultery against her; and if she divorces her husband and marries another, she commits adultery.'
>
> Mk 10.11-12

> 'But I say to you that anyone who divorces his wife, except on the ground of unchastity, causes her to commit adultery; and whoever marries a divorced woman commits adultery.'
>
> Mt. 5.32

> 'And I say to you, whoever divorces his wife, except for unchastity, and marries another commits adultery.'
>
> Mt. 19.9

'Anyone who divorces his wife and marries another commits adultery, and whoever marries a woman divorced from her husband commits adultery.'

Lk. 16.18

What at first glance appear to be five witnesses to the same saying of Jesus are in actual fact three at most. The first is the report of Paul in his letter to the Christ-believers in Corinth. The second is the attestation in the Gospel of Mark, which talks about how both men and women are liable for violating their former marital relationships if they divorce and remarry. Matthew has adopted this saying from Mark, but has edited it by inserting his exception clause and deleting the section dealing with divorce on a woman's initiative (Mt. 19.10). The third attestation comes from Q, where the idea is that a man is liable for violating a woman's marital relationship with her former husband if he remarries her. The Q variant probably looked something like the saying in Mt. 5.32, except that Matthew has added in the exception clause there too. It is not uncommon for Matthew to include double variants of a single saying of Jesus that appears in both Mark and Q. Luke, by contrast, prefers to choose one variant or the other or to combine the wording of Mark with that of Q. In this case, Luke's version is precisely a combination of the first section of the Marcan form (a man violates his own marital relationship through divorce and remarriage) with the second section of the form in Q (a man violates a divorced woman's marital relationship by marrying her).

Strictly speaking, the three witnesses – Paul, Mark and Q – are not independent of one other. They do not derive from different eyewitnesses to Jesus' activity but in all likelihood from a common tradition. They are, however, 'literarily' independent, meaning that the agreement among them is not due to the authors' having copied from each other's texts. This is an indication that the saying of Jesus in question was circulating in early, oral tradition, which thus increases the likelihood that it really does come from the historical Jesus.

Myth and history

But is it really feasible to extract historical data from the New Testament? Admittedly, as even an inexperienced reader of the Bible will quickly discover, the Gospels give a significantly more realistic and down-to-earth impression than the book of Genesis, for example, or Revelation. Nevertheless, it is clear that these are texts written by people with a worldview in which God, angels and demons exist and frequently manifest themselves in worldly events. The main character himself is certainly presented as a human being, but his entire life is marked by the miraculous: the virgin birth in Matthew and Luke, the encounter with Satan in the wilderness in the Synoptic Gospels, unexplainable wonders in every Gospel and the astonishing resurrection from the dead which the entire New Testament revolves around. For a source to be considered historically reliable, the claims it makes must not be obviously implausible in light of what we already know with certainty. The Gospels are full of implausible claims of this kind, in particular given our modern scientific understanding of how the world works. Can we use them for the purpose of historical research at all, then?

Despite all this, the answer to the question has to be yes. If we were to require ancient sources to be entirely free of what we think of as myth and legend for them to enter into consideration in historical research, there would be very little material left. Take Josephus, for example, whom we have already mentioned and whose work is an invaluable source for knowledge about how events unfolded in the Holy Land in the first century. Josephus, who otherwise does not refrain from ridiculing his uneducated countrymen for their gullibility and superstitiousness, recounts in all earnestness a series of curious omens that are supposed to have appeared in the years immediately preceding the fall of Jerusalem in 70 CE (*War* 6.289–300). A star resembling a sword stood over the city for a whole year. One night, around the temple and its altar it became inexplicably bright, like broad daylight. A cow gave birth to a lamb in the temple compound. An immensely heavy temple door of bronze opened by itself. Just before sunset one evening, all across the land heavenly chariots and warring armies were spotted in the clouds. The priests who came to officiate at night-time services in the temple felt the ground shaking and heard a multitude of voices saying 'we are departing from here'. Josephus admits that all of this might seem like just so many fables, were it not for the fact that the events were corroborated by eyewitnesses and furthermore fit well with the tragic fate which later befell Jerusalem and the temple (*War* 6.297–298). Josephus's conceptual world is not a reason for historians today to dismiss his work as myth from start to finish, but we must bear in mind that he looked at the world and at history in a way different from our own, and the same is true when we use the Gospels as historical sources.

Implausible elements in the Gospels

The implausible elements in the Gospels that a modern historian must disregard or explain in some other way are really of several different kinds. The first and most obvious category is reports that divine or demonic beings are directly involved in the course of worldly events, such as when the heavenly retinue announced their imminent departure from the temple, according to Josephus's chronicle. Supernatural interventions of this sort are relatively uncommon in the Gospels, but on a few occasions angels do appear and the voice of God himself is heard confirming that Jesus is the Son of God at Jesus' baptism as well as on the so-called Mount of Transfiguration – where incidentally Moses and Elijah, two heroes of old, also show up (Mk 1.11; 9.7). These are clear examples of mythological material that will be left out when we reconstruct historical events. It must be emphasized that historians do not claim to be able to determine whether or not gods, angels and demons exist. But it is a fundamental principle in historical research today that every event should theoretically be explainable as the effect of a known cause within the world, and supernatural beings do not meet these requirements.

Another type of historical implausibility consists of incidents that are given mythological interpretations by the evangelists but for which more historically satisfactory explanations can be given. From the start Jesus was known as an exorcist and wonder-worker, even in his own lifetime. The miraculous deeds attributed to Jesus in the Gospels are predominantly the sorts of wonders by which faith-healers in various times and cultures have made a name for themselves. Jesus manages to rid people of fever, skin disease, paralysis and haemorrhaging; he causes the blind to see and the deaf to hear; he makes those possessed behave normally again. The sicknesses and disabilities that Jesus attended to were so-called 'conversion disorders', that is, conditions that seemingly have a physical cause but may in reality be the result of intense psychological or social stress. Historically speaking, it is entirely plausible that people who came into contact with Jesus felt that he had the power to 'heal' them (Meier 1994: 617–45; Eve 2009). Certainly they likewise interpreted his successes in this area mythologically, just as the evangelists do later: Jesus' ability to heal people and drive out unclean spirits showed that the power of God was working through him. As historians, we must make a careful distinction between an event and the religious interpretation of it.

A third type of implausibility includes stories of Jesus raising the dead and the so-called 'nature miracles', such as the episodes where Jesus miraculously provides food for thousands of people in a deserted place (Mk 6.34-44), walks on water (Mk 6.45-52) or turns water into wine (Jn 2.1-11). No matter which angle we look at these stories from, they clearly make claims that cannot be reconciled with our scientific knowledge about how reality is constituted. Certain scholars have argued that some of these accounts may reflect experiences of 'altered states of consciousness' in which, for example, Jesus' disciples may really have believed that Jesus was walking on the surface of the water (Craffert and Botha 2005). A more plausible explanation of these episodes is that they are some sort of representation in narrative of the fact that the first Christ-believers, drawing inspiration from the Hebrew Bible, professed Jesus as the Lord (Eve 2009: 145–60). Jesus reveals himself by 'passing by' the disciples, as God himself does (cf. Exod. 33.22); like God, Jesus is able to walk 'through the sea' (Ps. 77.20; Isa. 43.16).

Finally, the Gospels contain information that conflicts with our other knowledge of history. A vivid episode in Mark's Gospel relates that Jesus went by boat 'to the other side of the lake, to the country of the Gerasenes', where he casts out several unclean spirits from a possessed man. When the spirits leave the man, they enter two thousand pigs, which rush straight down into the lake and drown (Mk 5.1-20). The story is doubtful to begin with because of the mythological touches and the unrealistic behaviour of the animals. But in addition Gerasa, lying approximately fifty kilometres south of the Sea of Galilee, is nowhere near a lake. Perhaps this story was never meant to be taken literally, but was intended as some sort of veiled criticism of Roman military presence in and around the Jewish homeland, as we will discuss further in Chapter 7. Another tradition that is difficult to reconcile with known historical realities is the prohibition of divorce as recorded by Paul and in the Gospel of Mark. As mentioned above, one difference between Roman and Jewish marriage law was that Roman law permitted both husbands and wives to initiate divorce, whereas Jewish law reserved that privilege for men. Thus, a woman's ability to seek a divorce was not an issue of immediate concern among Jews, which makes it hard to understand why the historical Jesus would have considered that eventuality at all when debating the subject of divorce with other Jews. Jesus can only have stated an opinion about men not being permitted to divorce, which is more or less what we find in the Q form of the prohibition, as reconstructed from Matthew and Luke. Later Paul and Mark adapted his statement for another cultural situation.

Portrait of a hero – with beauty spots

It almost goes without saying that a source should be as neutral as possible for us to be able to use it for the purpose of historical research. For example, if we set out to create a picture of a political conflict in some country, we cannot assume without further investigation that what is asserted in various partisan sources is reliable information. Ideally every claim made in such a source that seems to be influenced by the author's values should be checked against an external source that lacks an interest in correcting the account. A major problem for scholarship on the historical Jesus is that all of our sources are highly tendentious. The whole of the New Testament was written by people who believed that Jesus was the Messiah and the Son of God and who wanted to confirm themselves and others in that belief. There is never any doubt that Jesus is the great hero in the Gospels. In cases where his behaviour might be considered objectionable by an external observer, for instance when Jesus utters a curse on a fig tree simply because it lacks fruit (Mk 11.12-14) or when he bluntly denies a disciple the chance to bury his dead father (Mt. 8.21-22), there is no indication that the evangelists are being critical of Jesus. They start from the assumption that Jesus is always right and that those who oppose him – not least the ever-present Pharisees – are motivated by concern for prestige and evil intent.

Since Jesus stood as the great authority figure for the Christ-believers who transmitted and wrote down the traditions about him, the idea of putting their own beliefs into his mouth naturally presented itself. By this means, their ideas could appear to bear the ultimate endorsement. This tendency is especially marked in the Gospel of John, where Jesus time and again expresses highly developed theological ideas about himself. In fact, the verse sometimes called 'the gospel in a nutshell' is part of a longer speech that Jesus himself gives in John: 'God so loved the world that he gave his only Son, so that everyone who believes in him may not perish but may have eternal life' (Jn 3.16). This verse has been considered a concisely formulated expression of the entire Christian message, but it cannot possibly document something that the historical Jesus said. The themes of God's universal love for 'the world', Jesus' identity as the 'only Son' of God, and the possibility for humans to attain 'eternal life' are not ones that fit especially well with the traditions about Jesus that are found in Paul's writings and in the Synoptic Gospels. They are, on the other hand, very prominent in the so-called Johannine literature of the New Testament, and where we find such statements on Jesus' lips, we can be quite certain that it was the evangelist who invented them. This is not an isolated example; it is a regular phenomenon in John's Gospel, and scholars are therefore wary of trusting the sayings of Jesus in this work. Even so, the surrounding narrative sometimes does seem to contain details that make more sense than the Synoptics. For example, Jesus probably made several journeys to Jerusalem, as John writes, in contrast to the Synoptics.

Not all Christ-believers exercised as much liberty as the author of John's Gospel in having Jesus express ideas that they themselves favoured. Above we dealt with Paul's allusion to Jesus' prohibition of divorce and remarriage, which he refers to as a 'command of the Lord'. In the same discussion, when addressing the issue of the unmarried members of the congregation, Paul is clear in his opinion that these should preferably not get married. Interestingly, however, he does not try to make out that this stance is also based on a tradition from Jesus: 'Now concerning virgins, I have no command of the Lord, but I give my opinion' (1 Cor. 7.25). Paul's letters are certainly tendentious, too, but Paul was far more careful to distinguish between his own teachings and those of Jesus than was the author of John's Gospel. Somewhere between these two poles lie the Synoptic Gospels. On one hand, in some cases they clearly reformulate and embellish Jesus' words to such an extent that the words cannot be considered authentic. On the other hand, they do not permit themselves anything like the degree of unbridled creativity evident in the Gospel of John.

During the past decade, scholars have been increasingly discussing the question whether it is at all meaningful to distinguish between 'authentic' and 'inauthentic' elements in the Synoptic Gospels. James Dunn, Dale Allison and Chris Keith have in various ways drawn attention to the role played by memory in the early Christ-believing movement. As memory processes work, human beings tend to remember the general characteristics of events and persons, rather than the tiny details. When we recall something in the past, we also tend to reinterpret whatever we are remembering within the interpretative framework of our present concerns and convictions. Accordingly, these researchers have argued, it is unlikely that we will be able to find bits and pieces of unsullied 'authentic' information encapsulated within a bulk of 'inauthentic', theologically motivated, fabrications (Dunn 2003: 125–34; Allison 2010: 10–22; Keith 2011). This is a good point. We should bear in mind that, whenever we speak of authentic or historical information, this does not in any way mean that it has come down to us by any other channel than through the early Christ-believers, who remembered, reworded and reinterpreted it before and after putting it into writing. Nevertheless the method of historical source criticism enables us to maintain a distinction between, on the one hand, traditions that have a basis in actual perceptions of the historical Jesus, and the other hand, traditions that have a basis in the inventive activities of Christ-believers.

If the sources do seem to exhibit clear theological bents, then features that seem to go against the grain, so to speak, are particularly noteworthy. Some traditions about Jesus seem not to have been especially well-suited to the Christ-believers' goals of spreading their message about him and advancing their theology. The less useful a tradition is for these goals, the more certain we can be that it is not invented. A fascinating example is Jesus' usage of the phrase 'the Son of Man', which he uses about eighty times in the Gospels. Some occasions seem to be inspired by the vision of 'one like a human being' in the book of Daniel (Dan. 7.13), and according to the Gospels this refers to Jesus himself. What is interesting is that, with just one exception (Acts 7.56), there is no evidence that any of the first generations of Christ-believers called Jesus the Son of Man. Jesus is called Lord, Christ, Son of God and so on, but Son of Man was apparently not among his standard titles. For that reason it is also unlikely that Jesus' own use of the phrase in the Gospels is an invention of Christ-believers.

Sometimes we may suspect that a certain tradition was not simply not useful to those who passed it on and wrote it down, but positively inconvenient. Once again the prohibition of divorce provides a good example. The rule, as formulated by the historical Jesus, was an absolute ban on men divorcing and remarrying. But it seems to have been difficult to uphold such a radical ideal in Christ-believing circles. As we have seen, Matthew has added the qualification that 'unchastity' can constitute grounds for divorce. Paul argues that the rule cannot be applied as strictly in cases where a Christ-believer is married to a non-believer. If divorce is brought about on the initiative of the non-believing party, the believing 'brother or sister is not bound' (1 Cor. 7.15). Encroaching realities begin to chip away at the prohibition of divorce. The very fact that these writers held on to the principle even though it created practical difficulties suggests that they could not ignore its origins with Jesus himself.

Some aspects of the stories, it seems, were almost embarrassing for the evangelists. In the next chapter we are going to see how the memory that Jesus once received John's baptism of repentance was so well-known that it could not be ignored, despite the fact that it did not really fit with the image of him as the undeniable and infallible leader. Another awkward element in the accounts is Jesus' unfortunate choice of followers. All four canonical gospels explicitly state that Jesus himself chose 'the Twelve', the innermost circle of disciples, and that Judas Iscariot was one of these chosen disciples. The story ends in tragedy with Judas betraying Jesus and handing him over to the authorities. The evangelists go to great lengths to illustrate that this betrayal was part of God's plan and that Jesus knew what was going to happen, but these explanations were clearly contrived after the fact with the intention of masking a failure. In the Synoptics, at the last supper Jesus predicts that one of those present will betray him (Mk 14.18-21). According to John, Jesus knew that Judas was 'a devil' well in advance (Jn 6.70-71), even directly urging him to go through with the betrayal (Jn 13.27). Any impression that Jesus misjudged Judas had to be avoided, but the authors could not simply deny that Judas had belonged to the chosen few. These and other such traditions cannot have been added later. Rather, they are among the most secure information we have about the historical Jesus.

There are other details in the Gospels that likewise diverge from the tendentious portrayal of Jesus as a hero and can therefore be regarded as historically reliable. But the most important one is that their overarching plot is really an attempt to deal with the most embarrassing reality of all: that Jesus' life did not end with a triumphant enthronement in Jerusalem or with the heavenly army intervening, but with his being executed as one amongst several agitators against Roman authority. Although the authors of the New Testament are all convinced that in the end Jesus had his revenge in being raised by God, they have various strategies for dealing with the difficulty of why he needed to die such a degrading death at all. None of these theological explanations manage to completely disguise the problematic reality that Jesus did in fact fail. Some stories are said to be too good to be true. When it comes to the Gospels, we have to say that their stories are not 'good' enough to be altogether dismissed as fiction.

Summary

Any reconstruction of the life, mission and message of the historical Jesus has to be based on the New Testament gospels. These are written sources that pose a number of challenges to the historian. For one thing, they post-date Jesus by between thirty-five and seventy years and were not authored by eyewitnesses. For another, they are not independent of each other, as both the Gospel of Matthew and the Gospel of Luke appear to draw on the Gospel of Mark and on a now lost source commonly labelled 'Q'. Even more disturbingly for the purpose of historical reconstruction, the Gospels are strongly biased in favour of their main character, and to varying degrees Jesus is used as a mouthpiece for their authors' own theological convictions. The latter holds true especially for the Gospel of John, which is of very limited value as a source for sayings of the historical Jesus. Finally, and just like many other literary works of this period, the Gospels repeatedly make claims that clash with a modern scientific world-view or with general historical knowledge.

Fortunately, biblical scholars have developed strategies for getting around all of these obstacles. The time gap between Jesus and the written Gospels can be narrowed by taking into consideration Paul's letters, which provide evidence that sayings attributed to Jesus and stories about him were circulated orally in the early years following his death. By comparing the Gospel of Mark with the material that the Gospels of Matthew and Luke drew from Q, it is possible to establish an inventory of very early traditions about Jesus. Scientific and historical implausibilities can be filtered away, and the Gospels' theological biases are useful as foils that highlight those pieces of information that seem to diverge from their tendentious overall character. Hence, embarrassing details about Jesus and information that seems to go against the theological ideals of the authors are among the most valuable elements in any portrayal of the historical Jesus.

Of course, to make sense of these elements, we need to situate them within the network of relationships that linked Jesus with other individuals and groups. In order to understand Jesus' mission, first of all we need to know something about the person who had had a major influence on Jesus before Jesus embarked upon his public career. It is therefore time to turn to John the Baptist.

Bibliography

Allison, D. C. (2010), *Constructing Jesus: Memory, Imagination, and History*, London: SPCK.

Bauckham, R. (2017), *Jesus and the Eyewitnesses: The Gospels as Eyewitness Testimony*, 2nd edn, Grand Rapids: Eerdmans.

Bultmann, R. (1921), *Die Geschichte der synoptischen Tradition*, Göttingen: Vandenhoeck & Ruprecht.

Burkett, D. (2004), *Rethinking the Gospel Sources: From Proto-Mark to Mark*, New York: T&T Clark.

Burkett, D. (2009), *Rethinking the Gospel Sources: The Unity and Plurality of Q*, Atlanta: Society of Biblical Literature.

Burridge, R. A. (1992), *What Are the Gospels? A Comparison with Graeco-Roman Biography*, Cambridge: Cambridge University Press.

Craffert, P. F. and P. J. J. Botha (2005), 'Why Jesus Could Walk on the Sea but He Could not Read and Write: Reflections on Historicity and Interpretation in Historical Jesus Research', *Neotestamentica* 39: 5–35.

Dibelius, M. (1919), *Die Formgeschichte des Evangeliums*, Tübingen: Mohr.
Dunn, J. D. G. (2003), *Christianity in the Making, vol. 1: Jesus Remembered*, Grand Rapids: Eerdmans.
Eve, E. (2009), *The Healer from Nazareth: Jesus' Miracles in Historical Context*, London: SPCK.
Farrer, A. M. (1955), 'On Dispensing with Q', in D. E. Nineham (ed.), *Studies in the Gospels: Essays in Memory of R. H. Lightfoot*, 55–88, Oxford: Blackwell.
Gathercole, S. (2012), *The Composition of the Gospel of Thomas: Original Language and Influences*, Cambridge: Cambridge University Press.
Goodacre, M. (2002), *The Case Against Q: Studies in Markan Priority and the Synoptic Problem*, Harrisburg: Trinity Press International.
Goodacre, M. (2012), *Thomas and the Gospels: The Case for Thomas's Familiarity with the Synoptics*, Grand Rapids: Eerdmans.
Keith, C. (2011), 'Memory and Authenticity: Jesus Tradition and What Really Happened', *Zeitschrift für die neutestamentliche Wissenschaft* 102: 155–77.
Kloppenborg, J. S. (1999), *The Formation of Q: Trajectories in Ancient Wisdom Collections*, 2nd edn, Harrisburg: Trinity Press International.
Mack, B. L. and V. K. Robbins (1989), *Patterns of Persuasion in the Gospels*, Sonoma: Polebridge.
Meier, J. P. (1991), *A Marginal Jew: Rethinking the Historical Jesus, vol. 1: The Roots of the Problem and the Person*, New York: Doubleday.
Meier, J. P. (1994), *A Marginal Jew: Rethinking the Historical Jesus, vol. 2: Mentor, Message, and Miracles*, New Haven: Yale University Press.
Meier, J. P. (2009), *A Marginal Jew: Rethinking the Historical Jesus, vol. 4: Law and Love*, New Haven: Yale University Press.
Metzger, B. M. and B. D. Ehrman (2005), *The Text of the New Testament: Its Transmission, Corruption, and Restoration*, 4th edn, Oxford: Oxford University Press.
Olson, K. (1999), 'Eusebius and the Testimonium Flavianum', *Catholic Biblical Quarterly* 61: 305–22.
Patterson, S. J. (1993), *The Gospel of Thomas and Jesus*, Sonoma: Polebridge.
Porter, S. E. and B. R. Dyer, eds (2016), *The Synoptic Problem: Four Views*, Grand Rapids: Baker Academic.
Schmidt, T. C. (2018), 'The Testimonium Flavianum in Light of Jewish and Greco-Roman Reports about Jesus'. Paper presented at the Society of Biblical Literature Annual Meeting, Denver, November 18.
Theissen, G. and A. Merz (2011), *Der historische Jesus: Ein Lehrbuch*, 4th edn, Göttingen: Vandenhoeck & Ruprecht.
Vermes, G. (1987), 'The Jesus Notice of Josephus Re-Examined', *Journal of Jewish Studies* 38: 1–10.
Whealey, A. (2003), *Josephus on Jesus: The Testimonium Flavianum Controversy from Late Antiquity to Modern Times*, New York: Lang.

4

John the Baptist

When Jesus began his public career as a preacher and healer, he returned to familiar territory in Galilee, settling in Capernaum. On one visit to his home village of Nazareth, on the sabbath, he went to the synagogue, the natural meeting place, and taught there. From Mark's narrative it would appear that Jesus met with a mixed, though predominantly sceptical, response:

> On the sabbath he began to teach in the synagogue, and many who heard him were astounded. They said, 'Where did this man get all this? What is this wisdom that has been given to him? What deeds of power are being done by his hands! Is not this the carpenter, the son of Mary and brother of James and Joses and Judas and Simon, and are not his sisters here with us?' And they took offence at him. Then Jesus said to them, 'Prophets are not without honour, except in their home town, and among their own kin, and in their own house.'
>
> Mk 6.2-4

Mark adds: 'He could do no deed of power there, except that he laid his hands on a few sick people and cured them' (Mk 6.5). Because this passage contains comments that are critical of Jesus, which is quite rare, we may assume that the story depicts an event that did in fact take place (as we have seen, the evangelists are very unlikely to have invented criticism of Jesus). People reacted negatively to Jesus' new role. The villagers who had known Jesus as a child were surprised when he turned up, all of a sudden, as a prophet with his own disciples and they did not accept this new, self-assumed authority. One might wonder how this transformation occurred, 'Where did this man get all this?', as the people say in Mark. Although some scholars have suggested that Jesus was influenced by Graeco-Roman philosophy (Crossan 1991), we may instead seek an explanation of the transformation in the experiences Jesus had when he was part of John's baptismal movement.

In the four Gospels, the story of Jesus' adult life begins with the activities of John the Baptist. The first three Gospels give the impression that Jesus' baptism by John is a rite of initiation for his new mission. Afterwards Jesus withdraws to the wilderness and for forty days he is tempted by the devil and defeats him. Jesus then begins to preach. But what really happened? Why was Jesus with the Baptist at the River Jordan? From the Gospel of John it would appear that Jesus spent time with the Baptist beyond the baptism itself. According to the author, Jesus and his disciples stayed for some time with John the Baptist and baptized people (Jn 3.25-26). What is more, he depicts a friendly competition between Jesus and the Baptist over baptizing and gaining disciples (4.1-3): 'Now when Jesus learned that the Pharisees had heard, "Jesus is making and baptizing more disciples than John" – although it was not Jesus himself but his disciples who baptized – he left Judea and started back to Galilee.' Here, somebody – presumably the final editor – has added a note that Jesus did not baptize, which conflicts with the context (cf. Jn 3.22). We can infer from John's account in the Gospel that Jesus took part in the baptizing activity of John the Baptist and that he too baptized others. Thus, Jesus belonged to the group of disciples who assisted John (Mk 6.29; Mt. 11.2; Lk. 11.1; Jn 1.35). However, the claim found in the Gospel of John about Jesus having a baptismal movement of his own, alongside John the Baptist's, is doubtful. Rather, there is every indication that to begin with Jesus was a disciple of the Baptist, even if the evangelists want to give an altogether different impression. It is evident that Jesus began his own activity only after the Baptist had been arrested (Mk 1.14; Mt. 4.12), which fits with the picture of Jesus as one of John's former assistants. Some of the Baptist's disciples later followed Jesus, most likely after their master was arrested (Jn 1.35-39).

A comparison of the narratives depicting Jesus' baptism reveals some curious differences. Mark's description of Jesus' baptism is brief and to the point: 'In those days Jesus came from Nazareth of Galilee and was baptized by John in the Jordan' (Mk 1.9). The evangelist relates the baptism as a numinous event: 'Just as he was coming up out of the water, he saw the heavens torn apart and the Spirit descending like a dove on him. And a voice came from heaven, "You are my Son, the Beloved; with you I am well pleased"' (Mk 1.10-11). The divine speech in the narrative shifts the focus away from the historical event, the baptism, or 'immersion' as the Greek word *baptismos* means. The account of the immersion is altered in the other Synoptic Gospels. In Matthew, Jesus has to convince John that it is the Baptist who should baptize *him*, and not the other way around: 'John would have prevented him, saying, "I need to be baptized by you, and do you come to me?" But Jesus answered him, "Let it be so now; for it is proper for us in this way to fulfil all righteousness." Then he consented' (Mt. 3.14-15). Luke opts for a different strategy, reformulating Mark's description in such a way that it is unclear whether anyone besides Jesus is involved: 'Now when all the people were baptized, and when Jesus also had been baptized and was praying ...' (Lk. 3.21). Lastly, John's Gospel mentions the dove and the Spirit but does not mention the baptism itself (Jn 1.32-34). It is clear from these changes that several aspects of Jesus' baptism were frankly embarrassing to the early Christ-believers. If this baptism was at once a baptism of purification and an expression of repentance, it raised troublesome questions: did Jesus need to repent and could he really become impure? Such ideas did not fit with the dominant image of the exalted Christ in the early church. Matthew's version raises the issue of the role of the Baptist. It must have seemed strange that it was John the Baptist who baptized Jesus. Which was the superior of the two, in reality? Wasn't it the baptizer? We hear of disciples of John the Baptist who, long after his death, appear to have continued to baptize (Acts 19.1-7). It is conceivable that they claimed that the Baptist was superior to Jesus, with reference to such factors. We can observe how the Gospel authors use various means to deal with these problems, and not just in the actual scene of the baptism. John the Baptist heralds a future redeemer, and is seen clearly expressing his own inferiority to this figure: 'The one who is more powerful than I is coming after me; I am not worthy to stoop down and untie the thong of his sandals' (Mk 1.7). The Gospels portray John the Baptist as the forerunner of Jesus, in that he proclaims the coming of the saviour, a role fulfilled by Jesus. Through quotations from the Hebrew Bible, he is presented as the messenger who will prepare the way (Mal. 3.1) and, in the words of Isaiah, as a voice crying out in the wilderness: 'Prepare the way of the Lord; make straight the paths of our God' (Isa. 40.3, according to the version in the Septuagint). Here, texts originally about 'the Lord', that is, God, are applied to Jesus, the Son of God, for whom John the Baptist was to clear the way. In John's Gospel, the Baptist explicitly states, 'I am not the Messiah, but I have been sent ahead of him' (3.28) and 'He must increase, but I must decrease' (3.30). In his second work, the Acts of the Apostles, Luke makes it absolutely plain, through words he puts in Paul's mouth, that John the Baptist prepared the people to receive Jesus: 'John baptized with the baptism of repentance, telling the people to believe in the one who was to come after him, that is, in Jesus' (Acts 19.4). But to what extent did Jesus actually fit with the image of the liberator? And what was the meaning of John's baptism? It is time to take a closer look at John the Baptist.

Who was John the Baptist?

John the Baptist carried out his work on the bank of the River Jordan, but where precisely is somewhat uncertain. The evangelist John refers to two different places, Bethany, in Perea, and Aenon near Salim, within the territory of the Decapolis (Jn 1.28; 3.23), but the exact locations are unknown. Most scholars hold that he was active on the eastern side, in Perea, not too far from the Dead Sea and in the vicinity of Judaea, somewhere within reach for residents of Jerusalem. Christian pilgrims came here in droves from the fourth century on, which supports the idea that this is the right area. The region was governed by Herod Antipas, who later ordered the execution of John (see map). In geographical terms, John the Baptist very likely carried out his work just a few kilometres north of Qumran. There are certain similarities which have led scholars to ponder whether the Baptist may have been a member of the Qumran sect before he began his career as a public preacher (so Marcus 2018; for the opposite view, see Taylor 1997). This is also the story told at the Visitor's Centre at Qumran today. Luke's cryptic comments about the Baptist's early years lend support to this theory: 'The child grew and became strong in spirit, and he was in the wilderness until the day he appeared publicly to Israel' (Lk. 1.80). There is a strong association of John the Baptist with Isa. 40.3, which is used to introduce the Baptist in each of the Gospels (Mt. 3.3; Mk 1.3; Lk. 3.4; Jn 1.23). This text from Isaiah was an important one for the Qumran movement, who interpreted the passage as a reference to their own group. In the *Community Rule* we read about how they prepared for the Lord's coming by studying the Torah:

> When these become the Community in Israel, they shall separate themselves from the session of the men of deceit in order to depart into the wilderness to prepare there the Way of the Lord; as it is written: 'In the wilderness prepare the way of the Lord, make level in the desert a highway for our God.' This (alludes to) the study of the Torah wh[ic]h he commanded through Moses to do, according to everything which has been revealed (from) time to time, and according to that which the prophets have revealed by his Holy Spirit.
>
> 1QS 8.12-16

Yet there are also major differences. The apocalyptic beliefs that John the Baptist and the Qumran movement shared prompted them to completely different courses of action. Whereas the Qumran sect withdrew and looked forward to God's judgement, when the majority of the people of Israel would be destroyed, the Baptist worked to save the people ahead of the approaching doom. That a connection of some kind existed is possible – the Baptist may very well have been inspired by the Essenes – but a close link cannot be proved.

John was known for fasting, as emerges, for example, from criticism made of Jesus and his disciples. Jesus says: 'For John came neither eating nor drinking, and they say, "He has a demon"; the Son of Man came eating and drinking, and they say, "Look, a glutton and a drunkard, a friend of tax-collectors and sinners!"' (Mt. 11.18-19). Luke claims that John did not drink wine at all (Lk. 1.15). John's disciples fasted too: 'Now John's disciples and the Pharisees were fasting; and people came and said to him, "Why do John's disciples and the disciples of the Pharisees fast, but your disciples do not fast?"' (Mk 2.18). John the Baptist's ascetic way of life in the wilderness resembles that of a certain Bannus who was Josephus's mentor in his youth, around twenty years after the death of Jesus. After studying the three philosophical schools, Josephus undertook three years of training with this Bannus, an ascetic who lived in the wilderness and devoted a great deal of time to purity rituals involving cold water (*Life* 10–11). He subsisted entirely from nature, wearing clothes of materials made from trees and eating food that grew naturally without being cultivated. The descriptions of these two men's ascetic lifestyles appear somewhat farfetched and were written to present them as pious men who abstained from all luxury and comfort. Nevertheless, the reported diet of the Baptist, 'locusts and wild honey' (Mt. 3.4), are not necessarily indicative of asceticism per se since fried grasshopper as well as honey were 'a delicacy' (Stegemann 1998: 215). The special food rather signifies his dwelling place in the wilderness. Interestingly, both John and Bannus took on disciples like Jesus and Josephus.

As we read in the birth narrative in Luke, John the Baptist came from a priestly lineage, and although we may well doubt the accuracy of the rest of the Lucan narrative regarding his birth and kinship with Jesus, this detail is historically plausible. By presenting the birth of John the Baptist as a miracle – his parents, like Abraham and Sarah, have children in their old age (Gen. 17–18) – Luke builds up the audience's expectations that the child would receive a special mission. Growing up in a priestly household, John would have been well acquainted with purity rituals, a matter of particular concern for priests, who served at the temple, and to some extent this may explain why purifying immersion came to be a central element of his movement. As a preacher John the Baptist was a well-known figure who drew large crowds of people, among them Jesus: 'Then the people of Jerusalem and all Judea were going out to him, and all the region along the Jordan, and they were baptized by him in the River Jordan, confessing their sins' (Mt. 3.5). His popularity is confirmed by Josephus, who describes John the Baptist as a 'good man' and relates that in the end Herod Antipas had him executed because he was worried that he might stir up the people. In addition, Josephus, just like the evangelists, explains that John's message was one of living rightly: 'he was a good man and had exhorted the Jews to lead righteous lives, to practise justice towards their fellows and piety towards God, and so doing to join in baptism' (*Ant.* 18.117). Josephus does not, however, mention the Baptist's striking appearance or his distinctive diet, which are highlighted by Mark: 'John was clothed with camel's hair, with a leather belt around his waist, and he ate locusts and wild honey' (Mk 1.6). These were hardly fancy 'soft robes', as Jesus remarks ironically (Mt. 11.8). This description recalls prophets of former times, who wore clothing of hair as a sign of their prophetic status (Zech. 13.4), and particularly Elijah, who had a hairy appearance and wore a leather belt (2 Kgs 1.8). Moreover, John the Baptist is interpreted as Elijah in the Gospels (Mt. 11.14; Lk. 1.17). This was possible because, according to the legend in 2 Kgs 2, Elijah did not die but was rather taken up to heaven in a whirlwind by God. Hence, a belief arose that he would return at the end times, as is stressed in a secondary addition to the prophetic book of Malachi (Mal. 4.5, cf. Sir. 48.10). As we shall see, it is likely that John chose to present himself as Elijah, in dressing like him and in preaching about the approaching judgement in accordance with beliefs about the prophet.

Mark summarizes John's work in the following words: 'John the baptizer appeared in the wilderness, proclaiming a baptism of repentance for the forgiveness of sins' (Mk 1.4). 'Repentance' is a traditional Jewish concept grounded in the belief in a merciful God who forgives those who sincerely ask for forgiveness for their sins. Repenting was also about changing one's ways: distancing oneself from all evil and turning towards God, that is, living in accordance with God's will, acting rightly. In Luke's version, John explains what this involves in practice: 'The crowds asked him, "What then should we do?" In reply he said to them, "Whoever has two coats must share with anyone who has none; and whoever has food must do likewise" (Lk. 3.10-11). This repentance was made visible in a ritual immersion in the river.

The baptism of John

John's epithet 'the Baptist', which Josephus also uses of him, demonstrates that baptism was the characteristic feature of his work. As we have seen in Chapter 2 ritual bathing was commonplace within Judaism. But the baptism of John differs from traditional immersion in several crucial respects, in terms of both procedure and meaning. In contrast to standard purity rituals, which were performed as needed, our textual witnesses give the impression that the baptism of John was a singular event valid once and for all, or at least that it was a ritual that people underwent only rarely. But undergoing a water ritual with the Baptist did not mean that a person would subsequently stop performing other purification rituals; his baptism was not a substitute for these. A major difference as compared with standard ritual baths was that the Baptist assisted those who entered the purifying water, rather than letting them perform the purification rituals themselves. By adding new rites and linking the act of baptism with his own person, he transformed a common ritual into a very significant and memorable event for those who came to him (Uro 2016: 71–98). It is baptism of the kind practised by John that forms the basis for baptism as a rite of initiation into the church (1 Cor. 1.14-16; Acts 8.38).

John's baptism was a baptism of purification, just like ordinary ritual baths, but he lays particular stress on the importance confessing one's sins and committing to changing for the better prior to baptism (Mk 1.4-5). Josephus explains the meaning of the Baptist's ritual bath: 'first, the soul must be purified by practising righteousness, then the bodily (ritual) purification could be accepted' (*Ant.* 18.117). In this way, John the Baptist linked an outer purification from ritual impurity with an inner, moral cleansing. Although his emphasis on the importance of both inner and outer purity was unusually strong, he was far from unique in holding that the two went hand in hand. Texts from Qumran stress that purification is impossible for an unrighteous person. Here, purification is thus not regarded as a procedure that functions automatically, but rather as the action of the Holy Spirit which quite simply does not work when a person's inner being is not also pure. The *Community Rule* describes the condition of someone who refuses to enter into God's covenant and what is required to make a person pure:

> He cannot ... be cleansed by waters of purification, nor sanctify himself in streams and rivers, nor cleanse himself in any waters of ablution. Unclean, unclean is he, as long as he rejects the judgments of God, so that he cannot be instructed within the Community of his (God's) counsel. For it is by the spirit of the true counsel of God that the ways of man – all his iniquities – are atoned, so that he can behold the light of life. It is by the Holy Spirit of the Community in his (God's) truth that he can be cleansed from all his iniquities. It is by an upright and humble spirit that his sin can be atoned. It is by humbling his soul to all God's statutes, that his flesh can be cleansed, by sprinkling with waters of purification, and by sanctifying himself with waters of purity.
>
> 1QS 3.4–9

Here, just as in the teaching of John the Baptist, it becomes apparent that an outer, ritual purity depends upon a pure inner self. Similarly, in fragmentary prayers from Qumran we find prayers of atonement and forgiveness in connection with purification rituals. However, the reverse did not hold. People were not generally regarded as sinful for being ritually impure. If we remember that people became impure through giving birth and through burying their parents, which was a universal obligation, we see how unreasonable it would be to make a connection of this sort. Even so, certain diseases could be perceived as punishments, such as 'leprosy' (a term encompassing various skin conditions), which resulted in a grievous form of impurity (Num. 12). But ordinary forms of impurity were not associated with sin.

Proclaiming judgement

John the Baptist's message is concerned with a coming judgement, expressed in vivid terms in his sermon from the Q source: 'John said to the crowds that came out to be baptized by him, "You brood of vipers! Who warned you to flee from the wrath to come? Bear fruits worthy of repentance"' (Lk. 3.7-8; cf. Mt. 3.7). The vital importance of penitence becomes obvious – it is crucial that people prepare themselves for the impending doom. The hour is at hand: 'Even now the axe is lying at the root of the trees; every tree therefore that does not bear good fruit is cut down and thrown into the fire' (Lk. 3.9; cf. Mt. 3.10). Cutting down trees is an obvious metaphor of judgement with precursors in the Hebrew Bible (e.g. Isa. 10.33-34). John stresses that belonging to the people of the covenant will make no difference in the judgement; every individual must repent and live rightly (Mt. 3.9). We have no reason to doubt the general gist of John the Baptist's fiery proclamations of imminent judgement, since events did not turn out as he predicted. This aspect of the Baptist's preaching is entirely absent from Josephus, probably because of Josephus's aversion to apocalyptic movements. A picture thus emerges of John the Baptist as an apocalyptic prophet proclaiming that the end is nigh. Like earlier prophets such Amos and Jeremiah, he uses harsh words of warning to get his message across. He also announces the coming of someone 'more powerful' than he, whose sandal he is not worthy to untie (Mk 1.7). It is clear from the wider context of the Gospel narratives that the evangelists see Jesus, the Messiah, as the one heralded by John. But if we take a closer look at his message, we see that this identification is not wholly convincing. More likely, this is an example of what Joel Marcus calls a 'theological rereading of history' (Marcus 2018: 83). Interestingly, the Gospels also contain traces of a divergent understanding, when the Baptist, after his arrest, wonders what part Jesus had to play: 'When John heard in prison what the Messiah was doing, he sent word by his disciples and said to him, "Are you the one who is to come, or are we to wait for another?"' (Mt. 11.3; Lk. 7.19). The question that John the Baptist poses, which comes from Q, is surprising in that it goes against the description of the Baptist acknowledging Jesus as the Messiah earlier on in the baptism narratives. This suggests that when Jesus was coming to prominence through his work healing and preaching, John really did wonder about his role. It is doubtful, however, that the Baptist specifically asked whether Jesus was the one he had been waiting for. The one who was to come, according to John's proclamations, would be a future divine judge. This future figure would 'baptize with the Holy Spirit and fire.' Fire is a standard image for judgement (Isa. 10.17; Jer. 21.12). His 'winnowing-fork is in his hand, and he will clear his threshing-floor and will gather his wheat into the granary; but the chaff he will burn with unquenchable fire' (Mt. 3.11-12, Lk. 3.16-17). Hence we are dealing with a future figure who will judge the people on the last day, but also impart the Holy Spirit in accordance with hopes for the end time (Joel 2.28-29). These expectations hardly fit the historical person Jesus. Scholars debate who in particular the Baptist is alluding to: either God (Stegemann 1998: 216), who is, of course, judge (Isa. 30.27-28; Mal. 4.1) and who is often called strong and mighty (Gen. 49.24; Isa. 1.24), or one of the eschatological figures mentioned in various Jewish texts, like the Son of Man (Dan. 7.13–14), the angel Melchizedek (11QMelch, from Qumran) or a messiah (see Dunn 2003: 369–71; Meier 1994: 40). What is more, this vision for the future also fits with the role of Elijah, who was to prepare the people before the day of the Lord:

> Lo, I will send you the prophet Elijah before the great and terrible day of the LORD comes. He will turn the hearts of parents to their children and

the hearts of children to their parents, so that I will not come and strike the land with a curse.

Mal. 4.5

On that day it is God who acts and judges the people:

See, the day is coming, burning like an oven, when all the arrogant and all evildoers will be stubble; the day that comes shall burn them up, says the LORD of hosts, so that it will leave them neither root nor branch. But for you who revere my name the sun of righteousness shall rise, with healing in its wings. You shall go out leaping like calves from the stall. And you shall tread down the wicked, for they will be ashes under the soles of your feet, on the day when I act, says the LORD of hosts.

Mal. 4.1-3

At the same time, as we have seen, God is often expected to act through his agents, such as kings, angels and special end-time figures. John the Baptist's prediction in Mt. 3.11-12 deserves some special attention:

I baptize you with water for repentance, but one who is more powerful than I is coming after me; I am not worthy to carry his sandals. He will baptize you with the Holy Spirit and fire.

Similar sayings appear in Matthew, Luke and John (Mt. 3.11-12; Lk. 3.16-18; cf. Acts 13.25; Jn 1.26-27) and it belongs to one of the few cases where Q and Mark overlap. The multiple occurrences indicate an early provenance. In addition, the wording of someone being more 'powerful' or 'mighty' does not reflect typical Christological language, which speaks against it being a later Christian invention. The reference to someone 'stronger' who is wearing a sandal may point to more of an earthly figure than God or a supra-human character. Joel Marcus therefore argues that John awaits the Messiah, but that he does not identify Jesus as such (Marcus 2018: 47). Nevertheless, wearing a sandal can be compared to the other metaphors of a farmer cutting down trees, gathering wheat and burning chaff, which plays on traditional imagery for God (Meier 1994: 33–5). Still, wearing sandals would be an odd image for God, and better fit an eschatological agent of some kind (Dunn 2003: 369). We may say that the metaphors for God and his agent are blended together. Several commentators highlight the vagueness of the figure(s) that the Baptist speaks of and conclude that he was deliberately vague (Meier 1994: 40; Dunn 2003: 371). In other words, it is possible that he was not sure about whom God would be using as his agent for judgement and redemption, but he was sure that he would act in a decisive way very soon.

Jesus and John

Jesus' mission and work are closely linked to the work of John the Baptist. Jesus' occasional references to the Baptist reflect a belief that their activity was connected, that Jesus was continuing what John the Baptist had started and that both were agents of God in a divine plan. Jesus compares himself to John the Baptist; as mentioned above, they had different views on meals, but nothing satisfied the critics (Mt. 11.16-19; Lk. 7.31-35). When his authority is called into question by senior priests and others ('the chief priests, the scribes, and the elders') in the sanctuary, he counters with a question about their understanding of John the Baptist:

> 'Did the baptism of John come from heaven, or was it of human origin? Answer me.' They argued with one another, 'If we say, "From heaven", he will say, "Why then did you not believe him?" But shall we say, "Of human origin?"' – they were afraid of the crowd, for all regarded John as truly a prophet. So they answered Jesus, 'We do not know.' And Jesus said to them, 'Neither will I tell you by what authority I am doing these things.'
>
> Mk 11.30-33

The implication is that both Jesus and John had full divine authorization to preach as they did. This passage also reflects Jesus' extremely high estimation of his own importance, which was likewise a characteristic of John. As God's prophets they spoke with absolute authority and were not required to defer to any human being. This, of course, led to their downfall. Both of these proclaimers of judgement were put to death because the ruling powers saw them as a threat. In John the Baptist's case, he had also provoked the ire of Herod Antipas in publicly criticizing him for his marriage to Herodias, who was the wife of one of Herod's half-brothers (Mt. 14.4; Mk 6.18; Lk. 3.19) as well as being his niece (the daughter of another half-brother, Aristobulus). Herod's first wife was a Nabatean princess who left him when she found out about the union. In Jewish law, a man was expected to marry his brother's widow if the brother was childless, so as to provide his dead brother with children (Deut. 25.5-6). But if a man married his sister-in-law while his brother was still living, he would be violating the commandment 'You shall not uncover the nakedness of your brother's wife; it is your brother's nakedness' (Lev. 18.16; cf. 20.21). Marriage between a man and the daughter of his brother or sister was not, however, uncommon, and it was probably Herodias's status as Herod's sister-in-law that was the problem from John the Baptist's perspective, which Mark says too (Mk 6.18). Even so, the Qumran movement did oppose marriage between a man and his niece, regarding it as incest (CD 5.7–11). If John shared the sect's views on the issue, this aspect of Herod's relationship may also have played a role in his criticism.

The gruesome account of the execution of John the Baptist is replete with elements that stimulate the imagination – pride, cunning, violent death – and has inspired countless artists and composers, who have portrayed the drama in various mediums, as Oscar Wilde did, for example, in his play *Salome*. Herod is holding a great birthday feast, and Herodias's daughter dances before him and his many distinguished guests (Mk 6.17-29). As a token of his gratitude, Herod promises, foolishly, to give the girl a gift of whatever she desires, 'even half of my kingdom'. On the advice of her mother, she requests John the Baptist's head on a platter. The background to this request is that Herodias wanted to eliminate John the Baptist, whereas Herod was reticent: 'for Herod feared John, knowing that he was a righteous and holy man, and he protected him. When he heard him, he was greatly perplexed; and yet he liked to listen to him' (Mk 6.20). Mark's tale has been considerably abbreviated in Matthew's version, where Herod proves to be complicit (Mt. 14.1-12), while Luke refrains from including it at all, instead briefly mentioning John's imprisonment (Lk. 3.19-20). Josephus mentions that Herod brought John to his fortress at Machaerus, located on the eastern side of the Dead Sea, near the border between Perea and Nabatea in modern Jordan, and had him executed there (see map). He does not imply that there was anything unusual about the execution. The account of the sensational execution of John the Baptist in Mark's narrative is likely then a fictional tale that has been fabricated from other well-known legends, such as those of Jephthah's daughter (Judg. 11.29-40) and Esther (see especially 2.9; 5.3, 6; 7.2). The historical circumstances that remain are that Herod executed John the Baptist because John was a popular preacher who was publicly criticizing him. In addition, he was worried that the Baptist might incite the people to revolt. Evidently, many people were troubled by the execution. According to Josephus, when Herod Antipas later lost a battle to King Aretas of the Nabateans, who was the father of Herod's spurned first wife, many saw it as a punishment from God for his unjust execution of John. John the Baptist, as we shall see in the next chapter, was one of a series of potential revolutionaries executed for rebellious activities.

Summary

Jesus was baptized by John the Baptist in the River Jordan. Since there is a certain degree of embarrassment surrounding this episode, in that it is John who baptizes Jesus and not the other way around, we can be quite certain that the event took place. John warned the people about an impending judgement and called on them to repent. Heeding the warnings of the end time, people purified themselves of bodily impurities, confessing their sins. In an innovative twist on the traditional rite of purification, which a person would perform alone, John assisted the people undergoing this ritual.

In line with apocalyptic ideas of his time, John speaks in colourful terms of a future judge who would punish the wicked and reward the righteous. The Gospel authors present John as the messenger in the wilderness of Isaiah 40.3 (in the Septuagint), who prepares the way for the Lord, and this 'Lord' they in turn identify as Jesus. Nevertheless, the more likely historical background is that John preached of God as the coming judge and acting through a supra-natural agent. Through his special clothing and his message of doom, John presented himself as Elijah, a figure who, it was believed, based on the prophecy of Malachi (Mal. 4.5), would appear at the end time. In his role as God's spokesperson, John did not hesitate to criticize men in positions of power. He was eventually executed by Herod Antipas for criticizing the latter's marriage to his own sister-in-law, Herodias, in combination with a politically dangerous message. After the death of John, Jesus began his own public carrier, gathering disciples and travelling through the land. As a former disciple of John, Jesus spread John the Baptist's key message of an imminent new era, which he called the kingdom of God. We will turn to Jesus' role as a popular prophet next.

Bibliography

Crossan, J. D. (1991), *The Historical Jesus: The Life of a Mediterranean Jewish Peasant*, San Francisco: HarperSanFrancisco.

Dunn, J. D. G. (2003), *Christianity in the Making, vol. 1: Jesus Remembered*, Grand Rapids: Eerdmans.

Kelhoffer, J. A. (2005), *The Diet of John The Baptist: 'Locusts and Wild Honey' in Synoptic and Patristic Interpretation*, Tübingen: Mohr Siebeck.

Loader, W. (2005), *Sexuality and the Jesus Tradition*, Grand Rapids: Eerdmans.

Marcus, J. (2018), *John the Baptist in History and Theology*, Columbia: The University of South Carolina Press.

Meier, J. P. (1994), *A Marginal Jew: Rethinking the Historical Jesus, vol. 2: Mentor, Message, and Miracles*, New Haven: Yale University Press.

Stegemann, H. (1998), *The Library of Qumran: On the Essenes, Qumran, John the Baptist, and Jesus*, Grand Rapids: Eerdmans.

Taylor, J. E. (1997), *The Immerser: John the Baptist within Second Temple Judaism*, Grand Rapids: Eerdmans.

Uro, R. (2016), *Ritual and Christian Beginnings: A Socio-Cognitive Analysis*, Oxford: Oxford University Press.

5

The prophet leader

Jesus has often been portrayed as the founder of Christianity, a lone religious genius with utterly unique teachings. But like all historical figures, Jesus was part of a network of interrelations linking him with other people. For Jesus, this network was especially significant because to a great extent his identity came to be defined in relation to the movement that regarded him as their manifest leader. In this chapter, we shall focus on Jesus as a prophetic leader and on the various circles of followers that constituted the Jesus movement.

Professional and popular prophets

The Hebrew Bible contains numerous tales of prophets – men and women who were thought to have a special relationship with God – who appeared throughout the ages with messages for the kings and people of Israel. These messages did not consist exclusively, or even primarily, of forecasts for the future. Rather, they were criticisms of contemporary society, decrying the oppression of the poor and other forms of social injustice. The great prophetic books – including Amos, Isaiah and Jeremiah – are built around collections of oracles, both of disaster and of hope, which are said to have been delivered by prophets who bore these names. Prophets thus played a decisive role in the history of the Jewish people, but according to later rabbinic theologians 'the Holy Spirit ceased in Israel' with the death of the prophets Haggai, Zechariah and Malachi. In older scholarly literature, it is often assumed that prophets hardly ever appeared among the Jewish population at the beginning of the Common Era. If this picture is correct, it would explain why John the Baptist, according to both the Gospels and Josephus, attracted such great attention. In being 'clothed with camel's hair, with a leather belt around his waist' (Mk 1.6), and in living ascetically and proclaiming judgement and repentance, John was behaving like one of the prophets of old. Nevertheless, more recent scholarly work by Rebecca Gray (1993) and Richard Horsley (1999), among others, has demonstrated that the notion that Judaism at the beginning of the Common Era was without prophets is incorrect. In fact, the extant texts bear witness to several individuals from this period who claimed to be prophets with special abilities and missions. Some of these were 'professional prophets' who belonged to the social elite; they could read and write and were therefore considered well educated. Their 'prophecies' most often consisted of interpreting dreams or passages from the Hebrew Bible, and by such means they believed that they could predict the future. One widespread notion was that priests were particularly well qualified to prophesy. Josephus, who only barely escaped execution during the First Jewish–Roman War, at the end of the 60s CE, by predicting that Vespasian would become emperor, considered himself a prophet and associated this with his priestly heritage (*War* 3.351–354, 400–408). We find the same conception in the Gospel of John, where Caiaphas, the high priest, proposes that Jesus be done away with because 'it is better for you to have one man die for the people than to have the whole nation destroyed'. The evangelist adds that Caiaphas, without knowing it but by virtue of his high-priestly office, was speaking prophetically about the redemptive death of Jesus for the people (Jn 11.49-51). Professional prophets were thus often priests, but there were others, too, who were versed in the Scriptures and had prophetic pretensions. Josephus mentions prophets among the Pharisees as well as the Essenes (*Ant.* 17.41–43; *War* 2.159).

For his part, Jesus had little in common with such learned soothsayers. We have already seen that it is unclear whether Jesus could read at all. It is much more appropriate to compare him with the 'popular prophets' who came from the general population and whose successes were based not on book learning, but on charismatic personas and fervent conviction. One such popular prophet was Jesus, son of Ananias, who attained notoriety in Jerusalem around thirty years later than Jesus of Nazareth, that is, in the early 60s. According to Josephus, this man came to the city as a common pilgrim, but suddenly started declaring a fateful prophecy at the temple complex:

> 'A voice from the east, a voice from the west, a voice from the four winds; a voice against Jerusalem and the sanctuary, a voice against the bridegroom and the bride, a voice against all the people.'
>
> *War* 6.300–301

This son of Ananias was not content to deliver the message just once, but repeated it day and night. At last a group of enterprising individuals grew tired of the refrain and attempted to shut him up with a round of beatings. As soon as the son of Ananias had recovered from the blows, he resumed his prophesying. At this point some of the more cultivated citizens elected to take him to the Roman procurator, Albinus, who was responsible for law and order in Jerusalem. But not even the violent flogging that Albinus ordered could make the son of Ananias stop, which convinced him that the man was simply insane. Much to the chagrin of the citizens of Jerusalem, he released Jesus, son of Ananias, and the self-proclaimed prophet was able to continue delivering his message for more than seven years, until, during the siege of Jerusalem, he stepped into the path of a projectile and immediately perished. Just a few months later, the temple and the city fell.

There are a number of interesting similarities between Jesus, son of Ananias, and Jesus of Nazareth. Just like the Jesus of the Gospels, the son of Ananias refused to offer any defence or retract any aspect of his message, even when confronted by the emperor's representative. Just like Jesus of Nazareth, he foretold the destruction of the temple, and just like his better-known namesake, he expressed his message in words steeped in the language and ideas of the Hebrew Bible. His prophecy of doom alludes to the prophet Jeremiah's words about how God 'will bring to an end the sound of mirth and gladness, the voice of the bride and bridegroom in the cities of Judah and in the streets of Jerusalem' (Jer. 7.34). A modern hearer of this story might well suppose that the son of Ananias must have read the book of Jeremiah, but Josephus points out that he was an 'uneducated boor'. This would mean that he probably never learned to read much apart from possibly his own name. Nevertheless, both Jesus of Nazareth and Jesus, son of Ananias, had certainly heard the oracles of the ancient prophets read aloud and retold many times. When they themselves began to prophesy, they naturally used the imagery and phraseology of their holy tradition.

But the son of Ananias is unlike 'our' Jesus in one crucial respect. He acted in a decidedly antisocial way: he had no train of admirers, no disciples, and Josephus states that he did not even thank those kind souls who, despite everything, helped him survive by giving him food. In contrast, Jesus of Nazareth was no such loner, but rather surrounded himself with followers and was perceived as the leader of a popular movement. In this respect Jesus bears a closer resemblance to the popular prophet leaders about whom Josephus, thinly disguising his contempt, also has a great deal to say. These were leaders of mass movements that comprised several hundreds, or even thousands, of followers. Members were recruited with promises of apocalyptic miracles and divine acts that they would have the opportunity of witnessing if they simply followed the chosen prophet. In the mid-40s CE, a prophet leader called Theudas succeeded in convincing several hundred people to accompany him through the wilderness in the direction of the River Jordan, which was to part miraculously just as, according to the Hebrew Bible, it had done in the time of Joshua. A decade or so later, Jerusalem was surrounded by several thousand followers of a man known in Josephus' works and the book of Acts as 'the Egyptian prophet' or simply 'the Egyptian' (Acts 21.38). By one account, these were planning to breach the city by force; by another, they were expecting the city walls to collapse by themselves, just as, in the Hebrew Bible, the walls of Jericho had once fallen by divine intervention. Such equivocation, between the belief that God will act and the inclination nonetheless to take matters into one's own hands, is familiar to us from modern doomsday cults. In the early 1990s the Branch Davidians, a religious sect that was an offshoot of the Davidian Seventh-day Adventists, and their leader, the self-proclaimed Messiah figure David Koresh, became famous worldwide when American federal police laid siege to their compound in Waco, Texas, and stormed it. The sect was awaiting the imminent end of the world but, to be on the safe side, they had stockpiled guns and ammunition. Perceiving a growing danger to society, the American authorities decided to put an end to the movement, which tragically resulted in the death of not only Koresh, but eighty other men, women and children. In a similar way, the Roman authorities of the first century regarded the popular prophet leaders and their movements as politically dangerous and they stamped them out with violence. The 'Egyptian prophet' managed to escape, but Theudas was not so lucky. He was beheaded by Roman forces before any miracle could take place at the River Jordan, spelling an end to his movement.

Wouldn't it seem, then, that a great gulf separates these, often violent, agitators of the people from Jesus and his message 'Blessed are the peacemakers' (Mt. 5.9) and 'My kingdom is not from this world' (Jn 18.36)? Perhaps the gulf is not as great as we might think. We have already examined Jesus' background in John the Baptist's movement (ch. 4). When Herod Antipas had John executed it was because he feared, rightly or wrongly, that the mass movement centred on this prophet leader might develop into a political threat. In the same way, it is highly unlikely that Pontius Pilate would have ordered the execution of Jesus had it not been possible to make the claim that the 'prophet' and 'Messiah' Jesus of Nazareth, along with his followers, jeopardized the stability of the political status quo. And indeed it is hard to see how Jesus' prophetic oracles about the raising up of a 'temple ... not made with hands' in place of the existing temple in Jerusalem (cf. Mk 14.58) differ in any substantial way from the miracles promised by Theudas and the 'Egyptian prophet'. Jesus' ability to attract large numbers of followers must have been based on his success as a healer, combined with his personal charisma, and this gave rise to expectations that even greater miracles were to come. The dynamic interplay between leader and followers was the same in the Jesus movement as that which surrounded other popular prophet leaders.

To properly understand the historical Jesus, then, we need to view him as the prophetic leader of a large movement that had marked religious and political overtones. But we have more detailed information about Jesus than about any other early Jewish prophet. Consequently, we know a great deal, relatively speaking, about what the Jesus movement looked like. Within the movement broadly conceived – that is, everyone who took an interest in Jesus and was sympathetic to him and his message – we can distinguish relatively defined groups and even a few named individuals. So who were the people who joined the prophetic movement centred on Jesus?

The Jesus movement

'At once his fame began to spread throughout the surrounding region of Galilee' (Mk 1.28). So ends an episode at the beginning of Mark's Gospel in which Jesus teaches at the synagogue of Capernaum and drives out an unclean spirit. Without doubt, the claim that Jesus' fame immediately spread like wildfire to every single Galilean village is a rhetorical exaggeration, just as it can scarcely be true that 'people from the whole Judean countryside and all the people of Jerusalem' really came to John the Baptist at the Jordan and were baptized by him (Mk 1.5). As we saw previously (ch. 3), Jesus cannot have been regarded as especially significant in his own time, as most historians pass over him in silence. Nevertheless, Mark's stylized statement undoubtedly captures something of fundamental importance. In all likelihood the Jesus movement did indeed form and grow with the spread of rumour and hearsay about Jesus' supposed powers as an exorcist and a healer. We do not know how many people attended his public appearances – whether in hopes of being bodily cured, or because of longing for existential meaning or purely out of curiosity – but time and again the Gospels report that 'large crowds' gathered (e.g. Mk 4.1). There is no reason to doubt this picture, and as we have already discussed, this is the most plausible explanation as to why the Jesus movement was considered dangerous.

In many respects the Jesus movement can be considered an offshoot of the movement of John the Baptist. We have already seen that Jesus was himself part of the baptism movement and that his independent activity only began after John was put in prison. Some of Jesus' disciples may previously have been disciples of John the Baptist (Jn 1.35-42). The Jesus movement, like John the Baptist's, was a decidedly popular phenomenon, whose followers were not drawn from the societal elite. Both movements were marked by intensely apocalyptic beliefs and both spread the message that God's restoration of Israel was imminent and called for special readiness. The Gospel of John has preserved a credible report that the ritual of baptism associated with John was taken up and practised by the Jesus movement (Jn 3.22-26; 4.1-3).

The similarities are thus numerous, but there are also some crucial differences. One is that whereas John the Baptist was stationed in the wilderness by the Jordan, with prospective followers therefore having to make their way there to be baptized and to hear the prophet's message, the Jesus movement was quite literally a 'movement'. Jesus did have some kind of base for his work in Capernaum, but above all he made a name for himself through his itinerant lifestyle. The Gospels describe Jesus wandering from village to village, often with a crowd of people in tow. In one vivid account Jesus and his closest disciples attempt to withdraw to a deserted place, only to discover that word has got out and thousands of people have got there before them (Mk 6.32-44). Did Jesus have a particular rationale for roaming around as he did? Scholars have offered various suggestions, ranging from a desire to imitate the nomadic lifestyle of Abraham (Freyne 2004: 60–91) or the itinerant prophetic career of Elijah (Meier 2001: 623–25), to being inspired by the Cynic philosophers (Crossan 1991). The real reason may simply be that Jesus regarded mobility as a more effective strategy than the stationary one of John the Baptist. After all, several of the popular prophet leaders that we have already discussed required their followers to accompany them on some kind of journey. To a certain extent, this may have been a way of creating associations with Israel's legendary exodus from Egypt and its wanderings in the wilderness, but there must also have been a practical reason. Followers who had left their homes and familiar settings were naturally more loyal to the prophetic movement and its leader.

Another difference was that the Jesus movement was not characterized by the ascetic ideal associated with John the Baptist, who lived in the wilderness far from market places. Evidently he fasted so severely that he was rumoured to be possessed (Mt 11.18). In contrast, Jesus and his followers are suspected of wanton living. People wondered why the disciples did not practice regular fasting (Mk 2.18). Jesus had to defend himself against critical voices accusing him of being 'a glutton and a drunkard' (Mt. 11.19). The Gospels depict Jesus at meals on a surprising number of occasions, often dining alongside 'sinners', something he is criticized for (Mk 2.15-16; Mt. 11.19). Who were these people, and why was dining with them so controversial?

The concept of 'sin' is a very important one in much of the Hebrew Bible and New Testament. In traditional Greek and Roman religion, sin was synonymous with offending the gods, but for Jews the conception of sin included everything that conflicted with the will of God and with his laws for Israel and other nations. This meant that even acts that violated the divine order governing how human beings should treat one another counted as sins. As E. P. Sanders demonstrated long ago, a common view in early Judaism was that everyone committed sins and wrongdoings daily, even the pious and those faithful to the law. But despite this, God had made it possible, through the sacrificial cult and various systems of penance, for Israel to remain in the covenant (Sanders 1977: 423–27). In the *Psalms of Solomon*, a collection of poetic texts that may have been composed in the first century BCE in a Pharisaic setting, it is repeatedly stated that the righteous person atones for his sins through fasting and abstinence. Being 'righteous', then, does not mean never sinning, but rather availing oneself of the opportunity of atoning for one's sins. However, 'sinners' are people who cannot or will not avail themselves of this opportunity or whose sins are so grievous and persistent that penance will not suffice, as Sanders also pointed out. The typical examples given in the Gospels are tax-collectors and prostitutes, and both categories were represented in the Jesus movement. These were people who supported themselves by illicit means and were unable to change their ways without losing their livelihoods. Prostitution, unsurprisingly, was regarded as immoral. Tax collecting was not an objectionable occupation per se, but in practice tax-collectors were known to be corrupt and were often involved in extortion and other crooked deeds. These were people with whom no respectable Jew, especially not one with prophetic pretensions, ought to associate unless absolutely necessary.

Criticism of the Jesus movement for its meals, where the ambitious leader would dine with ordinary, decent Jews and notorious 'sinners' alike, was probably connected with the risk that established social and moral categories might dissolve. But the meals are also likely to have had a symbolic dimension that not everyone appreciated. In the Hebrew Bible and early Jewish texts, the future kingdom of God can be described specifically as a banquet, and Jesus himself makes use of such imagery (Mt. 8.11; Lk. 13.29). The meals were a kind of foretaste of the new reality that would emerge with the imminent establishment of the kingdom of God. Clearly in that reality, the lines that usually separated the righteous from sinners would no longer hold.

The disciples of the prophet

Even someone with superficial knowledge of the Gospels will surely know that in these narratives Jesus surrounds himself with 'disciples'. The word sounds old-fashioned in English and nowadays it is usually only used in this context, perhaps occasionally being applied to the devotees of other religious leaders too. The word that is found in the original Greek texts means something like 'one who learns'. We might translate it as 'student', but perhaps 'apprentice' would be a better alternative. This is because disciples are not simply engaged in the intellectual acquisition of a given teaching, but are also receiving practical training in how to perform the work of their master. Such is the case not only in the Gospels, but also in other biblical and early Jewish texts about prophets and their disciples (see Hägerland 2015).

The books of Kings from the Hebrew Bible contain detailed stories about Elijah and Elisha, two prophets who are said to have lived in the ancient Northern Kingdom in the ninth century BCE. Jewish narrative traditions of the first century CE show great interest in the relationship between these two prophets and Elisha was identified as Elijah's disciple. Even in the biblical text it is clear that Elisha is the prophetic heir to Elijah (1 Kgs 19.16). Early Jewish traditions embellish the story in which Elijah throws his prophet's mantle over Elisha's shoulders, thereby passing on the gift of prophecy. According to these traditions, Elisha, too, had disciples of his own. Similarly, the prophets Moses, Isaiah and Jeremiah were regarded within early Judaism as having had disciples, who learned to follow their masters' example and assist them in their work, so as to one day be able to strike out alone as prophets in their own right.

Prophets from the beginning of the Common Era also had disciples. Josephus talks, for example, of two professional prophets, Judas the Essene and Pollion the Pharisee, both of whom had disciples. The historian gives no indication that the popular prophets had disciples, but this may be due to his dislike of such troublemakers and hence a desire not to associate them with biblical prophets or with the educated men with whom he himself identified. We know that John the Baptist at least had disciples, as they are referred to at various points in the Gospels. In Mark's Gospel, for example, we read that 'John's disciples and the Pharisees' used to fast, unlike Jesus' disciples (Mk 2.18). In an episode that probably derives from Q (see ch. 3), John the Baptist uses his disciples as envoys to communicate with Jesus (Mt. 11.2-6; Lk. 7.18-23). John's disciples turn up throughout the Gospels and there is little reason to doubt that the popular movement centred on the Baptist included an inner circle of attendants to the prophet leader.

It must have thus seemed natural for Jesus to have a similar circle of apprentices and assistants. Prophets were not the only ones with followers; other kinds of teachers in antiquity – philosophers, Scripture experts and rabbis – were also accompanied by disciples who had chosen and sought out a master to learn from and emulate. The Gospels stress that the reverse was true of the relationship between Jesus and his disciples: he was the one who chose them, not the other way around. In Chapter 3 we saw one example of this in the episode where Jesus calls Levi (or Matthew). At merely a 'Follow me' from Jesus, Levi gets up without delay and becomes a follower (Mk 2.14). A similar thing is said to have happened when Jesus recruited the disciples who would come to be part of the very innermost circle: Simon (Peter), Andrew, James and John. These fishermen are in the middle of their work when Jesus orders them to follow him, and they leave everything right away: boats, nets and workmates (Mk 1.16-20). These narratives are undoubtedly highly stylized and adjusted to suit a later perspective. Early on there seems to have been an interest in highlighting the similarities between how Jesus and Elijah called their disciples. We can clearly see this in a scene in which a disciple asks Jesus whether he may first bury his father before joining Jesus. Jesus' response is surprisingly harsh: 'Follow me, and let the dead bury their own dead' (Mt. 8.22). This exchange is an allusion to when Elisha asked permission to bid farewell to his parents before going off with Elijah as his disciple (1 Kgs 19.20). We must be aware that this and other narratives, rather than reproducing historical events, reflect a tendency to root Jesus in biblical tradition. Nevertheless, the Gospels are so consistent on the issue of Jesus himself choosing his disciples that there must be a kernel of historical truth to the idea.

The disciples are an ill-defined group in the Gospel tradition. We do not know the names of all of the disciples or even how many of them there were. The Gospels contain lists of 'the twelve', who made up the inner core of followers, but the circle of those considered disciples was wider than this small group. What united all of the disciples was a feeling of being specially chosen and a readiness to accompany Jesus on his itinerant mission through the land. We should probably imagine a band that slowly grew in numbers, whose members came from various geographical locations, had disparate social and economic backgrounds and could be men as well as women.

Most of the named disciples came from Jesus' home region on the northern shore of the Sea of Galilee. According to the Gospel of John, Simon, also called Cephas or Peter, and his brother Andrew came from the fishing village of Bethsaida, as did Philip (Jn 1.44). Mark's Gospel, on the other hand, seems to assume that Simon was living with his family in Capernaum, about 10 km away (Mk 1.21-34), and archaeologists have excavated a building in Capernaum known as the 'house of Peter', which may well be just that. However these conflicting reports are to be interpreted, the key point is that most of the disciples were, like Jesus, Galileans. This probably exacerbated the sense of suspicion that the Jerusalem aristocracy felt towards Jesus and his following. The accent alone of the inhabitants of Galilee was regarded as a mark of stupidity and lack of refinement. An ancient Jewish joke pokes fun at a Galilean who wants to buy something and goes around asking for it; no one can understand him, though, because the similar Aramaic words for 'donkey', 'wine', 'wool' and 'lamb' all sound the same in the Galilean's mouth. And this accent is what gives the disciple Peter away as one of Jesus' followers in Jerusalem (Mk 14.70-71).

But there are also signs that some disciples may have begun following Jesus in Jerusalem. All four canonical gospels state that a man called Joseph, who came from the otherwise unknown town of Arimathea, arranged Jesus' burial after his death. According to Matthew and John, this Joseph, who evidently owned property in Jerusalem, was 'a disciple of Jesus' (Mt. 27.57; Jn 19.38). In John's Gospel, a mysterious figure known as 'the disciple whom Jesus loved' is said to be the main author of the Gospel (Jn 21.24). Since early church times, this disciple has commonly been thought to have been one of 'the twelve', specifically John, son of Zebedee, but this is probably incorrect. The beloved disciple is not mentioned in the introductory section of the Gospel, which is dominated by Jesus' activity in Galilee, but is said to have been present at Jesus' last supper, at his crucifixion and at one of the first collective visions that the disciples have of Jesus after his death. It is certainly possible, as some scholars maintain, that the beloved disciple is a purely literary character, and not a historical figure; but interestingly, John's Gospel displays a remarkable familiarity with the realities of the Jerusalem of Jesus' time – for instance, the pool of Bethesda, with its colonnades, is described in a way that agrees in detail with what modern excavations have revealed (Jn 5.2-3). At some level, behind the Gospel of John's heavily theological narrative about Jesus there must lie distinctive traditions passed on by people who were there at the time in Jerusalem, and there is no particular reason to distrust the reports in the Gospel that one such individual was numbered among the disciples. Perhaps, as argued at length by Richard Bauckham (2017: 358–471, 550–89), the beloved disciple should be identified with 'John the Elder', a figure distinguished from the group of 'the twelve' in some early Christian sources.

If Joseph of Arimathea really was one of Jesus' disciples, then the ideal of poverty that appears at many points in the Gospel tradition was clearly not absolute. After all, Jesus himself was a 'carpenter' or 'craftsman' (Mk 6.3) and while this hardly made him a member of the elite of society, he did not belong to its lowest level, either. Nor were the fishermen who accompanied him poor by the standards of the time. But it was a requirement for their joining that they abstain from excess and follow Jesus on his wanderings, at least periodically, in a kind of self-imposed poverty. Doing so was a sign of genuine devotion and we are told that not everyone who encountered Jesus was prepared to go to such lengths (Mk 10.17-22).

The Gospel of Luke contains an interesting report stating that Jesus was accompanied on his wanderings by 'the twelve . . . as well as some women who had been cured of evil spirits and infirmities: Mary, called Magdalene, from whom seven demons had gone out, and Joanna, the wife of Herod's steward Chuza, and Susanna, and many others, who provided for them out of their resources' (Lk. 8.1-3). What is especially noteworthy here is that the Joanna named in this passage was 'the wife of Herod's steward Chuza' and as such came from a higher social class than the disciples who were simple fishermen. She seems to have been one of several individuals of means who used their financial resources to support Jesus and the twelve. A more familiar figure from this passage is Mary Magdalene, who is also named as one of the women who witnessed Jesus' death and burial and later claimed to have found the tomb empty (Mk 15.40, 47; 16.1). In some branches of Christian tradition, Mary came to be regarded as a former prostitute. This image is a result of her being confused with the Mary at Bethany (Jn 12.1-8), who in turn was wrongly identified with an unnamed 'sinner' (Lk. 7.36-50). In fact, there are no grounds for believing that Mary Magdalene was a prostitute. Thus, perhaps the thing that is most surprising is that Jesus was accompanied by both men and women, as we already find stated in the Gospel of Mark (Mk 15.40-41). Nothing speaks against the idea that these women, too, were numbered among the disciples of Jesus. Does this mean, then, that Jesus was far ahead of his time? After all, in an ancient patriarchal society, wasn't a woman's place in the home? Were women really able to travel around and play an active role in something of this nature, a prophetic movement with subversive qualities?

It is, of course, true that ancient notions about how women and men could and should behave do not conform to the ideals of equality that predominate in Western societies today. For instance, in antiquity it went without saying that a wife's primary duty was taking care of the household – typical examples of women's work mentioned in the Gospels include baking (Mt. 13.33; Lk. 13.21), cleaning (Lk. 15.8) and waiting at table (Mk 1.31). But this did not mean that, generally speaking, women never left the house. On the contrary, it was also normal for women to take part in field work, fishing and other arduous tasks necessary to support the family. Only women from very wealthy households with a sufficient number of slaves could devote themselves entirely to managing the home. Even in matters of religious practice, ancient Jewish society was not marked by a pronounced segregation of the sexes. The so-called 'women's court' at the temple complex was in reality an area which both women and men had access to; the practice of separating men and women at synagogue services dates from a later period, and in all likelihood the purity laws that restricted physical contact on the basis of menstruation and childbirth would not have had a major impact on everyday life.

Nor would it have been especially unusual to see a woman travelling around without her husband. It is easy to forget how important the institution of slavery was in ancient society, including among Jews. Someone planning a long journey would rarely go without taking a slave with them. Josephus relates that during the Jewish war against Rome in the 60s CE, the messianic rebel Simon bar Giora was accompanied by his wife as well as her slaves. Slaves, both male and female, handled all manner of practical tasks, of course, but they were also expected to be sexually available to their owners. An external observer might very well have assumed that the women travelling with Jesus and 'the twelve' were serving as slaves in every respect, and this may have given rise to accusations of prostitution (see Mt. 21.31). In reality, a strict sexual morality was in effect among Jesus and the disciples, and the prohibition of remarriage that we discussed earlier (ch. 3) may in fact have been instituted precisely with the intention of preventing new family ties from being formed within a group of people who, as we have seen, had left their husbands and wives to devote themselves entirely to proclaiming the kingdom of God.

The disciples of Jesus were more than just helpers for the prophet leader; they were expected to be active in furthering the cause themselves, by preaching a message of repentance, performing exorcisms and miraculously healing the sick (Mk 6.7-13; Lk. 10.1-12). Naturally, a disciple was expected to absorb Jesus' teaching, but he or she should also observe certain special customs and rules and these enabled the group centred on Jesus to form its own identity over against other similar groups. These distinctive guidelines might cover the practices one should follow when fasting (Mk 2.18) and praying (Lk. 11.1) or how one should approach the purity laws (Mk 7.2, 5). Being the disciple of a prophet involved practising how to speak and act like the prophet leader and thus learning to play the part of the prophet for oneself (see Hägerland 2015).

The Twelve Judges and the restoration of Israel

Spring in Jerusalem, late evening. It will be Jesus' last before his execution. He has eaten the traditional Passover meal with his closest companions and during the blessing of the cup of wine he has made it known that the end – or the beginning of something new – is at hand. But he has also revealed that there is a traitor in their midst. The men's alarmed questioning about who the infiltrator might be quickly turns into an argument about which of them has shown himself most loyal and hence is preeminent among them. Suddenly Jesus interrupts the bickering and once more holds forth. He calmly explains that they will all be rulers with him in the new kingdom: 'you will sit on thrones judging the twelve tribes of Israel' (Lk 22.30).

This is more or less how the Gospel of Luke describes the last supper and the opening of Jesus' farewell speech. The account is in large part the evangelist's own composition. A comparison with the other Gospels reveals that Luke has taken various sayings of Jesus and short dialogues that were originally separate and has combined them into an extended speech. Jesus' statement that his followers will sit on thrones and judge the twelve tribes is also found in the Gospel of Matthew, but in a completely different context. There, when Peter wonders what reward he and the others who have left house and home to follow Jesus will receive, Jesus answers: 'Truly I tell you, at the renewal of all things, when the Son of Man is seated on the throne of his glory, you who have followed me will also sit on twelve thrones, judging the twelve tribes of Israel' (Mt. 19.28). Since this saying of Jesus is absent from Mark's Gospel, we can assume that Matthew and Luke have taken it from Q (see ch. 3), where it probably lacked any surrounding narrative context. The statement provides a key to understanding who 'the twelve' were and why Jesus designated an inner circle of disciples of this sort.

We can be fairly sure that this circle of twelve did indeed exist and is not a later invention. Meier's arguments in favour of the historicity of this datum are persuasive (Meier 2001: 125–47). For one thing, the group is referred to in several New Testament sources; in addition to Q, it is mentioned in Paul's works, in the Gospel of Mark and in John's Gospel (1 Cor. 15.5; Mk 3.14; Jn 6.67), which suggests that the tradition is very old. For another, is it unlikely that the 'twelve thrones' saying was formulated after Jesus' death, considering how in that saying Jesus actually includes the traitor Judas Iscariot among the twelve who will sit alongside him governing the new kingdom. We have already seen (ch. 3) that appointing Judas Iscariot as one of 'the twelve' was a strategic error on Jesus' part, one which the evangelists attempt to explain away in various ways, without much success. Had this saying of Jesus been composed at a later date, surely Judas would have been left off the list of those promised status and power. Rather, the only plausible interpretation of this evidence is that during his lifetime the historical Jesus surrounded himself with this circle and one its number betrayed him.

A much harder question to answer is, Who exactly were 'the twelve'? Their names are listed four times (Mk 3.16-19; Mt. 10.2-4; Lk. 6.14-16; Acts 1.13), but the lists differ and appear to derive from somewhat distinct traditions. According to all of the lists, the members of the innermost circle were all men. The lists all begin with Simon Peter, who stands as a kind of spokesman for 'the twelve', and finish with the traitor Judas Iscariot (only in Acts is Judas's name omitted, as he is already dead by that point in the narrative). The order of the following disciples differs from list to list: Andrew, brother of Peter; James and John, sons of Zebedee; Philip; Bartholomew; Matthew; Thomas; and James, son of Alphaeus. Towards the end of the lists, there is utter confusion: whereas the Gospels of Mark and Matthew record the otherwise unknown Thaddaeus and Simon the Cananaean, Luke and Acts have Simon the Zealot and James, son of Judas, instead. Attempts have been made to harmonize the lists with one another – 'the Zealot' and 'the Cananaean' might be different designations for the same man – but such efforts cannot fully explain the differences. One plausible explanation, also offered by Meier, is that shortly after Jesus' death most members of the circle ceased to be active in the movement and so uncertainty soon arose regarding their names. Simon Peter occupied a leading position among the early Christ-believers and was therefore well-known, and the memories of the sons of Zebedee and Thomas were kept alive by numerous tales about them, but who was that other Simon, again? And as for Thaddaeus – now, was he one of the twelve, or was he just part of the wider group of disciples? Questions like these must have presented themselves as efforts were made, several decades after the fact, to establish a definitive list of the men who had made up the esteemed inner circle during Jesus' lifetime.

Of course, Jesus' choice of precisely *twelve* men to be his closest collaborators was not incidental. According to the early Jewish understanding of history, the people of Israel originally consisted of twelve 'tribes', each of which traced its origins back to one of the twelve sons of Jacob (Gen. 49.1-28). When the Israelite kingdom was divided into two, ten of the tribes formed the so-called Northern Kingdom (Israel), while the remaining two resided in the Southern Kingdom (Judah). When the Northern Kingdom fell to Assyria and later the Southern Kingdom to Babylonia, the tribes were carried off into exile. After a few decades, the tribes of Judah and Benjamin returned to the land, but the ten tribes of the north had become scattered and remained so. At the beginning of the Common Era it was thought that only God could possibly know where the lost tribes had ended up and that God would one day bring them back to the promised land. In certain circles, it was believed that the prophet Elijah would return and 'restore the tribes of Jacob' (Sir. 48.10). In others, the re-establishment of the twelve tribes was imagined to be a task for the Messiah (see Hägerland 2014). In the *Psalms of Solomon* we read the following:

> He will gather a holy people whom he will lead in righteousness; and he will judge the tribes of the people who have been made holy by the Lord his God . . .
>
> He will distribute them upon the land according to their tribes. The stranger and the foreigner will no longer live with them . . .

> Happy are the people born in those days, who will see the good fortune of Israel that God will cause in the gathering of the tribes.
>
> *Pss. Sol.* 17.26, 28, 44

Steps were also taken in preparation for this ingathering of the tribes and restoration of the people. Talk of twelve played a central role in the Qumran movement, occurring frequently in the instructions found in the texts as to how the community should be led. According to the *Community Rule*, twelve laymen and three priests are to be the leaders of the council (1QS 8.1). Another scroll talks of how the assembly is to be judged by a group of twelve men (4Q159) which should include two priests. Of particular interest are the prescriptions in the so-called *War Scroll* for the final war. The scroll mentions twelve priests and twelve (1QM 2.1-2) serving in the temple and the chiefs of the (twelve) tribes guarding the gates of the sanctuary. The messianic 'prince', for his part, should have the names of the twelve tribes written on his standard (1QM 5.1). Once again, we may discern an example of eschatological dual thinking here: on the one hand, God is the one with the power to restore the people by gathering the tribes; on the other, members of the movement must be ready to lend concrete assistance.

Jesus, too, in appointing twelve representatives for the tribes, was making preparations for God's intervention. Few onlookers would have failed to grasp the symbolism as Jesus travelled throughout the 'promised land' with twelve specially selected men and a large group of followers besides. Although there must have been a variety of reactions – curiosity, fascination, derision – it was plain that here was a prophet with far-reaching ideas about a new beginning for the people of Israel. For Jesus and his supporters, however, such actions were merely preparation for what was soon to come. Presently, just as John the Baptist had prophesied, God would intervene to gather the scattered tribes and restore Israel to its former glory. And if ever the devoted members of the inner circle were troubled by doubts, they could at least draw comfort from the fact the prophet leader had honoured them with a great assignment: each one of them would 'judge' – that is, govern – one of the twelve tribes when God established his kingdom.

But it was not to be. The plans all failed to materialize, and the reason why most of 'the twelve' disappear from history without a trace may very well be that they gave up after their expectations ended in a fiasco.

Summary

Like many other first-century Jewish prophets, Jesus was the leader of a popular movement that was large enough to worry the establishment and to make the political authorities ultimately take action. Whereas Jesus and his followers understood themselves to be making preparations for God's intervention to restore Israel and to establish the kingdom, the religious and political elite sensed that this large movement of uneducated people longing for change could quite easily turn into an armed uprising that would put the relatively stable and peaceful conditions in Palestine at risk. For this reason Jesus' proclamation of the message about God's kingdom seemed so dangerous.

The Jesus movement was characterized by the itinerant lifestyle of its leader, who was followed by the crowd from one Galilean village to another, and by its famous meals at which decent folk and notorious sinners alike celebrated the coming of God's kingdom. Within this movement, there was a smaller group of more devoted disciples, selected by Jesus himself for the task of assisting him in his prophetic mission. This group probably included both women and men. Its innermost core was 'the Twelve', Jesus' closest companions, all of them men, the names of a few of whom are still known to us today. This circle of the Twelve pointed towards the coming restoration of the twelve tribes of Israel, and Jesus expected these disciples to play a continuing role as his co-regents once the kingdom had been fully established.

What, then, was this kingdom of God that Jesus preached and the prospect of which led so many people to join his movement? We shall deal with this question in the next chapter.

Bibliography

Bauckham, R. (2017), *Jesus and the Eyewitnesses: The Gospels as Eyewitness Testimony*, 2nd edn, Grand Rapids: Eerdmans.
Corley, K. E. (2002), *Women and the Historical Jesus: Feminist Myths of Christian Origins*, Santa Rosa: Polebridge.
Crossan, J. D. (1991), *The Historical Jesus: The Life of a Mediterranean Jewish Peasant*, San Francisco: HarperSanFrancisco.
Freyne, S. (2004), *Jesus, a Jewish Galilean: A New Reading of the Jesus-story*, London: T&T Clark.
Gray, R. (1993), *Prophetic Figures in Late Second Temple Jewish Palestine: The Evidence from Josephus*, New York: Oxford University Press.
Hägerland, T. (2014), 'A Prophet Like Elijah or According to Isaiah? Rethinking the Identity of Jesus', in S. Byrskog, T. Holmén and M. Kankaanniemi (eds), *The Identity of Jesus: Nordic Voices*, 70–86, Wissenschaftliche Untersuchungen zum Neuen Testament 2/373, Tübingen: Mohr Siebeck.
Hägerland, T. (2015), 'The Role of the Disciples in the Prophetic Mission of Jesus', in S. Byrskog and T. Hägerland (eds), Wissenschaftliche Untersuchungen zum Neuen Testament 2/391 *The Mission of Jesus*, 177–201, Tübingen: Mohr Siebeck.
Horsley, R. A. (1999), *Bandits, Prophets and Messiahs: Popular Movements in the Time of Jesus*, Harrisburg: Trinity Press International.
Meier, J. P. (2001), *A Marginal Jew: Rethinking the Historical Jesus, vol. 3: Companions and Competitors*, New Haven: Yale University Press.
Sanders, E. P. (1977), *Paul and Palestinian Judaism: A Comparison of Patterns of Religion*, London: SCM Press.
Sanders, E. P. (1993), *The Historical Figure of Jesus*, London: Allen Lane.

6

The kingdom

What was the core message of the historical Jesus? Was it possibly that everyone is of equal worth or that people should love their enemies? Or was it that every single person who believes in Jesus will have eternal life? No; in fact it was none of these. At the heart of Jesus' preaching and teaching, without a doubt, was something much more dramatic, brutal and difficult to comprehend – the idea that God was about to establish his kingdom on earth.

The coming of the kingdom

'Truly I tell you, there are some standing here who will not taste death until they see that the kingdom of God has come with power' (Mk 9.1). So said Jesus to his followers, according to Mark's Gospel, immediately after explaining that he was to suffer and die. Like the Aramaic word that Jesus himself used when he spoke, the Greek term that lies behind the English 'kingdom', here, can denote either an action, 'reigning as king', or a concrete 'kingdom'. Both dimensions are present in Jesus' use of the term in the Gospels. Regardless of which aspect is foremost, the term emphasizes the dominant position of the king, which is wholly in keeping with the view of society common in antiquity according to which a state tended to be defined by its ruler and not – as is most common today – by a particular territory, constitution or national identity. In Matthew's Gospel, Jesus usually talks of the 'kingdom of heaven' instead, a phrase that means the same as 'the kingdom of God', 'heaven' being a way of reverentially referring to God.

Mention of the kingdom of God is so widespread throughout the Gospels that all scholars, in a rare moment of consensus, agree that the message of the kingdom must have been central to Jesus' proclamation. This means neither that each and every saying about the kingdom that the evangelists attribute to Jesus does in fact come from him, nor that all experts of today have a common understanding of what Jesus meant by 'the kingdom'. John Dominic Crossan (1991), Mary Ann Beavis (2002) and other scholars – usually associated with the so-called 'Jesus Seminar', a North American research group active *c.* 1985–2005 – have suggested that Jesus' vision of the kingdom of God had nothing to do with apocalyptic predictions of the end of the world. Instead, Jesus was a teacher of wisdom who envisioned the kingdom of God to be established in the present world through his and his followers' counter-cultural lifestyle. According to these scholars, only after Jesus' death did some Christ-believers turn him into a prophet of apocalyptic doom. This non-apocalyptic interpretation of Jesus' message is rarely forwarded in recent scholarship, and that is for good reasons. Dale Allison (2010: 31–220) and others have pointed out that an apocalyptic world-view permeate the Gospels to the extent that if we attempt to filter it out, very little material will be retained for our reconstructions of Jesus. If our reconstructions lead us to conclude that the evangelists misunderstood the most central part of Jesus' proclamation, why should we take anything that they claim seriously? It is far more likely that Jesus, just like John the Baptist before him and Paul and other believers after him, viewed the world in apocalyptic terms. In the ominous prediction from Mark 9.1, then, we have a summary of what Jesus proclaimed concerning the kingdom of God: the kingdom will come soon – and 'with power'. Another of Jesus' pronouncements from later in Mark explains what it means to say that the kingdom will come 'with power' in greater detail:

> But in those days, after that suffering, the sun will be darkened, and the moon will not give its light, and the stars will be falling from heaven, and the powers in the heavens will be shaken. Then they will see 'the Son of Man coming in clouds' with great power and glory. Then he will send out the angels, and gather his elect from the four winds, from the ends of the earth to the ends of heaven.
>
> Mk 13.24-27

We will come back to the issue of who the mysterious 'Son of Man' might be later in the book (ch. 9). For the moment we may simply note that the Son of Man, just like the kingdom, will come 'with power'. This prediction is clearly inspired the book of Daniel in the Hebrew Bible, and exactly the same word for 'power' is used several times in the ancient Greek translations of Daniel and in the Gospel of Mark. In Daniel, the word does not refer to the wielding of power in the abstract, but rather to a celestial and terrestrial 'host' or military force (see Dan. 4.35; 8.10; 11.7, 13). Thus the coming of the 'Son of Man . . . with great power' means that he will come with an army of angels, ready to wage a decisive war for the kingdom of God. The 'powers in the heavens' that will be shaken are certainly first and foremost celestial bodies, but they are also invisible spiritual forces, which in antiquity were often thought to be behind the strange paths of the planets across the vault of heaven. To Jesus it was plain that if God was going to take action and claim his rightful position as king, he would have to defeat his adversaries. These adversaries included Satan and the demons, but also earthly rulers who had not submitted to the god of Israel, and seemed rather to be in allegiance with 'idols' like Zeus, Aphrodite, Apollo and their Roman counterparts.

Clearly Jesus, with his world-view, was a Jew of his time. To be sure, there were groups within Judaism, not least within the higher strata of society, who certainly did not harbour any hopes for a great act of divine intervention that would overturn the social order. Among these were the Sadducees, who no doubt regarded the temple's splendid services as sufficient manifestation of God's royal sovereignty. Certain Pharisees, who stressed studying of the Scriptures, devotion to the law and voluntary observance of purity rules, may also have numbered among such groups. Other Pharisees, as well as the Essenes at Qumran and, in all likelihood, numerous popular movements about which we now know scarcely anything, held the apocalyptic beliefs that we find in the teachings of Jesus. Several books in the Hebrew Bible (parts of Isaiah, Zechariah and Daniel) contain revelations about the end times, and from the turn of the Common Era a wide range of apocalyptic texts have been preserved. Authorship of these is often ascribed to some mythical figure from the distant past – Enoch, Abraham, Daniel and so on – who is said to have been granted a glimpse of the heavenly world and of the earth's future. The messages are cryptic and require interpretation, meaning of course that the intended reader of these texts feels privileged in having gained access to such valuable secrets. These texts were in many cases written in situations in which both author and audience felt particularly threatened. Given that the central theme of these apocalyptic texts is that everything that happens on earth is really part of a higher, divine plan, it is understandable that they were seen as offering comfort and hope in difficult times by their original readers and audiences.

Jesus' audience mostly came from the general population, whose daily struggle for the bare necessities meant arduous labour like farming, fishing and handicraft. By ancient standards their tax burden was high and did not carry with it any welfare provision. Many families were trapped in a devastating spiral of debt. On top of this, the Jewish homeland had been divided up amongst various political administrations, with Galilee being governed by a ruler who sometimes failed to respect the people's traditional piety – when Herod Antipas had his new capital city, Tiberias, built on an ancient burial ground, he showed no regard for the deeply rooted idea that contact with graves resulted in ritual impurity. In these times of economic, political and religious uncertainty, Jesus' message of imminent divine intervention was able to inspire hope. It is easy to overlook the fact that the prayer known to Christians as the Lord's Prayer or the Our Father, which in its basic outline stems from the historical Jesus, is in fact permeated with the apocalyptic notion that heavenly and earthly realities are intimately linked and that the kingdom of God is about to break into the visible plane. The prayer is found in two different versions in the Gospels (Mt. 6.9-13; Lk. 11.2-4), and on the basis of these we can surmise that in its earliest form it went approximately as follows:

> Father, hallowed be your name.
> Your kingdom come.
> Give us this day our bread for tomorrow.
> And forgive us our debts,
> as we have forgiven everyone indebted to us.
> And do not bring us to the time of trial.

Jesus' followers prayed that God's kingdom would come, but also that they would avoid being subjected to an overwhelming 'trial' during the period of civil chaos and natural disasters that was expected to precede the coming of the kingdom (see Mk 13.7-8, 14-20). At the same time, the prayer contains a very this-worldly petition for 'bread for tomorrow'. When members of the Jesus movement prayed for the forgiveness (or remission) of their 'debts', they may have had in mind both their sins, which they hoped would be forgiven on judgement day, and the snare of material debt from which they longed to be freed. The kingdom of God was an appealing solution to spiritual as well as corporeal woes.

Fairly soon after Jesus' death, changes began to take place in conceptions of the kingdom of God among the Christ-believers, and we shall come back to this at the end of the book (ch. 11). One such change was that the kingdom increasingly lost its concrete, earthly aspect and instead came to be understood in purely spiritual terms. By contrast, Jesus' vision was that 'people will come from east and west, from north and south, and will eat in the kingdom of God' (Lk. 13.29; cf. Mt. 8.11). For him, the kingdom of God was not some spiritual 'heaven' where people's immortal souls might go after death, but a real Israel, restored on earth. Yet earthly existence would be transformed so that God's presence would become visible in an entirely different way. Thus strange cosmic transformations would take place, a new temple 'not made with hands' (Mk 14.58) would be created and the righteous of bygone ages – including Abraham, Isaac and Jacob – would rise to a new and blissful life, presumably without end. There is little to suggest that the coming of the kingdom would mean the end of earthly existence; rather that existence was to undergo a radical and unprecedented change.

Another shift that occurred among early Christ-believers had to do with their temporal horizon. The authors of the works that make up the New Testament imagined that Jesus rose again after his death and was, for the time being, with God in heaven, awaiting the moment when he would make his glorious return.

Jesus himself proclaimed that 'the kingdom of God is at hand' (Mk 1.15). To be sure, he refrained from specifying exactly when the kingdom of God would in fact come. When describing the sudden and unpredictable arrival of the kingdom, he employed the somewhat surprising image of a thief who breaks into a house at an unknown time (Mt. 24.43; Lk. 12.39; cf. 1 Thess. 5.2-4; 2 Pet. 3.10; Rev. 3.3; 16.15). Yet all the evidence suggests that Jesus expected the great event to happen in his lifetime and believed that his activity would culminate in the establishment of God's visible kingdom. This hope lived on right to the bitter end. At his last meal with the disciples in Jerusalem, Jesus swore that he would 'never again drink of the fruit of the vine until that day when I drink it new in the kingdom of God' (Mk 14.25).

God – king of Israel, king of the world

The concept of God as king is deeply rooted in the Hebrew Bible. Several of the 'enthronement psalms' in the Psalter begin with the proclamation 'The Lord is king!' and extol God's sovereign might (Ps 93; 97; 99). In 1 Samuel, the establishment of the monarchy in ancient Israel is treated with great suspicion: the people demand a king like all the other nations, but in truth Israel ought to have no king but God, who is supposed to have led his people out of Egypt and into the promised land himself (1 Sam. 8.7; 12.12). During the Babylonian exile in the sixth century BCE, new hopes for deliverance from 'captivity' came to be associated with the notion of God as the true king of the Israelites (Isa. 33.22; Zeph. 3.15). The book of Isaiah speaks in poetic terms when it describes how the people and its god will return to Jerusalem, envisaging a messenger who calls out 'Your God reigns' (Isa. 52.7). The narrative in Mark's Gospel about Jesus 'proclaiming the good news of God, and saying, "The time is fulfilled, and the kingdom of God is at hand"' (Mk 1.14-15) alludes to this metaphorical messenger of Isaiah in both language and content, and Jesus must himself have had Isaiah's prophecies in mind when he spoke of the coming of the kingdom.

The bond that existed between the land, the people and their divine king and that had seemed so natural to many of the authors of the Hebrew Bible had weakened by the turn of the Common Era. For generations now Jews had been living in places all over the Mediterranean world, without harbouring any desire to relocate to the promised land. Considerable Jewish enclaves could be found in Alexandria, in particular, but also in Antioch, Asia Minor and Rome, and their allegiance to the god of Israel as king had more to do with their Jewish lifeways than with their geographic location. In one of his works, Josephus coined the term 'theocracy' to denote the form of government ordained by Moses in his capacity as lawgiver of the Jewish people (*Apion* 2.164-166). For Josephus, the law was the means by which God exercised royal authority over his people, regardless of where in the world they might be and no matter what earthly rulers they were subject to. To be sure, Josephus had not always held this view – in his youth in the 60s he had taken part in the Jewish revolt against Rome in Galilee – but in his old age Josephus enjoyed a rather comfortable existence under the protection of the Roman emperor and would hardly have had any personal interest in a more concrete manifestation of God's kingdom.

We also encounter advocates of a position resembling Josephus's in the Gospels: God's kingdom is realized through Jews' living according to the law, and not only is it unnecessary to hope for the overthrow of the prevailing social order, it is downright dangerous, even. It is hardly surprising that Jesus' most vocal opponents are often described as 'scribes' (e.g. Mk 1.22; 3.22; 7.5; 11.18), that is, men with some level of education, like Josephus, who therefore occupied a higher rung on the social ladder than the vast majority of the population. Among the elite, resistance to apocalyptic beliefs and subversive tendencies could, on the one hand, be seen as an expression of self-interest: revolution is rarely promoted by those who have reached the upper echelons of society. But on the other hand, also visible in the pragmatic conservatism of the scribes is a genuine concern for the welfare of the land and the people. In the Gospel of John, when the council in Jerusalem (ch. 2) convenes to discuss how to deal with Jesus and his movement, the chief priests and the Pharisees say:

> What are we to do? This man is performing many signs. If we let him go on like this, everyone will believe in him, and the Romans will come and destroy both our holy place and our nation.
>
> Jn 11.47-48

What John's Gospel presents here is hardly an accurate historical report of what was said – it is not even certain that such a meeting took place – but even so these comments convey the essence of the elite's critical outlook on Jesus. Most of them were old enough to remember 'Judas of Galilee', who, around the year 6 CE, led an armed uprising against the Roman authorities on the grounds that no one but God could be ruler of the Jewish people (*Ant.* 18.23); he failed and was treated with extreme brutality (Acts 5.37). Leading Jewish circles were well aware that although Rome permitted the Jews relative autonomy in internal affairs and freedom to follow their own customs, this permission hung by a thread. A large popular movement fantasizing about an army of angels that was about to appear and replace Roman rule with some kind of direct divine governance might prove too much. This could be the provocation that led the emperor to put his foot down once and for all and bring an end to that 'unruly race' from the remote south-eastern corner of the empire.

It becomes even more apparent why ideas about the kingdom of God made for political dynamite when we consider that in the writings of the Hebrew Bible God gradually moves from being the god of Israel to the god of the whole world: 'Before me no god was formed, nor shall there be any after me' (Isa. 43.10). In the Psalms, God is hailed as 'king of all the earth ... king over the nations' (Ps. 47.7-8). Thus, in its fullest extent God's kingdom comprises not just the Jews, but all people on earth. For Paul and other early Christ-believers, a central element of the gospel of Jesus was that it was meant not just for Jews but for all peoples. Some scholars have argued that universalism was also a feature of Jesus' conception of the kingdom of God, which would entail the dissolution or at least diminishing of the distinction between Jews and gentiles. As mentioned earlier in the chapter, Jesus predicted that 'people will come from east and west, from north and south, and will eat in the kingdom of God' (Lk. 13.29; cf. Mt. 8.11). Does this mean that Jesus was awaiting a kingdom where people of all ethnicities would belong on equal terms?

It may seem hard to swallow but all the indications are that Jesus' message was entirely ethnocentric. The few encounters between Jesus and gentiles recorded in the Gospels seem to have come about by chance, and in them Jesus keeps his distance (Lk. 7.1-10). In one episode we hear of how, when a non-Jewish woman asks Jesus to help her daughter who is possessed, Jesus calls her, indirectly, a 'dog' (Mk 7.24-30; Mt. 15.21-28). Initially the prophecy about people coming from every corner of the earth to take part in the feast in the kingdom of God probably referred, not to gentiles, but to the ingathering of the scattered tribes of the Jewish people. And while the report in Matthew about how Jesus and his disciples are only to seek out 'the lost sheep of the people of Israel' (Mt. 15.24; cf. 10.6) probably does not record an authentic saying of the historical Jesus, it captures the essence of his attitude well. Jesus had no intention of creating a new, universalistic religion; his message was that God's promises to the Jewish people would soon be fulfilled. This also explains why after Jesus' death such widely differing opinions prevailed on the issue of how gentiles should be incorporated into the Christ-believer movement, which is a subject we shall return to at the end of the book (ch. 11); the possibility that people of other ethnicities would desire to join the movement in large numbers was not something that Jesus had anticipated or planned for.

Was Jesus entirely uninterested in the future of the gentile nations, then? Were they to have no role whatsoever to play when the kingdom of God was established? In all likelihood Jesus held something like the equivocal attitude towards the gentiles that is articulated in the *Psalms of Solomon*. On the one hand, the future Messiah would bring about an ethnic cleansing, such that 'The stranger and the foreigner will no longer live with them' (*Pss. Sol.* 17.28), but on the other the author envisages gentile 'nations com[ing] from the ends of the earth to see his glory' (*Pss. Sol.* 17.31). This is a vision about roles one day being reversed, when Israel will be the great empire to which other nations and rulers must submit – given that Israel is God's special people, and God is king of all the earth.

A budding shoot

When Jesus talks of the kingdom of God in the Gospels, it is most often in the form of parables: short narratives (sometimes very short) grounded in everyday occurrences and familiar phenomena that are intended to illustrate some aspect of the message that Jesus wishes to convey. This manner of preaching is highly reminiscent of how certain prophets of the Hebrew Bible delivered their message (see, e.g. 2 Sam. 12.1-12; Isa. 5.1-7; Ezek. 15.1-8) and is a further indication that Jesus saw himself as a prophet. The parables about the kingdom usually begin 'The kingdom of heaven is like . . .' or 'The kingdom of God may be compared to . . .'. The kingdom is as if a man scattered seed on the ground and everything grows of itself (Mk 4.26-29), or as if a woman took yeast and mixed it in with flour (Mt. 13.33), or as if a man sowed wheat in his field, but an enemy came and sowed weeds (Mt. 13.24-30), or as if ten bridesmaids took part in a wedding procession, but five of them did not bring enough oil with them for their lamps (Mt. 25.1-12), and so on. These parables constitute our most extensive source for understanding what Jesus intended with his message about the kingdom of God, but at the same time they are very difficult to interpret, as it is rarely obvious in what respect the subject of the narrative is supposed to resemble the kingdom. As an example we may consider what it might mean to say that the kingdom is like treasure hidden in a field. In this short narrative, a man finds the treasure, hides it again, sells everything he owns and buys the field (Mt. 13.44). Is the point that the kingdom is a hidden secret, or that the kingdom is worth more than any possession, or that one must act shrewdly to obtain the kingdom – or all of these at once? What is more, when it comes to the parables found in the Gospels, scholars are not sure which derive from the historical Jesus and which were formulated later. From an investigation of the thirty or so narrative parables in the Gospels, Meier (2016) concluded that only four may be believed to have come from Jesus himself with any degree of certainty. In all probability, there are other authentic parables, but determining which those might be is difficult given the evangelists' apparent fondness for composing parables to put in Jesus' mouth.

Among the parables most likely to have been recounted by Jesus himself is that of the mustard seed. Mark depicts Jesus seemingly contemplating how best to explain what the kingdom of God is, before he finally finds the image he has been looking for:

> He also said, 'With what can we compare the kingdom of God, or what parable will we use for it? It is like a mustard seed, which, when sown upon the ground, is the smallest of all the seeds on earth; yet when it is sown it grows up and becomes the greatest of all shrubs, and puts forth large branches, so that the birds of the air can make nests in its shade.'
>
> Mk 4.30-32

The image of the tiny mustard seed that transforms in just a short while into a great bush was familiar to Jesus' audience, and they may have enjoyed his propensity for exaggeration – the mustard seed is not the smallest of all the seeds, nor is it a 'tree' (cf. Mt. 13.32; Lk. 13.19). One important aspect of Jesus' conception of the kingdom of God was that it would come when and because God wills it, not through human efforts. For this reason, the image of a seed was very apt; all that is needed is for it to be put in the ground, and the rest, as it were, takes care of itself. But the image of the mustard plant that shoots up says something else about the kingdom, too; the seed has already been sown and the emergence of the kingdom is even now perceptible, though as yet it has not manifested itself as the tree with large branches that offer shelter, but only as a little budding shoot.

Jesus' message was thus not simply that in the near future the kingdom of God would come 'with power', but further that in his work the kingdom had started to be realized. For Jesus, one sign that the kingdom was already beginning to emerge were his achievements as a miracle-worker and exorcist. We shall take a closer look at these in the next chapter, but even at this point we can note the response that, according to Luke's Gospel, Jesus gave to those who criticized his work as a caster-out of spirits: 'if it is by the finger of God that I cast out the demons, then the kingdom of God has come to you' (Lk. 11.20). It could hardly be stated more clearly that the kingdom of God is not merely something coming in the future, but also something currently being realized in Jesus' healing activity and in his vanquishing of evil spirits.

Another element of the Jesus movement that suggests that its adherents somehow wanted to celebrate the coming of the kingdom in advance are their communal meals. As we have seen, the Gospels portray Jesus at table with people who were usually regarded as having left God's covenant with Israel – 'tax-collectors' and 'sinners', which included prostitutes (Mk 2.15-17; Lk. 7.37-39; 15.2; cf. Mt. 21.31). Evidently, dining in questionable company was such a distinctive habit of Jesus' that he was accused of being 'a glutton and a drunkard' (Mt. 11.19; Lk. 7.34). When Jesus and his disciples were criticized for not fasting as was otherwise customary in pious Jewish circles, Jesus' response was that the 'wedding-guests cannot fast while the bridegroom is with them' (Mk 2.18-19). According to Jesus, the royal banquet had, in a sense, already begun around him, but it was not principally the pious or the scribes who were in attendance, but rather individuals who lived anything but exemplary lives. Another of Jesus' parables concerns a man who arranges a banquet and sends out invitations (Mt. 22.2-14; Lk. 14.16-24); when the intended guests prioritize other business and decline the invitation, the man tells his servants to bring people of all sorts, 'good and bad', to the banquet (Mt. 22.10). Those who were invited first are no longer welcome. Jesus must surely have hoped that his movement would receive the support of some of the scribes that he encountered in Capernaum, Bethsaida and other Galilean villages (cf. Mt. 11.20-24; Lk. 10.13-15). This hope did not materialize, however, and instead Jesus beheld a movement consisting largely of people of an even lower social status than himself. Those who chose to join him would be vindicated when the kingdom really did come 'with power' – as too would Jesus.

Living in the kingdom of God

According to one understanding, which is fairly common today, the core of all religion is ethics. It has been pointed out – rightly – that, with minor variations, the 'golden rule' (Mt. 7.12; Lk. 6.31) is found in the writings of many religions, as well as in numerous philosophical systems. Accordingly there is a tendency to present Jesus as a moral teacher, whose message was primarily concerned with how humankind might lead a good and upright life. There are, in early Judaism, several examples of wisdom teachers of this kind, such as the authors of the Wisdom of Solomon and the Wisdom of Sirach, but Jesus should not be numbered among them. He acted as a prophet, which is to say that at the heart of his preaching lay, not timeless ethical principles, but a proclamation of God's imminent intervention in the world. Nevertheless, just like the prophets of the Hebrew Bible, Jesus' message also had moral dimensions. In the new world order that he was awaiting the people of Israel would lead a new kind of life, and since the kingdom was in a sense already present in Jesus' activity, he and his followers were to endeavour to lead that new life without delay.

Reversed roles

'All who exalt themselves will be humbled, and all who humble themselves will be exalted', as one of Jesus' sayings has it (Mt. 23.12; Lk. 14.11; 18.14), or put another way: 'many who are first will be last, and the last will be first' (Mk 10.31; Mt. 19.30; cf. Mk 9.35; Mt. 20.16; Lk. 13.30). This might sound like general wisdom for living (pride goeth before a fall) or like another version of 'tall poppy syndrome' ('don't believe that you are special'), but for Jesus and his disciples, the idea that the privileged in society would be brought low in favour of the marginalized is closely connected with their apocalyptic world-view.

A recurring theme in apocalyptic works is the imminent reversal of roles: in but a little while the eminent rulers of the present will come to be reviled and vice versa. The book of Daniel, for instance, ends with a vision in which some of those who are to rise again at the end of time awake 'to shame and everlasting contempt', whereas those 'who are wise shall shine like the brightness of the sky' (Dan. 12.2-3). It is hardly surprising that this theme comes to the fore in such works since, as we have seen, they were written by and for people who knew what life was like at the bottom. For Jesus, this perception was strengthened by the fact that the local elites of the Galilean villages, rather than embracing his message, regarded his movement as positively harmful. Nor can he have had much faith in Herod Antipas, who held power in Galilee and who had John the Baptist executed. There are signs in the Gospels that the circle closest to Antipas likewise regarded the Jesus movement with concern and considered taking measures against it

(Mk 3.6; 8.15; Lk. 13.31). Jesus was aware that his message about the kingdom of God represented a provocation, both to the local Galilean ruler and to Roman claims of global dominion.

Jesus and his disciples reacted to the suspicion and setbacks they faced by playing the part of the oppressed and the persecuted with even greater conviction. The Beatitudes, as they are known (Mt. 5.3-12; Lk. 6.20-23), may well be the clearest expression of the ideal that came to characterize the itinerant Jesus movement: the worse things get now, the better it will be when the kingdom of God comes.

> Blessed are you who are poor, for yours is the kingdom of God.
> Blessed are you who are hungry now, for you will be filled.
> Blessed are you who weep now, for you will laugh.
>
> Lk. 6.20-21

Jesus and the disciples who journeyed with him had themselves chosen to leave their homes and occupations. They cultivated an identity as 'homeless' and 'poor', despite the fact that, in reality, the movement was not entirely lacking in financial resources, as we touched on in the last chapter. Those wanting to join the movement had to be prepared to live as if homeless (Mt. 8.19-20; Lk. 9.57-58) and to part with everything they owned (Mk 10.17-22). Wealth as an obstacle to gaining a share in the kingdom of God is a recurring theme in Jesus' teaching (Mk 10.23-25; Mt. 6.19; Lk. 12.33). In the Q source the reasoning for this is primarily that disciples should not concern themselves with worldly affairs like food, drink and clothing, but rather have complete trust that God will take care of such things and more besides (Mt. 6.25-34; Lk. 12.22-32). Anyone who holds on to money or possessions, as a precaution, has divided loyalties and is not serving God wholeheartedly (Mt. 6.24; Lk. 16.13). This indeed was probably how members of the Jesus movement thought, but at the same time there was a further, ulterior motive, of sorts, in that such self-imposed poverty would be rewarded with riches at the coming of the kingdom (cf. Mk 10.28-31).

Renouncing house and home was not enough to be sure of being rewarded. True disciples would even be prepared to die for their beliefs. One saying that appears several times in the Gospels states that anyone who seeks to save his life will lose it, while the one who loses his life will save it (Mk 8.35; Mt. 10.39; Lk. 17.33). This saying as found in the Gospels is coloured by the persecution and killing of Christ-believers that occurred after Jesus' death, but in substance it goes back to the historical Jesus, who anticipated that being involved in the movement might cost his followers their lives too. And to galvanize them not to betray him even in such dire circumstances they had the promise that they would rise again to their reward in the kingdom of God. Should they fail to remain loyal to the movement and its ideals, however, they would be condemned to the everlasting fires of Gehenna (cf. Mk 9.43).

Perfection

The Jesus movement thus demanded exacting standards. Earlier we observed that Jesus and his disciples invoked the god of Israel as 'Father', which suggests that they saw themselves as 'children' of God. In antiquity this also meant that they ought therefore to share in the father's attributes and model their behaviour on his. In a saying that is found, in different formulations, in Matthew and Luke, Jesus exhorts his disciples to be 'merciful' (Lk. 6.36) or even 'perfect' (Mt. 5.48), making reference to the fact that their divine father, for his part, was merciful or perfect. The theme is spelled out most clearly in the Gospel of Matthew, but the idea is present in other sources as well. When disciples prayed for God to forgive their sins, they were to make sure to practise forgiveness themselves (Mk 11.25; Mt. 6.12; Lk. 11.4). An inner tension in Jesus' teaching is discernible here between, on the one hand, a moral perfectionism of sorts that presupposes that the movement's followers can and should emulate the holiness and perfection of God, and, on the other, an acknowledgement that in the future they will also need to pray for God's forgiveness. This same tension can be seen in, for example, the *Thanksgiving Psalms* from Qumran, where, in one and the same psalm, humanity's shortcomings and its perfection can be expressed:

> But as for me, I know that righteousness does not belong to humankind,
> nor perfection of way to a mortal.
> To God Most High belong all the works of righteousness.
> The way of humanity is not established
> except by the spirit God has fashioned for it,
> in order to perfect a way for mortal beings
>
> 1QH 12.31–33

Several ancient Jewish apocalyptic texts, including *1 Enoch* and *4 Ezra*, speak of a future in which the people of God live a sinless existence in perfect reverence. A number of Jesus' sayings are so morally demanding that they almost seem to presuppose sinlessness. In this respect the teaching collected in Matthew's Sermon on the Mount (Mt. 5–7) is especially notable. In reality, of course, these chapters do not reproduce a lengthy sermon delivered by Jesus on a single occasion; they are rather a compilation of, and elaboration upon, various sayings that have ethical content. At numerous points it is clear that Matthew has seen fit to reformulate and supplement the material, and it is sometimes difficult to tell precisely which sayings really derive from the historical Jesus, but almost all scholars agree that the radical tenor of the Sermon on the Mount comes from Jesus himself.

In both the Sermon on the Mount and its lesser known counterpart in Luke's Gospel, sometimes known as the Sermon on the Plain, we find the lofty ideal of repaying evil with good:

> But I say to you that listen, Love your enemies, do good to those who hate you, bless those who curse you, pray for those who abuse you. If anyone strikes you on the cheek, offer the other also; and from anyone who takes away your coat do not withhold even your shirt. Give to everyone who begs from you; and if anyone takes away your goods, do not ask for them again.
>
> Lk. 6.27-30; cf. Mt. 5.39-44

Leading such a self-negating life was part of emulating the god whom Jesus and his disciples regarded as their 'father'. After all, God himself was 'kind to the ungrateful and the wicked' (Lk. 6.35; cf. Mt. 5.45)! Of course, when God's kingdom did come the oppressors and evildoers would disappear, but as long as they remained, a child of God should endure their oppression, so as to practise the perfection that would characterize life in the kingdom.

This morality could scarcely be upheld in reality, even within the Jesus movement. The emphasis on the necessity of God's forgiveness and on oneself having to forgive in order to have a share in it indicates that the members of the movement did not live up to the ethical standard that the children of the divine Father ought to embody. Consequently there is some truth to the term 'interim ethics' that has at times been used to describe Jesus' moral teaching. Its focus was on how the disciples were to conduct themselves in an evil and hostile world and thus it would become obsolete once the kingdom had come. It addressed how they were to live when God was both their king and their father, whilst leaving room for failure, as the kingdom of God had not yet come 'with power'.

As it was in the beginning

When at last the kingdom was established, then, which rules would govern life? For Jesus, the answer was, in fact, self-evident, as it was for other Jews: in God's kingdom, Israel would live by the laws in the Torah. When asked which commandment was the most important, Jesus answered by reciting the prayer most central to Judaism, about loving God (Deut. 6.4-5). To this he added the commandment to love one's fellow Israelites (Lev. 19.18). This saying is usually known as the double command of love:

> The first is, 'Hear, O Israel: the Lord our God, the Lord is one; you shall love the Lord your God with all your heart, and with all your soul, and with all your mind, and with all your strength.' The second is this, 'You shall love your neighbour as yourself.' There is no other commandment greater than these.
>
> Mk 12.29-31

Jesus did not question the status of the Jewish law as the highest moral authority. Nevertheless, some commandments were more important than others, and he was able to play various parts of the law off against one another. Earlier (ch. 3) we saw that Jesus forbade divorce and remarriage, despite the fact that the Hebrew Bible gives express instructions for what should happen when a man wishes to divorce his wife, who at that point becomes free to enter into a new marriage (Deut. 24.1-3). According to Mark's Gospel, some Pharisees called Jesus' attention to the fact that divorce was undoubtedly permitted by law, at which point Jesus is supposed to have responded that this contingency came about as a concession, whereas things had been different at the start:

> But from the beginning of creation, 'God made them male and female.' 'For this reason a man shall leave his father and mother and be joined to his wife, and the two shall become one flesh.' So they are no longer two, but one flesh. Therefore what God has joined together, let no one separate.
>
> Mk 10.6-9

The argument here is that the Torah presents two different ways of looking at divorce and remarriage; since the more radical of the two is expressed so early on, in the creation narrative (Gen. 2.24), it represents a more straightforward expression of the genuine will of God than the law that came later and that had to take into account humanity's imperfection. The *Damascus Document* also refers to the conditions at the creation as an argument against polygyny (taking several wives; see ch. 8). Similar reasoning probably lies behind Jesus' prohibition on oath-taking (Mt. 5.33-37). Even if other Jewish teachers from this period could sound warnings about taking oaths unthinkingly or out of habit (Sir. 23.9), there is no escaping the fact that the law not only permits oaths, but sometimes directly prescribes them (Exod. 22.10-11; Num. 5.11-31). According to Jesus this too was a concession to humanity's untrustworthiness, and he desired a return to an original, paradisiacal condition in which what needed to be promised could be said with merely a 'yes' or a 'no'. Jesus was striving for the seemingly impossible: to be more faithful to the will of God than Moses himself had been.

As far as we know, these specific ways of articulating that ambition are unique to Jesus, but the basic idea that the coming kingdom would represent a return to how things were 'in the beginning' is not uncommon in apocalyptic literature. The sinless existence that was awaited was a restoration of an original condition. The *Book of Jubilees* describes how, after the great flood, human beings lived wickedly, which explains why their lives were so much shorter than the fantastical lifespans recorded for several of the early figures in Genesis. In the future they shall turn back to righteousness and then once more live for a thousand years (*Jub.* 23.9-12, 26-29). When Jesus and other apocalyptics imagined their utopias, they looked to the past as much as to the future. The end would be like the beginning.

Summary

When it comes to the content of Jesus' preaching and teaching, the thing that we can say with the greatest certainty is that it involved the kingdom of God. His entire mission was driven by the conviction that – very soon and in a very tangible way – God would reclaim his position as the sole ruler of Israel, indeed, of the entire world. Jesus expected the visible coming of the kingdom to occur within his own lifetime and called on his followers to prepare for this apocalyptic event.

At the same time, Jesus and his movement also thought that the kingdom was already establishing itself in and through their ongoing mission. Their communal meals, which challenged conventional socio-religious boundaries, were anticipations of the final banquet associated with the powerful coming of the kingdom. Their healings and exorcisms were further signs of the kingdom in the making. Moreover, they idealized a lifestyle which included, among other things, the renunciation of wealth, strict sexual morals, a willingness to forgive one another, and the readiness at any point to die for their beliefs if needed. All of this was meant as an imitation of the perfection of God, their 'father', and as a way of living in accordance with God's original intentions.

Next we will turn to one of the most tangible manifestations of the kingdom in Jesus' mission, his work as a healer and exorcist. Did Jesus really heal people and expel demons? If so, in what sense and to what ends? These are the questions we shall tackle in the next chapter.

Bibliography

Allison, D. C. (2010), *Constructing Jesus: Memory, Imagination, and History*, Grand Rapids: Baker Academic.

Beavis, M. A. (2002), *Jesus and Utopia*, Santa Rosa: Polebridge.

Crossan, J. D. (1991), *The Historical Jesus: The Life of a Mediterranean Jewish Peasant*, San Francisco: HarperSanFrancisco.

Ehrman, B. D. (1999), *Jesus: Apocalyptic Prophet of the New Millennium*, New York: Oxford University Press.

Meier, J. P. (2009), *A Marginal Jew: Rethinking the Historical Jesus, vol. 4: Law and Love*, New Haven: Yale University Press.

Meier, J. P. (2016), *A Marginal Jew: Rethinking the Historical Jesus, vol. 5: Probing the Authenticity of the Parables*, New Haven: Yale University Press.

7

In conflict with Satan

After two thousand years of Christian usage the phrases 'kingdom of God' and 'kingdom of heaven' are so time-worn that it is easy for us to forget how politically loaded they were to begin with. As 'king' of his realm, God is not some toothless constitutional monarch, but rather a real ruler, who extends and preserves his dominion by force. And naturally, should any other princes or kingdoms fail to bow to his will of their own accord, God must fight against them and defeat them. Jesus saw himself as being in the middle of this fight for God's kingdom. This fight, however, was not above all directed against human foes, nor even against the Roman Empire, but against much tougher opponents: Satan himself, his demons and their works. In this chapter we turn to the question of Jesus as a healer and exorcist in the service of the kingdom of God.

Sickness and healing then and now

'Unfortunately, due to sickness I will be unable to come in today'. Most of us have probably used a sentence like this at some point, without reflecting further on what we mean by 'sickness'. Have I seen a doctor and been given a diagnosis? Is it a matter of my experiencing the sensation of my body or mind not working as it should? Or am I perhaps feeling better, but have been advised to refrain from certain activities so as not to get immediately sick again? The term can encompass a range of meanings that are in fact quite different. Indeed, we have several different words that make it possible to distinguish these different meanings. This may prove necessary as we try to understand the significance of the fact that Jesus was known as one who could 'heal the sick'.

Different ways of looking at sickness

In the first place, sickness may be a medical condition, such as when the body contracts a bacterial infection. We use the word 'disease' to denote this physiological kind of sickness. A doctor might cure this kind of disease by, for example, administering antibiotics for the infection. Secondly, sickness can be the same thing as 'illness', that is, the subjective experience of feeling unwell, which need not tally with any particular medical diagnosis. The condition known as Electromagnetic hypersensitivity (EHS) is a good example of this kind of illness. No one disputes whether individuals with EHS do indeed feel ill, but since clinical studies have not been able to demonstrate that electromagnetic fields per se can cause the symptoms reported, cognitive behavioural therapy is probably a more effective treatment for them than abatement work. A third concept is sickness in a social sense, that is, the state of being regarded as sick by others, and we sometimes express this specifically with the word 'sickness'. In order to understand what is meant here, we can consider the familiar situation of someone being signed off work sick. For someone to be signed off a doctor must judge that his or her capacity to work is impaired because of disease or illness, but usually there is no reason to tell that person's co-workers what is wrong with him or her. All anyone else needs to know is that the individual is not fit for work.

These different conceptions of sickness are not mutually exclusive. In most cases the subjective feeling of illness corresponds to some medical condition – many mental illnesses, for instance, have physiological causes. Thus we are not primarily dealing with different kinds of sickness but with different ways of looking at sickness, and it will be worthwhile to be alert to these various perspectives as we address the question of Jesus as healer. The order in which we introduced these different conceptions – first the biological, then the subjective and finally the social – is typical of our modern way of looking at reality and at human life. In antiquity, if anything the order would have been reversed. The most important dimension was the social one: what chiefly determined whether someone was considered sick was how other people reacted to his or her condition. Only after this came the individual's own experience, and lastly notions from primitive medicine about how disease manifested itself and what caused it. The wide divergence in ways of looking at sickness through history means that something that might readily be classed as sickness today would not necessarily have been understood as such in antiquity, and vice versa. For example, ancient physicians were aware of diabetes, but the number of diagnosed cases known from antiquity is very low. And although this might be largely due to the fact that the disease is undoubtedly more prevalent today, we may also suppose that many people had diabetes in ancient times without knowing it. Conversely numerous conditions that we would nowadays hesitate to class as sickness were understood as such at the turn of the Common Era. This includes various sorts of congenital and acquired disabilities, such as blindness, but also some kinds of mental disorder, typically interpreted as demonic possession in antiquity.

Various diseases meant social exclusion in ancient Jewish society. When Luke relates that ten 'lepers' sought out Jesus to be freed from their disease, he describes them as 'keeping their distance' (Lk. 17.11). Early on in the Hebrew Bible, in Leviticus, we find detailed instructions about how various types of skin disease referred to as 'leprosy' should be examined and treated, and we read that anyone afflicted by this skin disease must take steps to stay away from others:

> The person who has the leprous disease shall wear torn clothes and let the hair of his head be dishevelled; and he shall cover his upper lip and cry out, 'Unclean, unclean.' He shall remain unclean as long as he has the disease; he is unclean. He shall live alone; his dwelling shall be outside the camp.
>
> Lev. 13.45-46

Several episodes in the Hebrew Bible highlight the social stigma that skin disease of this kind brought with it. King Azariah, or Uzziah, of Judah, in the eighth century BCE, is said to have developed this skin disease. Evidently the worst aspect of the condition was not the physical suffering it caused but rather the fact that the king 'to the day of his death ... lived in a separate house' (2 Kgs 15.5; cf. 2 Chron. 26.21). This requirement of isolation must originally have arisen because the disease was observed to be infectious, but over time it also came to be associated with ritual impurity and with the idea that it was a punishment from God. Likewise, individuals who were possessed, that is, who were thought to be under direct demonic control, might need to be quarantined so as not to harm themselves or others. The vivid account of Jesus' encounter with a possessed man at Gerasa (Mk 5.1-20) contains several strange details that must be fictional, but what is not unrealistic is the introductory description of how 'among the tombs and on the mountains [the man] was always howling and bruising himself with stones' (Mk 5.5) and of how people had tried to bind him hand and foot. Less dramatic 'sicknesses' – what we would refer to rather as disabilities today – could also lead to marginalization. Someone who was blind or paralyzed often had no option but to beg and in so doing to become dependent on the compassion of others for survival (Mk 10.46; Jn 9.8; Acts 3.1). Clearly such individuals lacked what they would have needed to start their own families and to perpetuate their ancestral names and honour.

Sin and sickness

We have already mentioned, in the introductory chapter, that the population of Galilee in the time of Jesus was afflicted with numerous diseases that were seldom curable. People reflected, as they always have done, on the problem of evil. Where does evil come from? Why do some people suffer while others do not? How does this fit with the notion of a benevolent god who is creator of all? In the past, just as today, people could reach various answers. One was that diseases and other forms of suffering were the work of Satan. In Luke's Gospel we hear about a woman whom 'Satan bound for eighteen long years' with 'a spirit that had crippled her' and given her a stoop (Lk. 13.10-17). Another, more common answer was quite the opposite: that diseases were God's doing, punishments for the sins people had committed. 'He who sins against his Maker, may he fall into the hands of the physician', as the Wisdom of Jesus Ben Sira (Sirach) puts it, a work from the beginning of the second century BCE (Sir. 38.15). This proverb is a fairly apt summary of the idea that sickness is a punishment for sin, an idea earlier expressed in the Hebrew Bible and also evident at several points in the Gospels. One episode in the Synoptics tells of a paralyzed man who has been carried into Jesus' presence. Only after saying to the man 'your sins are forgiven' does Jesus tell him to 'stand up, take your mat and go to your home', whereupon the man gets up and walks (Mk 2.1-12). In a similar episode in the Gospel of John, after his miracle Jesus says to the man, 'you have been made well! Do not sin any more, so that nothing worse happens to you' (Jn 5.14). Here the Gospels assume that there is a link between the forgiveness of sins and physical healing. Particularly striking is the dialogue between Jesus and his disciples that introduces the episode in John of the curing of a man born blind. Here the disciples ask Jesus whether the man's blindness is a result of his own sin or of his parents' (Jn 9.2). The question may sound strange but it should be understood in the light of speculations about whether someone was capable of sinning even in the womb – for, if not, a congenital disability must be the result of God from time to time punishing the *children* of those who sin too. Jesus answers that neither the man nor his parents have sinned, though this should hardly be taken as a rejection of the idea, on principle, that sin can lead to bodily ailments. On the contrary, Jesus seems to have acknowledged a link between forgiveness and healing, as we saw from the episodes just discussed.

Curing and healing

By this point a careful reader may have remarked upon the term 'healing' and been wondering why we have not been writing about Jesus 'curing' diseases instead. The reason is that, just as it makes sense to distinguish various types of 'sickness', similarly there is good reason to differentiate between curing and healing. Curing someone means eliminating a state of disease with a physiological basis, whereas healing involves the removal of the subjective experience of illness. This insight has been fruitfully applied to Gospels studies by biblical scholars, most notably John Pilch (2000) and Eric Eve (2009), and we are following their lead here. Describing Jesus as a healer allows us to study the effects of his activity as a miracle-worker without being limited to what is in fact medically possible. For historians, the important thing is really that Jesus was known as a worker of miracles even in his own time and that both he and people he met became convinced that he had a special power to heal. What may have happened on a physiological level – and how that was brought about – is of secondary interest.

Of course, Jesus was not the only person in antiquity with a reputation for being able to heal people. Within the discipline known as medical anthropology, a society's health-care system is usually divided into three different sectors. The first is the popular sector, and most illnesses are actually handled within it. We are all fairly good at recognizing the symptoms of a cold, for instance, which we then treat in various ways. Usually nothing else is required, but sometimes we have to proceed to the second sector, the professional. This is mainly, though not exclusively, made up of trained and accredited health-care workers who are occupied primarily – though not exclusively – with preventing and curing diseases, in the medical sense. In ancient times the stringent controls that apply in this sector today were lacking, and the field was not only open to the reputable physicians whose talents are celebrated in Sir. 38.1-15, but also to charlatans. Mark's Gospel provides a poignant insight into the helplessness that many people who were afflicted by sickness experienced, in the introduction to the episode in which a woman with haemorrhages is healed at Capernaum:

> Now there was a woman who had been suffering from haemorrhages for twelve years. She had endured much under many physicians, and had spent all that she had; and she was no better, but rather grew worse.
>
> Mk 5.25-26

A person who lacks access to care in the professional sector for whatever reason, or who judges that his or her needs will not be met there, can often turn to the third sector for help. In this sector, which is called the folk sector, operate individuals who are thought to possess the ability to heal perceived illnesses without having any formal training or accreditation. What we label 'alternative medicine' today includes a wide range of techniques for treating illness, including everything from practices that have been discredited by science, like homeopathy, to contentious ones, such as acupuncture and reflexology. All of these belong in the folk sector, insofar as they are not prescribed by professional doctors but are nonetheless used by many people, in the belief that they provide good results. So, too, does the woman with haemorrhages in Mark's Gospel decide to turn to the folk sector for help, when the professional one fails her:

> She had heard about Jesus, and came up behind him in the crowd and touched his cloak, for she said, 'If I but touch his clothes, I will be made well.' Immediately her haemorrhage stopped; and she felt in her body that she was healed of her disease.
>
> Mk 5.27-29

The detail, here, that the woman 'immediately ... felt in her body' that healing had taken place is quite typical. In contrast to the gradual recovery that often marks curing in the professional sector, healing in the folk sector generally happens instantaneously. The 'proof' that healing has taken place is usually the disappearance of the symptoms of illness, together with a sense of certainty on the part of the recently sick person that he or she is well once more. Follow-ups are rarely carried out.

In ancient times folk healings were often associated with particular sites and shrines where the gods were thought to be especially active, in the same way that many Roman Catholics today regard Lourdes in southern France as a site of supernatural healings. Epidaurus in the Peloponnese, in modern day Greece, is the most famous ancient place of healing, where pilgrims came to sleep in the sanctuary of the god Asclepius in hopes of thereby being healed or at least of receiving instructions as to their healing in dreams. Jerusalem had the pool of Bethesda, whose water was regarded as exerting a healing influence on those with paralysis, blindness and other disabilities (see Jn 5.2-7). But in addition, charismatic wonder-workers of the first century CE were sometimes known to act as folk healers. The itinerant philosopher Apollonius of Tyana is said to have healed the sick, cast out spirits and even raised the dead. Vespasian, as newly appointed Roman emperor, reluctantly performed acts of healing, spitting on the eyes of a blind person and touching the leg of a paralytic. In the Jewish realm, Hanina ben Dosa is supposed to have healed the sons of two prominent teachers of the law through prayer. Josephus claims to have personally witnessed an exorcist named Eleazar casting out a demon from a possessed man by means of special objects and incantations.

The line dividing magic and religion is not clear-cut and our choice of terminology can often reflect a value judgement on the phenomenon under discussion. Whereas in our society religion has come to be seen above all as a system of ideas about the supernatural and humanity's relationship with it, the word 'magic' tends to be used disparagingly to describe strategies for 'manipulating' the world by means of rituals and special tools. Most religions, however, have rituals that their practitioners regard as being effective by virtue of simply being performed – consider the sacraments within Christianity or the recitation of the Quran in Islam – and it is practically impossible to establish a neat boundary to mark when rituals of this kind cross over into 'magic'. At first glance Jesus' approach to healing people and casting out demons, merely by issuing a command in most cases, appears to differ substantially from the technique used by the exorcist Eleazar to cast out spirits, which involved a special ring, herbs and formulas. However, the episode in Mark's Gospel about the woman with haemorrhages reveals that the healings carried out by Jesus could likewise be described with what we might call magical overtones. According to the narrative, all that was needed was for the woman to touch Jesus' clothing to be healed. Mark continues with a description of how Jesus became 'immediately aware that power had gone forth from him' (Mk 5.30). On other occasions we hear of Jesus using special gestures and materials, as when he heals a deaf man who has a speech impediment by putting his fingers in the man's ears, spitting and touching his tongue (Mk 7.32-35), or when he rubs a paste of saliva and earth onto the eyes of the man born blind (Jn 9.6). Someone who wanted to might well brand such acts magic and witchcraft without great difficulty. Hardly surprisingly, Jesus' critics accused him of being possessed himself and of receiving Satan's help to perform his miraculous works (Mk 3.22).

The healer

The Gospels omit a great many details about their protagonist, details that we would have expected to find if we were reading a modern biography. For example, what happened the first time Jesus succeeded in healing someone? Was it planned? Was he surprised by his own success or had he been preparing for it for some time, perhaps even learning various techniques from a master?

What sort of miracle-worker was Jesus?

The silence of the Gospels on these points has led to much curiosity and speculation throughout history. As early as the second century CE the philosopher Celsus, a critic of Christianity, claimed that Jesus had spent several years in Egypt and that he learnt his magic tricks there. That century also saw the composition of the so-called *Infancy Gospel of Thomas*, which we have already mentioned (see ch. 3). This work consists of a series of anecdotes (which lack any real value as historical sources) about the exploits of Jesus from the age of five up to the episode about Jesus as a twelve-year-old at the temple (cf. Lk. 2.41-52). Even as a little boy Jesus displays miraculous abilities (*Infancy Gospel of Thomas* 2.1; 3.1-3):

> When this child Jesus was five years old, he was playing by the ford of a stream; and he gathered the flowing waters into pools and made them immediately pure. These things he ordered simply by speaking a word. . . . Now the son of Annas the scribe was standing there with Joseph; and he took a willow branch and scattered the water that Jesus had gathered. Jesus was irritated when he saw what had happened, and he said to him: 'You unrighteous, irreverent idiot! What did the pools of water do to harm you? See, now you also will be withered like a tree, and you will never bear leaves or root or fruit.' Immediately the child was completely withered. Jesus left and returned to Joseph's house. But the parents of the withered child carried him away, mourning his lost youth. They brought

him to Joseph and began to accuse him, 'What kind of child do you have who does such things?'

translation Bart D. Ehrman (2003)

The narrative continues in the same vein: another boy has the misfortune of happening to bump into Jesus, who at once curses him, and he falls down dead. When the parents of the dead boy approach Joseph and ask him to teach his son to bless rather than curse, Jesus immediately makes them blind. Admittedly, the *Infancy Gospel of Thomas* does have a happy ending as later on Jesus revives those he had killed and heals those he had rendered sick or disabled, but the text creates a singular impression of a Jesus who uses his limitless powers capriciously and for questionable ends.

This is a major contrast to how Jesus' wonder-working is presented in the more historically reliable Synoptic Gospels. On a few occasions animals (Mk 5.11-13) and plants (11.12-14, 20-24) are stricken by Jesus' miracles, but for humans his wonders always have a positive outcome. We are repeatedly told that Jesus' miracles of healing are manifestations of pity and compassion (e.g. Mk 5.19; 10.47-48). His success as a healer results in word of Jesus spreading and to more and more people joining the movement (Mk 1.28, 32-34), but this seems to be more of a side effect than a worked-out strategy of Jesus'. In contrast to the plagues of the *Infancy Gospel of Thomas* and the 'signs' that prophet leaders offered (see ch. 5), Jesus' healing acts are not demonstrations of his power. At several points in the Synoptic Gospels we encounter sceptical critics who want Jesus to prove his legitimacy as God's messenger by performing a 'sign' – but Jesus refuses (Mt. 12.38-42; 16.1-4; 16.1-4; Mk 8.11-12; Lk. 11.16, 29-32). He does not work wonders so that people will believe in him; rather the wonders presuppose that faith is already present. In John's Gospel, however, again and again Jesus performs 'signs' that 'reveal his glory' (see Jn 2.11; 11.4, 42; cf. 10.38). Here, Jesus' aim with the miracles is to prove his legitimacy and to draw attention to his own person. What explains this difference?

The Gospel of John clearly represents a later point of view on this issue, when interest was increasingly directed towards the person of Jesus and his relationship to God. The early Christ-believers firmly believed that the greatest miracle of all, 'the resurrection' of the dead Jesus, should be allowed to throw light on the stories of his earthly life. This attitude is not absent from the Synoptic Gospels; the more spectacular – and scientifically impossible – miracle stories of Jesus walking on the Sea of Galilee, for instance (Mk 6.45-52), very likely arose as reflections about the risen Jesus that employed motifs drawn from the Hebrew Bible. Yet even so the Synoptics preserve traces of more historically plausible realities. We have already seen (ch. 3) how Matthew attempts to soften the troublesome report in Mark about Jesus being unable to work any miracles in Nazareth on one occasion. The context makes it clear that this failure was due to the unbelief of the people in Jesus' hometown (Mk 6.6); they adopted the same sceptical attitude as the Pharisees who demanded that Jesus convince them with a 'sign'. In this latter situation, although the gospel authors want to give the impression that Jesus freely chose not to offer any miraculous proof of his powers, a far more historically likely scenario is that in reality he was unable to. Jesus' success as a miracle-worker was dependent upon people believing in his abilities.

Faith and miracles

On numerous occasions the Gospels emphasize just how important faith is for miracles to happen. According to one saying of Jesus in the Gospel of Mark there are no limits to what can be accomplished with faith:

> Jesus answered them, 'Have faith in God. Truly I tell you, if you say to this mountain, "Be taken up and thrown into the sea", and if you do not doubt in your heart, but believe that what you say will come to pass, it will be done for you. So I tell you, whatever you ask for in prayer, believe that you have received it, and it will be yours.'
>
> Mk 11.22-24; cf. Mt. 21.21-22

The same assertion, though couched in different imagery, also appears in material that Matthew and Luke have taken from Q (Lk. 17.6; Mt. 17.20) and we can be reasonably confident that this particular line of thought derives from the historical Jesus. One formulaic expression found in several episodes that corroborates the link between faith and healing is 'your faith has made you well' (Mk 5.34; 10.52; Lk. 7.50; 17.19). Even in cases where Jesus does not use this expression, the gospel authors can point out that it was faith that brought about healing (Mk 2.5; 5.36; 9.23-24; Lk. 7.9; Mt. 15.28). It is important to note that the 'faith' that these episodes refer to differs from the faith that would later occupy a central position in the Christ-believer movement. In the New Testament epistles what matters is believing that Jesus is the Messiah and that God has raised him from the dead – faith of this sort leads to salvation and eternal life. For the historical Jesus, on the other hand, what was important was that people believed in his ability to heal them physically.

Across different times and cultures, religious or faith healing displays a number of common features. The disabilities and illnesses that respond to this kind of healing may, as we have already noted, be understood as 'conversion disorders', psychologically and socially conditioned illnesses with evident physical manifestations. At the shrine of Asclepius at Epidaurus, as at other temples in antiquity where healing was thought to take place, visitors would leave votive offerings that tended to depict the part of their body that had been healed. This was often a leg or an arm, which shows that paralysis was one malady that lent itself to such healing. At the cave at

Lourdes several thousand crutches hang on the walls, left behind by pilgrims who travelled there to be healed. For a believer, these abandoned walking aids are evidence of divine intervention, but a sceptic can always ask the question that Émile Zola is said to have posed: Why aren't there any wooden legs left behind at Lourdes? Aches and pains, paralysis and blindness are frequently said to vanish in connection with healing, but an amputated leg does not grow back. The difference is due to what is causing the physical symptoms. If the fundamental cause is psychological, then a belief in the possibility of healing may, when combined with a strong emotional experience, make the symptoms vanish or ease. Modern medical research has shown that the 'placebo effect' – that is, when expecting a positive outcome can aid a patient's recovery – is not simply a figment of the imagination, but is related to the fact that brain activity can produce various chemical changes in the body. For example, in experiments placebos of various kinds, such as 'sugar pills' with no medicinal properties or 'surgery' involving only superficial cuts, have proven to be particularly successful remedies for chronic pain.

The healing trade is, of course, susceptible to deliberate hoaxes. In modern times, for example, several American 'televangelists' have been exposed as frauds who made fortunes by getting perfectly healthy individuals to pose as people in need of healing. The same thing must also have happened in antiquity, but Jesus' miracle-working is probably not best explained as such. With a few exceptions, like the idiosyncratic report in Luke's Gospel of Jesus healing a severed ear with a single touch (Lk. 22.50-52), the healings described are not so spectacular as to be beyond explanation without reference to collusion. In the Synoptic Gospels the most common type of healing is the casting out of demons. Besides this, Jesus heals people of paralysis, blindness, deafness, muteness, haemorrhages, 'leprosy', fever and other, less specific illnesses. There is every indication that Jesus truly believed in his ability to heal, and that he reflected on why at times he was unsuccessful, as when the people of Nazareth questioned his mission.

The charismatic healer

The Gospels do not provide us with many details in their descriptions of how Jesus went about his work as a healer. The narratives are condensed and stylized and their focus tends to be on the successful outcome and on the amazement of the onlookers. At times scholars have made much of the fact that Jesus seems to act entirely on his own authority, in contrast to other wonder-workers of the time who used incantations or prayers to bring about healing. Nevertheless, the assumption that Jesus differed radically in his technique from other exorcists can be challenged on several grounds. Mark claims that Jesus instructed his disciples to use prayer when casting out unclean spirits (Mk 9.29). Moreover, certain technical terms and established techniques in the field of exorcism are also preserved in Mark. In the story about the Gerasene demoniac, Jesus forces the spirit to reveal its name, by asking 'What is your name?' This practice is known from an incantation text from Qumran (11Q11). By gaining knowledge of the evil spirit's name, the exorcist attempts to get the upper hand. Furthermore, Jesus commands the unclean spirit to be silent in Mark 1.25, which is common expression in ancient Greek magical papyri, as is the command to 'come out' (Mk 1.25; 5.8; 9.25). The phrase 'I command you' (Mk 9.25 cf. 1.27) is also well known from Greek magical texts. Other commands include 'Stand up!', 'Receive your sight!', 'Be opened!', 'Be made clean!' In several instances this moment evidently made such a strong impression on the onlookers that Jesus' utterances in Aramaic were etched in their memory and ended up being preserved in even the Greek gospel text (Mk 5.41; 7.34).

These are highly formalized accounts, as has been mentioned, but there are hints that these exorcisms could be quite dramatic and violent. In Mark's account, those possessed by demons, 'demoniacs', come across as distraught. Their distress is toned down in Matthew's and Luke's descriptions, suggesting that there would seem to have been some embarrassment in the early church about this aspect of the exorcisms. In Mark's story the possessed man cried out for fear of his life ('Have you come to destroy us?', Mk 1.23); the unclean spirit 'convulsed' the man and subsequently came out of him 'with a loud voice' (Mk 1.26). Similarly, in Mk 5.7 the man living among the tombs shouted 'Do not torment me!' In addition, as part of Jesus' exorcism of an unclean spirit that was possessing a boy in Mk 9.20-29, the unclean spirit was 'crying out and convulsing' the boy 'terribly', such that the boy then appeared 'like a corpse'. Jesus, on the other hand, is reported to have 'rebuked' the unclean spirits (Mk 1.25). At a general level there is likely some historical reality behind the stories that indicate the violent nature of exorcisms. That exorcism could be violent should not surprise us since it was perceived as a fight against evil spirits, even against Satan himself. At other points Jesus seems to exhibit some intense emotions. We read that, in connection with healings, he was 'moved with anger' (Mk 1.41) and that 'looking up to heaven, he sighed' (7.34). These are likely traces of behaviour that was anything but proper and restrained. It is safe to assume that exorcism was often a messy business.

One episode, found only in the Gospel of Mark, which may have been 'censored' by Matthew and Luke, suggests that things didn't always go so easily:

> They came to Bethsaida. Some people brought a blind man to him and begged him to touch him. He took the blind man by the hand and led him out of the village; and when he had put saliva on his eyes and laid his hands on him, he asked him, 'Can you see anything?' And the man looked up and said, 'I can see people, but they look like trees, walking.' Then

Jesus laid his hands on his eyes again; and he looked intently and his sight was restored, and he saw everything clearly.

Mk 8.22-25

A host of legends always grows up around accomplished healers. Usually it begins with rumours that spread during their lifetime and it often intensifies after their death. In Jesus' case, the narratives about his miracles are such a central part of our source material that they must go back to events witnessed during his lifetime. What is also clear, however, is that they have been embellished, they have multiplied and they have in some cases spawned still more fantastical episodes that reveal little about the historical Jesus. We are often unable to determine whether a particular tradition has a historical core or is altogether a product of theological reflection. What about the episodes in which Jesus raises the dead, for example? Even the most fervent of healers is not capable of restoring life to someone who really is dead. Perhaps the synagogue leader's daughter in Capernaum was not really dead after all (Mk 5.35-43), but when it comes to the episode in John's Gospel where Jesus raises Lazarus, there is no scope for such rationalizing explanations. Lazarus has lain in the tomb for four days and 'already there is a stench' (Jn 11.39). For the author of John's Gospel this is the whole point: Jesus is not bound by human limitations – he is the son of God, with power over life and death.

Liberation from the demons

We have already established that the most common form of healing in the Gospels is exorcism. This term is from a Greek verb meaning 'to adjure, to conjure', but the word is not used in the Gospels, which usually describe Jesus as 'casting out' the demons or 'unclean spirits' instead. The individuals said to be possessed by demons conduct themselves in a decidedly antisocial manner (Mk 5.5; 9.22) and engage in self-harm. These demonic expulsions are, in a very palpable sense, a trial of strength between God's messenger, Jesus, and Satan's minions, the unclean spirits.

Possession and exorcism

In many parts of the world possession remains a tangible phenomenon to this day. The relentless torrent of horror films on the subject that the 1973 premiere of *The Exorcist* unleashed is a clear indication that people's fascination with the influence of evil remains, even in societies otherwise regarded as enlightened. A YouGov survey in 2013 concluded that 51 % of the entire US population believed that possession by the devil or by evil spirits was a real phenomenon, with 46 % believing in the power of exorcism rituals and only 28 % being convinced that possession was certainly not real. In churches and other religious organizations, belief in the existence of evil spirits and the efficacy of exorcisms is of course even more widespread. Father Gabriele Amorth, a Catholic priest and exorcist of the Diocese of Rome, reportedly claimed to have performed more than 160,000 rites of exorcism before his death in 2016. Concepts of the devil and the demons live on and are of course always drawing renewed energy from the Gospels.

It may be surprising to learn that the Hebrew Bible does not contain many accounts of possession or of spirits being driven out. The exceptions that prove the rule are the narratives that tell of how the young David had to play the lyre to calm King Saul when the latter was tormented by 'an evil spirit from the Lord' (1 Sam. 16.14-23; 18.10-11; 19.9-10). In these narratives the figure behind the evil spirit is God, not Satan, whose existence it is at most hinted at in the Hebrew Bible. Only in later Jewish texts do we find a burgeoning of ideas about Satan, or Beliar, and with it a growth in interest in possession and casting out demons. We do not know for sure whether the Qumran movement practised exorcism, but several of their texts describe the phenomenon. The *Genesis Apocryphon*, among others, contains an account of the pharaoh of Egypt asking Abraham to drive away an evil spirit through prayer and the laying on of hands. A statement Jesus makes in the Q source assumes that several Galilean exorcists were active during his time (Lk. 11.19; Mt. 12.27). As already mentioned, Josephus provides a detailed description of what casting out a spirit could look like. According to him it was Solomon who instituted the rituals of exorcism, a notion that resurfaces much later in a text known as the *Testament of Solomon*. Josephus is convinced of the powerful effect the rituals have:

> I have seen a certain Eleazar, a countryman of mine, in the presence of Vespasian, his sons, tribunes and a number of other soldiers, free men possessed by demons, and this was the manner of the cure: he put to the nose of the possessed man a ring which had under its seal one of the roots prescribed by Solomon, and then, as the man smelled it, drew out the demon through his nostrils, and, when the man at once fell down, adjured the demon never to come back into him, speaking Solomon's name and reciting the incantations which he had composed. Then, wishing to convince the bystanders and prove to them that he had this power, Eleazar placed a cup or foot-basin full of water a little way off and commanded the demon, as it went out of the man, to overturn it and make known to the spectators that he had left the man.
>
> *Ant.* 8.46–48

The accounts of Jesus casting out spirits are generally much more succinct. In a few cases we find an introductory dialogue between Jesus and the demons, where the latter protest against being cast out and try to best Jesus by demonstrating that they know full well who he is (Mk 1.24; 5.7). The only episode containing more vivid details is that in which Jesus casts out one or several unclean spirits from a possessed man – two men are involved according to Matthew – in the region of Gerasa south-east of the Sea of Galilee (Mk 5.1-20; Mt. 8.28-34; Lk. 8.26-39). Here we read that Legion, as proves to be the demon's name, asks to be sent into a herd of swine. The memorable scene in which two thousand possessed swine rush down the steep slope and drown in the lake serves as an even stronger proof of a successful exorcism than Eleazar's overturned basin. However, this episode displays so many peculiarities that it is doubtful whether it was ever intended to be taken as a realistic depiction of true events. As already noted, Gerasa is nowhere near a body of water, lying about 30 miles from the Sea of Galilee, and even so, since pigs are strong swimmers, the animals ought not to have drowned. The demon's name, Legion, is the term for an organizational unit in the Roman army. Numerous scholars have wondered whether it is merely a coincidence that standards borne by one part of the tenth legion (*Legio X Fretensis*), consisting of a few thousand soldiers, depicted a wild boar, among other things. This legion took part in the fight against the Jewish rebels in the war of 66–70 CE. Could the episode about the drowned swine be a piece of anti-Roman polemic in the form of symbolic narrative? Whatever the case may be, it is not a typical example of Gospel accounts of Jesus casting out spirits, and it tells us little about the historical Jesus as an exorcist.

The spirit of God and the evil spirits

Whereas the Synoptics relate several episodes of demons being cast out, the Gospel of John does not contain a single one. Evidently the traditions concerning Jesus' showdowns with evil spirits were not judged to be of use in John's portrayal of a Jesus who is never perturbed and is always in control of the situation. Exorcisms are mentioned a few times in the Acts of the Apostles (Acts 16.16-18; 19.11-12), but otherwise exorcism is not a prominent theme in the early Christ-believer movement. On this point Jesus' own practice diverged from the actions of later groups who saw themselves as his successors.

So far we have been discussing possession as something negative and harmful, but in fact ancient Judaism also recognized the possibility that people could be possessed by the spirit of God, a positive state of affairs. Philo of Alexandria regarded the prophets – including Moses, the greatest prophet of all – as 'possessed' by the Spirit: their inspiration lay in their own, natural abilities having been set aside and replaced by the very power of God. One major point of conflict between Jesus and his contemporary critics revolved precisely around whether he was 'possessed' by the spirit of God or by some evil spirit. Jesus' understanding of himself as a prophet must have arisen from 'charismatic' experiences of the Spirit taking possession of him. The narrative that relates how the heavens opened and the Spirit descended upon Jesus when he was baptized by John is heavily stylized, but ultimately it probably goes back to some such experience that Jesus underwent and took as his 'calling' to be a prophet. The sceptics, of course, saw things differently. Jesus' relatives were frankly of the opinion that 'he has gone out of his mind' and needed to be taken into custody (Mk 3.21). Lovers of order – scribes from Jerusalem, in Mark's Gospel – were even harsher in their judgement: they 'said, "He has Beelzebul, and by the ruler of the demons he casts out demons"' (3.22). Jesus had become too successful to be dismissed as a fraud. Nevertheless there was scope to wonder whose side he was really on in the battle that was continually being fought between unseen forces.

The coming of the kingdom of God

Jesus' response to the accusations of being possessed by Satan or an unclean spirit was to assert that such thinking was ludicrous. There was no way that he, the very one who had managed to cast out evil spirits on numerous occasions, could be under demonic influence!

> Every kingdom divided against itself becomes a desert, and house falls on house. If Satan also is divided against himself, how will his kingdom stand?—for you say that I cast out the demons by Beelzebul. Now if I cast out the demons by Beelzebul, by whom do your exorcists cast them out? Therefore they will be your judges. But if it is by the finger of God that I cast out the demons, then the kingdom of God has come to you.
>
> Lk. 11.17-20

This sharp dividing line between good and evil is typical of the apocalyptic world-view that Jesus espoused. You are either on God's side or on Satan's, and the exorcisms must be a sign that the kingdom of God is gaining ground. The phrase 'the finger of God' is so unusual that Matthew has changed it to the more readily understood 'Spirit of God' (Mt. 12.28), but behind it lies the tale of Moses and the exodus from Egypt, where it is used by Pharaoh's magicians in reference to God's plagues (Exod. 8.19). Jesus interpreted his achievements as an exorcist as minor victories for the kingdom of God in the struggle that would end with the total defeat of Satan. Jesus' claim that he 'watched Satan fall from heaven like a flash of lightning' (Lk. 10.18) may hark back to a visionary experience he had in which he believed he had seen how it would all end. Nor were these events that lay far ahead in the distant future: God's kingdom was already on its way.

The book of Isaiah and the miracles of Jesus

In the previous chapter we saw that Jesus shaped and interpreted his mission as proclaimer of the kingdom in part based on his understanding of the book of Isaiah. From the Q source Matthew and Luke have taken words of Jesus' that demonstrates that he interpreted his healing in light of Isaiah's prophecies as well. The setting of the episode is that John the Baptist has been wondering whether Jesus is 'the one who is to come'. Jesus answers:

> Go and tell John what you hear and see: the blind receive their sight, the lame walk, the lepers are cleansed, the deaf hear, the dead are raised, and the poor have good news brought to them. And blessed is anyone who takes no offence at me.
>
> Mt. 11.4-6; Lk. 7.22-23

With these words Jesus summarizes his achievements as a healer and preacher. The answer to the Baptist's question is that the eschatological prophecies in the book of Isaiah are in the process of being fulfilled. With the exception of 'lepers' being 'cleansed', each item in Jesus' answer corresponds to an element in Isaiah's prophecies of how things will be in the end times, when God will restore the people of Israel. At that time the blind shall see (Isa. 29.18; 35.5; 42.7, 18), the lame walk (Isa. 45.6), the deaf hear (Isa 29.18; 35.5; 42.18), the dead be raised (Isa 26.19) and the poor have good news brought to them (Isa. 61.1). In general, however, these prophecies were not taken literally. In the Isaiah Targum, an ancient and very free translation of the Hebrew book of Isaiah into Aramaic, they are interpreted metaphorically. For example, the Hebrew original describes the people's return to Zion as follows: 'Then the eyes of the blind shall be opened, and the ears of the deaf unstopped' (Isa. 35.5). The Isaiah Targum has: 'Then the eyes of the house of Israel, that were as blind *to the law*, shall be opened, and their ears, which were as deaf *to listen to the sayings of the prophets*, shall listen'. Another early Jewish work that also alludes to the miracles outlined in Isaiah is the text from Qumran about the messianic age (4Q521), which was introduced earlier (ch. 2). We will come back to this text later on, but for now we can point out that it is hard to know whether it talks concretely of miracles or whether here, too, the wording is meant to be taken figuratively. Jesus, evidently, interpreted the prophecies literally, in light of his own experiences.

Healing and forgiveness went hand in hand for Jesus. Neither sin nor physical defects would be found in God's kingdom. Here, too, he was able to recall verses from the book of Isaiah:

> Then prey and spoil in abundance will be divided; even the lame will fall to plundering. And no inhabitant will say, 'I am sick'; the people who live there will be forgiven their iniquity.
>
> Isa. 33.23-24

The word translated 'lame' here occurs again later in the book, where it is written: 'then the lame shall leap like a deer' (Isa. 35.6). When the lame, the paralyzed and the sick are healed, they will also receive forgiveness for their sins. Both of these elements are present in the episode in which Jesus heals a paralyzed man in Capernaum, but only after declaring that the man's sins are forgiven (Mk 2.1-12). When Jesus pronounced the words of forgiveness over the lame man and immediately afterwards exhorted him to get up and walk, he did not look on it as merely the healing of one individual. On the contrary, Jesus interpreted his own miracle-working as a sign that the end time had come, the time for the restoration of Israel and the coming of the kingdom of God.

Summary

There is no reason to doubt that Jesus had a reputation for being a successful healer and exorcist. As a typical 'folk healer', he shared with his contemporaries a view of sickness and healing that is far removed from present-day scientific understandings. Jesus would have agreed that the cause of many illnesses was people's sins, and he believed that faith in God and in his own abilities could lead to bodily healing. In fact, his power to heal seems to have been dependent on the faith of those whose health he sought to restore, which indicates that the placebo effect was at work. Some of the Gospel episodes about Jesus' healings retain traces of the techniques he used. Around this historical core of Jesus the folk healer, later tellers of stories about Jesus, including the evangelists, spun their narratives about a miracle-worker who was even able to walk on water and raise the dead.

Jesus interpreted his exorcisms as signalling the coming of God's kingdom. Casting out the demons was an important part of the ongoing battle between God, as represented by Jesus, and Satan, as represented by the evil spirits. Among Jesus' contemporaries those who were sceptical of his claim to be acting under the influence of God's spirit took the opposite view of the matter – they suspected him of being Satan's representative.

Jesus' primary framework for understanding his success as a healer was the prophecies about the end time in the book of Isaiah. Like other early Jewish interpreters of Isaiah, Jesus thought that the beginning of the messianic age would be signalled by miracles. Later we will come back to the question of what this entailed for his view of his own role in the kingdom, but before that we need to turn to another key issue, Jesus' attitude towards the Torah.

Bibliography

Ehrman, B. D. (2003), *Lost Scriptures: Books that Did Not Make It into the New Testament*, Oxford: Oxford University Press, 2003.

Eve, E. (2009), *The Healer from Nazareth: Jesus' Miracles in Historical Context*, London: SPCK.
Hägerland, T. (2012), *Jesus and the Forgiveness of Sins: An Aspect of his Prophetic Mission*, Society for New Testament Studies Monograph Series 150, Cambridge: Cambridge University Press.
Meier, J. P. (1994), *A Marginal Jew: Rethinking the Historical Jesus, vol. 2: Mentor, Message, and Miracles*, New Haven: Yale University Press.
Pilch, J. J. (2000), *Healing in the New Testament: Insights from Medical and Mediterranean Anthropology*, Minneapolis: Fortress.
Wassén, C. (2019), 'The Impurity of the Impure Spirits in the Gospels', in T. Wasserman and M. Tellbe (eds), *Healing and Exorcism in Second Temple Judaism and Early Christianity*, 33–52, Wissenschaftliche Untersuchungen zum Neuen Testament 2/511, Tübingen: Mohr Siebeck.

8

Jesus and the laws

Just like other Jews, Jesus followed the laws set out in the five books of Moses, or Torah, and held the traditional scriptures to be authoritative. Yet he is remembered as having been involved in various conflicts that centred on how to live in accordance with the law, and especially the rules of the sabbath. What might have lain behind these disputes? One common misconception is that Jesus rejected certain laws, such as the sabbath commandment and the purity regulations, but there is no evidence for this view. Rather, these disputes should be understood in a historical context in which various Jewish parties and individual teachers differed in their ideas about how to live in accordance with the laws, but not about whether to live by them at all. As we shall see in this section, Jesus is taking part in this ongoing debate and arguing for his own interpretation. We begin by looking at some general statements about the law that are attributed to Jesus.

The laws of Moses

Jesus' fundamental attitude towards the Jewish laws comes across clearly in the double command of love in Mark:

> One of the scribes came near and heard them disputing with one another, and seeing that he answered them well, he asked him, 'Which commandment is the first of all?' Jesus answered, 'The first is, "Hear, O Israel: the Lord our God, the Lord is one; you shall love the Lord your God with all your heart, and with all your soul, and with all your mind, and with all your strength." The second is this, "You shall love your neighbour as yourself." There is no other commandment greater than these.'
>
> Mk 12.28-31

Jesus' answer would not have surprised his audience since he often cites key verses of the Torah, as we have seen (see ch. 6). The first commandment (Deut. 6.4-5) is traditionally known as the Shema, from its first word 'Hear' in Hebrew, and it was part of the daily prayers. In this context, 'love' is not primarily a matter of emotions, but rather of loyalty within a relationship, of obeying God and keeping his commandments with all one's strength (cf. Deut. 10.12). The verse is also about being exclusively loyal to the god of Israel and not worshipping other gods. The point of the next part of the passage, 'Keep these words that I am commanding you today in your heart' (Deut. 6.6), is that the words must be remembered. The passage ends with the exhortation 'Bind them as a sign on your hand, fix them as an emblem on your forehead, and write them on the doorposts of your house and on your gates' (Deut. 6.9). This exhortation was taken literally and, together with other verses from Exodus and Deuteronomy, the passage was copied out onto parchment scrolls in extremely small script and placed inside phylacteries, or *tefillin*, and inside *mezuzot*, small containers that were fixed onto doorposts. The former were placed on the forehead and on the arm and tied in place with straps for use in prayer, a tradition that has survived from the time of Jesus to the present day. In Mt. 23.5 Jesus criticizes the Pharisees because 'they make their phylacteries broad' merely to show their piety in public. The comment, which may derive from the time of Matthew rather than Jesus, demonstrates that the use of phylacteries was common practice in the first century CE. Josephus, too, relates that people bore verses on their arms and foreheads and wrote inscriptions on doorposts (*Ant.* 4.213). At Qumran more than twenty phylacteries used for housing tiny scrolls have been found, as well as a large number of small slips made to fit the *tefillin* (Adler 2017). In these Deut. 6.4-9 is often included, demonstrating how central this text was within Judaism.

The second of Jesus' commandments is a quotation from Lev. 19.18, 'you shall love your neighbour as yourself'. Here, too, the verb 'to love', rather than emphasizing an emotional state, expresses loyalty and the need to carry out certain duties and obligations towards others. In its original context, the commandment represents a summary of several precepts found in Lev. 19.9-18 relating to right treatment of others, for example, that one should not reap all the way to the edges of a field because there should be something left over for immigrants and the poor (Lev. 19.9). In this way, with these two commandments Jesus summarizes two primary focuses of all the laws, namely, right behaviour towards God and fellow human beings. These two focuses are clearly visible in the Ten Commandments, for example, the first of which lay down the proper way of relating to God, and the rest the proper relationship with fellow human beings (Exod. 20). Although love it is not a predominant theme in the Synoptic Gospels, Jesus also speaks of the importance of 'love' towards others in Q, even towards one's enemies (Mt. 5.44/Lk. 6.27; cf. to 'one another' in Jn 15.12). Obviously, doing good towards others and living according to God's law is a key message in Jesus' teaching in general. Hence, it is likely that these comments derive from Jesus. However, in the narrative framework in Mark surrounding Jesus' comments, the author's own interests clearly come into view when the scribe with whom Jesus is conducting this dialogue, impressed, exclaims 'You are right, Teacher; you have truly said [these things]' and then proceeds to repeat the commandments in his own words (Mk 12.32). Here we see Mark using the tradition of the double commandment of love to portray (the uneducated) Jesus as a teacher and the learned scribe as a student.

Jesus is also credited with explaining what constitutes the core of the commandments in another statement, in what has come to be known as 'the golden rule': 'In everything do to others as you would have them do to you; for this is the law and the prophets' (Mt. 7.12; cf., Lk. 6.31). In Luke's version of this Q saying the reference to 'the law and the prophets' is missing. Since this is a favourite expression in Matthew (cf. 5.17; 22.40) this part most likely originated with the Evangelist. The dictum is known in various forms from many other sources, both Jewish and Hellenistic. In the book of Tobit, from around 200 BCE, we read 'What you hate, do not do to anyone' (Tob. 4.15), and Philo, too, mentions a similar rule (*Hypoth*. 7.6). The famous Pharisaic rabbi Hillel, who was significantly older than Jesus and may have lived until around 10 CE, is also known for his 'golden rule'. Legend has it that Hillel was challenged by a gentile who promised to convert to Judaism if Hillel could explain the entire Torah to him while he was standing on one leg. Hillel told him: 'What is hateful to you, to your fellow don't do. That's the entirety of the Torah; everything else is elaboration' (b. Shabb. 31a). Jesus' version of the golden rule is yet another example of this traditional principle which is perhaps more related to common sense than to the law. Because the principle was so widely spread, many scholars, including Meier (2009: 551–7) assume that it was attributed to Jesus at a later time by Christ-believers who liked to think that it originated with their master. But, as James Dunn points out, that the principle was well known is no reason for why Jesus would not also have appropriated it (Dunn 2003: 589). We can conclude that the ethical dictum did not originate with Jesus and that he may have approved it, but it is hard to tell.

In Matthew's Sermon on the Mount we find a certain degree of criticism of how the law was interpreted and followed. We have already seen (ch. 6) that Jesus' command to love one's enemies from Q (Mt. 5.44/ Lk. 6.27) expressed a demand for perfection of a kind befitting life in the kingdom. The Sermon on the Mount provides further examples of Jesus' stringent rules.

The Sermon on the Mount

In the introduction to Matthew's Sermon on the Mount, Jesus expresses a very positive view of the law in general terms:

> Do not think that I have come to abolish the law or the prophets; I have come not to abolish but to fulfil. For truly I tell you, until heaven and

earth pass away, not one letter, not one stroke of a letter, will pass from the law until all is accomplished.

Mt. 5.17-18

The exhortation 'Do not think that I have come to abolish the law or the prophets' reveals that this part of the speech, at least, can hardly have been uttered by Jesus, as who could have thought that Jesus' aim was to abolish the law? By Matthew's time, however, when many Christ-believers were gentiles who did not follow the Jewish laws, this kind of understanding of Jesus' teachings may have developed. Matthew criticizes such an interpretation by putting the words 'Do not think . . .' in the mouth of Jesus and by stating that those who hold it – that is, some amongst Matthew's audience – are wrong. Rather, Jesus demands absolute faithfulness to the law, or Torah – not one letter, not one stroke of a letter will pass from it. A similar statement is found in Luke's Gospel, and the tradition thus stems from Q: 'But it is easier for heaven and earth to pass away, than for one stroke of a letter in the law to be dropped' (Lk. 16.17). Jesus possibly said something of this sort. In that case Jesus himself considered his teaching to be thoroughly grounded in the Torah. According to Matthew, it was only by following the teachings of Jesus that one could live entirely in accordance with the law (Mt. 5.20). As we have already noted (ch. 6), the Sermon on the Mount contains numerous pronouncements of Jesus', gathered together by Matthew into one long speech in which Jesus, like a new Moses on the mountain, sets out various laws. These begin with 'You have heard that it was said . . .', which is followed by 'but I say to you . . .'. Even though we cannot be certain that all of these expositions go back to Jesus, a clear trajectory can be discerned in his message. His concern was not to abolish commandments, but rather to make the commandments significantly stricter. He demanded of his listeners a morally perfect way of life that was impossible to live up to. At this point we can take a look at some further examples of this kind of intensification:

You have heard that it was said to those of ancient times, 'You shall not murder'; and 'whoever murders shall be liable to judgement.' But I say to you that if you are angry with a brother or sister, you will be liable to judgement; and if you insult a brother or sister, you will be liable to the council; and if you say, 'You fool', you will be liable to the hell of fire.

Mt. 5.21-22

Here Jesus quotes one of the Ten Commandments (Exod. 20.13) and outlaws the underlying cause of murder, anger directed towards someone. In a similar way, Jesus forbids looking 'at a woman with lust', because it is the underlying cause of adultery, which is, of course, forbidden (Mt. 5.27-28; Exod. 20.14). We shall come back to Jesus' prohibition of divorce below (Mt. 5.31-32). A similar intensification lies behind his comments about swearing oaths and about retaliation. According to Matthew, Jesus has the following to say about oaths:

> Again, you have heard that it was said to those of ancient times, 'You shall not swear falsely, but carry out the vows you have made to the Lord.' But I say to you, Do not swear at all, either by heaven, for it is the throne of God, or by the earth, for it is his footstool, or by Jerusalem, for it is the city of the great King. And do not swear by your head, for you cannot make one hair white or black. Let your word be 'Yes, Yes' or 'No, No'; anything more than this comes from the evil one.
>
> Mt. 5.33-37

The idea that Jesus opposed oath-taking is strengthened by an independent, albeit shorter, remark in the Letter of James (5.12) that may reflect a tradition from Jesus: 'Above all, my beloved, do not swear, either by heaven or by earth or by any other oath, but let your "Yes" be yes and your "No" be no, so that you may not fall under condemnation.' The point is that oaths are not needed because one should always tell the truth. If the historical Jesus rejected the use of oaths, was he, then, rejecting the laws of Moses? A few laws do prescribe oaths (Exod. 22.10-11), but the purpose of the laws concerning oaths, like the laws Jesus alludes to, is above all to moderate their use. Examples include Lev. 19.12: 'And you shall not swear falsely by my name, profaning the name of your God: I am the Lord'; and one of the Ten Commandments, Exod. 20.7: 'You shall not make wrongful use of the name of the Lord your God, for the Lord will not acquit anyone who misuses his name.' In forbidding the use of oaths, Jesus was also eliminating the risk that a person would break these commandments. Jesus' admonishment is reminiscent of another law of the Torah, Deut. 23.21-22, which stresses that vows are unnecessary: 'If you make a vow to the Lord your God, do not postpone fulfilling it; for the Lord your God will surely require it of you, and you would incur guilt. But if you refrain from vowing, you will not incur guilt.'

This negative stance of Jesus' can be compared to forms of warning against oath- and vow-taking found in wisdom literature. Ecclesiastes calls attention to the dangers of not keeping an oath, since it rouses the wrath of God (Eccl. 8.2), and concerning vows he urges his readers: 'It is better that you should not vow than that you should vow and not fulfil it' (Eccl. 5.5). In the Wisdom of Jesus Ben Sira (Sirach) the reader is warned against breaking oaths and against swearing frequently (23.9-11). An indirect criticism may also be noted in the works of Philo and Josephus, who point out, approvingly, that the Essenes abstained from swearing oaths. According to Philo this was an expression of their love of God: 'Their love of God they show by a multitude of proofs, by religious purity constant and unbroken throughout their lives, by abstinence from oaths, by veracity, by their belief that the Godhead is the cause of all good things and nothing bad' (*Omn. Prob. Lib.* 84). Philo, for his own part, likewise holds that the best thing to do is to avoid swearing oaths (*Dec.* 82–95; *Spec. Leg.* 2.1–38). Concerning the Essenes, Josephus writes: 'Any word of theirs has more force than an oath; swearing they avoid, regarding it as worse than perjury, for they say that one who is not believed without an appeal to God stands condemned already' (*War* 2.135). This idea is close to the teaching of Jesus. Josephus adds, however, that new members did swear oaths on entry to the sect. In the majority of texts from Qumran, the use of oaths is taken for granted, whereas the use of the name of God is restricted (CD 15.1-5). Against this background it is hard to see how anyone could have understood Jesus' forbidding his listeners from swearing oaths as his being opposed to the laws of Moses. His was one among many voices intoning on the practice of swearing oaths.

The best known of Jesus' sayings from the Sermon on the Mount is perhaps his interpretation of Exod. 21.24: 'You have heard that it was said, "An eye for an eye and a tooth for a tooth." But I say to you, Do not resist an evildoer. But if anyone strikes you on the right cheek, turn the other also' (Mt. 5.38-39). This exposition of the law from Exod. 21.24 has often been misunderstood because it has been interpreted out of context. 'Eye for eye, tooth for tooth' is an attempt to put a limit on retribution for crimes: death, for example, should not be the penalty for a person who puts out someone's eye; the punishment should be proportionate. Hence Jesus' teaching once again represents an intensification: do not exact even the rightful penalty – forgo punishment altogether instead. As discussed earlier (ch. 6), in cases where Jesus' moral rules seem utopian, they should be seen against the background of his belief in the coming of the kingdom.

The sabbath

In the Synoptic Gospels conflicts arise in connection with the sabbath in two situations: when disciples of Jesus pluck grain in a cornfield, and when Jesus heals people on the sabbath. There are numerous narratives of Jesus healing on the sabbath, a tradition also noted by John (Jn 7.22-23; 9.14-16). So what was problematic about plucking grain or healing? Well, such activities might be construed as work, something that a person was to abstain from on the sabbath. Among the Ten Commandments, the sabbath commandment (Exod. 20.8-11) is one of the fullest:

> Remember the sabbath day, and keep it holy. For six days you shall labour and do all your work. But the seventh day is a sabbath to the Lord your God; you shall not do any work – you, your son or your daughter, your male or female slave, your livestock, or the alien resident in your towns. For in six days the Lord made heaven and earth, the sea, and all that is in them, but rested the seventh day; therefore the Lord blessed the sabbath day and consecrated it.

What exactly counted as work, however, is not stated. It was tradition, above all, that dictated what was or was not done on the sabbath, although there were several rules and examples in the Torah that served as guidance. From these it emerges that, among other things, it was forbidden to light a fire, to plough, to reap, to gather manna, to gather firewood, or to bake or boil anything (Exod. 16.22-23; 34.21; 35.2-3; Num. 15.32-36). Starting from the basic principle that the seventh day was a day of rest on which work was forbidden, men well-versed in the law recorded their own interpretations of what rules should apply for the sabbath. Early interpretations are preserved in *Jubilees* and the *Damascus Document*, which represent strict interpretations of the law that date to before 100 BCE. The *Damascus Document* states, for instance, that on the sabbath one should not speak of work nor conduct business through a gentile agent (CD 10.19; 11.2). The author of *Jubilees*, in line with Exodus (Exod. 31.14; 35.2), imposes the death penalty upon those who work on the sabbath. In *Jubilees* travelling, lighting a fire, riding, slaughtering an animal and waging war number among unlawful activities (*Jub.* 50.12-13). Some of the laws on these lists were controversial, such the ban on waging war. The right to defend oneself on the sabbath was widely accepted. This principle was developed during the Maccabean revolt (1 Macc. 2.39-41) after Jewish men were massacred when they would not defend themselves on the sabbath. Thus in *Jubilees* we find a rather stricter position.

Plucking grain in the cornfield

Mark presents two conflicts in succession, starting with the narrative about grain:

> One sabbath he was going through the cornfields; and as they made their way his disciples began to pluck heads of grain. The Pharisees said to him, 'Look, why are they doing what is not lawful on the sabbath?' And he said to them, 'Have you never read what David did when he and his companions were hungry and in need of food? He entered the house of God, when Abiathar was high priest, and ate the bread of the Presence, which it is not lawful for any but the priests to eat, and he gave some to his companions.' Then he said to them, 'The sabbath was made for humankind, and not humankind for the sabbath; so the Son of Man is lord even of the sabbath.'
>
> Mk 2.23-28

First let us note the somewhat artificial scenario described here of the Pharisees following Jesus and his disciples through the fields. What are they doing there? In all probability the narrative framework for this dispute has been devised by Mark and reflects the general tendency to make the Pharisees the primary opponents of Jesus (ch. 2). In Sanders' words (1985: 265), 'Pharisees did not organize themselves into groups to spend their Sabbaths in Galilean cornfields in the hope of catching someone transgressing.' But even if the narrative is fictional, the dispute itself need not be. One of the sabbath rules from the *Damascus Document* is reminiscent of the opinion expressed by the Pharisees in Mark's narrative, which shows that a conflict of this kind fits well with the historical context: 'Let no man eat anything on the Sabbath day except that which is prepared. And of that which is lost in the field he shall neither eat nor drink unless it was in the camp (before the Sabbath)' (CD 10.22–23). Plucked grain did not count as prepared food and would not have been accepted as such by the Qumran movement which advocated a fairly strict stance. Jesus' opinion on the matter may well represent more of a popular position. Even so, he supports his interpretation with reference to the fact that the case in question was an emergency. Just as David and his men ate the bread of the Presence when they were hungry (1 Sam. 21.1-9), so too Jesus and his disciples could pluck grain on the sabbath because of hunger. Jesus' version of the narrative about David, however, does not fully match the text of 1 Samuel: the high priest was not Abiathar, but Ahimelech. The error may be the reason why Matthew and Luke choose not to include this comment (Mt. 12.1-8; Lk. 6.1-5). Jesus' argument is built on the notion that David broke the laws of the temple because he was in need, as Jesus himself states (Mk 2.26): 'the bread of the Presence, which it is not lawful for any but the priests to eat'. Such were the rules of the Jerusalem temple in the time of Jesus, but according to the narrative about David in 1 Samuel 21 (which involves a different sanctuary), it was permissible for laymen, if they were ritually pure, to eat the bread, and David avers that the laymen in question meet this requirement. Jesus' point is that it is permissible to break the sabbath commandment (not to work) in a situation of acute hunger. In Mark's version Jesus articulates the basic principle that 'The sabbath was made for humankind, and not humankind for the sabbath', and most Jews would agree. Thus, according to Jesus, in an emergency it is right to violate the sabbath commandment (Kazen 2013: 100–5). He advances a similar argument when it comes to the question of healing on the sabbath, and in reality these are one and the same issue. We might say that Jesus makes the case that the 'healing' of either the hungry or the sick, something that counts as work, has priority over the sabbath commandment.

Healing

Reports of Jesus healing on the sabbath, and thereby provoking discontent, appear several times in the Gospels in different versions (Mt. 12.9-14; Mk 3.1-6; Lk. 6.6-11; 13.10-17; 14.1-6; Jn 7.22-23; 9.14-16). Their multiplicity indicates that the underlying tradition is an early one. Although the particular stories are literary creations they lack later Christological interpretations and likely reflect underlying, early traditions which provide some insight into the background to the conflicts and the motives for Jesus' healings (Kazen 2013: 105–11). Mark depicts a heated exchange at a synagogue on the sabbath (Mk 3.1-6). A man with a withered hand is present at the synagogue and Mark states that 'they' (who are not identified) 'watched [Jesus] to see whether he would cure him on the sabbath, so that they might accuse him'. In Mark's account Jesus challenges their approach: 'Then he said to them, "Is it lawful to do good or to do harm on the sabbath, to save life or to kill?" But they were silent. He looked around at them with anger; he was grieved at their hardness of heart' (Mk 3.4-5). The man is cured when, at Jesus' bidding, he stretches out his hand. The pericope ends with a sense of foreboding as the opponents, now identified as 'the Pharisees', depart and at once begin to conspire with supporters of Herod as to how to do away with Jesus.

What the rules were when it came to curing or helping the sick on the sabbath is not straightforward. In the lists in *Jubilees* and the *Damascus Document* of what should count as work no prohibition of tending the sick or curing people appears. It is important to note that Jesus does not criticize the sabbath commandment per se. In arguing for his view, he focuses on what it was lawful to do on the sabbath: 'Is it lawful to do good or to do harm on the sabbath, to save life or to kill?' He carries the first argument, 'to do good or to do harm', to extremes when he continues with 'to save life or to kill'. The case of the man with the withered hand is not, after all, a matter of life or death. According to later rabbinic tradition, the principle was self-evident: saving human life always had priority over the sabbath commandment. Obviously a person should assist those in life-threatening situations even if it meant violating the sabbath commandment; no one disputed this (t. Shabb. 9.22). It was common sense. Given Jesus' reference to 'saving life' we can assume that an explicit principle about it was already established in his time. Thus everyone would agree that life-saving measures in cases of emergency had priority over sabbath rules, but this was not a situation of that kind. What arguments, then, might the opponents be able to cite for their view? Mark does not say, but in a similar narrative in Luke (Lk. 13.10-17), in which Jesus cures a woman with a stoop on the sabbath, Luke does present his readers with a counterargument: 'But the leader of the synagogue, indignant because Jesus had cured on the sabbath, kept saying to the crowd, "There are six days on which work ought to be done; come on those days and be cured, and not on the sabbath day."' This seems like a perfectly reasonable argument; when life-threatening illnesses weren't involved, couldn't the curing wait a day?

The narratives about controversies relating to Jesus' conduct presuppose that there was debate about what rules applied in non-life-threatening situations. In this case Jesus' actions may reflect a common view based not so much on scriptural interpretation as on normal practice, a view that those who espoused a stricter understanding would not have accepted. Still, we should remember that in the time of Jesus it was hard to tell the difference between illnesses that were life-threatening and those that were not, since even the slightest fever could be fatal. We should also note that in these narratives the Gospel authors emphasize the idea that some of those whom Jesus cures had chronic health conditions, which makes Jesus' healing even more miraculous. At the same time this renders the disputes even more acute, since the conditions in question cannot be interpreted as life-threatening.

In Matthew's reworked version of Mk 3.1-6, the author provides Jesus with an additional argument: 'Suppose one of you has only one sheep and it falls into a pit on the sabbath; will you not lay hold of it and lift it out? How much more valuable is a human being than a sheep! So it is lawful to do good on the sabbath' (Mt. 12.11-12). A similar argument appears in a healing narrative in Luke (14.1-6): 'If one of you has a child or an ox that has fallen into a well, will you not immediately pull it out on a sabbath day?' As these arguments differ from one another, they do not come from the common Q source, but from Matthew's and Luke's unique sources, and the fact of a doublet suggests that this is an early tradition. Though they differ in terms of specifics, the principle behind the arguments, mostly clearly expressed in Matthew, is the same. Jesus wins the debate in both Matthew's and Luke's narratives since everyone agrees with his point about the sheep (Matthew) or the child/ox (Luke). We now know from the Dead Sea Scrolls that not everyone would have agreed with Jesus' principle of rescuing an animal on the sabbath. The text *Miscellaneous Rules* (4QSD; 4Q265) addresses the issue of saving human and animal lives on the sabbath:

> On the day [ ] of the Sabbath, [ ] Let no ma[n] ca[rry out] any vessel or foo[d] from his tent on the day [ ] of the Sabbath, [ ] Let no man raise up an animal which falls into the water on the Sabbath day. And if it is a human being that falls into the water [on] the Sabbath [day], let him cast his garment to him to raise him up therewith, but an implement he may not carry [to raise him up on] the Sabbath [day].
>
> 4Q265 fragment 6, 4–8

From this it would appear that whereas one should rescue a human being from a hole, one may not rescue an animal. Restrictions apply to the rescue, however. Specifically, one may not carry an implement to the place, but rather should use clothing, that is, the things a person already has with him or her. A similar rule appears in the *Damascus Document* (CD 11.13-17). These texts demonstrate the existence of an opinion contrary to Jesus' views on helping animals on the sabbath. We may presume that the authors of the Qumran texts would likewise have disapproved of Jesus' work as a healer on the sabbath. It is thus highly likely that Jesus did take part in a debate about sabbath rules, and that in this debate he adopted a liberal attitude when compared with the members of the Qumran movement, who occupied an extreme position on this issue. Jesus' reasoning about healing on the sabbath does, however, conform with later rabbinic thinking. It was permissible, for example, to heat water for tending the sick (t. Shabb. 15.14-15) and to administer medicine (t. Shabb. 2.7). Midwives, too, worked on the sabbath (m. Rosh Hash. 2.5). Such exceptions could be justified, just as in Jesus' arguments, through the principle stating that saving human life always has priority over the sabbath commandment. The principle also held in uncertain cases, when a person did not know for sure whether life was at stake (t. Shabb. 15.15).

The conflict narratives in the Gospels should be taken to reflect a historical situation in which Jesus carried out his healing work even on the sabbath and was eventually challenged for doing so by those who held stricter views. This also implies that those who were coming to Jesus for help on the sabbath shared his perspective on the matter, which could represent a more popular view. As a teacher, Jesus used the Scriptures to argue for his opinion as well as interpretative traditions current in his day.

Divorce and sexuality

We have already considered Jesus' prohibition of divorce, which is well founded, historically speaking, in that his thinking on the matter is recorded in Mark (Mk 10.2-12, with a parallel in Mt. 19.3-9), Q (Mt. 5.32; Lk. 16.18) and Paul (1 Cor. 7.10-11). At this point we shall explore further aspects of the issue in order to illustrate how Jesus' interpretation of the law fits with his historical context. Traditionally a man had the right to divorce his wife, something that is taken for granted in the Wisdom of Ben Sira (Sirach), for instance: 'Allow no outlet to water, and no boldness of speech to an evil wife. If she does not go as you direct, separate her from yourself' (Sir. 25.25-26; cf. 25.13-24; 26.7). Divorce was permitted within the Qumran movement as well (CD 13.17; 4Q266 fragment 9 iii), though with the reservation that it should be approved by one of the leaders. In the narrative in Mark, Jesus' comments on divorce form part of a confrontation with the Pharisees, who have set out 'to test him' (Mk 10.2). In what sense the question posed by the Pharisees might be a test is not clear and they disappear from the narrative after the introduction. As with the episode of plucking grain on the sabbath, we may assume that Mark has opted to provide a saying of Jesus' with a narrative framework, in which the Pharisees feature as critics. In this particular case, however, it is unlikely that the Pharisees as a group would have disagreed with Jesus' opinion, as they themselves were divided on the issue. The two rabbis Hillel and Shammai held differing opinions and Jesus' view is closer to Shammai's. Mark describes the dialogue as follows:

> Some Pharisees came, and to test him they asked, 'Is it lawful for a man to divorce his wife?' He answered them, 'What did Moses command you?' They said, 'Moses allowed a man to write a certificate of dismissal and to divorce her.' But Jesus said to them, 'Because of your hardness of heart he wrote this commandment for you. But from the beginning of creation, "God made them male and female." "For this reason a man shall leave his father and mother and be joined to his wife, and the two shall become one flesh." So they are no longer two, but one flesh. Therefore what God has joined together, let no one separate.'
>
> Mk 10.2-9

In this debate the Pharisees refer to the permission of divorce that Moses granted, as is written in Deut. 24.1: 'Suppose a man enters into marriage with a woman, but she does not please him because he finds something objectionable about her, and so he writes her a certificate of divorce, puts it in her hand, and sends her out of his house . . .'. The Pharisaic rabbis debated the meaning of the phrase 'something objectionable', with Hillel holding that absolutely anything could qualify, for instance if a wife burnt the food (m. Git. 9.10). Shammai, on the other hand, held that divorce was only permissible in cases of infidelity. In the text of Mark, Jesus voices a prohibition of divorce on principle, like Shammai, but he does not raise the issue of what would happen, for example, were the woman to be unfaithful. Jesus probably considered an exception of this sort to be self-evident, since the very point of Deut. 24.1-4 is that a man may not take a wife back if she has been with another man (through having been married to someone else, in this case), a situation that is described in stark terms: 'for that would be abhorrent to the LORD' (Deut. 24.4). Only Matthew inserts a clause relating to 'unchastity' (Mt. 19.8-9; cf. Mt. 5.31-32):

> It was because you were so hard-hearted that Moses allowed you to divorce your wives, but at the beginning it was not so. And I say to you, whoever divorces his wife, except for unchastity, and marries another commits adultery.

'Unchastity' or 'fornication' here is marriage within prohibited degrees of kinship (Lev. 18.6-18), those unions that are regarded as incest in the Torah. As long as the Jesus movement was primarily made up of Jews, the laws of incest were uncontroversial, but as Gentiles joined in greater and greater numbers, problems could arise if new members were married to close relatives (cf. 1 Cor. 5.1-5). From a Jewish perspective, reflected in Matthew's addition, such marriages were invalid and ought to be dissolved.

Why was Jesus opposed to divorce? Some scholars argue that he was especially concerned about the situation of women. A divorced woman received a settlement as part of the divorce but she also had to leave the home. Depending on her financial circumstances, life could be hard for a commandment from the very beginning: 'Be fruitful and multiply' (Gen. 1.28). It was, however, a grievous sin to enter the temple, a holy place, in a state of impurity. In Chapter 2 we saw how priests as well as ordinary Jewish visitors to the temple had to be ritually pure to set foot in the holy site, as impurity was a major threat to the presence of God. But even at great distances from the temple people were concerned with ritual purity, which may be indicated by almost six hundred stepped pools that have been found throughout the country from this time. The majority of these were discovered in Judaea, but archaeologists have unearthed approximately seventy in Galilee as well (Adler 2013).

As we saw earlier (ch. 2), ritual impurity was a normal feature of everyday life, since common occurrences rendered a person unclean: sexual intercourse, ejaculation, menstruation, childbirth and so on. Priests, too, who had to be pure when serving at the temple and partaking of sacrificial meals, were married and consequently unclean on a regular basis. Common forms of impurity could always be removed by means of rituals involving water in combination with a specified waiting period. Thus after intercourse, for instance, a couple had to bathe and wait until the evening before they were pure again (Lev. 15.18). Certain types of disease also entailed impurity, for example serious skin disease of a particular sort ('leprosy') and diseases involving penile discharge or long-term vaginal bleeding. When a person became well again he or she could be cleansed, but if the illness turned out to be chronic, as it did for some sufferers of serious skin disease, the impurity, too, was permanent. Scholars frequently associate impurity with women in particular, since menstruation entailed a week of impurity. This view is anachronistic, however; in premodern societies such as Palestine in the time of Jesus women did not menstruate particularly often. Married women were often pregnant or, if not, they were breastfeeding, which suppresses menstruation in many women. Thus, given that women had on average between six and nine children, menstruation was not a common part of daily life.

Impurity could be transmitted from person to person and between people and objects. Leviticus 15 offers detailed guidelines concerning the transmission of impurity and gives instructions as to how someone who, for instance, has touched a bed that a menstruating woman has lain on may be cleansed. To an outsider these rules may sound complicated, but to the people who observed them they seemed quite natural; they were merely following the traditions that they had grown up with. We should also remember that throughout the Roman Empire the principle of making a distinction between the pure and the impure was a given, even if the rules about how a person became unclean and how a person could be cleansed differed from one nation to another. Understandings of the purity laws also varied between different groups. Indeed, differences regarding laws of purification for the temple were one of the main points of conflict between the Qumran movement and the temple priests, as 4QMMT makes clear.

Among other things the author of this text complains about the deaf and the blind being allowed to enter the temple, because, he argues, their disabilities mean that one cannot count on such people being pure. That there were varying interpretations of the purity laws among Jewish groups will be an important point to keep in mind below as we attempt to understand a dispute about purity laws and meals.

Jesus and the purity laws

Most scholars of the New Testament argue that Jesus rejected the purity laws or at least that he viewed them with some indifference. Their reasoning is flawed, however. The mistake that scholars often make is to compare Jesus to the Pharisees or the Essenes, both of whom had an unusually strict approach to purity rules. In a comparison of this sort Jesus' behaviour may appear lax, as when he dined with people of all sorts, for example, something that members of those groups would not have done. But these sects are not representative of the population at large and the comparison is thus misleading. Another mistake that scholars make is to assume that people actively avoided impurity. They argue that Jesus was not concerned about purity laws because in his work as a healer he touched people who were unclean and came into contact with dead bodies. Naturally he, too, became unclean in these situations. But, as we stressed earlier, impurity was a normal aspect of everyday life. There was nothing strange about becoming unclean and afterwards, of course, a person could be cleansed. The Gospel narratives contain many examples of Jesus touching the sick when he cures them, for instance in Mk 8.22-26, when he cures a blind man by spitting and laying his hands on the man's eyes (cf. Mt. 9.29; Jn 9.6). Similarly, to heal a deaf man with a speech impediment Jesus 'put his fingers into his ears, and he spat and touched his tongue' (Mk 7.33). It seemed obvious that healing would involve physical contact and we see this in Mark's introduction to his narrative of Jesus' raising the synagogue leader's daughter from the dead: 'when he saw [Jesus], [he] fell at his feet and begged him repeatedly, "My little daughter is at the point of death. Come and lay your hands on her, so that she may be made well, and live."' (Mk 5.23). From this we can conclude that, like other healers and physicians, Jesus did touch the sick when seeking to cure them. He did not avoid becoming ritually impure in his activities. Yet this does not mean that Jesus was unconcerned about purity laws, but rather that he was simply carrying out his work. Mark's narrative of Jesus reviving the synagogue leader's daughter is telling in this regard:

> While he was still speaking, some people came from the leader's house to say, 'Your daughter is dead. Why trouble the teacher any further?' But overhearing what they said, Jesus said to the leader of the synagogue, 'Do not fear, only believe.' He allowed no one to follow him except Peter, James,

and John, the brother of James. When they came to the house of the leader of the synagogue, he saw a commotion, people weeping and wailing loudly. When he had entered, he said to them, 'Why do you make a commotion and weep? The child is not dead but sleeping.' And they laughed at him. Then he put them all outside, and took the child's father and mother and those who were with him, and went in where the child was.

Mk 5.35-40

For Mark, who is fully familiar with Jewish customs and practices, the fact that lots of people are gathered in a house where someone has just died is unremarkable. According to the laws of Moses, in so doing all of these people had become unclean as well, and this impurity lasted for seven days (Num. 19.14). But even so, neighbours, friends and relatives of a family who lost a child did not hesitate to visit the household to support the bereaved; on the contrary, it seems to have been what was expected (Wassén 2016). Once again we see how impurity was part of everyday life in Jewish society. Hence Jesus' behaviour does not indicate that he viewed the purity laws with indifference, but rather that he behaved as ordinary people did. What's more, Jesus was taught by John the Baptist, a man who, as we have seen, set out to cleanse people both inwardly and outwardly. In all likelihood this aspect of John's teaching also had an influence on Jesus; for one thing, as we have seen, he underwent a ritual act of bathing that John presided over. That Jesus did care about the purity laws is evident from Mark's narrative of Jesus healing a leper (Mk 1.40-45). There Jesus orders the man to 'go, show yourself to the priest, and offer for your cleansing what Moses commanded' (Mk 1.44), that is, to observe the purity laws of Lev. 13. There is one conflict narrative, however, – about washing one's hands in connection with meals – that is usually interpreted as meaning that Jesus rejected the purity laws, though as we shall see this interpretation is not convincing.

A dispute about handwashing at meals

In Mark 7.1-23 several statements of Jesus' relating to purity laws have been combined with a dispute with the Pharisees about handwashing, and the author has also inserted a dispute about vows respecting temple offerings (*Corban*). Mark begins by explaining how Jewish purity laws work, at which point he describes the traditions of the Pharisees, which he states, generalizing somewhat, hold for all Jews:

> For the Pharisees, and all the Jews, do not eat unless they thoroughly wash their hands, thus observing the tradition of the elders; and they do not eat anything from the market unless they wash it; and there are also many other traditions that they observe, the washing of cups, pots, and bronze kettles.

Mk 7.3-4

This description quite clearly reveals that Gentiles made up the majority of Mark's Christ-believing audience, since they are expected to be unfamiliar with these rules. Matthew opts not to include the explanation of the purity laws when borrowing the narrative from Mark (Mt. 15.1-20), while Luke chooses not to include the narrative at all.

In Mark's narrative the Pharisees and the scribes ask Jesus, 'Why do your disciples not live according to the tradition of the elders, but eat with defiled hands?' (Mk 7.5). This prompts Jesus to unleash a tirade upon them:

> Isaiah prophesied rightly about you hypocrites, as it is written, 'This people honours me with their lips, but their hearts are far from me; in vain do they worship me, teaching human precepts as doctrines.' You abandon the commandment of God and hold to human tradition.
>
> Mk 7.6-8

Behind this criticism lies the fact that washing one's hands before meals was a relatively new custom, observed by the Pharisees but not found in biblical law. But does this criticism really come from Jesus? Given the tendency of the Gospel authors to paint the Pharisees in a negative light, which we noted earlier (ch. 2), the inordinately harsh attack on the Pharisees may well reflect Mark's views rather than Jesus'. If we examine the quotation from the Bible more closely it becomes clear that these remarks cannot go back to Jesus. The quote from Isa. 29.13 about *'teaching* human precepts' occurs only in the Septuagint, not in the Hebrew text (cf. NRSV's 'their worship of me is a human commandment learned by rote'). Now, obviously Jesus did not use the Greek text of Isaiah, but Mark did. In the conflict that emerged between the church and the synagogue, Christ-believing groups could accuse Jews of keeping 'human commands and teachings', in the words of the author of the Letter to the Colossians (2.22), and thus the passage from Mark reflects a time later than that of Jesus. This also casts doubt over the historical reliability of the other accusations found here – about how vows relating to temple offerings (*Corban*) are human inventions as opposed to divine commandments (Mk 7.9-13) – at least in the form that Mark presents them. Still, it is not impossible that, citing the Mosaic law (Exod. 20.12; 21.17), Jesus was opposed to the idea of vowing a donation to the temple if such a donation would have negatively affected the well-being of one's parents. An attitude similar to that voiced by Jesus is found in the *Damascus Document*, which forbids people from vowing to give donations of food to the temple rather than helping their neighbours afflicted with hunger (CD 16.14–15).

Although the form in which Jesus' criticism of the Pharisees is presented in Mark 7 is the likely work of the author of that Gospel, some historical core probably lies behind the dispute about handwashing in which Jesus and the Pharisees occupy differing positions. Several verses later Mark has Jesus express his fundamental view on this issue: 'there is nothing outside a person that by going in can defile, but the things that come out are what defile' (Mk 7.15). This is a distinct, short saying, or *chreia* (ch. 3), that many scholars presume goes back to Jesus (see Dunn 2003: 574). Later, according to Mark, Jesus explains this statement of principle to the disciples:

> He said to them, 'Then do you also fail to understand? Do you not see that whatever goes into a person from outside cannot defile, since it enters, not the heart but the stomach, and goes out into the sewer?' (Thus he declared all foods clean.) And he said, 'It is what comes out of a person that defiles. For it is from within, from the human heart, that evil intentions come: fornication, theft, murder, adultery, avarice, wickedness, deceit, licentiousness, envy, slander, pride, folly. All these evil things come from within, and they defile a person.'
>
> Mk 7.18-23

Mark provides his audience with his own interpretation: 'Thus he declared all foods clean' (Mk 7.19). The Greek word for food, *broma*, refers to what is eaten and not to the unclean animals that are prohibited in Lev. 11. Interestingly, when Matthew incorporates the passage he omits this comment, likely because he disagrees with Mark. Although Mark's explanatory comment is in line with Jesus' saying, he goes a step further than Jesus; whilst Jesus does reject the idea that eating ritually impure food defiles a person, that is not the same as saying that all food is clean. For Mark, writing for an overwhelmingly gentile audience, the Jewish purity laws were no longer relevant in the way they were for Matthew. Jesus' argumentation in the narrative is fairly complex. The subject is ultimately ritual purity, which is conceptualized as a physical condition. But in the explanation of the overarching principle that Jesus offers in v. 15 ('there is nothing outside a person...') Mark contrasts physical realities (food passing through the stomach) with inner, moral ones (7.18-23); this, of course, was not the point of the Pharisees' question. A comparable list of different types of sin, a catalogue of sins, does not occur anywhere else in the teachings of Jesus and is not in keeping with his style. The list is of a general nature and it does not fit particularly well with Jesus' remarks in 7.15. Most likely it was added at a later stage (Kazen 2013: 182). Nor does the somewhat forced comment about the path that food takes through the stomach and out again (7.19) fit particularly well here, because what is eaten both goes in *and* comes out of a person. Matthew has altered the saying in Mk. 7.15 by adding references to 'the mouth' (Mt. 15.11), hence limiting the meaning to what goes in and out of the mouth. This however creates new problems, since the sins in the ensuing list are not restricted to oral utterances. Rather than being limited to the mouth, the earlier form of the sentence as we find it in Mark may likely had a wider frame of reference.

How should we understand the central statement in Mk 7.15, which Jesus may well have uttered? Most scholars understand 7.15 to mean that

Jesus declared all animals prohibited for consumption clean (e.g. Sanders 1985: 260; Dunn 2003: 573–7). It is hard to believe that Jesus would have rejected the Mosaic laws relating to prohibited animals, which are described as 'unclean' in the Hebrew Bible (Lev. 11). Had Jesus advocated the eating of unclean animals, something that ran counter to fundamental norms of Jewish culture (ch. 2), we ought to be able to discern this view elsewhere in the traditions about Jesus. As we shall see in the final chapter, the issue of food does later come to be a point of dispute within the early church, when Christ-believers debated what rules should apply if Jews and Gentiles ate together. That debate shows no signs of having been influenced by some declaration that purportedly came from Jesus and stated that the food laws could be ignored. Consequently some scholars regard the statement as unhistorical (Sanders 1985: 260–9; Dunn 2003: 574; Meier 2009: 393–7). But in so doing they overlook the fact that in the context of Mk 7 this is not a statement about prohibited foods like pork, but rather one about food that has been defiled, ritually speaking. It was common at meals for everyone to dip bread into the same dish (cf. Jn 13.26) and the question that Jesus was debating with the Pharisees was how impurity was spread at such meals. According to the Pharisees, the spread of impurity could be prevented if everyone washed their hands before a meal. Matthew makes it clear that ritual impurity is what is at issue when he puts an additional explanatory sentence in the mouth of Jesus: 'These [sins] are what defile a person, but to eat with unwashed hands does not defile' (Mt. 15.20).

Alternatively, other scholars argue that Jesus is weighing the two categories against one another prioritizing ethical standards over purity concerns: no outward impurity defiles a person as much as inner impurity – sin – does. With this Jesus is not abolishing purity rules surrounding food but commenting on their relative value in comparison with moral rules (Dunn 2003: 576; Kazen 2013: 190–1). This interpretation is not impossible, but it would still mean that Jesus' attitude towards the purity laws was nonetheless fairly negative. As was shown above, there is nothing elsewhere in the sources to suggest that he devalued or relativized the purity laws (Wassén 2016). Instead, a more likely interpretation is that the entire statement in Mk 7.15 should be understood literally and thus that it is indeed concerned with ritual impurity. Jesus is therefore rejecting the Pharisees' view that handwashing is necessary since, his view, eating food that has become ritually impure does not defile a person ('there is nothing outside a person that by going in can defile'). At the same time the continuation affirms that certain substances do defile: 'the things that come out are what defile'. The second part of the verse, then, refers not to immorality but to substances that were regarded as defiling according to the purity laws of Lev. 15, for example menstrual blood and semen, substances which do, of course, come out of a person (Furstenberg 2008). On this interpretation Jesus is criticizing the Pharisees' requirement regarding handwashing, while affirming the traditional laws that govern the transmission of impurity.

Summary

Many people might assume that a commandment to love others, in the sense of having certain positive feelings towards them, is at the heart of Jesus' message. But, perhaps surprisingly, 'love' is not a common theme in Jesus' teaching, nor does 'love' primarily express emotions, but rather loyalty and a willingness to do good to others, values which correspond to traditional Jewish teaching. As we have seen, Jesus acted in accordance with traditions current in his day. He was a law-abiding Jew who argued for his interpretation of the Torah with authority. Still, his conduct on the sabbath sparked controversy and his behaviour was called into question. He held more liberal views in these conflicts than the Pharisees and the Qumran movement, yet in many cases his opinion probably accorded with that of the common person, that is, with Jews outside the sects. For example, even on the sabbath sick people came to Jesus for help. Jesus and his disciples may have plucked grain in the field on the sabbath, a practice that Jesus defended by pointing to emergency conditions while admitting that it was a transgression of the sabbath law. On ethical issues and in the debate about divorce, however, Jesus adopted an unusually strict position, in effect prohibiting men from divorcing their wives. Jesus rejected oath-taking in general, since it was unnecessary for completely honest people and made people liable to commit transgressions. While many New Testament scholars do characterize Jesus as a law-observant Jew, they nevertheless claim that Jesus rejected the purity laws, or at least that he did not care much about them. Nevertheless, we have argued that Jesus lived in accordance with these Jewish laws, too, albeit in keeping with his own interpretation of them. Although, in his healing and exorcism practices, he would have touched ritually impure people, this does not mean that he was indifferent to purity laws, as scholars often claim. Instead, touching the sick, even those who were impure, was part of his job as a healer. Like other people who were regularly impure, for example from sexual intercourse or contact with menstruating women, Jesus does not seem to have striven to avoid human impurities. In addition, he objected to the Pharisaic practice of handwashing before meals, which was a novel purity practice. What emerges from Jesus' legal interpretation and teaching is that, like his contemporaries, Jesus took the authoritative status of the books that would later make up the Hebrew Bible for granted. Jesus often referred to the Torah in his teaching and in particular he highlighted a person's duty to be loyal to the god of Israel and to his or her fellow human beings. There is thus no reason to think that Jesus abolished Jewish laws. Why Christ-believers would later come to reject certain laws, such as purity laws and laws concerning prohibited foods, is a topic we shall explore in the final chapter.

In this chapter we have examined Jesus' role as a teacher in matters of legal interpretation. Earlier we focused on his role as a healer and a prophet. It is now time to reflect on his role as Messiah or Christ. The notion that

Jesus was the anointed one came to predominate in views of who Jesus was within the early church. Where did this idea come from? Did Jesus in any way understand his mission in the light of the messianic beliefs that flourished in his day, or was it the followers of Jesus who started regarding him as a Messiah after his death? In the next chapter we look for the answer.

Bibliography

Adler, Y. (2013), 'Purity in the Roman Period', in *The Oxford Encyclopedia of the Bible and Archaeology*, vol. 2, 240–49, New York: Oxford University Press.

Adler, Y. (2017), 'The Distribution of Tefillin Finds among the Judean Desert Caves', in M. Fidanzio (ed.), *The Caves of Qumran: Proceedings of the International Conference, Lugano 2014*, Leiden: Brill.

Collins, N. L. (2014), *Jesus, the Sabbath and the Jewish Debate: Healing on the Sabbath in the 1st and 2nd Centuries CE*, Library of New Testament Studies 474, London: Bloomsbury T & T Clark.

Dunn. J. D. G. (2003), *Christianity in the Making, vol. 1: Jesus Remembered*, Grand Rapids: Eerdmans.

Furstenberg, Y. (2008), 'Defilement Penetrating the Body: A New Understanding of Contamination in Mark 7.15', *New Testament Studies*, 54: 176–200.

Ilan, T. (1996), *Jewish Women in Greco-Roman Palestine*, Peabody: Hendrickson.

Kazen, T. (2013), *Scripture, Interpretation, or Authority? Motives and Arguments in Jesus' Halakic Conflicts*, Wissenschaftliche Untersuchungen zum Neuen Testament 320, Tübingen: Mohr Siebeck.

Loader, W. (2010), 'Jesus and the Law', in S. E. Porter and T. Holmén (eds), *Handbook for the Study of the Historical Jesus*, vol 4, 2745–72, Leiden: Brill.

Meier, J. P. (2009), *A Marginal Jew: Rethinking the Historical Jesus, vol. 4: Law and Love*, New Haven: Yale University Press.

Sanders, E. P. (1985), *Jesus and Judaism*, London: SCM Press.

Wassén, C. (2005), *Women in the Damascus Document*, Society of Biblical Literature Academia Biblica Series 21, Atlanta: Society of Biblical Literature/ Leiden: Brill.

Wassén, C. (2016). 'The Jewishness of Jesus and Ritual Purity', *Scripta Insituti Donneriani Aboensis*, 27: 11–36, https://journal.fi/scripta/issue/view/4663

9

The anointed one

Throughout large parts of the Western world today, people tend to think of religion as first and foremost a set of ideas and opinions. Religion is about 'believing in' something, which we can do (or not do) without it affecting or being noticed by other people. In the Hebrew Bible there is no clear-cut boundary between the material world and what we might call the 'spiritual' realm; the divine manifests itself in human actions and physical objects as well. When someone is specially chosen by God for an important office – as priest, king or prophet – that person is marked out by being anointed with aromatic oils. The intense fragrance is to show that the chosen individual has God's favour. The Messiah, 'the anointed one', was a liberator and leader specially chosen by God. The authors of the New Testament are convinced that Jesus is that chosen one. In this chapter we shall find out whether the historical Jesus viewed himself the same way.

Who do people say that I am?

The author of Mark's Gospel relates that Jesus was out walking in the area of Caesarea Philippi, a city at the foot of Mount Hermon that was the chief settlement in what is today the disputed Golan region. So far Mark's narrative has described Jesus working miracles, casting out spirits, speaking in parables and getting into disputes with the scribes, but now all of a sudden Jesus poses an unexpected question about himself: 'Who do people say that I am?' The disciples report various possible suggestions. Some people have apparently been speculating that Jesus is in fact John the Baptist come back from the dead. Others believe that he is Elijah, that great prophet who was taken up to heaven in a chariot of fire and who would return in the last days. Still others think that Jesus may be some other prophet. But then comes a more sensitive question: 'But who do you say that I am?' We can imagine a profound silence falling at this point. Jesus' followers must also have been wondering and cautiously discussing amongst themselves whether their charismatic leader might be concealing a very special identity. Now all of a sudden they are called upon for an answer. They know their master well enough not to dare venture an incorrect guess. Simon is the one who finally breaks the silence: 'You are the Messiah' (Mk 8.27-29).

Was this answer right or wrong? In Mark's Gospel Jesus himself offers no clear answer. The episode of Simon Peter identifying Jesus as the Messiah is a turning point in the Gospel, in that up to this point in the narrative no human being has grasped who Jesus is, despite the fact that God (Mk 1.11) as well as the unclean spirits (Mk 1.24; 3.11) have acknowledged him as God's 'Beloved', 'the Holy One of God' and 'the Son of God'. Humans, however, – supporters and opponents alike – appear to find it almost absurdly difficult to comprehend Jesus' identity in the slightest until he puts the question to the disciples himself. The disciples are left in suspense here, too, as Jesus neither praises nor censures Peter, but rather 'sternly' forbids them 'to tell anyone about him' (Mk 8.31). Much later in the narrative the high priest puts the question directly to Jesus himself: 'Are you the Messiah, the Son of the Blessed One?' (Mk 14.61). Jesus' answer sounds like a confirmation – 'I am' – but the phrase is not absolutely crystal-clear in Greek, and according to both Matthew and Luke Jesus deflects the question, leaving it unanswered (Mt. 26.64; Lk. 22.68). Elsewhere in the Synoptic Gospels Jesus never states that he is the Messiah or Son of God.

Still, there is no doubt that the author of Mark's Gospel was utterly convinced that Jesus was the promised Messiah. It is clear from the very start: 'The beginning of the good news of Jesus Christ [= Messiah], the Son of God' (Mk 1.1). If there really is anything that unites the twenty-seven writings ultimately included in the anthology that is the New Testament, it is precisely the thought that Jesus is the Christ, the Messiah, 'the anointed one'; only in the very brief Third Letter of John is the term absent. Earlier we saw that the letters of Paul sometimes grant us access to very early, oral narratives about Jesus (ch. 3). One such narrative, which Paul himself says was among his and his congregations' most fundamental beliefs, states that 'Christ died for our sins in accordance with the scriptures, and that he was buried, and that he was raised on the third day in accordance with the scriptures, and that he appeared to Cephas, then to the twelve' (1 Cor. 15.3-5). 'Christ', here, is already serving as something like a proper name, but underlying it, of course, is the belief that Jesus is the Messiah. As far as we can tell, after his death there were never any 'Jesus-believers' who questioned the messianic identity of Jesus. Even so, clear confirmation from Jesus himself is not found in the Gospels.

How should we account for this state of affairs? At the beginning of the twentieth century the German biblical scholar William Wrede wrote a highly influential book addressing the 'messianic secret' in the Gospels (Wrede 1971). He observed that the Jesus of Mark's Gospel does not stop at simply refraining from describing himself as the Messiah; he even makes a point of actively preventing others from doing so. Jesus appears to forbid demons (Mk 1.34; 3.12) as well as human beings (Mk 8.30) from revealing his messianic identity. The explanation for this, according to Wrede, is that belief in Jesus as the Messiah only arose after his death, and that the early Christ-believers were well aware that Jesus never made any messianic claims himself. To overcome the discrepancy between memories of the earthly Jesus and belief in the risen Christ, Mark came up with the idea that Jesus' identity as the Messiah was a closely guarded secret up until his death. The notion of a 'messianic secret' was thus an ingenious later invention. Is the question that Jesus asks his disciples fictional, then, part of a plot formed long after his death? Or could it have been meant sincerely? Might Jesus have been genuinely uncertain as to who he really was?

Jesus' identity is formed

Much like other ancient biographies, the Gospels do not factor in any real psychological growth when portraying their protagonist. Luke may well write that Jesus 'increased in wisdom and in years' (Lk. 2.52), but, in line with the thinking of the age, he does not suppose that his hero's attributes are the product of various environmental factors; instead, they are the complete realization of a potential that was already within him to begin with. A typical example of this way of looking at personal development can be seen in the episode about the twelve-year-old Jesus making a great impression among the teachers in the temple with his knowledge (Lk. 2.46-47): even as a young boy Jesus demonstrated the abilities that would come to fruition in adulthood.

It is also obvious in the Gospels that Jesus knows who he is and what his mission involves. With his last Passover approaching, John presents Jesus as 'knowing that the Father had given all things into his hands, and that he had come from God and was going to God' (Jn 13.3). Even in the Synoptic Gospels, where Jesus is portrayed in a more human light, he seems fairly self-assured. He even anticipates his own death and resurrection (Mk 8.31; 9.31; 10.33-34).

Part of the work of the historian is putting aside the point of view that the narrative sets out to convey. Today we know that someone's personality is not simply a result of his or her inborn character. Instead, the development of personality is bound up with identity formation, a process that takes place, to a great extent, in the interplay between people. For one thing, our identities are formed by our sense of belonging to various groups and of having certain unique characteristics in relation to others. How we are treated by the people around us is critical for how we are shaped as individuals. In ancient times less was known about these processes than is known today, but of course they were just as active then as now, and Jesus' understanding of his own identity is no exception. As a historical individual Jesus can hardly have come into the world with a ready-made image of himself and his life's mission. He must have come to self-understanding by degrees, with reference to various factors in identity formation: his cultural milieu, his subjective experience and the response others showed towards him. What degree of clarity he reached in his self-concept must remain unknown.

Jesus was born into a cultural context in which it was assumed that visible and invisible forces were equally real and equally powerful. Angels and demons, the Spirit of God and unclean spirits were forces to be reckoned with (see ch. 2). This cultural setting was the basis on which Jesus was able to have certain key spiritual experiences. It is highly likely that his baptism in the River Jordan, which by all reports marked the beginning of Jesus' public ministry, was one such experience. Earlier we saw that the account of the baptism in the Gospel of Mark includes a mythological description of how Jesus 'saw the heavens torn apart and the Spirit descending like a dove on him' (Mk 1.10). Here and in Matthew we seem to be dealing with a vision that Jesus is granted at the time of his baptism. Luke, on the other hand, gives the impression that the descent of the Spirit was something that everyone could see, and the Gospel of John explicitly states that John the Baptist was the one who saw the Spirit descending like a dove on Jesus (see Mt. 3.16; Lk. 3.11; Jn 1.32-33). It seems plausible that the original narrative would have told of a powerful subjective experience that Jesus himself had of the Spirit of God taking possession of him. It is impossible to know whether Jesus had felt the calling to launch a prophetic career before this point, but in any event being subjected to this spiritual experience in association with his baptism served to confirm for Jesus that God was on his side.

Further confirmations of this kind followed when Jesus discovered his ability to heal the sick and cast out demons. Francis Schlatter, a cobbler and healer of Alsatian origin who in the 1890's, after experiencing God's special calling, toured the American West on foot, is said to have had a fairly unsuccessful beginning. Several of his early attempts at healing failed, and it was only after a couple of years that he was able to trust his miraculous power fully. We do not know what happened the first time Jesus noticed that he could make people well, but presumably, like other folk healers, he began cautiously and grew increasingly confident with the positive response others had to his success. These 'miracles' led to speculation – on the part of both Jesus himself and his followers – about his identity and his relationship to God. There is nothing especially remarkable about people possibly concluding that Jesus must be a prophet in the mould of Elijah – that figure from olden times who, according to the Hebrew Bible, had performed spectacular wonders (1 Kgs 17.8-24; 2 Kgs 1.12; 2.8). Such speculation about Jesus' prophetic identity provided further stimulus to his already strong sense of being guided by the Spirit. In the end he was certain that he should indeed assume the role of a prophet of God completely.

Although it may today seem strange to imagine Jesus interpreting his role in light of the Scriptures, our first assumption should be that that is precisely what he did. In the time of Jesus a great wealth of written texts and oral narratives already existed that embellished Holy Writ and gave it new meaning. In certain circles, particular interest was cultivated in those obscure passages which, it was thought, might tell of a saviour figure to come. For example, God's promise to Moses in his old age to send 'a prophet like you' (Deut. 18.18) gave rise to speculation about a future prophetic messiah figure. It would hardly be surprising if Jesus and his circle of supporters used the Hebrew Bible as an interpretative key and began to wonder if perhaps his accomplishments had been predicted in its writings. John's question to Jesus, sent through his disciples – 'Are you the one who is to come?' (Mt. 11.3; Lk. 7.19) – makes it sound as if there was some clearly defined task that was just waiting to be carried out by the right person; but as we saw in Chapter 2 there were many different messianic conceptions circulating at the time. Jews at the turn of the Common Era could hope for a messiah who had the power of a king, but they could also imagine a messiah figure who was chiefly a priest or a prophet. Some thought that the Messiah would appear as an ordinary human being, while others envisaged a heavenly, angelic saviour. The sectarians at Qumran even expected two or more messiahs! This abundance of ideas added to the opportunities one had for regarding oneself or someone else as 'God's anointed'. Jesus may have never been entirely sure whether he really could claim to be a messiah, but there are many indications the thought did occur to him and his disciples.

The messianic Son of Man

Although Jesus may not speak of himself as 'the Messiah' in the Gospels, there is another term that he does use with much greater frequency: 'the Son of Man'. Earlier (ch. 3) we observed that this term was rarely or never used by the early Christ-believers and that it must therefore derive from the historical Jesus. Another indicator of this is the fact that 'Son of Man' occurs in all of the Gospels and in all of their putative underlying sources. Jesus uses the term in the Gospel of Mark (e.g. 9.9; 10.45), in Q (e.g. Mt. 8.20; Lk. 9.58), in the material unique to Matthew (e.g. 10.23) and that unique to Luke (e.g. 12.8) as well as in the Gospel of John (e.g. 1.51). 'The Son of Man' is even to be found in the *Gospel of Thomas* (*Gos. Thom.* 86).

The term – literally 'the son of the human being' – sounds at least as strange in Greek as it does in English, and this strangeness surely stems from the fact that it is an early translation from the original Aramaic, the language of Jesus and his disciples. In both Aramaic and Hebrew 'a son of a human being' is simply a synonym for 'a man'. In addition, in various texts the Aramaic term serves as something like an indefinite pronoun that can mean 'humanity in general', 'a particular person' or 'this person', 'I' (cf. English 'one'). The term's usage appears to have changed over time, and scholars therefore debate which of these various meanings the term might have had when Jesus used it. At the very least it is clear that in several sayings of Jesus 'Son of Man' can easily be understood in one of these mundane senses. Such sayings include, for example, the almost proverb-like statement about the harsh conditions that Jesus and his companions endure on their wanderings: 'Foxes have holes, and birds of the air have nests; but the Son of Man has nowhere to lay his head' (Mt. 8.20; Lk. 9.58).

There have been prominent scholars, not least Geza Vermes (1973: 160–91) and Maurice Casey (2009), who have argued that Jesus only used the Aramaic expression in such an everyday sense. But in other utterances of Jesus', the meaning of 'Son of Man' is anything but mundane. In what is considered the most apocalyptic portion of Mark's Gospel, the Son of Man is a heavenly figure:

> But in those days, after that suffering, the sun will be darkened, and the moon will not give its light, and the stars will be falling from heaven, and the powers in the heavens will be shaken. Then they will see 'the Son of Man coming in clouds' with great power and glory. Then he will send out the angels, and gather his elect from the four winds, from the ends of the earth to the ends of heaven.
>
> Mk 13.24-27

This description of the Son of Man's coming to gather 'his elect' at the end times fits well with the apocalyptic message that Jesus preached. It clearly builds on motifs from the book of Daniel in the Hebrew Bible. In one of Daniel's night-time revelations, the protagonist sees four strange and terrible beasts rising up out of a stormy sea (Dan. 7.2-12). These beasts represent four major political powers and their rulers: in order, the Neo-Babylonian Empire, the Median Empire, the Persian Empire and the (Hellenistic) Seleucid Empire. This nightmarish account takes a new turn when an 'Ancient One' with snow-white clothing and a throne of fire – evidently God himself – takes his seat on the stage and presides over a trial. At this point a new figure is introduced, 'one like a human being' (literally 'one like a son of man'):

> As I watched in the night visions, I saw one like a human being coming with the clouds of heaven. And he came to the Ancient One and was presented before him. To him was given dominion and glory and kingship, that all peoples, nations, and languages should serve him. His dominion is an everlasting dominion that shall not pass away, and his kingship is one that shall never be destroyed.
>
> Dan. 7.13-14

In Daniel, this human-like figure is a symbol of the people of Israel collectively, just as the four beast-like figures symbolized various empires collectively. Even so, this does not preclude the possibility that the figure also stands for an individual – the four beasts are interpreted not just as four empires but also as four kings. In Israel's case, however, the individual in view is not some earthly ruler but rather a heavenly protector, the angelic 'prince' Michael (Dan. 10.13, 21; 12.1).

When speaking about the 'Son of Man', Jesus seems to have been thinking of an individual, and it is not unlikely that he identified this individual as a messiah figure. This is because, by the turn of the Common Era, Daniel's vision of the figure resembling a human being had come to be interpreted in a new way. Though the book of Daniel mentions an entity that is merely 'like a human being', it was increasingly thought that what was meant was just that, a human being, who would receive power and dominion – a messianic ruler. In the so-called *Fourth Book of Ezra*, Ezra the scribe is shown 'something like the figure of a man' who comes up out of the sea, flies with the clouds of heaven, annihilates his enemies and gathers his people together (*4 Ezra* 13.1-13). God himself explains to Ezra that the 'man' whom he has seen coming up from the sea is God's 'Son', whose identity is as unknown as the depths of the sea, but who will one day appear and gather the tribes of Israel (*4 Ezra* 13.25-52). At another point in the book we hear that God's 'Son', who is furthermore explicitly called 'the Messiah' here, will live on earth for four hundred years and then die – after which time the resurrection of the dead and the last judgement will take place (*4 Ezra* 7.28-35).

The same tendency to interpret Daniel's vision messianically can also be seen in the so-called 'Book of Parables', which forms part (chapters 37–71) of the loose collection of writings known as the *First Book of Enoch* (or *1 Enoch*). In this text Enoch ascends to heaven where he is shown God's 'Elect One', the Messiah, who is also referred to as 'the Son of Man'. After seeing the Ancient One from Daniel's vision, Enoch goes on:

> And with him was another whose countenance had the appearance of a man, and his face was full of graciousness, like one of the angels. And I asked the angel who went with me and showed me all the secret things, concerning yonder Son of Man, who he was, and whence he was. . . . And he answered and said unto me: This is the Son of Man to whom belongs righteousness . . . because the Lord of spirits has chosen him.
>
> *1 En.* 46.1-3

The Son of Man is also styled the 'Anointed One' and he is portrayed as an earthly ruler (*1 En.* 52.4). For now he is with God, hidden (*1 En.* 48.6), but he will judge the ungodly and lead the righteous and elect in the last days.

In the Judaism of Jesus and his contemporaries there was no uniform set of beliefs about the 'Son of Man'. The enigmatic imagery of the book of Daniel is used in various ways in *4 Ezra, 1 Enoch* and other writings, but among these a common tendency can be observed. What Daniel saw long ago is imagined to be not merely a symbol of the Jewish people or an angelic heavenly prince, but a real individual, the Messiah whom God would send to liberate Israel. It would be strange if such messianic interpretations did not colour Jesus' understanding of Daniel's vision.

Jesus claimed that the 'Son of Man' would come when people least expected it (Mt. 24.44; Lk. 12.40). The Son of Man would send 'the angels' to gather 'his elect' (Mk 13.27), as we saw earlier. His coming would take place when the kingdom of God came 'with power' – not in the partial and incomplete manner in which the kingdom had already come in the exorcisms and wonders wrought by Jesus, but definitively, such that no one could fail to notice it (Mk 8.38–9.1). All of this accords with the messianic conceptions of the Son of Man that were circulating among Jewish groups in the time of Jesus. He was, if not actually an angel, then at the very least an angel-like figure who could command the heavenly army. The precise timing of his coming was unknown – God alone knew when it would come to pass. But once that time came, the Son of Man would gather the elect and grant the faithful their reward.

Does this mean that Jesus did openly proclaim himself to be the Messiah after all? If so, perhaps the reason the term 'Messiah' does not appear on his lips is that he preferred 'Son of Man'. Perhaps, but the issue is a little more complicated than that. Among the authentic sayings of Jesus that mention the Son of Man, those that clearly associate this figure with the vision from the book of Daniel are relatively few, and all of those are about his magnificent coming at the ultimate fulfilment of the kingdom of God (Mk 8.38; 13.27; 14.62; Mt. 24.44; Lk. 12.40). Thus the Son of Man is a figure who is to come at some future point. If Jesus believed that he was this future Son of Man, that would presumably mean that he was expecting to be exalted to that office as part of the realization of God's kingdom. If so, the early Christ-believers, who knew that Jesus had died and who believed that he had risen again and was with God, reinterpreted this expectation of his as referring to a second coming at the end of time.

There are, to be sure, several points in the Gospels where Jesus speaks of himself as the present Son of Man. Some of these display no clear association with messianic ideas, such as the saying about the Son of Man lacking a home, for instance (Mt. 8.20; Lk. 9.58). Others seem to have been added by early Christ-believers. For instance, the statements in Mark's Gospel about how 'the Son of Man has authority on earth to forgive sins' (Mk. 2.10) and is 'lord . . . of the sabbath' (Mk 2.28) – statements which certainly do hint at the Messiah's power and dominion – are unlikely to have been uttered by the historical Jesus. In addition, the solemn predictions about the suffering, death and resurrection of the Son of Man (Mk 8.31; 9.31; 10.32-33) are in all probability later inventions. In Matthew, 'Son of Man' has become such an unmistakable designation of Jesus that he can ask his disciples, 'Who do people say that the Son of Man is?' (Mt. 16.13), apparently without any of them reacting to the fact that in so doing he has already revealed his identity. In other words, it is clear from the Gospels that an increasing number of statements in which Jesus is identified as the Son of Man, not just in some coming age but even during his earthly life, are later fabrications. Is it possible that at first the Son of Man did not refer to Jesus at all, but rather to some other saviour figure?

The idea is not as strange as at first it might sound. John the Baptist's message about the coming of a future judge was subsequently reinterpreted as a message about Jesus. Conceivably Jesus awaited the coming of a Son of Man figure in the future, whom the disciples and other Christ-believers only came to identify with Jesus after his death. But this reconstruction can also be challenged. If Jesus really did herald the coming of a Son of Man other than himself, how, then, would this prediction have transformed into the belief that Jesus himself was the Son of Man without any trace of the original conception being left behind? Even though the authors of the Gospels were convinced that John the Baptist was the forerunner of the Messiah, they could not completely cover up the fact that John had not equated the coming judge with Jesus (Mt. 11.2-3; Lk. 7.18-19). Similarly, shouldn't we also find some indication of Jesus and the Son of Man being regarded as distinct somewhere in our sources of knowledge about the early Christ-believers (see Hägerland 2016)?

A further possibility is that Jesus' message was vague on this point and open to interpretation. Given that Jesus spoke of the Son of Man in the third person, his listeners could not be entirely sure if he meant himself or someone else. Presumably, the fact that the everyday expression 'a son of a human being' could be used in a number of different ways further added to the uncertainty. The ambiguity in Jesus' use of language might reflect genuine uncertainty on his part, given that the only one who really knew who the anointed one was and when he would appear was God. Jesus may have wondered for a long time, perhaps right up to the end, whether he was in fact the Son of Man whom God had chosen.

The Anointed One of the Spirit

We saw above that in time Jesus became convinced that he was a prophet. Among the various messianic conceptions in early Judaism, one was centred on a prophetic messiah, and it seems to have been this prophetic role that presented itself most readily to Jesus. In this area, too, he was able to tap into existing interpretations of the Holy Scriptures, and, above all, of Isaiah, the book of the Hebrew Bible that had the greatest influence on Jesus. We have repeatedly seen that Jesus used the book of Isaiah to give meaning to his accomplishments as a popular prophet, preacher and miracle-worker. We have observed that his preaching about the 'kingdom' of God was inspired by the proclamation of God as king by the 'messenger' in the prophecy of Isaiah. In addition, we saw that the Q source contained a question from John the Baptist about whether Jesus was 'the one who is to come' along with Jesus' answer, which brings together various quotations from Isaiah about healing and restoration in a manner which closely resembles a text from the Dead Sea Scrolls, *Messianic Apocalypse* (4Q521; Mt. 11.4-6; Lk. 7.22-23). To these we may also add Jesus' declaration of

God's forgiveness (Mk 2.5), a theme that is likewise associated with healing in the book of Isaiah, as well as the blessing he pronounces over the poor, which recalls Isaiah's 'good news to the oppressed' (Isa. 61.1): 'Blessed are you who are poor, for yours is the kingdom of God' (Lk. 6.20; cf. Mt. 5.3).

Similarly, when Jesus encountered opposition, he turned to the passages he had heard read aloud from the book of Isaiah to discern a meaning in his opponents' actions. When the inhabitants of the villages and towns of his youth would not join him in spite of his miracles, Jesus cursed them in terms inspired by Isa. 14.13-15 (Mt. 11.20-24; Lk. 10.13-15). That not everyone grasped the meaning of his parables, Jesus explained with reference to Isaiah's much earlier commission from God to 'make dull' the heart of the people of Israel (Mk 4.11; cf. Isa. 6.9-10). Jesus' parable of the tenants is a kind of pastiche of Isaiah's 'song of the vineyard'; the parable alludes to the continued persecution and killing of God's prophets by the establishment and suggests that the same fate will likely befall Jesus (Mk 12.1-9; cf. Isa. 5.1-7).

Jesus would certainly have presumed, as did all other Jews at the time, that this lengthy book had been written in its entirety by the prophet Isaiah, son of Amoz, who was active in the ancient Southern Kingdom of Judah in the latter half of the eighth century BCE. Modern biblical scholarship has shown that the book was in fact composed in different stages over a period of several hundred years. One section of the book contains a series of references to a figure who described, in God's voice, as 'my servant' and 'my chosen':

> Here is my servant, whom I uphold,
> my chosen, in whom my soul delights;
> I have put my spirit upon him;
> he will bring forth justice to the nations.
>
> Isa. 42.1

Upon the Servant rests the Spirit of God. Not only will the Servant gather the scattered tribes of Israel once more; he will also be 'a light to the nations' (Isa. 49.6). Among the passages about this figure, the one which tells of the suffering of the Servant has come to be the most widely known (Isa. 52.13–53.12), as it has been regarded by Christians as an extremely detailed prediction of the innocent suffering of Jesus and of his atoning death. The Servant is not an individual but a symbol for the people collectively, more or less like the human-like figure in the book of Daniel (see Isa. 44.1-2, 21; 49.3). We also encounter in Isaiah an anonymous prophet, who speaks in the final part of the book: 'The spirit of the Lord God is upon me, because the Lord has anointed me; he has sent me to bring good news to the oppressed' (Isa. 61.1). Just like the Servant, this prophet possesses the Spirit of God, and his commission to bring good news in turn recalls 'the messenger' who cries out 'Your God reigns' when the people return to Jerusalem (Isa.

52.7). The Servant and the messenger started out as metaphors, but with time the poetry of Isaiah, like the visions of Daniel, came to be interpreted in an increasingly concrete and literal way. Jesus was not alone in fusing the Servant, the prophet and the messenger into a single prophetic messiah figure.

Jewish biblical interpretation at the turn of the Common Era was capable of taking liberties to an extent that might seem surprising. Almost anything could be read into the Hebrew Bible, even if it was seemingly the exact opposite of the holy texts' original meaning. An extremely striking example of this can be seen in in the so-called Isaiah Targum, dating from around 70–135 CE. The Servant is repeatedly identified in this work as 'the Messiah', but the passage about the Servant's suffering (in the Hebrew Bible) is completely altered, so much so that the messianic Servant is presented as a capable and triumphant king, priest and prophet. The notion that the Messiah would endure suffering and die a painful and humiliating death is not at all attested in early Jewish sources; rather, it is a Christian idea that emerged to give meaning to Jesus' death.

Two texts from the Dead Sea Scrolls, encountered earlier, use motifs drawn from the book of Isaiah to express ideas about a prophetic messiah. The first text, known as *Melchizedek* (11QMelch), features a figure called 'the anointed one of the spirit', referring to the prophet from Isa. 61.1, who is at the same time identified here with the messenger of 52.7. This prophetic messiah, according to the *Melchizedek* text, will make the people 'return . . . and he will proclaim to them an emancipation to release them [from the burden of] all their sins'. The second text is the *Messianic Apocalypse* (4Q521). The preserved text is incomplete but the most significant fragment begins with a reference to God's 'anointed'. Through this messiah figure God will 'heal the badly wounded, and will make the dead live, he will proclaim good news to the poor'. Once again we see this same verse, Isa. 61.1, being interpreted as a statement about a future prophetic messiah. In the *Messianic Apocalypse*, the description of the prophet as herald is combined with allusions to verses from other parts of Isaiah and from the Psalter that speak of healing and restoration. What is not entirely clear is whether the scribe who composed this text hoped for a messiah who would eradicate sickness, death, hunger and poverty in the literal sense. Such language may be meant to be taken figuratively. But if we consider that by the turn of the Common Era the mystical symbolic language of Daniel tended to be interpreted concretely, then this particular reinterpretation of the book of Isaiah should most likely be understood literally as well. At God's bidding the messianic prophet would perform spectacular miracles.

There are many indications that the ideas expressed in the *Messianic Apocalypse* text about the prophetic messiah's miracle-working were also known outside Qumran. If so, then Jesus' answer to the Baptist's question about whether he was the Messiah could be a way of confirming John's speculation indirectly. But as with Jesus' predictions regarding the Son of Man, there is something vague and ambiguous about his answer to John the Baptist. His response is not 'Yes, I am', but rather 'Go and tell John what you hear and see: the blind receive their sight, the lame walk, the lepers are cleansed, the deaf hear, the dead are raised, and the poor have good news brought to them'. Given the tremendous respect and reverence Jesus had for John the Baptist, it is perhaps not surprising that he sends the question back, as it were, to the master in prison. Jesus does indeed appear to have held that his miracles signified that he might be the promised messianic prophet, but he himself avoided taking a definite position on the issue. Jesus left the question of his messianic identity to others – ultimately it was up to God to determine.

The Son of David

A lot of things start to make sense once we recognize that the messianic role that Jesus mainly had in view was a prophetic one, yet one piece of the puzzle is still missing. After all, Jesus was executed as 'King of the Jews' (Mk 15.26). What this is likely to mean is that the Roman authorities perceived him not simply as a dangerous popular prophet in the same vein as Theudas and 'the Egyptian'; Pilate must also have seen in Jesus a delusional pretender to the throne who was claiming to be a royal messiah.

Sometime in the late 50s CE Paul wrote his canonical letter to the Christ-believing Gentiles in Rome. In his introduction, which may be based on an existing, older confession of faith, Paul writes that Jesus 'was descended from David according to the flesh and was declared to be Son of God with power' (Rom. 1.3-4). A modern reader, especially one familiar with the Christian teachings of the fifth century about the 'two natures of Christ', might be tempted to detect a major contrast, here, between Jesus' Davidic descent, on the one hand, and his status as Son of God, on the other. 'Son of David' signifies that Jesus was considered to come from the line of David and as such was a possible candidate for heir to the throne. 'Son of God', by contrast, increasingly came to be understood within the development of Christian doctrine as an expression of Jesus' unique relationship with God and of his being himself divine. Indeed, he even came to be regarded as 'true God from true God, begotten, not made, of one being with the Father', to quote the confession of faith most widely used among Christians today. Initially, however, the terms 'Son of David' and 'Son of God' were nearly synonymous, both designating the specially chosen, but altogether human, ruler of Israel.

David and his son Solomon after him reigned over the united kingdom of Israel in a remote golden age (tenth century BCE). After this kingdom was divided in two, descendants of David continued to reign over the so-called Southern Kingdom up until the fall of Jerusalem in the 580s BCE and accompanying deportation of the inhabitants to Babylon. The monarchy was not restored until after the Maccabean revolt in the 160s BCE, and the house that assumed power lacked any familial connections to King David. There must have been numerous families that had stronger or weaker grounds for regarding themselves as being descended from the venerable father of the nation. That Jesus' relations numbered among those with claims to Davidic descent is entirely possible. Paul was not the only one who believed that Jesus belonged to the line of David; the authors of Matthew and Luke also suppose that Jesus' genealogy can be traced back to David. For this reason the anonymous author of the Letter to the Hebrews, a work which goes to great lengths to present Jesus as a heavenly high priest, is forced to acknowledge that Jesus definitely did not belong to the priestly tribe, the Levites: 'it is evident that our Lord was descended from Judah' (Heb. 7.14), that is, the tribe from which David also came. Thus we have several, independent sources which together provide credible information that from very early on, very likely during his own lifetime even, Jesus was considered to be descended from David and hence was potentially a 'Son of David'.

The Synoptic Gospels report cases of Jesus being called 'Son of David' by others. In Mark and Luke we find the episode of Bartimaeus the blind beggar, who cries 'Son of David, have mercy on me!' (Mk 10.47-48; Lk. 18.38-39), and in Matthew the term is used on several occasions in connection with Jesus' healings and exorcisms (Mt. 12.23; 15.22; 20.30-31). Only once does Jesus refer to himself as 'Son of David', in comments from Mark's Gospel that are rather hard to interpret:

> While Jesus was teaching in the temple, he said, 'How can the scribes say that the Messiah is the son of David? David himself, by the Holy Spirit, declared, "The Lord said to my Lord, 'Sit at my right hand, until I put your enemies under your feet."' David himself calls him Lord; so how can he be his son?'
>
> Mk 12.35-37

This argument starts from the premise that the standard understanding among 'the scribes' is that the Messiah will be a son of David. Against this Jesus sets his own interpretation of Ps. 110, which, according to the traditional way of understanding the superscript (110.1), was composed by David and which Jesus assumes is about the Messiah. But if David calls the Messiah 'my Lord', then surely the Messiah must be superior to David, since in the thinking of the time it would have been unimaginable for a father to show such great respect towards his son. Does this mean that Jesus questioned the common notion that the Messiah was a son of David? Did he mean that 'Son of David' was an inadequate, albeit accurate, description of the Messiah? Or was he perhaps uncertain what to think on this issue as well?

Considering the great respect that Jesus evidently showed for the Holy Scriptures, it is unlikely that he would have questioned the notion that the

Messiah would be a descendant of David. To be sure, several of the scriptural passages that were later taken to prophesy a royal messiah did not, to begin with, speak of a future messianic figure; rather they were expressions of the belief that David's dynasty would never end (e.g. 2 Kgs 7.11-16). When Jerusalem fell in 586 BCE, the ideological foundations of the Israelite monarchy were also in ruins. The 'eternal' rule of the line of David came to an abrupt end. Many of those exiled in the sixth century clung to prophecies that promised that the House of David would be established anew. The prophet Jeremiah, for instance, beheld a future in which God would cause the people to return to Jerusalem, where they would once more live under an heir to the throne of David (Jer. 33.14-17). Jeremiah was certainly proved right about Jerusalem and its temple being rebuilt, but the Davidic dynasty did not return.

To pious Jews, however, it was unthinkable that God would fail to keep his promises. Sooner or later a son of David would once more reign over the people. Earlier, in Chapter 2, we referred to the collection of texts known as the *Psalms of Solomon*, which took shape in the first century BCE, possibly in Pharisaic circles. In the two psalms that conclude the collection the hope for the coming of an anointed king is expressed more clearly than anywhere else in ancient Jewish literature (*Pss. Sol.* 17–18). The seventeenth of the psalms opens with a dismal description of the land: foreign powers rule over it, large numbers of Israelites are driven into exile and of those Jews who remain in the land many are 'sinners' who do not live by the law. There is hope that God will send a king, the 'Lord Messiah' (*Pss. Sol.* 17.32), who will banish the intruders by force and restore the people:

> Look, O Lord, and raise up for them their king, a son of David, to rule over your servant Israel in the time that you know, O God. Undergird him with the strength to destroy the unrighteous rulers, to purge Jerusalem from the Gentiles who trample her down to destruction.
>
> *Pss. Sol.* 17.21-22

The Messiah will lead the lost tribes back to the land – the tribes of the old Northern Kingdom, who were thought to be living scattered among the nations – and reign over them as a just and holy king.

The Dead Sea Scrolls paint a similar picture. Referring to the Hebrew Bible, several texts prophesy that the Davidic dynasty will be restored and that Israel will become a politically important power, e.g. *Florilegium* (4Q174); *Commentary on Genesis A* col. 5 (4Q252). In the *Apocryphon of Daniel* text (4Q246), mentioned in Chapter 2, it is said of the future king that 'He will be called the Son of God, they will call him the son of the Most High'. The text goes on to describe how under the leadership of this king the people will live righteously and justly and will subdue all other nations and kingdoms. Here, too, we find the hope expressed that the Messiah will achieve world domination, to reflect God's universal power.

We know that at times men from the general population took on the role of a royal messiah, particularly in times of unrest when there was instability of political power. In the vacuum that followed the death of the harsh client-king Herod the Great in 4 BCE, mobs revolted across the land and proclaimed various leaders their 'kings', as Josephus relates (*Ant.* 17.271-285). Of particular interest is the report of Athronges, 'a shepherd completely unknown to everybody although he was remarkable for his great stature and feats of strength'. In spite of Josephus's disdain for this rustic, who was entirely lacking in good breeding or ancestry, we get the impression that Athronges was reputed to be a new David. He wore a royal diadem and, with the help of his brothers, marshalled an army which succeeded for quite some time in doing battle with the forces of both the emperor and Herod in the area around Jerusalem.

Similar scenes played out during the Jewish war with Rome at the end of the 60s CE. After the Jewish resistance split up into various factions, Simon bar Giora took up the role of king in Jerusalem. He had started out as a rebel leader in Galilee and later consolidated his positions in a violent offensive across the entire land. Simon's supporters, who offered him the allegiance due to a king, were attracted by his proclamation of 'liberty for slaves and rewards for the free' (*War* 4.508) – a message with a clear messianic resonance (cf. Isa. 61.1, 6; Lk. 4.18-19). He occupied, among others, the ancient city of Hebron, in the present-day West Bank, where David was twice anointed as king, first over the tribes of Judah and later over the tribes of northern Israel (2 Sam. 2.4; 5.1-3). Afterwards Simon, like King David (5.6-7), marched to Jerusalem to seize power. For the last year of the war Simon wielded absolute power in Jerusalem. When Roman forces breached the city after a long siege and destroyed the temple, he dressed himself in royal purple and silently gave himself up to the conquerors.

So what about Jesus? Was he, too, a messianic candidate in the mould of Athronges and Simon bar Giora? As we have seen, he seems to have been primarily influenced by conceptions of a prophetic messiah. But in the ancient Jewish texts the different categories overlap and Jesus may have drawn inspiration from several of them. In the narratives of Jesus' last days in Jerusalem, to which we will turn in the next chapter, there are clear indications that Jesus may have begun to accept the role of a messianic king.

Summary

We cannot know for certain what Jesus' thoughts about his own identity were – in fact, we cannot even be certain that he ever formed a clear idea on the matter. There are, however, several factors that point to the conclusion that at the very least he did not dismiss the possibility that he was Israel's Messiah.

Jesus did speak about the Son of Man, an angel-like figure who he thought had been prophesied by Daniel and who in the future would come with the clouds to execute judgement on God's behalf and gather the elect into the fully realized kingdom of God. It is most likely that he equated the Son of Man with the Messiah; the evidence suggests that Jesus pictured himself in this future role, although it is quite possible that he considered it presumptuous to make unequivocal claims to that effect. A related, yet distinct concept that Jesus' ministry could have brought to mind was that of the prophetic Messiah, an idea based primarily on the book of Isaiah and developed in a small number of early Jewish texts. As a healer and proclaimer of prophetic messages, Jesus seemed to some of his contemporaries to match their expectations of one 'anointed of the spirit', and his use of Isaiah's predictions about the end time in answer to the Baptist's question about whether he was the Messiah indicates that he was favourably inclined towards such speculation.

What about Jesus' identity as 'Son of David', the royal Messiah? Was this formed and shaped during the very last days of his life? All four Gospels tell of Jesus riding into Jerusalem and being hailed by the crowds in a manner that recalls the formal entry of a king. Also present in all four is the credible report about the inscription that stated that Jesus was executed because he claimed to be 'the King of the Jews'. What did happen in that final week?

Bibliography

Bird, M. F. (2009), *Are You the One Who Is to Come? The Historical Jesus and the Messianic Question*, Grand Rapids: Baker Academic.

Casey, M. (2009), *The Solution to the 'Son of Man' Problem*, London: T&T Clark.

Collins, A. Y. and J. J. Collins (2008), *King and Messiah as Son of God: Divine, Human, and Angelic Messianic Figures in Biblical and Related Literature*, Grand Rapids: Eerdmans.

Hägerland, T. (2016), 'Jesus and the Scriptures: Problems of Authentication and Interpretation', in T. Hägerland (ed.), *Jesus and the Scriptures: Problems, Passages and Patterns*, 3–30, London: Bloomsbury T&T Clark.

Le Donne, A. (2009), *The Historiographical Jesus: Memory, Typology, and the Son of David*, Waco: Baylor University Press.

Vermes, G. (1973), *Jesus the Jew: A Historian's Reading of the Gospels*, London: Collins.

Wrede, W. (1971), *The Messianic Secret*, Cambridge: Clarke. (German original published in 1901.)

10

The final week

Jesus' death on the cross is the one episode that all scholars of the historical Jesus agree really did happen. How can they be so sure in this case when their opinions are so divided on the historicity of so many other Gospel narratives? Well, the answer is quite simply that the early Christ-believers would never have invented a story in which their master met so horrible an end. Today, because the cross is the Christian symbol par excellence, we may find it hard to fully grasp how utterly devastating the first disciples would have found their leader's death on a cross. For one thing, crucifixion represented the worst kind of torture. For another, this particular punishment was typically reserved for individuals of the lowest social standing, such as slaves who had committed crimes or rebels who stood up against Roman rule. The condemned were often hung near the city gate so that everyone might behold their naked bodies and their appalling suffering. It was, in other words, an extremely shameful method of execution. Below we shall see what Jesus had done to receive this punishment.

The last week of Jesus' life is described in great detail in the four Gospels. In terms of length, the narratives about the last days in Jerusalem found in Mark, the earliest Gospel, make up approximately a third of the entire work. Thus, in comparison to Roman biographies, an unusually large proportion of the narrative centres on the protagonist's death and the events surrounding it. To Roman readers, this intense focus on Jesus' tragic death must have seemed rather odd. Why do the authors put so much emphasis on Jesus' final days? There are a number of explanations. The main reason is probably that the early followers of Jesus had to struggle to understand why their leader was put to death. They were not prepared for such an ignoble end; instead of death and dishonour they had been expecting victory and triumph. Despite this, some among them held on to their belief that Jesus was God's chosen agent, and so, little by little, they came to the conclusion that his death must have been part of God's plan. They went back to the scriptures to see if they could shed light on Jesus' death. Luke's resurrection narrative, if we read between the lines, depicts precisely this process. Luke tells of how two disciples were walking on the road to Emmaus when Jesus revealed himself to them. Not realizing who he is, the disciples instead carry on a conversation about the death of Jesus with Jesus himself, who is pretending not to know what happened. Full of sorrow (Lk. 24.17), they explain: 'Our chief priests and leaders handed him over to be condemned to death and crucified him. But we had hoped that he was the one to set Israel free' (Lk. 24.20-21). Clearly, the first disciples were not at all prepared for Jesus' death. The disciples then bring up the rumours of the empty tomb. At this point Luke puts the following words in the mouth of the risen Jesus: '"Oh, how foolish you are, and how slow of heart to believe all that the prophets have declared! Was it not necessary that the Messiah should suffer these things and then enter into his glory?" Then beginning with Moses and all the prophets, he interpreted to them the things about himself in all the scriptures' (Lk. 24.25-27). That is to say, Luke explains to his readers that the Messiah's death was part of God's plan and is foretold in books of Moses and the prophetic writings. One can see this, Luke claims, if only one reads the scriptures properly, as he likewise stresses in his other work, the Acts of the Apostles (Acts 8.30-35; 10.43; 17.2-3). Given that Luke makes the same point again and again, we get the impression that the idea that the Messiah had to die was not an easy sell.

In that final week Jesus performed two actions in public that were charged with symbolism: he rode into Jerusalem on a donkey and he attacked the sellers, buyers and money-changers at the temple. The last supper, too, was of great significance for the disciples. We shall focus on these memorable incidents and endeavour to understand their meaning. We shall also examine the accounts of the proceedings of the trial and the death itself. As we do this it is important that we bear in mind the circumstances under which these works were produced. The Gospels were written at a time when a number of Christ-believing congregations (consisting of a mix of both Jewish and gentile members) had come into conflict with (other) Jewish groups, something we shall consider in the next chapter. This conflict has had an effect on the narratives concerning the legal proceedings. It should also be remembered that the Gospels were written within the Roman Empire by Christ-believers who worshipped a man found guilty of seditious activities against Rome and executed for his crimes; he was, from a Roman perspective, a rebel. These Christ-believers found themselves in a very difficult situation. The authors had to choose their words carefully when retelling what did actually happen. They obviously had to show that Jesus was innocent; yet they also had to account for why he was executed. They opted to blame the Jewish priests and the Jewish people while minimizing the responsibility of the prefect. Consequently, an anti-Jewish tendency comes across in the accounts.

Passover

Passover was the largest of the three annual pilgrimage festivals (Deut. 16.16). Like so many other Jewish pilgrims from all over the Roman Empire, Jesus journeyed to Jerusalem with his supporters to celebrate Passover. During the holiday Jerusalem's population exploded as pilgrims filled the city. It was a politically unsettled time and Pilate, the prefect, left his ordinary residence on the coast at Caesarea and travelled to Jerusalem to oversee security. It was not just the large crowds that made him uneasy; the theme of the festival was troubling as well. After all, the Jews were recalling with jubilation how God had once liberated them from oppression by a foreign power, when the people escaped from Egypt and were led by Moses through the wilderness. This combination of a festival to freedom and the large crowds made for an explosive situation. Not only Jerusalem but also the surrounding villages swelled with pilgrims. Thus we see Jesus' group staying in the village of Bethany outside Jerusalem (Mk 11.12). While many visitors found lodgings at inns or in people's homes in the city, others brought their own tents and stayed in large encampments outside the city walls (Ant. 17.217).

Walking from Galilee to Jerusalem took about three days by the quickest route, through Samaria. Another, longer route involved following the River Jordan to Jericho, instead, and then taking the long road up to Jerusalem. That way one could avoid passing through Samaria, which could be dangerous because of the prevailing hostility between Samaritans and Jews. For safety people travelled in large groups (cf. Lk. 2.41-45). It is easy to imagine that a general atmosphere of joyous celebration accompanied the pilgrims on their journey towards Jerusalem. It was a chance for them to enjoy a break from their everyday toils, to see new surroundings and to take part in special ceremonies at the temple. Many of them probably looked forward to indulging in good food and drink as well, and especially meat, something that ordinary people rarely ate, of course.

The party that came with Jesus from Galilee was made up of both men and women. Mark's account makes it very clear that the group was greater than just the Twelve and that many women came, too (Mk 15.40-41). The pilgrims arrived a few days before Passover to purify themselves ahead of the paschal meal itself, since everyone who partook of it was supposed to be ritually pure. Many of them were unclean from having touched a corpse or from having been in close proximity to one, and this necessitated several days of purification rituals involving being sprinkled with special water that was kept at the temple (Num. 19.11-22). Jesus and his band likewise came to Jerusalem to be cleansed ahead of the holiday. John, although unlikely to have any precise information about when Jesus reached Jerusalem, does know what was customary, and he claims that Jesus got to Bethany, just outside Jerusalem, six days before Passover (Jn 12.1; cf. War 6.290).

The entry into Jerusalem

As we saw earlier (see ch. 1), Jesus had probably been to Jerusalem many times before, among other things to celebrate Passover. This hypothesis is supported by the fact that Jesus' group had contacts in the area who helped to organize their visit: they were able to borrow a donkey, to stay in people's homes in Bethany and to arrange a meal at a house in the city. Yet even from the start this Passover seemed different. Both John (Jn 12.12-19) and the Synoptic Gospels portray Jesus' entry into Jerusalem as a highly symbolic gesture. Jesus rides on a donkey as the people sing 'Hosanna . . .' from the Psalms (Ps. 118.25) and lay branches on the road before him. In so doing Jesus fulfils the prophecy of Zechariah 9.9 about the coming of a prince of peace, according to Matthew (Mt. 21.4-5):

> This took place to fulfil what had been spoken through the prophet,
>   saying,
> Tell the daughter of Zion,
> Look, your king is coming to you,
> humble, and mounted on a donkey,
> and on a colt, the foal of a donkey.

Of course, we cannot know for sure whether this narrative reflects a genuine historical episode or whether it arose later, under the influence of the prophecy, but it does appear in both John and the Synoptics. John's account differs at various points from the Synoptics'; for instance, he associates Bethany not with 'Simon the leper' (cf. Mk 14.3; Mt. 26.6), but with Lazarus, Mary and Martha, friends of Jesus' (Jn 12). The differences in the accounts suggest that John had access to a different, independent tradition, which strengthens the assumption that this memorable entry did in fact take place. Another reason why the tradition concerning the entry probably does reflect a real occurrence is that it fits well with what happened later, specifically, with the fact that Jesus was executed. If Jesus was hailed as a king on entering the city, it would go some way towards explaining why he was subsequently executed precisely for having royal pretensions.

The story of the ceremonious entry reflects the joyful mood of the band of pilgrims that accompanied Jesus, which enthusiastically proclaimed him king. It shows how unprepared they were for what was about to happen, as Mark reveals when he describes the arrest: 'All of them deserted him and fled' (Mk 14.50). Who took part in this acclamation of Jesus? Mark tells us that 'many people' were acclaiming Jesus (Mk 11.8), while Matthew gives the impression that a large group of pilgrims was involved: 'The crowds that went ahead of him and that followed were shouting, "Hosanna . . ."' (Mt. 21.9). Luke, for his part, plays down the incident in stating that the disciples were the ones who 'began to praise God' in this way (Lk. 19.37). Finally, according to John, Jesus was met by a multitude that came out of the city to pay homage (Jn 12.12-13). The most plausible supposition is that this incident primarily involved the band that had accompanied Jesus. Had Jesus been hailed as king by a great multitude, he would scarcely have made it into the city before being arrested. The supporters, according to the Synoptics and John, were singing from Ps. 118: 'Blessed is the one who comes in the name of the Lord' (Ps. 118.26). Mark inserts an extra line: 'Blessed is the coming kingdom of our ancestor David! Hosanna in the highest heaven!' (Mk 11.9-10). Psalm 118 is one of the so-called Hallel Psalms (Ps. 113–118), which were sung by pilgrims on the way to Jerusalem. Again, there is therefore nothing strange about the crowd who were with Jesus singing Ps. 118 and, presumably, other Hallel Psalms, too. Still, the words acquired new meaning among his followers in that they were hailing Jesus specifically as 'the one who comes in the name of the Lord' and believed that deliverance was coming.

Riding a donkey may not seem very regal to us today. Wouldn't a horse have been more fitting for a king? Even so, in Zechariah's prophecy the perfect king does, as we have seen, ride on a donkey, and when David's son Solomon was to be anointed king after his father, he rode on a mule (1 Kg. 1.32-40, 44). There is no episode in the Hebrew Bible in which a king rides a horse. But the royal symbolism in Jesus' actions was obvious to those who acclaimed him. When Jesus' supporters laid cloaks and leafy branches in his path, they were hailing him as king. According to John, they laid palm fronds (Jn 12.13) – emblems of nationalism (1 Macc. 4.36; 13.51; 2 Macc. 10.7) and of freedom – which expressed their hope for a new era. As we have seen, hopes were widespread that God would appoint a messiah or saviour figure of some kind and would deliver his people and restore Israel. But there was also great variety when it came to conceptions of what this saviour would be like. One common expectation was that a new king, in the spirit of David, would arise. Earlier we observed that that role was not one that Jesus took on and that Jesus appears to have avoided calling himself the Messiah. Here, however, we see him acting as a new king, which raises many questions. Had Jesus ultimately reached the conclusion that he was the Messiah? Did he announce that the eschatological transformation would take place now? This symbolic act indicates that the royal-messiah role was not far from Jesus' mind, even though he did not limit himself solely to the expectations commonly attached to this figure. In contrast to other messianic pretenders, Jesus was not a proponent of armed revolt; on the contrary, all such things should be left to God. God would be the one to create the kingdom, by punishing sinners and exalting his faithful. Through his sign-act Jesus was expressing a belief that the kingdom of God was about to manifest itself. Paula Fredriksen convincingly argues that the backdrop to the dramatic events in the last week is found in Jesus' and his followers' expectations of the imminent arrival of the kingdom of God (Fredriksen 1999: 251–2). Those enthusiastic songs of salutation indicate that his followers were convinced that God was going to intervene now, at this very Passover, in world history to create his kingdom. They were certain that all the promises about the end times would imminently be fulfilled through his agent, the Messiah. The hopes tied up with that last Passover must derive from Jesus. From the outset, the core of his message had been the approaching kingdom. In assuming the role of a messianic king, Jesus spurred his eager supporters on. The time was now; Jesus was about to assume his God-given role as God's regent on earth. At that point, the role of king did fit.

The attack in the sanctuary

Mark's account of the grand entry into Jerusalem ends in something of an anticlimax with Jesus behaving almost like a tourist visiting the city: 'Then he entered Jerusalem and went into the temple; and when he had looked around at everything, as it was already late, he went out to Bethany with the twelve' (Mk 11.11). Exactly what happened next is very unclear, but at some point before the feast of Passover Jesus acted violently within the sanctuary. The authenticity of this incident is strengthened by the fact that both the Synoptics and John report it, even if John does place the event at the beginning of Jesus' public life (Jn 2.13-22). Scholars favour Mark's timeline, for one thing because Jesus' actions at the temple complex, just like the sensational entry into the city, would fit very well as one of the reasons he was arrested. Above all, it is very hard to explain why this tradition would have arisen at all if it is not based on a real event. Jesus' actions in the temple is therefore a given topic in the list of 'key events in the life of the historical Jesus' in a book by that title (Bock and Webb 2010). In addition, had the incident been invented at a later point, possibly after the temple was destroyed, we would have expected the meaning of the episode to be more readily apparent, which Adela Collins points out (Collins 2001). But in its current form, the intention behind Jesus' actions is not wholly clear. Mark offers a concise account of what happened:

> Then they came to Jerusalem. And he entered the temple and began to drive out those who were selling and those who were buying in the temple, and he overturned the tables of the money-changers and the seats of those who sold doves; and he would not allow anyone to carry anything through the temple. He was teaching and saying, 'Is it not written, "My house shall be called a house of prayer for all the nations"? But you have made it a den of robbers.'
>
> Mk 11.15-17

Was the action an attempt to 'cleanse' the temple as the subtitles to the passage in modern Bibles often suggest (cf. NRSV: 'the cleansing of the temple')? In this line of interpretation, Jesus is supposed to have protested against different aspects of the sacrificial cult, such as the focus on animal sacrifices, its mediation of atonement, notions of purity or the alleged priestly corruption. In other words, he aimed at reforming the worship in the sanctuary, to cleanse it from abuses. But such a motive does not fit well with Jesus' previous sayings since he does not voice criticism of the temple cult per se elsewhere. In fact, we see quite the opposite in, for instance,

Mt. 5.23, where Jesus expresses the importance of having a clear conscience 'when you are offering your gift at the altar', and in Mk 1.44, when Jesus sternly warns a recently cured 'leper' to make the offering that Moses prescribed for his cleansing. The scriptural passages that Jesus quotes in Mark – 'My house shall be called a house of prayer for all the nations' and the description of the temple as 'a den of robbers' – are taken from Isaiah (56.7) and Jeremiah (7.11). In John's version, instead Jesus says, 'Take these things out of here! Stop making my Father's house a market-place!' (Jn 2.16), which is an allusion to Zechariah 14.21. These allusions most likely reflect the ways in which some early Christ-believers interpreted the episode rather than Jesus' authentic words. For one thing, it does not seem that the historical Jesus was especially eager for 'all the nations' – that is, the gentiles – to come and pray at the temple, which is, of course, what the verse from Isaiah anticipates. Instead, when a Syrophoenician woman approaches Jesus about her demon-possessed daughter, he likens gentiles to dogs, and she has to persuade him to cure her daughter, as he is reluctant given that she is not Jewish (Mk 7.24-30). Gentile involvement did, however, became very important in the later church, as we shall see in the final chapter, and the quote from Isaiah fits well with that context. In interpreting the incident, then, we should be guided by Jesus' actions, not the words attributed to him.

Was Jesus taking a stand against commerce per se? Buying and selling traditionally formed part of temple business and was especially aimed at pilgrims, since the sacrificial animals these required naturally had to be bought at their destination rather than being brought with them from home. The money-changers and the sellers were also necessary for the smooth running of the whole operation. Jesus had been to the temple a number of times before and the money-changers, sellers and buyers were around then, too. It would be strange if he were protesting against practices that he had been exposed to for a long time. At the same time, Jesus was clearly angry at something. But it may be a mistake to try to pin-point the object of his temper more specifically, which scholars often do. For example, Craig Evans (1997) argues that Jesus protested the alleged corruption by priests, Hans Dieter Betz (1997) highlights the commercialism while Adela Collins (2001) points to the use of Tyrian shekels which have an image of the god Melqart on them, among other things. Nevertheless, it is possible that Jesus protested more widely against a perceived general corruption and defilement, which sprung from his vision of the future. According to Sanders his actions can be understood as a symbolic act, one signalling the end times and the coming of God's kingdom (Sanders 1993: 254–62).

How can we know if Jesus' actions were a sign-act, and if he wasn't just taking a swing at a handful of individuals for some unknown reason? In this context, it is important to remember that prophets frequently conveyed their message both by means of words and of actions. The prophets of the Hebrew Bible sometimes used striking sign-acts that illustrated their message in order to reinforce their rhetorical impact. When Jeremiah predicted the conquest of Judah by the Babylonians and the destruction of Jerusalem he smashed an earthenware jug on the ground (Jer. 19.10). One of the more bizarre sign-acts was Isaiah's walking naked for three years (!) to illustrate the coming captivity that would afflict the nations (Isa. 20.1-6). Josephus recounts that the Essene prophet Menahem predicted, while Herod was still a boy, that he would become king of the Jews. Menahem symbolically struck Herod several times to signify the punishment God would ultimately mete out to him (*Ant.* 15.374). Although the story is likely legendary it demonstrates that people were quite familiar with prophetic sign-acts as a phenomenon in the time of Jesus. Therefore they would have been able to interpret Jesus' actions. The interpretation that immediately suggests itself is that Jesus' aggressive actions symbolized the destruction of the temple (Sanders 1993). This understanding fits well with the traditions about Jesus warning of the destruction of the temple in his preaching (Mk 13.1). Although it is reasonable to wonder whether the prediction was attributed to Jesus at a later time – after the temple had been destroyed – there are reasons to think that it originated with Jesus after all. For one thing, he was not unique in anticipating the destruction of the temple; so did also Jesus son of Ananias that we've already mentioned (ch. 5). Furthermore, had Mark invented the saying it would likely had been more accurate; Jesus predicts 'Not one stone will be left here upon another; all will be thrown down' (Mk 13.1). But the temple was actually burnt down. Moreover, a message about the destruction of the temple also fits well with the accusations that he threatened to destroy the temple himself, which is an indication that the fall of the temple was part of his vision of the end times (Mk 14.57-58; 15.29; Jn 2.18-22; so Sanders 1985:71-6). If so, he probably also anticipated a new temple, which was a fairly standard feature of the apocalyptic conceptual universe. In a vision report, Ezekiel offers a detailed description of a future Jerusalem and a new temple where the 'glory of the Lord' would dwell (40–48), which formed the basis of hopes for a new, perfect temple. The Temple Scroll from Qumran also sets out precise plans for an ideal temple and lays down stringent purity rules to be followed throughout Jerusalem by all. Similarly, the reconstructed text of Florilegium (4Q174 frag. 1–2 at 2-3) concerns a temple that is to be built by God: 'This is the house which [he will build] for [him] in the latter days, as it is written in the book of [Moses, "The sanctuary,] O Yahweh, which your hands have fashioned"' (cf. *1 En.* 90.28-36; *T. Benj.* 9.2; *Jub.* 1.15-18). Similar utopian hopes probably lie behind the charge levelled against Jesus in Mk 14.58: 'I will destroy this temple that is made with hands, and in three days I will build another, not made with hands.' In both Mark and John (Jn 2.18-22), Jesus' prophecies concerning a future temple have been reinterpreted in light of traditions about his resurrection, such that Jesus is instead seen to be foretelling his own future resurrection.

It is hard not to see Jesus' aggressive actions as an expression of judgement as well. If God was to destroy the temple, then presumably there ought to be a reason for it. We saw earlier that the book of Daniel played an important role in Jesus' understanding of God's plan for the world and of his own role in the end times (ch. 9). The same holds for his view of the temple. The idea that the temple would be desecrated at the end of days formed part of apocalyptic beliefs. The temple had been defiled before, in the 160s BCE, by the heinous actions of Antiochus IV Epiphanes; for one thing, he had a pagan sacrificial altar erected there (1 Macc. 1.41-58), an object which the book of Daniel refers to as 'the abomination that desolates' (Dan. 9.27; 11.31; 12.11, in various formulations). In Daniel, as well as in other books such as *Jubilees* (23.21), the *Testament of Levi* (16.1) and parts of *1 Enoch* (89.73), the events of the period under Antiochus IV are interpreted as signs of the end times. The priesthood of the time, who were regarded as accomplices, often come in for harsh criticism. But, as is typical in apocalyptic tradition, these events from the authors' own time are described, using ambiguous language and imagery, as prophecies of the future horrors of the end times. As a result, later generations were able to reinterpret these messages and apply them to their own times, since the end had not yet come. Jesus' view of the temple was likely influenced by ideas of this kind. He was certain that the temple had been desecrated and he warned of the judgement and devastation to come. To put it another way, it did not matter how the priests ran the cult or organized the temple – they were going to fail spectacularly, in Jesus' eyes; it was part of the general collapse that accompanied the end times (Wassén 2016).

From Jesus' prophecy about the 'desolating sacrilege' (Mk 13.14) from Daniel it becomes clear that he expected the temple to be desecrated:

> But when you see the desolating sacrilege set up where it ought not to be (let the reader understand), then those in Judea must flee to the mountains; someone on the housetop must not go down or enter the house to take anything away; someone in the field must not turn back to get a coat. Woe to those who are pregnant and to those who are nursing infants in those days! Pray that it may not be in winter. For in those days there will be suffering, such as has not been from the beginning of the creation that God created until now, no, and never will be.
>
> Mk 13.14-19

Here, Jesus prepares his disciples for the imminent fulfilment of Daniel's prophecy. Scholars usually understand Jesus' message about the 'desolating sacrilege' as a later invention of the Gospel author (e.g. Crossley 2004: 23); the comment 'let the reader understand' is thus an invitation for readers to recognize that the prediction has come true. Scholars point to Caligula's attempt to have a statue of himself erected at the temple in 39/40 CE or to the actions of the general Titus when he entered the holy of holies right before the final destruction of the temple in the year 70 CE. The problem with these interpretations is that they do not line up with Jesus' words particularly well. If the prophecy had been made up by Mark (or someone prior to him), we would expect it to have been tailored to fit events more closely. But instead we see Mark inviting his readers to interpret Jesus' words in such a way that they should be deemed to have been fulfilled. As with other aspects of Jesus' predictions about the end times that never came, this is a case of a prophecy that went unfulfilled (so Pitre 2005: 314-59). His prophecy about the 'desolating sacrilege' can be compared to the coming of the Son of Man (see ch. 9), which everyone was going to behold: 'Truly I tell you, there are some standing here who will not taste death before they see the Son of Man coming in his kingdom' (Mt. 16.28; cf. Mk 14.62). It was a prediction that never materialized.

Why wasn't Jesus arrested then and there?, we might wonder. If the temple guards had witnessed Jesus' violent actions, they would doubtless have arrested him at once. For now, he escaped detection. Mark reports that in the days that followed Jesus continued to preach at the temple, but it seems unlikely that he would have returned and risked drawing attention to himself with such behaviour. Rumour must have spread of his actions and of the enthusiasm of his supporters and their belief that Jesus was the Messiah, and a few days later he was arrested. We shall explore this in further detail below.

The last supper and the arrest in the garden of Gethsemane

Jesus, a security risk

At Passover, with the enormous crowds all jostling in a confined space in Jerusalem, Jesus posed a major risk to security. Josephus writes that festivals were when riots could most easily break out (*War* 1.88). The slightest unrest might be the spark that ignited an enormous powder keg. Senior priests were worried that Jesus and his supporters would cause a riot; they knew from experience that riots always ended in massacres. One massive protest would suffice for Pilate to send soldiers into the crowds. This had happened before, as we mentioned in Chapter 1, after Pilate commandeered funds from the temple treasury to finance an aqueduct into Jerusalem and people turned out in protest. The fact that Jesus was not planning to use violence to bring about the kingdom of God didn't matter: all talk of a coming kingdom of God was political dynamite. Such a message presumed that the current political order, the Roman Empire, was not God's, which indirectly made for scathing criticism of Rome. In other words, Jewish and Roman leaders alike had every reason to put Jesus out of action.

The royal entry into Jerusalem and the actions at the temple reflect an atmosphere of tense anticipation; now was the time when God would intervene in history and establish his kingdom. A judgement was part of the end of days – the time had come for the temple to be destroyed and for judgement to take place. The forces of evil – Satan and his minions and anyone who had turned away from God – would be wiped out once and for all. Soon Jesus would assume his rightful role as God's representative on earth and his disciples would sit on thrones dealing out judgement (Mt. 19.28; cf. Lk 22.30). The vulnerable and the oppressed would be rewarded and the oppressors would be punished (Mt. 25.46), and a paradisiacal existence would ensue (Mt. 13.43). Expectations were high when the Passover festivities commenced. Did the mood change at the last supper? Had the celebratory atmosphere turned into unease? Apparently so.

The last supper

According to the Synoptic Gospels, Jesus and his disciples ate a Passover meal together in the evening (Mk 14.12-17). As we have seen, in Jewish tradition a day ran from sunset to sunset and hence in these accounts Jesus was crucified on the same day, on Passover. Nevertheless, in John's version the last supper took place a day earlier instead, and Jesus was executed on the day of Preparation (Jn 13.1-2; 18.28; 19.14). In consequence Jesus would have been crucified at the time when the lambs were being slaughtered in the sanctuary. Several factors suggest that John's dating is correct. Most importantly, it is hard to imagine that it would have been possible for Jesus to be tried or questioned on the day of Passover itself, as this day counted as a sabbath (Lev. 23.7). Conducting an interrogation must have been considered work and it is unlikely that Jews – especially leading priests and members of the council – would have performed any such work on a holiday. Furthermore, people were busy celebrating Passover with their families – priests and laymen alike – and would hardly have assembled for an interrogation. It is far easier to understand how the proceedings against Jesus were able to go ahead if they took place before the holiday began. Similarly, in Mark 14.2, the chief priests and the scribes say that they should avoid apprehending Jesus during the festival itself. In addition, the main dish at any paschal meal, the lamb, is not mentioned in the accounts of the last supper. It is indeed possible to hypothesize that John, in placing Jesus' death at the time when the lambs were being slaughtered in the temple, was intending to make a theological point (Jn 19.36 alludes to the Passover lamb; cf. 'Lamb of God' in Jn 1.29, 36). Nevertheless, in this case John would rather appear to have developed his theological interpretation on the basis of the information he had access to about the timing.

Who was there that final evening? Mark states that it was just the Twelve present (Mk 14.17), whereas John describes Jesus washing the feet of the 'disciples' (Jn 13.5), a term that can include a group wider than his innermost circle. Jesus had come from Galilee with a large band of people, and this included women, too, as Mark stresses at the time of the crucifixion: 'There were also women looking on from a distance; among them were Mary Magdalene, and Mary the mother of James the younger and of Joses, and Salome. These used to follow him and provided for him when he was in Galilee; and there were many other women who had come up with him to Jerusalem' (Mk 15.40-41). It is hard to imagine them not all dining together as a group. Passover, after all, was a joyous holiday, but this last supper turned sombre.

The wine and the bread occupy a prominent position in accounts of the meal. There was nothing strange about saying blessings and prayers of thanks over bread and wine; such rituals were part of every meal. This meal, however, made a strong impression on those involved, who recalled it as something far out of the ordinary. Jesus most likely declared that this was his last meal before the arrival of the kingdom: 'Truly I tell you, I will never again drink of the fruit of the vine until that day when I drink it new in the kingdom of God' (Mk 14.25). The meal had a symbolic meaning; it pointed towards the final banquet, after the kingdom of God had been established on earth, an image that is familiar from Jesus' earlier preaching (Lk. 13.29-30; cf. Mk 10.35). In partaking of a communal meal, with blessings over the bread and the wine, the group was looking ahead to that future meal in God's kingdom. Given that the kingdom of God did not come as Jesus predicted it would, there is no reason to suppose that later Christ-believers invented this saying. Even so, Jesus' words are ambiguous. When was Jesus to 'drink it new in the kingdom of God'? Was God's great intervention in world history going to happen immediately, before the next meal, or would it take longer? The context offers a clue that Jesus was starting to suspect he wouldn't live through this Passover, something that becomes clear from what else Jesus had to say at the meal.

Jesus' words concerning the bread and the wine are heavily influenced by later interpretation of Jesus' death. They are recorded in four versions (Mk 14.22-25; Mt. 26.26-29; Lk. 22.15-20; 1 Cor. 11.23-26); the wording of Luke resembles that of 1 Corinthians, while the texts of Mark and Matthew are fairly similar to one another. In that Paul has a report of the words of Jesus at the last supper (see ch. 3), we are informed about a tradition that was written down around twenty years after Jesus' death. Of course, even though Paul's version of Jesus' words is the oldest, a lot could have changed in the course of twenty years. Paul is lamenting that the Corinthians celebrate the group's communal meal, which he calls 'the Lord's supper', in an unworthy manner. Some receive no food whilst others get drunk, and Paul offers a reminder of the origins of the meal:

> The Lord Jesus on the night when he was betrayed took a loaf of bread, and when he had given thanks, he broke it and said, 'This is my body that is broken for you. Do this in remembrance of me.' In the same way he took the cup also, after supper, saying, 'This cup is the new covenant in my blood. Do this, as often as you drink it, in remembrance of me.'
>
> 1 Cor. 11.23-25

These verses are an expression of Paul's theology, which views the death of Jesus as a necessary sacrifice; earlier on in the letter he has spoken of Jesus as a slaughtered 'paschal lamb' (1 Cor. 5.7). In his version, Paul links celebration of the Lord's supper with Jesus' final meal and subsequent death, in having Jesus invite those present to eat and drink in remembrance of his sacrificial death. Mark writes:

> While they were eating, he took a loaf of bread, and after blessing it he broke it, gave it to them, and said, 'Take; this is my body.' Then he took a cup, and after giving thanks he gave it to them, and all of them drank from it. He said to them, 'This is my blood of the covenant, which is poured out for many.'
>
> Mk 14.22-24

But do any of these words go back to Jesus? Dunn argues that the accounts reflect 'living oral tradition' based on the celebrations of the Lord's Supper in the early church (Dunn 2003: 229–31). Against this one may note that the earliest sources that describe the celebration, including the early Christian document *Didache* (*c*. 100 CE; *Did*. 9-10) and the church father Justin Martyr (*c*. 100–165 CE; *1 Apol*. 65.3-4; 67.5), lack any evidence that Jesus' words would have been used liturgically (Schröter 2006).

Of course, it is impossible for us to know the exact wording, but it is not unlikely that Jesus spoke of his approaching death in metaphorical language in connection with the bread and the wine, something that may also be seen as a sign-act. He certainly had a suspicion about what was going to happen. It did not take a prophet to recognize that Jesus' provocative actions at the temple might lead to arrest and execution. All that was needed was for someone to inform on him to a senior priest or Roman soldier and he would be taken away. Yet it is hard to imagine that Jesus formed a clear idea of how this new development fitted into God's plan right away. Instead, this talk of establishing a renewed covenant should probably be seen as a token of the efforts of later Christ-believers to understand Jesus' death. There were, however, established notions about how the death of an innocent person could be of benefit to others (2 Macc. 6.18–7.41; Isa. 53), and if Jesus wanted to prepare himself and his disciples for the idea that he had to die, he may have alluded to these. Still, according to Mark, Jesus struggled with the realization that he might soon die, when after dinner, in Gethsemane on the Mount of Olives, he asked if he could be spared. Gone was the triumphant tone he displayed earlier – when he looked forward to assuming the role of God's viceroy who would judge the tribes of Israel together with his disciples (Mt. 19.28; Lk. 22.30):

> 'I am deeply grieved, even to death; remain here, and keep awake.' And going a little farther, he threw himself on the ground and prayed that, if it were possible, the hour might pass from him. He said, 'Abba, Father, for

you all things are possible; remove this cup from me; yet, not what I want, but what you want.'

Mk 14.34-36

Because this narrative does not portray Jesus as a stoical hero who goes to his death willingly, we can assume that it contains a historical core that goes back to Jesus' anguish, even though, in the narrative, he prays in private. The difference is striking when compared, for example, with the martyrdom narratives of a fictional nature in the books of Maccabees, which were in circulation in the time of Jesus (2 Macc. 6.18–7.41). Though Jesus had tried to prepare the disciples for what was about to happen, the shock and panicked behaviour that Jesus' execution prompted among the disciples indicates that they were not ready for such an end; far from it.

Jesus' arrest and the role of Judas

Jesus was betrayed by one of those closest to him, Judas. This piece of information is very historically reliable; it occurs in several sources (Mk 14.10-11, 43-45; Jn 18.2-3; Acts 1.16) and makes for an inconvenient tradition from the point of view of the first followers. There would have been no reason for later Christ-believers to invent a story about traitor from within the inner circle if it had not been the case. It makes sense that Judas would have gone to senior priests, as they had a unit of guards and were responsible for maintaining order. In Mark's account, the band of men who arrest Jesus appear to be from the temple guard, in that he describes them as 'a crowd with swords and clubs, from the chief priests, the scribes, and the elders' (Mk 14.43), with one of them being 'the slave of the high priest'. Jesus then mentions that he has been spending time at the sanctuary, which shows that Mark does have the temple guard in mind, and Luke even makes this explicit (Lk. 22.52). Dramatically, but entirely unrealistically, John claims that an entire 'cohort' (NRSV: 'detachment') – a Roman unit of 600 men – showed up and then threw themselves on the ground when Jesus addressed them. John intended this to show that Jesus was in complete control, that the Son of God could not be arrested without his approval. Someone in Jesus' party was armed and wounded a guard's ear (Mk 14.47; Jn 18.10). That marked the last time that anyone would try to defend Jesus. From that moment on he was all alone. Mark highlights this by having Jesus foretell such an outcome with a quotation from Zech. 13.7: 'You will all become deserters; for it is written, "I will strike the shepherd, and the sheep will be scattered"' (Mk 14.27). Later on Mark points out that at the time of the arrest: 'All of them deserted him and fled' (Mk 14.50). Peter, though, did follow Jesus at a distance, but, according to Mark, he denied knowing him (Mk 14.54, 66-72), and John, too, is aware of this tradition (Jn 18.12-18). Peter's denial of Jesus is an embarrassing episode, and thus it probably did happen, even if not as described in the worked-out version in the Gospels, which includes Jesus' prediction of it happening three times (cf. Mk 14.30; Jn 13.38).

People have speculated about the motive behind Judas's actions. Did he do it for the money? The precise sum, thirty pieces of silver (Mt. 26.15), is inspired by Zechariah (11.12), but he may nonetheless have received some kind of reward. No matter what, Judas must have lost confidence in Jesus' leadership, after having presumably given up a great deal to follow him. Disappointment and frustration underlie actions of this sort. How exactly did Judas aid the authorities? According to the Gospels, Judas showed a band of armed men the way to Jesus. With pilgrims crowded into every corner of Jerusalem and thousands of people camped outside the city, finding any given person in the throng was not easy, which is why Judas was needed to act as a guide. Perhaps he betrayed Jesus in more than one sense. As we have seen, Jesus did not openly present himself as the Messiah or as a royal pretender, yet he was executed for the very reason that he had claimed to be the 'King of the Jews', in the words of the inscription detailing his crime that was nailed on the cross. Where did this charge come from? Perhaps from Jesus' entry into Jerusalem, when he rode in like a king. But perhaps from Judas as well. Given his position in the inner circle, Judas knew all about Jesus' proclamation of the coming kingdom; in it, the king was God, but it also included a vision of Jesus' own status as God's agent and deputy, that is, as a ruler of sorts. The details of Judas's demise are legendary in nature and of doubtful value (Mt. 27.3-10; Acts 1.17-19). In Matthew's version Judas was overcome with great anguish and gave back the 'thirty pieces of silver', later hanging himself (Mt. 27.3-10). According to Luke, Judas instead bought a piece of land with the money but soon afterwards died a dramatic death: 'falling headlong, he burst open in the middle and all his bowels gushed out' (Acts 1.18).

The interrogations

The sequence of events that followed Jesus' arrest is clear in broad outlines and appears to be historically plausible: first Jesus was questioned by the high priest and his associates, then by Pilate, and he was subsequently sentenced to death, a sentence which was swiftly executed. Here the Gospel authors are in agreement and this also broadly matches what Josephus has to say, when he mentions very briefly that Pilate sentenced Jesus to crucifixion on the initiative of 'men of the highest standing amongst us' (*Ant.* 18.63-64). Paul's letters likewise presume both Jewish and Roman involvement in Jesus' death, in that he lays emphasis on the crucifixion (1 Cor. 2.2) – which was a Roman punishment – whilst also writing that it was 'the Jews who killed both the Lord Jesus and the prophets' (1 Thess. 2.15). Yet the Gospels differ on several crucial points: When did the examination led by the high priest take place? In the evening, with a further gathering in the morning, as Matthew and Mark would have it (Mt. 26.57-59; 27.1; Mk 14.53-55; 15.1; cf. Jn 18.12), or in the morning, as in Luke's version (Lk. 22.66)? Or was it more of an informal questioning by the high priest, as John describes (Jn 18.12)? Which high priest was it? It was Caiaphas, according to Matthew (Mt. 26.57), while John assigns that role to Annas instead, the father-in-law of Caiaphas (Jn 18.12-24). Furthermore, Matthew and Luke insert information that only they are aware of. Was Jesus also questioned by Herod Antipas, as Luke claims (Lk. 23.6-12)? Did Pilate wash his hands, as Matthew alone reports (Mt. 27.24)? In what follows we shall try to tease out what would seem to be the most plausible course of events. As was mentioned above, a clear anti-Jewish polemic is evident in the narratives, as is a tendency to lessen Pilate's responsibility. This bias can be explained by reference to strained relations that existed between Christ-believers (both Jewish and gentile) and, on the one hand, Jewish congregations, and, on the other, the Roman authorities, something that we shall discuss in the next chapter.

When we compare the details of the four versions of the passion – that is, the story of Jesus' final hours, from arrest up until death – it becomes clear that we are dealing with two main traditions, Mark's and John's. Luke and Matthew have made use of Mark as a source, modifying his text independently of one another and supplying additional information. John, for his part, displays many unique features. The agreement of the two main traditions in their basic outline is due to their being based on similar traditions (most likely both written and oral). This also suggests that, at an early stage, the narratives about what happened to Jesus in Jerusalem were circulating in a relatively stable and fairly logical order: arrest; examination by Jewish authorities and, later, Roman ones; crucifixion; and burial.

In Mark's version, Jesus was taken to the high priest (who is not named) on the same night he was arrested. There was assembled the entire council, the Sanhedrin, which served as a tribunal, and a formal trial ensued with witnesses who testified falsely against him (Mk 14.53-65). The council assembled again in the morning and then handed him over to Pilate (Mk 15.1). In Luke, these two gatherings have been condensed into one. According to the Mishnah, the council was made up of seventy-one members (m. Sanh. 1.6), which is often taken as accurate information for the time of Jesus. But since this figure is a theologically significant one and derives from the story of Moses and the seventy elders (Num. 11.16), it reflects an ideal rather than reality, and therefore we do not know how many members the council had. In John, the examination is instead presented as an informal questioning by Annas, who had been high priest previously. Annas then sends Jesus to Caiaphas (18.24) but there is no mention of a hearing before the council. It seems implausible that the entire council would have assembled at such short notice, as Mark maintains, especially on a night when everyone was busy with preparations for Passover (assuming that John's dating is correct). But a less formal questioning, like that which John describes, does seem possible and a number of leading scholars therefore favour John's account on this point. This does not mean that his description of what was said at the interrogation should be believed. Which high priest was it, Annas or Caiaphas? If we consider how these divergent traditions may have come about, it is easy to see why Matthew would have specified that the high priest Mark was referring to was Caiaphas; he did, after all, occupy the high-priestly office at the time. On the other hand, it is harder to explain the reference to Annas, Caiaphas' relative who was not high priest, if it was not the case that he did in fact conduct the interrogation, which therefore seems likely. We may suppose that Annas was not alone, but rather had the assistance of other priests and members of the council.

What were the charges? In John's version, Annas asks questions about Jesus' teaching to which Jesus only gives indirect answers. The interrogation in Mark, who is followed in this by Matthew, is concerned with what Jesus said about the temple. According to Mark, false witnesses came forward who claimed to have heard Jesus threaten to tear down the temple and rebuild it in three days (Mk 14.58). The reason that Jesus had been arrested was that he had acted violently at the temple, in a symbolic act that someone might very well have taken as a warning about the destruction of the temple. Thus it seems entirely logical that the questions centred on this topic. The alleged involvement of false witnesses, however, is a sign of Mark's antipathy towards the Jewish leadership; there was probably no need of false witnesses to find Jesus guilty. John does not mention any witnesses at all. The reference to three days, here, reflects a later view and derives from Christ-believers who interpreted Jesus' talk of the temple symbolically, in light of their belief in his resurrection. According to Mark, the witnesses give conflicting testimony. Then the hearing takes a new turn:

> Again the high priest asked him, 'Are you the Messiah, the Son of the Blessed One?' Jesus said, 'I am; and "you will see the Son of Man seated at the right hand of the Power", and "coming with the clouds of heaven."' Then the high priest tore his clothes and said, 'Why do we still need witnesses? You have heard his blasphemy! What is your decision?' All of them condemned him as deserving death.
>
> Mk 14.61-64

There is a problem with this exchange, in that Jesus' statement does not involve any kind of blasphemy. Blasphemy meant using God's name irreverently (cf. Lev. 24.16), not calling oneself 'Messiah' or the Son of the Blessed One. It is hard to believe that this dialogue really happened. Instead, the question about Jesus' identity as the Messiah and Son of God reflects a time when Jesus' identity was at the centre of a conflict between Christ-believers (both Jewish and gentile) and non-Christ-believing Jews, a conflict about the Christ-believers' worship of Jesus as a deity, the Son of God, which could indeed be seen as blasphemy (Brown 1994: 526-7).

When Jesus is handed over to Pilate, a different charge surfaces, that of claiming to be the king of the Jews. This also contains within it the main accusation against him, insurrection against the Roman Empire, a very serious charge that could carry the death penalty. Both Mark and John know of the tradition that the charge was nailed onto the cross (Mk 15.26; Jn 19.19), which indicates that it was an early one. What is more, 'King of the Jews' is not an epithet that the Christ-believers used and so there is no reason to think that the title originated with them. Why was Jesus dangerous from the point of view of the Jewish leaders? In their eyes he was a disruptive figure, who spoke with great, self-assumed authority and respected neither the priests nor the temple. He was a ticking time bomb; he might easily incite the people to revolt. It would not take much for riots and unrest to break out, which would be followed by massacres of the populace. Given that it was the responsibility of the priests and the council to maintain order and further peaceful relations with Rome, they felt forced to put Jesus out of action. John doubtless captures something of their outlook when he has Caiaphas tell the council: 'it is better for you to have one man die for the people than to have the whole nation destroyed' (Jn 11.50; cf. 18.14).

The council did not have the power to impose the death penalty, except in cases when a gentile had set foot in the temple proper (that is, the women's court), which only Jews were permitted to enter. John sets out this legal situation in a fictional dialogue between Pilate and the high priest and his associates (in reality, Pilate would of course have known the laws dictated by Rome):

> So Pilate went out to them and said, 'What accusation do you bring against this man?' They answered, 'If this man were not a criminal, we would not have handed him over to you.' Pilate said to them, 'Take him yourselves and judge him according to your law.' The Jews replied, 'We are not permitted to put anyone to death.'
>
> Jn 18.29-31

Josephus confirms that the judicial system operated in this way. As we described in Chapter 5, Jesus son of Ananias, who had been prophesying the destruction of the temple, was arrested by leading Jewish men and, just as in the case of Jesus of Nazareth, these handed him over to the then procurator Albinus. During these proceedings he was flogged by both authorities (*War* 6.300-309). Josephus also relates that the high priest Ananus used a change in Roman governors as an occasion to assemble a council to try Jesus of Nazareth's brother James and that he sentenced him to be stoned, which he was in around 62 CE (*Ant.* 20.200-201). Ananus was removed from office because this constituted overstepping his authority. The governor himself, however, did have the power to put rebels to death, as emerges from the report that Tiberius Alexander (governor 46–48 CE) had two brothers from Galilee crucified for incitement to revolt (*Ant.* 20.102-103).

Pilate sentenced Jesus to crucifixion. The Gospel authors go to great lengths to show that his hand was forced by Jewish leaders, and above all by the chief priests. The Gospels all maintain that some parts of the proceedings were conducted in public, before a large crowd, egged on by the priests, that demanded Jesus' death. Mark claims that Pilate 'realized that it was out of jealousy that the chief priests had handed him over' (Mk 15.10). According to Luke and John, Pilate explicitly states that Jesus is innocent (Lk. 23.4; Jn 18.38). Pilate repeatedly tries to persuade the people to change their minds, offering to let Jesus go. Matthew inserts material of a legendary nature when he describes how Pilate's wife, having dreamt that Jesus was innocent, warned her husband of this (Mt. 27.19). He also adds intensity to the episode by having Pilate perform a dramatic gesture that receives an ominous response from the people:

> So when Pilate saw that he could do nothing, but rather that a riot was beginning, he took some water and washed his hands before the crowd, saying, 'I am innocent of this man's blood; see to it yourselves.' Then the people as a whole answered, 'His blood be on us and on our children!'
>
> Mt. 27.24-25

Writing after the destruction of Jerusalem and the temple in the year 70 CE, Matthew, like other Christ-believers, was able to interpret the devastation as God's punishment of the city that had killed his Son, a punishment that, in Matthew's telling, the people themselves requested.

That Pilate should have come to Jesus' defence and yet let himself be swayed by priests and an angry mob seems implausible to most scholars. Aside from it not being in his interests to protect a potential rebel, this characterization does not tally with other information we have about the prefect. First, we may note that Jesus is not alone in being crucified; rather, he is one of several (three according to Mk 15.27 and Jn 19.18). In Mark, these others are identified as men 'who had committed murder during the insurrection' (Mk 15.7). Which insurrection this is supposed to have been is not stated. In other words, Pilate was not averse to handing out death sentences – Jesus' was just one more. That several men were crucified before Passover corresponds well with the report in the Tosefta (t. Sanh. 11.7) about how criminals sentenced to death were kept in prison until the festivals came around, at which point they would be crucified so that as many people as possible would see them. Crucifixion was, after all, meant first and foremost as an effective warning to nations under occupation about what awaited those who engaged in opposition to Rome. As for other sources of information about the prefect, the Jewish philosopher Philo of Alexandria, writing around 41 CE, a few years after Pilate had been removed from office (36 CE), notes that he was infamous for his cruelty (Leg. Gai. 28). Philo may, however, have had a particular reason for sullying Pilate's reputation – to extol the new Jewish client-king Agrippa I (41–44 CE) – and his portrayal should not be relied upon unreservedly. From Josephus, of course, we know of several crises under Pilate's administration, and in a few cases he did opt to use military force to intervene. When, as mentioned in Chapter 1, there were large protests against the construction of an aqueduct in Jerusalem, Pilate had soldiers dressed in civilian clothing infiltrate the crowd, who, at a given signal, fell upon those who were demonstrating (Ant. 18.60-62). It should be noted that these protests took place during a festival, when Pilate made a point of being in Jerusalem, and it is an indicator of why the pilgrimage festivals in Jerusalem were uneasy periods for Pilate. In the year 36 CE, a few years after Jesus' death, he sent a detachment of soldiers to Mount Gerizim in Samaria to prevent a popular prophet and his large retinue from climbing the mountain in order to view some holy vessels reputedly hidden there by Moses. The band of Samaritans was armed, which explains Pilate's attack. In the assault on them, several Samaritans were killed, others were arrested and their leaders were executed. A group of Samaritans protested against this conduct to Pilate's superior, the Syrian legate Vitellius, who took the reports very seriously. He sent Pilate to Rome for questioning and a short time later removed the high priest Caiaphas from office (*Ant.* 18.85-89, 95), though it is unclear whether the latter had any involvement in the decision taken by Pilate. Yet violence was not always Pilate's answer to protests, as we know from the dispute over the presence of Roman standards in Jerusalem (see ch. 1.). Taken together, these incidents attest that Pilate did not hesitate to use violence when necessary, from a Roman perspective, but he was not excessively cruel either; rather, he acted as a competent Roman governor should. In the Gospels, Pilate is depicted as an ineffectual individual doing everything possible to keep the peace, who felt forced to crucify a man whom he personally regarded as innocent. But most scholars agree that this depiction is unhistorical. It is far more plausible that Jesus' execution was a further example of effective collaboration between Roman and Jewish authorities; individuals who could potentially cause riots were got rid of. In this particular case, unlike with the band of Samaritans, only the leader, Jesus, was executed, not any of his followers. This is evidence of a certain degree of restraint after all, and shows that the group was considered fairly harmless without its figurehead.

The accounts of the trial proceedings also include the detail that at Passover the prefect used to set one prisoner free, and Pilate therefore lets the people choose between Jesus and Barabbas, in the hope that they will choose the former (Mk 15.6-15). The tradition about Barabbas is present in John, too (Jn 19.39-40). In spite of the attestation in two possibly independent sources the historicity of this incident is doubtful for several reasons. No other sources give any indication that it was customary to release a prisoner for Passover. Nor is there any evidence in ancient Roman literature of any comparable practice. The name 'Barabbas' is a bit odd since in Aramaic it means 'son of a father' which has led to the assumption that the name was made up. But, Raymond Brown highlights occurrences of the name Abba and therefore there is no reason to doubt the existence of a prisoner by that name. Hence most likely, one of Jesus' fellow prisoners named Barabbas was indeed released. It would be understandable if on retrospect the disciples were indignant about the fact that Jesus was killed while someone else went free. Perhaps little more was needed for a tale to emerge about how Pilate had given the people a choice (Brown 1994: 799–800, 819–20).

As the Christ-believers continued to hand on the traditions concerning the trials, they interpreted the events from an anti-Jewish perspective. Within a short time the fault lay entirely with the Jewish people and the priests. In contrast to how Pilate is presented, however, the description of the Roman soldiers is more accurate; they behave like the vicious henchmen they probably were.

Suffering and death

During the proceedings Jesus was taunted and abused several times. There was nothing unusual about the use of threats and torture to interrogate suspects, and flogging could be part of the punishment (Mk 15.15), but the specific details of what happened to Jesus were probably not known to the Christ-believers. Mark's account follows a certain pattern: Jewish councillors and guards mock Jesus for being a false prophet by making him guess, while blindfolded, who is striking him (Mk 14.65); Roman soldiers dress him up in royal appurtenances that include a crown of thorns, and taunt him with being a false king (Mk 15.16-20; Mt. 27.28-31; Jn 19.2-5). In Luke, Herod Antipas takes care of the royal parody instead, which renders the point even more ironic as the reader knows that the person being mocked by a worldly ruler is in fact the real king (Lk. 23.6-12).

The Gospel authors do not provide many details about how the execution itself was carried out. The Greek word usually translated 'cross' does not tell us about whether Jesus was hung on a cross as traditionally understood, or on a T-shaped structure or a stake. Together with other ancient texts about crucifixions, the partly conflicting reports of Jesus carrying the apparatus for execution himself (in John's Gospel) and of him getting help with carrying it from a man by the name of Simon (so Mark) have given rise to various speculations as to the cross's design. However, the Swedish scholar Gunnar Samuelsson (2011) has shown that the sources are not sufficiently clear for us to be able to say anything with certainty on this point or on the issue of how executions of this sort tended to be carried out. In antiquity the distinctions between different forms of the death penalty – hanging, impalement and crucifixion – do not seem to have been fixed, and the specific ways in which they were carried out could vary endlessly. What was most important was that the person being executed suffered, was degraded and was hung up as an example to deter others.

According to John, Jesus was fixed to the 'cross' with nails (Jn 20.25) and there is nothing in the Synoptic Gospels to contradict this report. Even before being hung on the cross, Jesus must have been seriously weakened by the torture he endured, and loss of blood may have hastened his death. How long someone subjected to this penalty could survive thus suspended varied, and there are reports of crucified people living several days. The Gospels unanimously report that Jesus' death came after just a few hours. The immediate cause of death was likely suffocation, as it was hard to breathe, and painful, with one's arms suspended.

The narratives of Jesus' suffering and death are marked by influence from the Septuagint versions (LXX) of several biblical books, and especially Psalm 22, a psalm of lament. The report about the guards spitting on Jesus and striking him on the face (Mk 14.65) is inspired by Isa. 50.6 (LXX), which talks of the Lord's suffering servant: 'I have given my back to scourges and my cheeks to blows, but I did not turn away my face from the shame of spittings.' There is also a biblical background to the derision Jesus receives while hanging on the cross: 'Those who passed by derided him, shaking their heads' (Mk 15.29; Mt. 27.39). We can compare this to 'All who see me mock at me; they make mouths at me, they shake their heads' (Ps. 22.7). Matthew has the members of the council taunt Jesus as he hangs on the cross, putting words from Ps. 22.8 in their mouths:

> In the same way the chief priests also, along with the scribes and elders, were mocking him, saying, 'He saved others; he cannot save himself. He is the King of Israel; let him come down from the cross now, and we will believe in him. He trusts in God; let God deliver him now [cf. Ps 22.8], if he wants to; for he said, "I am God's Son."'
>
> Mt. 27.41-43

The polemic of a later period can be detected, here, when Christ-believers faced counterarguments like, 'If he was God's Son, as you say, why didn't God help him?'

In some cases the biblical background to these descriptions is explicit. Referring to 'the scripture', John describes the soldiers as dividing up Jesus' clothes. Once again it is the biblical text, rather than events themselves, that have guided the author:

> When the soldiers had crucified Jesus, they took his clothes and divided them into four parts, one for each soldier. They also took his tunic; now the tunic was seamless, woven in one piece from the top. So they said to one another, 'Let us not tear it, but cast lots for it to see who will get it.' This was to fulfil what the scripture says, 'They divided my clothes among themselves, and for my clothing they cast lots.'
>
> Jn 19.23-34, quoting Ps. 22.18

Here John portrays the incident as the fulfilment of a prophecy, as he also does when it comes to the report that while Jesus was on the cross, no one broke his bones, something that the two others who were crucified were subjected to. Instead the soldiers pierced Jesus' side to make sure he was dead: 'These things occurred so that the scripture might be fulfilled, "None of his bones shall be broken." And again another passage of scripture says, "They will look on the one whom they have pierced"' (Jn 19.36-37; cf. Zech. 12.10). The reference to the bones not being broken recalls the Passover lamb of Exodus 12.46. It is interesting to note, here, that not just the books of the prophets but biblical psalms and the Torah, too, could be regarded as prophecy that offered clues about 'the future', which is to say, the authors' own time. The same view of scripture can be seen in those Dead Sea Scrolls that contain expositions of biblical psalms, where the psalms are interpreted, in much the same way, as bearing witness to the sect's own time.

The words Jesus utters on the cross are likewise inspired, in part, by biblical passages, and in the Gospel authors' accounts of Jesus' last moments on earth, their interpretations of who Jesus was show through very clearly. At the moment of his death in Luke, Jesus cries out in a loud voice: 'Father, into your hands I commend my spirit' (Lk. 23.46). Mark stresses that Jesus is the suffering Messiah, who not only endures physical torment, but is also abandoned by everyone (Mk 14.50). Feeling that, in the end, God, too, has abandoned him, Jesus' last words are: 'My God, my God, why have you forsaken me?' (Ps 22.1). His suffering is profound. In John, by contrast, Jesus comes across as a strong figure who is fulfilling a defined role. His last words on the cross are 'It is finished' (Jn 19.30), in keeping with John's portrayal of Jesus as a lofty, godlike figure.

From a purely historical perspective, we can assume that there was no one in the vicinity of the cross when Jesus died apart from soldiers. However, certain women who show up in the narrative of the empty tomb are said by Mark to have been watching at a distance as Jesus died (Mk 15.40). If so, none of the followers were close enough to Jesus to hear what he said. What the narratives of Jesus' death reveal instead are the attempts of the first Christ-believers to understand why Jesus had died, something that came as an enormous shock to them. During this process they found consolation and guidance in biblical texts, and especially in the psalms and in hymns from Isaiah about the Lord's suffering servant, texts which deal with innocent suffering. For them, Jesus, in a unique way, personified the righteous, innocent individual who suffers in those texts. Importantly, God delivers the one who cries out to him (Ps. 22.23-32); suffering gives way to rejoicing when God acts. Psalm 22.28 inspires hope of an eschatological future: 'All the ends of the earth shall remember and turn to the LORD; and all the families of the nations shall worship before him' (Ps. 22.27). The Christ-believers became convinced that God had exalted Jesus after his death.

Summary

All four Gospels include long and detailed accounts of Jesus' last days in Jerusalem, demonstrating both the importance of these events for the early church and the wealth of information that was circulating among the followers. Clearly, what happened during the last days of Jesus' life became the subject of much discussion and reflection early on. With the claim that within a short time Jesus was raised from the dead, the story ends in triumph. Even so, the accounts reveal that the path from a hopeful, grand entry into the city to the brutal execution was a tumultuous and devastating one for the followers. They did not expect Jesus to die. The clear and detailed predictions that Mark ascribes to Jesus (e.g. 8.31-33) about his upcoming suffering and death, which Jesus delivers long before the journey to Jerusalem, were evidently made up after the fact. Rather, the disciples most likely expected the kingdom to come that very Passover, as Jesus' prophetic sign-acts suggest.

Jesus staged a triumphal entry into Jerusalem in which he was hailed as a messianic king. The followers were in good spirits and seemed confident that their leader was about to take on the role of the royal Messiah. Later, however, they may have been confused when Jesus attacked people in the sanctuary and threw the furniture around, causing a great disturbance. The quotations from scripture placed on Jesus' lips present these actions as protests against aspects of the cult, criticisms of the priesthood for turning the place into a 'den of robbers'. Yet Jesus' original purpose is far from clear. The most likely interpretation is that he was symbolically predicting the destruction of the temple, something which was part of visions of the end time. The corruption of the priesthood was also part of these expectations about the end times, and Jesus' protest says more about his apocalyptic beliefs than about the priests themselves.

The atmosphere at the last supper seems ominous, with Jesus speaking of his imminent death and the coming of the kingdom. The narrative highlights Jesus' worry by having him pray in the garden of Gethsemane; this report reveals Jesus' human side – he appears highly distraught, fearful for his life and unsure about whether events are proceeding according to God's plan. Jesus was arrested when Judas led the temple guard to the garden. While Judas's betrayal is a highly reliable piece of information, his ensuing death is not. The reports of the interrogations in the Gospels differ in matters of detail as to where, when and by whom they were carried out. Nevertheless, a skeleton of the main events is fairly clear. Jesus was first questioned by Jewish authorities, including priests and members of the Sanhedrin – and then by Roman officials, including Pilate. The precise wording differs among the various accounts and the early followers are not likely to have known what was said. In contrast to the presentation in the Gospel accounts, the cooperation between Jewish and Roman authorities was probably quite smooth. Both of these governing bodies had the same overarching goal: to keep the peace during the holiday. Jesus was charged with having royal pretensions and he was swiftly found guilty of rebellion, and executed. He died on the Friday (Mk 15.42), most likely before the Passover began.

The story of the final days of Jesus' life is told against the backdrop of the Scriptures. A large number of allusions and quotations, and also some fabricated events inspired by 'prophecies' in the Septuagint, guide readers towards interpreting the tragic ending as divinely ordained and necessary. These discourses of intense scriptural interpretation testify to the followers' continued belief that Jesus was the chosen instrument of God. But why was it that they did not give up their belief in spite of the fact that their master was dead, executed as a common rebel? Moreover, how did a small group of Jewish men and women based in Jerusalem come to grow into a major movement that spread far beyond the borders of Palestine? We shall consider these questions next.

Bibliography

Betz, H. D. (1997), 'Jesus and the Purity of the Temple (Mark 11:15-18): A Comparative Approach', *Journal of Biblical Literature* 116 (3): 455–72.

Bock, D. L. and R. L. Webb, eds (2010), *Key Events in the Life of the Historical Jesus: A Collaborative Exploration of Context and Coherence*, Grand Rapids: Eerdmans.

Brown, R. E. (1994), *The Death of the Messiah: From Gethsemane to the Grave: A Commentary on the Passion Narratives in the Four Gospels*, 2 vols, New York: Doubleday.

Collins, A. Y. (2001), 'Jesus' Action in Herod's Temple,' in A. Y. Collins and M. M. Mitchell (eds), *Antiquity and Humanity: Essays on Ancient Religion and Philosophy: Presented to Hans Dieter Betz on His 70th Birthday*, 45–61, Tübingen: Mohr Siebeck.

Crossley, J. G. (2004), *The Date of Mark's Gospel: Insight from the Law in Earliest Christianity*, London: T&T Clark.

Dunn, J. D. G. (2003), *Christianity in the Making, vol. 1: Jesus Remembered*, Grand Rapids: Eerdmans.

Evans, C. A. (1997), 'Jesus' Action in the Temple: Cleansing or Portent of Destruction?' in B. D. Chilton and C. A. Evans (eds), *Jesus in Context: Temple, Purity and Restoration*, 395–439, Leiden: Brill.

Fredriksen, P. (1999), *Jesus of Nazareth, King of the Jews: A Jewish Life and the Emergence of Christianity*, New York: Vintage Books.

Pitre, B. (2005), *Jesus, the Tribulation, and the End of the Exile: Restoration Eschatology and the Origin of the Atonement*, Wissenschaftliche Untersuchungen zum Neuen Testament 2/204, Tübingen: Mohr Siebeck.

Samuelsson, G. (2011), *Crucifixion in Antiquity: An Inquiry into the Background and Significance of the New Testament Terminology of Crucifixion*, Wissenschaftliche Untersuchungen zum Neuen Testament 2/310, Tübingen: Mohr Siebeck.

Sanders, E. P. (1985), *Jesus and Judaism*, London: SCM Press.

Sanders, E.P. (1993), *The Historical Figure of Jesus*, London: Penguin Books.

Schröter, J. (2006), *Das Abendmahl: Frühchristliche Deutungen und Impulse für den Gegenwart*, Stuttgart: Verlag Katholisches Bibelwerk.
Wassén, Cecilia (2016), 'The Use of the Dead Sea Scrolls for Interpreting Jesus's Action in the Temple', *Dead Sea Discoveries*, 23: 280–303.

11

From a Jewish group to a multi-ethnic movement in the Roman Empire

Jesus' death represented a failure, not just for Jesus himself but also for the movement that had formed around him. The mood of dejection that followed Jesus' execution is captured well by the author of Luke's Gospel when he has two disciples admit with disappointment that 'we had hoped that he was the one to set Israel free' (Lk. 24.21). Nothing had come of it. Jesus had met the same fate as several other popular prophets from the first century of the Common Era (see ch. 5). But there is one key difference between these other prophets and Jesus: whereas other prophetic movements disbanded and disappeared as soon as their leader was eliminated, the Jesus movement lived on. In fact, it didn't just survive; once the initial shock subsided, it appears to have unexpectedly gained new strength. In a short time the Christ-believers established themselves as a significant faction within Judaism, and within a few decades the movement had expanded across large parts of the Roman Empire to include people of other ethnicities as well. Eventually it developed into a religion of its own: Christianity. In this last chapter of our book, we shall take a very brief look at how such a dramatic transformation came about.

The first Christ-believers

For the Jewish group that, by the mid-30s CE, had begun to spread its message that Jesus was the Messiah, the belief that God had 'raised' this prophet from the dead was fundamental. No such notion had a place in Jesus' own preaching. It is true that Mark's Gospel does have him predicting his death and resurrection (8.31; 9.31; 10.32-33), but no trace of a prediction of this kind is found in the material that Matthew and Luke have taken from Q. What is more, the panicked actions of the disciples in response to Jesus' execution indicate that it was certainly not part of any plan. How, then, did some of those very disciples come to believe that Jesus had risen again? And how does this relate to the fact that the Christ-believer group not only survived but very rapidly grew in numbers and significance?

Belief in the resurrection

It has long been known to behavioural scientists that members of religious groups which emphasize prophetic revelations and apocalyptic beliefs tend to react in certain ways when their prophecies fail to materialize. In a famous study from the 1950s, the psychologist Leon Festinger and his colleagues described developments within a small new religious movement in Chicago, which thought it could communicate with extraterrestrial beings (Festinger, Riecken and Schachter 1956). Its leader had informed the members that on a fixed date North America would be destroyed in a great flood, but also that they themselves would be saved when aliens arrived to collect them in their spaceships. When the fateful day came and went with no sign of a flood or of spaceships, the sense of disappointment defied description, and anyone might have thought that the group would break up right away. But just as Festinger and his colleagues had suspected, the opposite happened. The group quickly united around a shared interpretation of the grand finale that never came – their devotion and faith was what had averted the catastrophe – and members who were gathered at the movement's headquarters began to evangelize much more actively and ardently than before. Thus, what had seemed like a blow turned into a success; far from breaking the group, it made it stronger. The researchers explained this by observing that members had made such great sacrifices for their beliefs, including leaving their jobs and severing relations with family and friends, that they had quite simply come to depend on the continued existence of the movement. Actively carrying out missionary work, in the hopes of winning others over, became a way for them to allay their own disappointments and doubts.

Human behaviour does not operate according to rigid laws, and theories of the sort that Festinger and others have formulated cannot fully explain the survival and growth of the Jesus movement. But it is hard to overlook the relationship between several factors: the great cost, in terms of social exclusion, that following Jesus in the hopes of future rewards had meant for the disciples; the complete and utter disappointment that Jesus' execution represented; and the missionary zeal with which Christ-believers later proclaimed his resurrection. In the eighteenth century, Hermann Samuel Reimarus, an early scholar of the historical Jesus, argued that the disciples had deliberately fabricated the resurrection story in order to be able to keep up their lucrative enterprise (Lessing 1879: 88–108), but such an explanation is altogether improbable. Just as the members of the new religious movement in Festinger's study really did believe that they had saved the world from a deluge, so the first Christ-believers were genuinely convinced that Jesus had been raised from the dead and was alive once more. This conviction was based on two factors: visions of the risen Jesus and the discovery of the empty tomb.

Experiences described as encounters with the risen Jesus are attested as early as the writings of Paul, who maintained that he himself had such an encounter with Jesus (Gal. 1.15-16; 1 Cor. 15.5-8). The story of how Jesus had 'appeared' to various people was, according to Paul, among the fundamental 'traditions' that he had learnt from others, and this indicates that it arose very early on. The Gospels, too, in varying levels of detail, tell of such encounters with the risen one. A number of these accounts are very brief, and the sources offer conflicting reports as to when, where and in what order these perceived encounters occurred. This, too, suggests that a multitude of different testimonies, stories and rumours of perceived encounters with a living Jesus were circulating among the supporters soon after his death. We read of private encounters as well as experiences in groups. What exactly the 'witnesses' believed they had seen is unclear. When Luke describes Paul's encounter with Jesus in the book of Acts, Paul hears a voice but sees only a dazzling light (Acts 9.3-4; 22.6-7; 26.13-14). Other accounts suggest that the visionaries had trouble recognizing Jesus (Lk. 24.16, 37; Jn 20.14; 21.4). In a number of the narratives, the encounters amount to Jesus giving the disciples commissions of various kinds (Mt. 28.10, 19; Lk. 24.48-49; Jn 20.17, 21-23; 21.15-19). We may suspect that that the wider circle of disciples aided in elucidating the murky experiences that the visionaries recounted.

Among the perceived encounters with Jesus, the vision of the disciple Simon, known as Cephas or Peter, occupied a unique position. According to the early tradition known to Paul, Cephas's vision was the first (1 Cor. 15.5), an idea that Luke confirms in passing (Lk. 24.34). It is likely to have taken place in Galilee, where Jesus' innermost circle appears to have returned soon after the fiasco in Jerusalem (cf. Mk 16.7; Mt. 28.16). In its most original form the concluding episode of John's Gospel, in which Peter encounters Jesus on the shore of the Sea of Galilee, very likely goes back to this vision, even though the account has accrued various later embellishments. In the original narrative, Peter recognizes Jesus and receives a commission from him to act as leader (Jn 21.1-19). The same vision may lie behind the commission that Peter receives from Jesus in Matthew's Gospel, which the author has incorporated into the episode where Peter calls Jesus the Messiah (Mt. 16.17-19) and which does not really fit the context very well. Simon Peter's perceived encounter with Jesus served a dual purpose: first, it confirmed that Jesus' ignominious death was not the end after all, but was part of a greater plan; secondly, it legitimized Peter's position as the leader of the movement.

After this initial vision of Peter's, several others followed. On one occasion, those who were still part of 'the Twelve' are said to have had a collective vision of Jesus (1 Cor. 15.4; Mt. 28.16-20; Lk. 24.36-49; Jn 20.19-

23; cf. Mk. 16.7). Paul mentions that he appeared to James, too, the brother of Jesus (1 Cor. 15.7). As already noted, Paul was convinced that he himself had encountered the risen Jesus. This is likely to have occurred within two years of Jesus' death, and when, almost twenty years later, Paul writes of it to the community in Corinth, he presumes that it was the last vision of its kind (1 Cor. 15.8). Accounts of Jesus visibly being 'carried up' into heaven forty days after his resurrection are only found in Luke's works (Lk 24.50-52; Acts 1.9-11), and there is no indication that any such vision was known to either the other Gospel authors or to Paul. Numerous visionary experiences probably occurred in the period immediately following Jesus' death. Gradually they grew more infrequent, before almost ceasing altogether. Later some Christ-believers would nevertheless have visions of a very different kind of the resurrected Christ, such as the author of the book of Revelation, John of Patmos (Rev. 1).

The principal argument for Jesus' resurrection was thus that the supporters themselves had seen him, but what also played a role were the reports that certain female members of the movement had found Jesus' tomb empty (Mk 16.1-8; Mt. 28.1-15; Lk. 23.55–24.12; Jn 20.1-2). To be sure, many scholars – James Crossley (2005) is one of them – maintain that the stories of the empty tomb are of a later date, both on the grounds that Paul makes no mention of it and on account of the many legendary elements that the accounts contain. Even so, it appears more plausible that the narratives are based on some historical event. For one thing, an author who had free rein entirely is hardly likely to have come up with the idea of having a group of women discover the tomb. It would have suited the purposes of the Christ-believers far better if 'the Twelve' had been there at the tomb that Sunday morning and able to verify that it was empty. In fact, the author of John's Gospel does offer a partly amended version of the story, in which Simon Peter is the first to enter the empty tomb (Jn 20.6-7); but John cannot entirely cover up the more original tradition either, as he mentions that Mary Magdalene was the first on the scene (20.1-2). For another thing, it is hard to account for the belief that Jesus rose again 'on the third day' (1 Cor. 15.4) other than by supposing that the supporters did indeed believe that they found the tomb empty on the Sunday after the execution. If the first vision of the risen Jesus took place in Galilee, it cannot have been 'on the third day', as Peter would not have made it back to the area so soon. One plausible scenario, therefore, is that a few of the female supporters claimed to have discovered that the tomb was empty early on, on the Sunday – whether because the body had been moved or they had gone to the wrong tomb or for some other reason, we cannot know – and that after this there followed a fairly short period of uncertainty and confusion. After returning to Galilee, the inner circle began to have visions which they interpreted to mean that Jesus was no longer dead. They therefore came to the conclusion that the reason that the tomb was empty was that God had raised him 'on the third day'.

The disciples also interpreted the visions as a commission to return to Jerusalem and hold their positions there while they awaited the kingdom, whose coming had been deferred. In time, the mixture of shock, confusion and uncertainty of those first days became merely a short interlude in the collective memory of the Christ-believer movement. When Luke, at least half a century later, gives an account of this initial period, little of the turmoil is left: on the very same day as the empty tomb is discovered, Jesus appears to his followers, alive, and, ordering them to remain in Jerusalem, he explains that everything that had happened was foretold in the Holy Scriptures (Lk. 24.36-49).

An inner-Jewish missionary group

'All who believed were together and had all things in common; . . . Day by day, as they spent much time together in the temple, they broke bread at home and ate their food with glad and sincere hearts, praising God and having the goodwill of all the people' (Acts 2.44, 46-47). Luke's romanticized description of the first Christ-believers in Jerusalem shows all the nostalgia we would expect in a portrait of the good old days. To get a true historical picture, we have to read it critically and also take into account the older, and less idealized, information that Paul supplies in his letter to the Galatians.

In a number of respects the Jerusalem community was a continuation of the movement that had been centred on the historical Jesus. There were healings, for example, which could be used as proofs when the movement preached to outsiders (Acts 2.43; 3.1-16; 4.8-12; 5.12-16). Peter's leadership contributed a further element of continuity between the band of 'the Twelve' and the community. Yet if we read between the lines in both Paul's works and Luke's, it becomes clear that Peter's position did not go unchallenged; Jesus' brother James was also regarded as an important authority (Gal. 2.9, 12; cf. Acts 15.13-21). Perhaps there was a rivalry, here, between two strong personalities who could both claim to have been close to Jesus, one as a member of his family, the other as the informal leader of the Twelve. Both Peter and James could also, of course, cite their encounters with the risen Jesus.

In other respects the community differed from the earlier Jesus movement. Once the prophet leader was gone, greater emphasis seems to have been placed on charismatic phenomena, which were construed as the presence of the Holy Spirit among the movement's general membership (Acts 2.1-13; 8.14-17). An intensive preaching effort was also undertaken with the aim of bringing more people into the movement. The sermons delivered in Acts, despite being largely Luke's own compositions, probably correspond fairly closely in substance to the message that the Christ-believers first preached to outsiders. This spoke of how Jesus had been executed unjustly and placed great emphasis on the idea that in raising Jesus from the dead, God had confirmed his status as the Messiah, and it ended with an exhortation to 'repent' and be baptized, or in other words, to join the Christ-believer movement (Acts 2.14-40; 3.11-26; 5.30-32).

Christ-believers were still, at this point, very clearly an inner-Jewish group, and their missionary activity was directed solely towards other Jews. From the outside they might be regarded as yet another school of thought within Judaism, like Pharisees, Sadducees or Essenes. But unlike the Pharisees and the Sadducees, the Christ-believing Jews were radical apocalyptics, and unlike the Essenes, they did not keep themselves apart, but rather attracted new adherents at a great rate. The authorities took a negative view of this new group for the same reasons they had been troubled by Jesus' successes. Popular movements of this sort, with evident fanatical tendencies, could easily evolve into political revolutions, with disastrous consequences. According to Acts (4.11-22; 5.17-42), the priestly elite of Jerusalem repeatedly took measures against the Christ-believers as well.

Not even Luke with his romanticized depiction can hide the fact that tensions soon arose within the group. In Acts 6.1-6 he recounts a dispute between the 'Hellenists' and 'the Hebrews' in the community, a dispute which concerns the allocation of common resources, and which the leadership resolves by appointing a group of seven 'Hellenists' to take care of this aspect of operations. From the text we cannot know whether these Hellenistic Jews had moved to Jerusalem from the diaspora or were the descendants of earlier returnees. In any case, what is clear is that their first language was Greek and that to some extent they were culturally different from the Aramaic-speaking, 'Hebrew' Jews who had made up the Christ-believer movement since its inception. From what the book of Acts has to say about the 'Hellenists' Stephen and Philip, we get the impression that they represented a Judaism with a more open and cosmopolitan bent than that of the more traditionalist Aramaic speakers. Stephen is stoned to death by a mob for relativizing the significance of the Jerusalem temple (Acts 6.8–8.1). Philip preaches the message to Samaritans (Acts 8.4-8) and baptizes an Ethiopian man (Acts 8.26-39). Although though these narratives exhibit many features of anecdotes, there is likely a historical core to their presentation of the 'Hellenists' as a group whose approach and activity laid the groundwork for a mission to those who were not Jewish.

The mission beyond Palestine

The Christ-believer movement was driven by a firm conviction that Jesus would return, and that this would happen very soon. The divine kingdom that Jesus had preached about would then become manifest on earth. Given that time was scarce, the Christ-believers actively sought to convince others about their faith, so as to save as many people as possible. With apocalyptic fervour they also looked beyond Palestine and addressed themselves to gentiles, as well. Judaism was not, generally speaking, a missionary religion, so why did these groups of Christ-believers start looking for members beyond the Jewish people? The answer lies in their apocalyptic world-view. Even if the dominant theme in visions of the future involving other nations is judgement in the Hebrew Bible, there are nonetheless a considerable number of prophecies that describe how, at the end times, the nations will come to see that the God of Israel is the one true God. Zechariah prophesies that 'the Lord will become king over all the earth' and that 'on that day the Lord will be one and his name one' (Zech. 14.9). Israel will then be a light to the nations (Isa. 42.6; 49.6) and, in the words of Isaiah, the nations will come as pilgrims to Jerusalem (Isa. 2.2-3; 66.18-21; cf. Zech. 14.16-19):

> In days to come
> the mountain of the Lord's house
> shall be established as the highest of the mountains,
> and shall be raised above the hills;
> all the nations shall stream to it.
> Many peoples shall come and say,
> 'Come, let us go up to the mountain of the Lord,
> to the house of the God of Jacob;
> that he may teach us his ways
> and that we may walk in his paths.'
> For out of Zion shall go forth instruction,
> and the word of the Lord from Jerusalem.
>
> Isa. 2.2-3

Since the Christ-believers saw the death and resurrection of the Messiah as the beginning of the eschatological transformation, they were also convinced that the 'nations' should be allowed to join the movement. What is more, as they succeeded in attracting gentiles, they sensed that the biblical prophecies were starting to come true, which in turn galvanized their apocalyptic beliefs.

Paul

Apocalyptic hope was also a strong driving force for the most famous missionary of all, Paul. In 1 Thessalonians, for example, he states those in the community who have already died will rise again when Christ returns. When that happens, Paul is confident that he himself will not be among them:

> For since we believe that Jesus died and rose again, even so, through Jesus, God will bring with him those who have died. For this we declare to you by the word of the Lord, that we who are alive, who are left until the coming of the Lord, will by no means precede those who have died.
>
> 1 Thess. 4.14-15

We know a reasonable amount about Paul, as a number of his letters are preserved in the New Testament. Luke also describes Paul's work in the book of Acts. Of the thirteen letters ascribed to Paul, scholars are in agreement that at least seven were written by him, while three (Ephesians, Colossians and 2 Thessalonians) are debated and three show clear signs of having been written at a later period (1 & 2 Timothy and Titus). Paul was a Pharisee of the Jewish diaspora, from Tarsus in present-day southern Turkey (Phil. 3.5-6; Acts 21.39; 22.3). The authentic epistles grant us some insight into his background and personality. In Gal. 1.13-14 he tells of his former life:

> You have heard, no doubt, of my earlier life in Judaism. I was violently persecuting the church of God and was trying to destroy it. I advanced in Judaism beyond many among my people of the same age, for I was far more zealous for the traditions of my ancestors.
>
> Gal. 1.13-14

What this persecution exactly involved is hard to know. Describing Paul's earlier life, Luke presents him as 'breathing threats and murder' and claims that he was authorized by the high priest to travel to Damascus to detain any members of the movement he found in the synagogues there and bring them to Jerusalem (Acts 9.1-2). The notion that the high priest would have had the authority to imprison Jews outside Palestine does not correspond with Roman law and Luke's account appears to be something of an exaggeration. But Paul did actively oppose the Christ-believing Jews, which tells us a great deal about him as a person. He was an extremely intense man who was ardent in his convictions, both before and after he began believing that Jesus was the Messiah. He must also have been fervent as a law-observant Pharisee, since, by his own account, he was exemplary in following the law. He changed course after an experience of encountering the risen Christ and began to seek to persuade others of his new belief.

Luke offers an account of what happened when Paul changed his course of life on the road to Damascus. He describes the episode three times (Acts 9.1-9; 22.6-11; 26.9-18) with differing details about how Paul and his travel companions miraculously saw a light or heard a voice. Paul also refers to some kind of revelation in the next part of Gal. 1 (vv. 15–16):

> God, who had set me apart before I was born and called me through his grace, was pleased to reveal his Son to me, so that I might proclaim him among the Gentiles.

Paul's new belief in Christ has traditionally been understood as a conversion. But the former Harvard professor Krister Stendahl (1976: 7–23) argued that the term is misleading since this is not a case of someone converting from one religion – Judaism – to another – Christianity. Instead, and in line with Paul's own description, it is a matter of being called to a new commission. As Stendahl stresses, it is important not to perceive Paul the missionary as Christian, since it was as a Jew that he continued his work. Still, Paul did undergo a radical change in his life, a change that may appropriately be described as conversion so long as we recognize that it was a conversion from one Jewish school of thought to another. According to church tradition, Paul is supposed to have changed his name on converting, but there is no evidence of this in the writings of the New Testament. Rather, like many other Jews in the diaspora, the man had two names; Paul was his Greek name, whereas his Hebrew name was Saul.

Sometimes Paul is presented as the founder of Christianity. Given that during his time the movement remains Jewish, this is inaccurate; what is more, there were a large number of missionaries and the movement gained ground early on in cities such as Rome, Alexandria, Antioch and Damascus without Paul's efforts. Yet as a missionary he was a leading figure in a network of like-minded individuals. In his letter to the Romans he sends greetings to several people, men as well as women, who have been working towards the same goals.

Paul's letters came to exert a very strong influence on the theology of the emerging church, and this is especially true of his interpretation of Jesus' death and of what it meant for the salvation of humanity (see Rom. 6). For Paul, Jesus' death and resurrection was an absolutely crucial part of God's plan for humanity and it signalled the opening of a new path to salvation for those who were not Jewish.

Paul – The apostle to the gentiles

In Gal. 1.16 Paul sets out the task that God has given him: to proclaim the gospel to the gentiles. He travelled around the eastern Mediterranean, founding new communities in various cities. Luke describes what Paul would do after arriving in a new city in order to reach new audiences (in this particular instance he is accompanied by one of his travelling companions, Silas):

> After Paul and Silas had passed through Amphipolis and Apollonia, they came to Thessalonica, where there was a synagogue of the Jews. And Paul went in, as was his custom, and on three sabbath days argued with them from the scriptures, explaining and proving that it was necessary for the Messiah to suffer and to rise from the dead, and saying, 'This is the Messiah, Jesus whom I am proclaiming to you.'
>
> Acts 17.1-3

Paul debated with other Jews in the natural place for Jews in the diaspora to congregate, the synagogue. Luke notes that the 'devout' were particularly interested in Paul's message, continuing: 'Some of them were persuaded and joined Paul and Silas, as did a great many of the devout Greeks and not a few of the leading women' (Acts 17.4). The group that Luke refers to as 'devout Greeks' were not Jews but other local people who also attended the synagogue and who observed Jewish traditions to varying degrees. Synagogues in the diaspora were open to gentiles and according to Josephus many people from non-Jewish backgrounds were drawn to the synagogues' sense of community (*War* 7.45; *Apion* 2.282). Often these people would add Israel's god to the other gods they worshipped, whilst continuing to participate in the official cult. Among this group in particular, Paul found a receptive audience. Their positive response towards Paul's teaching is related to the standing of these gentiles in the synagogues. Prior to this point, the option of converting and thus becoming Jews was already available. But for men the process was both painful and shameful as it meant being circumcised, a step few were willing to take. These sympathizers were known as 'devout Greeks' or 'God-fearers' (Acts 16.14), a status indicating that they were worthy gentiles but not Jews, and thus they occupied a position between other pagans, who were often thought to be sinners, and Jews. Their status was no doubt debated in the synagogues before the Christ-believer movement came into being and there must have been various views on the matter. But Paul brought an entirely new perspective: those who believed in Christ were to be full and equal members of the people of the covenant, regardless of whether or not they were Jews. Accepting Jesus as the Messiah and joining this new movement became the new criterion for belonging to the covenant. Hence it was not necessary for gentiles to convert; they were welcome as they were. In Paul's eyes, it was wrong, even, for them to convert.

Paul's was one of several views among Christ-believers and the issue of the status of non-Jewish members became so divisive that there was a risk that the movement might split in two. The question of how everyone could eat together proved especially problematic, an important subject given that the Christ-believers used to meet for communal meals (see 1 Cor. 11.17-34). Luke reports that leading men within the movement assembled in Jerusalem for a meeting to address the status of, and rules for, those of non-Jewish ethnicity who wished to join the Christ-believers. Thus, the problem for the movement was the status of the gentiles, which shows beyond doubt that the movement was Jewish.

The apostolic council and the Jewish laws

Paul and Barnabas took part in the meeting in Jerusalem as representatives of the community in Antioch, where early on the movement had gained a large following. One group held that circumcision, that is, conversion, was necessary for gentiles and with it observance of the law of Moses as well (Acts 15.5). Luke puts particular stress on the fact that this was the opinion of a group of Christ-believing Pharisees. He then has both Peter and James speak before the assembly, and he presents James as the clear leader in that he is the one who states the decision, referring to the fulfilment of the Scriptures:

> Therefore I have reached the decision that we should not trouble those Gentiles who are turning to God, but we should write to them to abstain only from things polluted by idols and from fornication and from whatever has been strangled and from blood.
>
> Acts 15.19-20

The decision meant that gentiles were to keep certain basic commandments from the laws of Moses (Lev. 17-18) that applied not just to Israelites but also to foreigners dwelling in the land: the prohibitions against meat from sacrifices offered to other gods (Lev. 17.8-9), against incest and homosexual relations (Lev. 18.6-29), and against dead animals that had not been properly slaughtered (Lev. 17.10-16), as well as the prohibition against consuming anything containing blood (Lev. 17.2). In Jewish literature, idol worship and sexual transgressions frequently appear together in generalized descriptions of what was typical of gentiles. Christ-believers, though, were not to walk in the ways of such wicked heathens (cf. Rom. 1.18-32). Consuming blood was considered a great sin and the prohibition, which is also given to Noah and his sons, was thought to apply to the whole of humanity (Gen. 9.4). The decision taken in Jerusalem meant that the main obstacles would be removed, so that non-Jews would be able to join the movement without needing to convert. According to Luke, this information was warmly received in Antioch, and Paul and Barnabas continued to teach there and proclaim 'the word of the Lord' (Acts 15.36). But Paul's letter to the Galatians several years after the meeting paints another, more realistic picture. Paul confirms that those present at the meeting resolved that circumcision was not necessary for gentiles. However, he makes absolutely no mention of any special laws that might apply to this group, perhaps because he adopted a more pragmatic approach, at least to meat from sacrifices (Gal. 2.1-10; 1 cor. 8–10). After the meeting Paul returned to Antioch and Peter joined him there. Eating together was apparently not causing problems for the community, that is, until 'certain people came from James'. At this point, according to Paul, Peter 'drew back and kept himself separate for fear' of the Jews (literally, 'those of circumcision'; Gal. 2.12) and other Jews did the same. Thus, the matter was far from settled.

In his letter to the Galatians, Paul warns the recipients against converting to Judaism, as part of a polemic against a branch of the Christ-believer movement that continued to campaign for men to be circumcised. He cites a multitude of different arguments, setting works of the law against faith, for example, and comparing life under the law to slavery. The epistle also contains an explanation of why it was so important to Paul that gentiles not convert. He writes, 'if righteousness comes through the law, then Christ died for nothing' (Gal. 2.21). Paul understands the role of the law in light of his firm belief that the Messiah has come and died. This change in his conception of the law's significance for salvation had nothing to do with first-hand experience of his own imperfection, as is often supposed in Protestant tradition. Paul had no problem keeping the law; on the contrary, by his own account he was better than others (Gal. 1.14). His reasoning is the reverse: because the Messiah came and died, that path to salvation cannot have worked. If obedience to the law had worked, God would not have sent his Son to die for humankind. Paul writes this to gentiles whom he is warning against converting. He is not commenting on whether Jews should observe the laws, which, of course, they did. Paul writes in negative terms about obedience to the law, at times scathingly. To understand Paul's views on the laws of Moses it is important to remember that he is not commenting on the laws in general; rather, he is writing to gentiles with the aim of deterring them from following the laws, and for that reason he puts his arguments more forcefully. In other contexts he can have positive things to say about the law (Rom. 9.5). A Jewish reader would doubtless have been horrified by the way Paul polemically contrasts the law with faith (Gal. 3.10-11, 22-23), or his view in Galatians that obedience to the law is slavery (Gal. 4.21-5.1). Devotion to the law was based on a belief in a merciful God who forgave sins – naturally faith and works went hand in hand, as the author of the letter of James, for example, points out (Jas 2.14-26). Personally, Paul appears to have adopted a flexible approach to keeping the laws, as he writes in 1 Cor. 9.20-21:

> To the Jews I became as a Jew, in order to win Jews. To those under the law I became as one under the law (though I myself am not under the law) so that I might win those under the law. To those outside the law I became as one outside the law (though I am not free from God's law but am under Christ's law) so that I might win those outside the law.

Nevertheless, it is mistaken to argue that Paul preached a law-free gospel, as Fredriksen (2017: 108-21) and others have rightly stressed. Paul demanded a tremendous amount of these new members, fully in keeping with the Jewish laws. In his first letter, 1 Thessalonians, he expresses his joy at the progress the recipients have made:

> For they report about us what kind of welcome we had among you, and how you turned to God from idols, to serve a living and true God, and to wait for his Son from heaven, whom he raised from the dead – Jesus, who rescues us from the wrath that is coming.
>
> 1 Thess. 1.9-10

Gentiles in the movement were expected to reject 'idols', that is, their traditional Roman and Greek gods. To our ears this sounds simple and harmless enough, but what did it involve?

Stringent demands on gentile members

The inhabitants of the Roman Empire were expected to take part in the official cult. Veneration and worship of the gods was also an essential feature of all public occasions, such as athletic contests, theatrical performances and all sorts of celebrations during the festivals. Many professional organizations had their own societies at whose meetings a particular god or gods were worshipped. Part of any banquet with good friends was a libation to the gods. Were Christ-believers supposed to reject all of this? How far did it go? In people's homes, the worship of the household deities involved specific rituals at the household shrine. What should Christ-believing slaves do in these cases? Should a Christ-believing woman stop performing the religious rituals if she was married to a man who did not share her faith, a situation that according to Paul was not uncommon (1 Cor. 7.12-16)? It came down to striking a balance between being part of society and setting up boundaries. But in Roman society this balancing act could be dangerous.

The Romans were used to Jews being different. They did not participate in public worship of the gods, including the important imperial cult. Jews had received dispensation from emperor worship, but all of a sudden non-Jews were starting to behave the same way, after joining this Christ-believer group. From a Roman point of view, this was outright provocation. It might also be dangerous if the Christ-believing non-Jews failed to carry out their ritual obligations towards the gods, as these were the protectors of the cities. This growing gang of Christ-believers looked like a subversive movement arousing contempt. It was not enough that they worshipped a Jewish prophet who had been executed as a rebel to Rome; they also called him 'Lord', 'Saviour' and 'Son of God', titles used of the emperor. They were a charismatic group where people would spontaneously speak in tongues or prophesy (1 Cor. 14), rousing suspicions among others about what went on at these meetings. In addition, many of them, citing their apocalyptic beliefs, refrained from marrying (1 Cor. 7), in conflict with social mores as well as directives from the Roman authorities about having many children. According to Luke's accounts in Acts, quarrels frequently broke out at synagogues between the Christ-believer missionaries and 'the Jews'. Behind this there doubtless lies a historical reality. Since Jews formed a religious and ethnic minority that did not participate in local cults, their position in Roman societies was often precarious. In many areas Jews enjoyed peaceful relations with their neighbours, but elsewhere things could be very tense. The first pogroms against Jews in Alexandria occurred in 38 CE. At the end of the 40s CE, the Roman emperor Claudius expelled a large number of Jews from Rome (Acts 18.2) because they were accused of causing unrest. Anti-Jewish propaganda was spread by Greek and Roman writers. In this situation it is not surprising that Christ-believers would not have been especially welcome in Jewish communities. Jews were not looking for any more attention from the Roman authorities. Paul is well aware of the difficult balancing act that the Christ-believers faced. Offering guidance to the Corinthians on issues relating to meat from sacrifices, he admonishes them to 'Give no offence to Jews or to Greeks or to the church of God' (1 Cor. 10.32). It was hard for the Christ-believers not to 'give offence' and over time we can see them having to adapt more and more to the prevailing social system and its cultural norms.

Moving towards Christianity

The question of when Christianity emerged as a religious system of its own, distinct from Judaism, does not have a straightforward answer. In a number of places, the separation was complete as early as the beginning of the second century, but elsewhere it appears to have taken far longer. In any case, it is clear is that the process of separation began in earnest after Paul's activity and the fall of Jerusalem.

The new race

The great success that Christ-belief met with in the Mediterranean region in the second half of the first century CE meant that the movement's ethnic composition and identity underwent a change. At the apostolic council in Jerusalem the question had still been how gentiles were to be integrated into a movement that was entirely dominated by Jews. Half a century later, Jewish members were clearly in the minority, and in the second century it gradually became obvious that Christianity and Judaism were two different and incompatible religions. This development was partly a result of the gentiles' superior numbers, but it was also connected to the destruction of Jerusalem in the year 70 CE and the consequent need to define Judaism more precisely, and in slightly different terms, than before.

As long as Jerusalem remained and its temple still stood, the city formed a natural focal point, for Jews in general, of course, but also for the Christ-believer movement. There was a strong sense that the original community was the one in Jerusalem. A few years after being convinced that Jesus was the Messiah, Paul visited Jerusalem and met with the two most important leading figures, Peter and James, to legitimize his own activity (Gal. 1.18-19). Later, when he visited again to take part in the apostolic council, it was agreed that during his travels he should be sure to raise funds for 'the poor' of the Christ-believer community in Jerusalem (Gal. 2.10). This collection, which Paul comes back to several times in his letters (Rom. 15.26; 1 Cor. 16.1-4; 2 Cor. 8–9), served as an outward sign of the affinity of these Christ-believer communities with the 'mother church' in Jerusalem. The collection thus served a function comparable to the annual tax that all Jewish men were supposed to pay to the temple of Jerusalem, regardless of where they lived in the Roman Empire. And, just as the destruction of Jerusalem in 70 CE heralded the end of something as important for Jewish identity as the temple tax, so too it led to the disappearance of the city's Christ-believer community. For the movement, this meant the weakening of its Jewish identity.

Another effect that the fall of the temple had was that Jewish religious leaders needed to find new ways of formulating how to lead a Jewish life. After all, up until that point the temple and the sacrifices offered there had been the hub around which the entire religion and nation had revolved. Now offering sacrifices was no longer possible and Judaism therefore came to be centred even more on the reading of the Holy Scriptures and the interpretation of the law – practices that were already important, for example for Pharisees and Essenes. The 90s saw efforts among Jews to define, more clearly than before, which writings should be considered sacred, but also what teachings categorically could not be regarded as falling within the bounds of 'true' Judaism. The Christ-believers' confession of Jesus as the Messiah was one such teaching. Prayers began to be read aloud in synagogues that implied repudiating Christ-believers and other 'heretics'. Jews faced the option of either renouncing Christ-belief and remaining in the communion of the synagogue or abandoning their Jewish identity and joining a community where the average member was not Jewish.

But if, by the end of the first century, the majority of Christ-believers were no longer Jews, then what were they? Needless to say, they came from every possible ethnic background, but they also shared a common experience of not really fitting in anywhere. As we saw earlier, the Christ-believers were viewed with suspicion as deviants for relinquishing religious obligations and societal duties that they held to be incompatible with their belief. In such a scenario it should not strike us as odd that some Christ-believers began to think of themselves as a people of their own. In the letter known as 1 Peter – which is unlikely to have anything to do with Peter the disciple – the author writes that the recipients 'Once . . . were not a people' but that they have become 'God's people', and he admonishes them to conduct themselves well 'among the Gentiles' (1 Pet. 2.10, 12). The Gospel of Matthew, too, refers to the Christ-believer movement using 'ethnic' terminology (Mt. 21.43). During the latter part of the second century this idea developed so far that the anonymous author of the *Epistle to Diognetus* can explicitly speak of 'this new race' who are neither Jews nor gentiles but who set themselves apart by their special way of life.

New temporal horizons and new power structures

Jesus expected God's kingdom to be established imminently. The first Christ-believers held on to this belief, although the timeline, so to speak, was revised: the risen Jesus was currently 'at the right hand of God' in heaven and no one knew exactly when he would return, but it was assumed that it would not be long. In what is the oldest work preserved in the New

Testament, Paul anticipates that he will be 'alive ... left until the coming of the Lord' (1 Thess. 4.15). As we have already mentioned (ch. 6), one of the lines along which the Christ-believer movement most clearly developed during the first century is the waning of these intense apocalyptic sentiments. The Gospels contain traces of an idea which believers were able to hang on to for a long time: Jesus would come again while one of his original disciples was still living (Mk 9.1; Jn 21.20-23). But they, too, died. At the beginning of the second century, the anonymous author of 2 Peter is forced to deal with the awkward issue of why the second coming has not yet happened:

> First of all you must understand this, that in the last days scoffers will come, scoffing and indulging their own lusts and saying, 'Where is the promise of his coming? For ever since our ancestors died, all things continue as they were from the beginning of creation!' ... But do not ignore this one fact, beloved, that with the Lord one day is like a thousand years, and a thousand years are like one day. The Lord is not slow about his promise, as some think of slowness, but is patient on your account, not wanting any to perish, but all to come to repentance.
>
> 2 Pet. 3.3-4, 8-9

When the visible kingdom never arrived, it was tempting to reinterpret it in spiritual terms. Even Paul states that 'the kingdom of God is not food and drink but righteousness and peace and joy in the Holy Spirit' (Rom. 14.17). Jesus, who had anticipated a time when people would 'eat in the kingdom of God' (Lk. 13.29), would probably have had difficulty agreeing with such subtle thinking. Nor is it the historical Jesus' voice that we hear when, during the hearing before Pilate, the author of John's Gospel has Jesus utter the famous line 'My kingdom is not from this world' (Jn 18.36) – Jesus, after all, had expected that he and the men closest to him would reign over the reassembled tribes of Israel.

As the kingdom of God was being spiritualized and the visible second coming put off to a future which was more or less remote, coming up with fixed structures to organize the Christ-believer movement became increasingly important. From the beginning, apocalyptic suspense and the perception that the Spirit was manifesting itself in miracles, prophecy and the gift of tongues had been strong enough to create a common identity among Christ-believers. By the end of the first century this initial charismatic enthusiasm had been replaced by the need for greater organization. Now it was a matter of handing on Christ-belief to new generations and making sure that the movement did not fragment into countless smaller units. The idea came to prominence that each local congregation was really a manifestation of the single, worldwide 'church' which possessed common structures.

The emergence of the church as an institution can be seen in several developments, including defining more clearly what counted as correct doctrine; writing down the orders for religious services; and adopting certain writings – which in time would be known collectively as the 'New Testament' – for reading alongside the Hebrew Bible at those services. One particularly important trend in this process of institutionalization was the gradual formation of the office of bishop. Early on, Paul had used the Greek word that gave rise to our 'bishop' when he wrote specifically to the 'overseers' of the community at Philippi (Phil. 1.1), but here it evidently refers to a group of leading individuals and not a particular office. In the so-called Pastoral Epistles, which bear Paul's name but which were most likely written towards the end of the first century, the 'overseer' has become a key figure who is expected to be of exceptionally good moral character, in order to be able to exercise authority over the community (1 Tim. 3.1-7; Tit. 1.9). One of the overseer's most important responsibilities is to watch over 'the teaching' (Tit. 1.9). In the first decades of the second century, Ignatius of Antioch campaigned staunchly for a leadership structure that eventually became the standard model throughout Christendom. According to Ignatius, in every city the community should be led by a single bishop whose authority was almost absolute. The unity of the universal church would be ensured by the mutual recognition of the bishops from different communities. But it took a long time for this model to gain widespread acceptance. There are many indications that in the time of Ignatius the community in the city of Rome had not yet adopted it, and it would be quite some time before the bishop of Rome would claim to be the visible head of the worldwide church.

With the emergence of a clear hierarchy within the church, where bishops were the official leaders, the leadership also came to be predominantly male. Previously, men as well as women had been in charge of 'house churches', groups of Christ-believers who gathered regularly in private residences. Luke reports that Christ-believers used to gather at the home of a certain Lydia, a wealthy woman in Philippi who was persuaded by Paul's teaching (Acts 16.14-15, 40). The concluding section of Colossians includes greetings to 'Nympha and the church in her house' (Col. 4.15), according to the reading of the earliest Greek text. But later scribes who copied the text were uncomfortable with the idea of a woman being the leader of a house church and they therefore altered the wording so that it referred to a man, Nymphas (cf. KJV). A Jewish couple, Prisca/Priscilla (feminine) and Aquila (masculine) with whom Paul worked closely, were leaders of house churches in Ephesus and Rome at different periods (1 Cor. 16.19; Acts 18.18-20). Paul is clear that both of them are leading figures in the movement:

> Greet Prisca and Aquila, who work with me in Christ Jesus, and who risked their necks for my life, to whom not only I give thanks, but also all the churches of the Gentiles. Greet also the church in their house.
>
> Rom. 16.3-4

Women, continued to be in charge of house churches into the second century CE, like Tavia in Smyrna, as emerges from a letter of Ignatius of

Antioch (Ignatius, *Smyrn.* 13.2). In the period when the movement first began to spread throughout the Roman Empire, we also come across women who occupy other leading positions in communities. Phoebe was a 'deacon', a leader of some kind within the community, and a 'benefactor' of Paul's (Rom. 16.1-2). Women prophesied and led the congregation in prayer (1 Cor. 11.5) and they served as teachers, like Priscilla (Acts 18.26) and the popular female prophet in Thyatira whom John curses in the book of Revelation (Rev. 2.20-23). In his farewell greetings in Romans, Paul names both men and women who are active in the movement. He refers to a Jewish couple, Andronicus and Junia, as apostles, 'emissaries', using the honorific title that he otherwise applies to disciples of Jesus and to himself (Rom. 16.7).

According to prevailing ideals, the absolute head of a traditional Roman household, which had a definite power structure, was the father. Even so, a married woman had considerable power in the home insofar as she was responsible for the household finances, supervised the daily chores and gave orders to the slaves (cf. Prov. 31.10-31; see Osiek and MacDonald 2006: 144–63). Whilst women were in charge at home, men's arena was public life, where they were supposed to be engaged in politics and the like. In between the domestic and public spheres there was a social sphere where guilds and voluntary associations belonged. Recent research has indicated that both men and women could and did assume leadership roles in such associations (Harland 2009: 82–96). Male and female benefactors are often called by parental titles ('father' and 'mother') which implied some leadership functions. Still, inscriptions with male titles of honour far outnumber those of female titles. It was quite natural that women were leading figures in the Christ-believing congregations as long as these associations gathered in the private homes; when the churches moved more towards the public sphere, their power structures also changed, in favour of male leaders. This development, of course, looked very different in different places and was influenced by various internal and external factors.

At the beginning of the second century, the author of 1 Timothy forbade women from teaching in the assembly. To lend weight to his letter, he wrote in Paul's name:

> Let a woman learn in silence with full submission. I permit no woman to teach or to have authority over a man; she is to keep silent.
>
> 1 Tim. 2.11-12

The prohibition is reminiscent of Paul's order in 1 Cor. 14.33-34 that women should be silent in the assembly. Since earlier in the letter Paul gives instructions about how a woman should dress while prophesying or praying (1 Cor. 11.2-16), he would appear to be contradicting himself here. It is possible, however, that this passage, 1 Cor. 14.33-35, has been added by a later scribe who was familiar with the rules given by 'Paul' in 1 Tim. 2. The fact that the passage appears at two different points in the various manuscripts suggests that the verses were not an integral part of the original epistle.

A respectable religion

When the temporal horizon was readjusted and the Christ-believers began to think that their movement was set for a more lasting existence, the need to maintain good relations with the surrounding society also became more pressing. The earliest community was regarded with suspicion by the authorities, as Jesus and his followers had been. Its charismatic focus, its proclamation of a kingdom that was soon to come, along with other aberrant behaviours contributed to the perception that the Christ-believer movement had subversive aims. Paul exhorted the community in Rome to counteract this perception:

> Let every person be subject to the governing authorities; for there is no authority except from God, and those authorities that exist have been instituted by God. Therefore whoever resists authority resists what God has appointed, and those who resist will incur judgement. … For the same reason you also pay taxes, for the authorities are God's servants, busy with this very thing. Pay to all what is due to them – taxes to whom taxes are due, revenue to whom revenue is due, respect to whom respect is due, honour to whom honour is due.
>
> Rom. 13.1-2, 6-7

The notion that Christ-believers ought to be upstanding inhabitants of the Roman Empire is thus present from early on. As time passes, the importance attached to traditional, respectable morality increases in descriptions of the ideal way of life for a Christ-believer. We have already seen that the encouragement that 1 Peter offers to its recipients is 'conduct yourselves honourably' so that outsiders' prejudices about the movement may be proved wrong (1 Pet. 2.12). In this work, as in a few other epistles that date from a period later than the authentic writings of Paul, we find something like a catalogue of morals – usually referred to as a household code (*Haustafel*) – which prescribes how the various classes of members of the community should best carry out their assigned roles (1 Pet. 2.18-3.7; Col. 3.18-4.1; Eph. 5.21-6.9; Tit. 2.1-10). The values that feature in the household codes are essentially no different from the conservative ideals typically espoused by Greek and Roman moral philosophers. Children should obey their parents, who, for their part, should not provoke their children unnecessarily. Women should submit to their husbands, while husbands should treat their wives well. Similarly, slaves should obey their masters – the writings of the New Testament never question the institution of slavery – and Christ-believers who own slaves themselves should take the best care of them. This is far cry from Jesus' words about how he had 'come to set a man against his father, and a daughter against her mother, and a daughter-in-law against her mother-in-law' (Mt. 10.35). On the contrary, harmonious relations, both within the family and with the surrounding society, are a Christ-believer's virtue.

A striking change is observable when it comes to views on women and marriage. Paul, who was himself unmarried, called upon Christ-believers to abstain from marrying, and this was apparently a common view among the Corinthians, as well:

> To the unmarried and the widows I say that it is well for them to remain unmarried as I am. But if they are not practising self-control, they should marry. For it is better to marry than to be aflame with passion.
>
> 1 Cor. 7.8-9

The justification for abstinence was that the end of the present age was nigh and the second coming of Christ was at hand, and so one should not allow a husband or wife to be a distraction (1 Cor. 7.29-34). Exhorting young people not to marry went flatly against social mores which said that marriage was part of a person's duties to his or her family and empire. Accordingly, the household codes represent a return to traditional views on the family and a move towards conformity with the established order. The author of 1 Timothy goes even further, stating that women's salvation is dependent upon their having children (1 Tim. 2.15), which is essentially the opposite of Paul's teaching.

Summary

Who is the founder of Christianity? Most people would probably claim that the title obviously belongs to Jesus. After all, one of the fundamental tenets of Christianity is that it was the life, death and resurrection of Jesus of Nazareth that both brought God's saving work in the world to its climax and resulted in the formation of the church. Others acknowledge the insights scholarship has provided – that Jesus himself did not set out to bring about a new religion and that what the Gospels offer is a reinterpretation of his significance from several decades after his death – and have proposed that Paul should be recognized as the real inventor of Christianity. In Paul's letters, they would argue, not only do we find the idea attested for the first time that everything revolves around Jesus' death, resurrection and imminent return; but we also encounter the notion that Jews and non-Jews alike are invited to join the Christ-believing communities. Still others would point to the fact that Paul, for all we know, remained a faithful and Torah-observant Jew up to his death. They might suggest that the author of the letter to the Ephesians, the author of 1 Peter, or even Ignatius of Antioch was the first to come up with the notion of Christianity as an independent, manifestly non-Jewish, religion.

We would do well to let go of the idea that Christianity is a theological system that was founded by an identifiable person at a distinct point in history. Rather, the formation of Christianity was a gradual process, a process that in one sense began as soon as some of Jesus' disciples became convinced that God had raised him to new life after his death, but also one that required time as well as the involvement of Paul, Ignatius and so many other men and women whose names are mostly lost to us. It was also, like the birth of any religious movement, the product of various social, cultural and political circumstances. Even the very first Christ-believing community in Jerusalem was already part of the larger Jewish and Greek-speaking world, and the highly developed infrastructure of the Roman Empire facilitated the rapid spread of the movement. A massive influx of non-Jewish believers, coupled with the failed Jewish insurrections that were quashed by the Romans and the subsequent decline of Jerusalem as a religious and political centre, ultimately transformed this Jewish messianic movement into the Christian religion.

By the late second century, Christ-belief was on its way to becoming respectable within the Roman Empire. It was in the process of cutting its last ties with Judaism, and increasingly came to be perceived as an appealing synthesis of the most sophisticated currents in religion and morality. When Emperor Theodosius I declared Christianity the official religion of the Roman Empire in the year 380, naturally this represented a triumph for the Christian church. Oddly enough, this was, in a way, an indirect outcome of Jesus' prophetic activity and of his proclamation of the kingdom of God. Whether, ultimately, he succeeded or failed is very much in the eye of the beholder.

Bibliography

Barclay, J. M. G. (1996), *Jews in the Mediterranean Diaspora: From Alexander to Trajan (323 BCE–117 CE)*, Berkeley: University of California Press.

Crossley, J. (2005), 'Against the Historical Plausibility of the Empty Tomb Story and the Bodily Resurrection of Jesus: A Response to N.T. Wright', *Journal for the Study of the Historical Jesus* 3: 171–86.

Festinger, L., H. W. Riecken and S. Schachter (1956), *When Prophecy Fails*, Minneapolis: University of Minnesota Press.

Fredriksen, P. (2017), *Paul the Pagan's Apostle*, New Haven: Yale University Press.

Fredriksen, P. (2018), *When Christians Were Jews: The First Generation*, New Haven: Yale University Press.

Harland, Ph. A. (2009), *Dynamics of Identity in the World of the Early Christians: Associations, Judeans, and Cultural Minorities*, New York: T&T Clark.

Hedner Zetterholm, K. (2012), *Jewish Interpretation of the Bible: Ancient and Contemporary*, Minneapolis: Fortress.

Lessing, G. E. (1879), *Fragments from Reimarus: Consisting of Brief Critical Remarks on the Object of Jesus and His Disciples as Seen in the New Testament*, London: Williams and Norgate. (German original published in 1778.)

Nanos, M. D. and M. Zetterholm, eds (2015), *Paul within Judaism: Restoring the First-century Context to the Apostle*, Minneapolis: Fortress.

Osiek, C. and M. Y. MacDonald (2006), *A Woman's Place: House Churches in Earliest Christianity*, Minneapolis: Fortress.

Stendahl, K. (1976), *Paul among Jews and Gentiles*, Philadelphia: Fortress Press.

GLOSSARY OF NAMES AND TERMS

Agrippa I	Grandson of Herod the Great. Tetrarch of Galilee 39–41 CE. Afterwards client king of Palestine until his death in 44 CE. Referred to as 'King Herod' in Acts 12.
Antiochus IV Epiphanes	Ruler of the Seleucid Empire 175–164 BCE, of which Palestine was a part. His attempt to ban Jewish religious traditions led to the Maccabean revolt, described in 1 & 2 Maccabees. Symbolically described as a 'little horn' in Dan. 7.8 (cf. 7.25).
Apocrypha	A collection of books that formed part of the Greek translation of the Hebrew Bible, the Septuagint. These books are not, however, part of the Old Testament in Hebrew. In Roman Catholic and Orthodox Bibles, the books are included in the canon, while in Protestant Bibles they form a section of their own or are omitted entirely. (Hence, they are also known as the deuterocanonical books.) The term is derived from the Greek word *apokryphos*, 'hidden', in reference to the obscurity of their meaning.
Apollonius of Tyana	Greek philosopher and teacher from the Pythagorean school who was active during the first century CE. He was famous as a healer and miracle-worker and his life is told by Philostratus in the third century CE.
Asclepios	God of medicine. At the sanctuary of Asclepios, people with illnesses could perform an 'incubation', which meant staying the night in order to receive a cure during sleep. The god was thought to come to the patient in the form of a doctor or sometimes a snake.
Augustus Caesar	Born Gaius Octavius. Roman emperor whose reign began in 31 BCE. Lived 63 BCE–14 CE.
Beelzebul	A name for the principle power of evil and, what's more, lord of the demons. The name is originally derived from 'Baal-zebub', one of the gods of the Philistines.
Belial	A word meaning 'wickedness' or 'worthlessness' in Hebrew which appears in the Hebrew Bible. In the Dead Sea Scrolls the term is commonly used as a name for the personified principle of evil and as an alternative designation for Satan. In the New Testament the related name Beliar is used (2 Cor. 6.15).

Bethesda, Pool of	A pool in Jerusalem that was thought to possess healing powers. The pool has been identified with ancient remains at the Church of St Anne in East Jerusalem.
Bible	The term is derived from the Greek word *biblia*, 'books', referring to a collection of books. According to Christian tradition, the Bible consists of the Old and New Testaments. Jewish tradition recognizes only the Old Testament, which is known as the Bible or Tanak. This latter term is an acronym formed from the Hebrew names of the three divisions – the Torah, the Prophets and the Writings. The Old Testament is predominantly written in Hebrew, and is therefore also known as the Hebrew Bible. The New Testament is written in Greek. Strictly speaking, use of the term 'Bible' for the books of the Hebrew Bible in the time of Jesus in anachronistic, as the canon was not fixed until a later date.
Caiaphas	High priest 18–36 CE. Active as high priest and head of the Sanhedrin when Jesus was sentenced.
Caligula, Gaius	Roman emperor 37–41 CE. He resolved to have a statue of himself erected in the temple of Jerusalem, but died before putting this into effect.
canon	From Greek *kanon*, 'measuring stick' or 'rule'. A term for a collection of written works regarded as authoritative within a religious tradition. In Jewish tradition the canon consists of the Hebrew Bible. A tripartite collection of Jewish writings is first mentioned in 117 BCE in the preface to the Wisdom of Sirach. Christians adopted the Hebrew Bible and added Christian books to their canon. A list of authoritative Christian texts from the end of the second century, the Muratorian Canon, lacks the Johannine epistles, among others. The process of canon formation continued for centuries.
Daniel	A figure of legend, a wise and righteous man. The name is also used by the author of the book of Daniel, whose true name is unknown.
David	King of a unified Israel from *c.* 1000 BCE. Under his reign the land expanded, but it was later divided into a northern kingdom (Israel) and a southern kingdom (Judah). David's kingdom is seen as a golden age by biblical authors.
Decapolis	A term meaning 'ten cities' in Greek. It denotes a group of ten cities strongly influenced by Hellenistic and Roman culture in an area that today corresponds to north-western Jordan, southern Syria and a small portion of northern Israel (Beth-shean/Scythopolis). The cities enjoyed a relatively autonomous status.
Diognetus. Epistle to	A letter written to a certain Diognetus by an unknown Christian author who set out to give an account of

GLOSSARY OF NAMES AND TERMS

	what Christian faith involved. Likely from the second century CE.
1 & 2 Enoch	Ancient Jewish books of legends surrounding the figure of Enoch, who, according to Gen. 5.21-32, was the father of Methuselah, Noah's grandfather. *1 Enoch* is the older of the two and consists of five works of an apocalyptic nature. Aramaic fragments of four of these have been found in the caves at Qumran. *2 Enoch* is from the first century CE.
4 Ezra	A Jewish apocalypse from the end of the first century CE. The author interprets the fall of Jerusalem and destruction of the temple as a sign that the end times have begun. The Messiah features prominently in the book.
Gehenna	A term for hell derived from the Hebrew name for the Valley of Hinnom, south of Old Jerusalem. The site had evil associations as children had been sacrificed to the god Moloch there.
Gerizim	The holy mountain of the Samaritans in central hill country of the former northern kingdom of Israel. The mountain was once the site of their temple but this was destroyed by John Hyrcanus I in *c.* 110 BCE.
Gethsemane	A garden on the Mount of Olives outside Jerusalem.
Gnosticism	A current of thought within Christianity regarded as heretical by the school which was to become normative. One principal doctrine was that matter was evil and that liberation from this evil world could be attained through right knowledge (*gnosis* in Greek). The texts that are usually labelled 'gnostic' demonstrate significant theological variation.
Gospel	From Old English *godspel*, 'good news', which ultimately translates the Greek *euangelion*. In Mk 1.1 Mark begins his story of Jesus with this word. The term was later used as a name for books about the works and teachings of Jesus.
Hasmoneans	Another name for the Maccabees, a priestly dynasty who led a revolt against the Seleucid Empire in the time of Antiochus IV Epiphanes. Hasmonean dynasts ruled the land from *c.* 167 BCE up until the time Palestine became part of the Roman Empire in 63 BCE.
Herod Antipas	Son of Herod the Great. Ruled over Galilee and Perea as client ruler 4 BCE–39 CE. It was Herod Antipas who had John the Baptist executed.
Herodias	According to Mark, Herodias was the wife of **Philip the Tetrarch** (see below), but in terms of chronology this cannot be correct. From the works of Josephus it would appear that she was married to the son of Herod the Great with Mariamne II, whose name was also Herod

	(*Ant.* 18.136). Herodias's daughter Salome was, however, married to Philip.
Hillel	A Pharisaic teacher who, to a great extent, laid the foundations for the emerging rabbinic movement. He was an older contemporary of Jesus. He is known solely from rabbinic sources.
Idumea	A region to the south of Judaea inhabited by the Idumeans, a Semitic people. The region was conquered by John Hyrcanus I in *c.* 110 BCE. According to Josephus, the population was forced to convert to Judaism (*Ant.* 13.257). Herod the Great came from a leading family of Idumea.
Ignatius of Antioch	Bishop of Antioch (died *c.* 110 CE) who was taken to Rome as a prisoner. On the way he wrote seven letters, the so-called *Letters of Ignatius*.
John Hyrcanus I	High priest 134–104 BCE and regent. Belonged to the Hasmonean dynasty.
Josephus, Flavius	(37–95/96 CE) A priest from Jerusalem and a general during the revolt against Rome of 66–70 CE. After being taken prisoner, he was used by the Romans as a go-between at the siege of Jerusalem. He was rewarded for his efforts by the emperor Vespasian and thus was able to write several substantial books on Jewish history and the Jewish War.
Jubilees, book of	A book from the second century BCE that represents a rewriting of Gen. 1 to Exod. 19. The author alters the biblical text on the basis of his theological agenda, including in chronological matters. The work is presented as the words dictated to Moses by an angel on Mount Sinai.
Kittim	In Gen. 10.4 and 1 Chron. 1.7 Kittim is possibly a term for Greeks. In the pesher literature and the *War Scroll* from the Dead Sea Scrolls the term refers to eschatological non-Jewish foes, often the Romans.
leprosy	The Hebrew word traditionally translated as 'leprosy' (Lev. 13–14) includes various skin diseases, as well as mould on clothes and houses. Today these skin conditions are commonly called 'scale disease'. Leprosy proper, Hansen's disease, first spread to the Near East with the conquests of Alexander the Great in the fourth century BCE. In the Septuagint and New Testament the Greek word *lepra* is used, which can likewise describe a wide range of skin diseases.
Levi, Testament of	Part of the *Testaments of the Twelve Patriarchs*, in which each of Jacob's twelve sons delivers a speech on his deathbed. The *Testament of Levi* contains the speech ascribed to Levi, who is traditionally considered to be the ancestor of the priestly tribe.

Maccabees	The name of the family which was the driving force in the revolt against Seleucid rule that began in 166 BCE under Judas Maccabeus. See **Hasmoneans**.
Median Empire	A dominant regional power with its base in what is now Iran c. 680–549 BCE.
Melchizedek	A name possibly meaning 'righteous king'. According to the legend in Gen. 14.18-20, this was the name of the priest and king of Salem (Jerusalem) who blessed Abraham. He is also mentioned in Ps. 110.4. In the Dead Sea Scrolls Melchizedek is one name for the highest angel. In the letter to the Hebrews Melchizedek is seen as a model for Jesus, who is presented as a perfect, heavenly high priest.
mikveh	A Hebrew word meaning 'collection' (of water). The term for a pool used for Jewish ritual purification. A typical *mikveh* is hewn into rock, with steps leading down into the pool. Such pools were especially popular during the first century BCE and the first century CE.
Mishnah	A compilation of previously oral Jewish traditions concerning how the law, the Torah, should be interpreted. Some of the traditions it contains are attributed to rabbis of various periods, but it is unclear how reliable these reports about origins and dating are. The compilation was put together in the third century CE.
Mithras, cult of	A Roman 'mystery religion', whose adherents were initiated with secret, dramatic rituals. At the centre of the cult stood Mithras, a deity of Persian origin. Its rites included ritual bathing as well as holy meals, and they were viewed, especially in earlier scholarship, as a background to the Christ-believers' rituals of baptism and meals.
Nabateans	An Arabic-speaking trading nation. The Nabatean kingdom controlled the region to the south and east of the Dead Sea at the turn of the Common Era. The rock city of Petra in present-day Jordan was the Nabatean capital city.
Nag Hammadi	A city on the Nile in Egypt, close to the ancient town of Chenoboskion. In 1945 a library of Coptic texts was discovered here, texts believed to have been hidden when Bishop Athanasius of Alexandria condemned the use of non-canonical books in 367 CE. Among the texts thus preserved is a Coptic version of the *Gospel of Thomas*.
Neo-Babylonian Empire	Also known as the Chaldean Empire. A dominant regional power which had its base in what is now Iraq from 626 to 539 BCE.
Palestine	The name is derived from the Philistines, an ethnic group mentioned in the Hebrew Bible, often in hostile terms. In

	antiquity the region corresponding to present-day Israel could be referred to as Palestine by Jews and non-Jews alike. The name gained official status in 135 CE through the actions of the emperor Hadrian, who, with a view to erasing the Jewish homeland, elected to rename the province of *Iudaea* (Judaea) '*Syria Palaestina*'.
parousia	A Greek word meaning 'presence' or 'arrival'. It could be used, for example, for the ceremonial arrival of the emperor or his messenger at a city in the Roman Empire. Among Christ-believers it came to refer to the anticipated second coming of Jesus to judge the world.
Persian Empire	The first Persian empire, also known as the Achaemenid Empire, was a dominant regional power which had its base in what is now Iran *c.* 550–330 BCE.
Peter (Cephas)	The name of the best known of 'the Twelve' was in fact Simon son of Jonah (or John). According to the Gospels, it was Jesus who gave him the Aramaic alias Cepha(s), which was later 'translated' into Greek as Petros (Mk 3.16; Jn 1.42). This alias means 'stone' or 'rock', which the Gospel of Matthew explains as meaning that Peter would stand as the foundation of the church (Mt. 16.18). The historical reason why Peter was so called is not known.
Philip the Tetrarch	Son of Herod the Great. Ruled over the region east of Galilee as client ruler 4 BCE–34 CE. Also known as Herod Philip II.
Philo	A Jewish philosopher who lived in Alexandria *c.* 25 BCE–40 CE and who sought to combine Jewish theology with Greek philosophy. He frequently interprets biblical texts allegorically in order to find a deeper meaning behind the literal.
Pliny the Elder	A Roman general and geographer, died 79 CE. His magnum opus *Naturalis Historia* is a kind of encyclopaedia covering a multitude of subjects relating to humankind, nature, culture and philosophy.
Pliny the Younger	A Roman lawyer and author, died *c.* 112 CE. He was the nephew and adopted son of **Pliny the Elder**. He is best known for his many extant letters, many of which are from his correspondence with the emperor Trajan.
Plutarch	A Greek philosopher and author, died *c.* 120 CE. Best known for his long series of biographies of the Roman emperors and other eminent persons.
Pontius Pilate	Prefect of the Roman province of Judaea 26–36 CE. He is named in an inscription of the period from his place of residence, Caesarea Maritima, as well as in various literary sources, where he is presented as quite a tough political realist. Best known for sentencing Jesus to death.

GLOSSARY OF NAMES AND TERMS 239

Pseudepigrapha	The term is derived from a Greek word meaning 'falsely attributed', initially referring to a work which presents itself as having been written by a particular person who is not the real author. In New Testament scholarship, for example, the term is sometimes used to describe the letters that bear Paul's name but that do not derive from him. More commonly it is applied to non-canonical writings such as the *Testament of Abraham* and the *Books of Enoch*.
Q	The hypothetical document which many scholars suppose that the authors of Matthew's and Luke's Gospels made use of is known as Q, which likely originated as an abbreviation of the German *Quelle*, 'source, spring'. See also Chapter 3.
(Khirbet) Qumran	An ancient settlement immediately north-west of the Dead Sea. Most scholars agree that from the first century BCE the site was inhabited by an Essene community. The documents found in 1947 and onwards in nearby caves, the Dead Sea Scrolls, have provided scholars with new and invaluable information about Jewish life and thought at the turn of the Common Era. The settlement was destroyed around 68 CE at the latest, during the Jewish–Roman War.
Samaritans	Inhabitants of Samaria, the territory between Galilee in the north and Judaea in the south. Samaritans and Jews shared a common ethnic and religious origin, but the Samaritans differed from the Jews in having their cult centre on Mount Gerizim, not in Jerusalem, and they recognized only the Pentateuch (the five books of Moses) as sacred scripture. This ethnic group has survived into modern times; today it consists of around just 750 individuals.
Sanhedrin	This is a Hebrew word but it is originally from Greek and means 'council'. The Sanhedrin in Jerusalem exercised legislative, executive and judicial power in matters of religion.
Saul	The first king of Israel and Judah, according to the Hebrew Bible. He is thought to have reigned at the end of the eleventh century BCE, but historical information about him is highly uncertain.
Seleucid Empire	A dominant regional power with its base in Syria in the period 312–63 BCE. It was formed when the empire of Alexander the Great was divided after his death in 323 BCE. In time three great Hellenistic states emerged: the Seleucid Empire, the Ptolemaic Empire in Egypt, and Macedonia.
Septuagint	The ancient Greek translation of the Hebrew Bible which originated in Alexandria. The name means 'seventy' in Latin, and derives from the legend that tells

	of how the translation was the work of seventy Jewish men. Hence the abbreviation LXX (70 in Roman numerals). The Septuagint also contains the Apocrypha, or deuterocanonical writings, which did not make it into the Jewish canon.
Shammai	A Jewish jurist of the Pharisaic school, died c. 30 CE. He founded a school of legal interpretation which grew to compete with the school of Hillel, and which usually adopted what is regarded as the stricter position.
shekel	A currency of silver coins minted in Tyre. The Jewish temple tax consisted of half a shekel (roughly corresponding to two days' wages) to be paid every year by all Jewish men aged twenty or older.
Sheol	The 'underworld', which in the Hebrew Bible was originally the dreary region of the dead where both the righteous and the wicked were thought to go when they died. The first clear Jewish attestation of the concept of the resurrection of the righteous is found in the book of Daniel, from the 160s BCE.
Simon bar Giora	Rebel leader during the Jewish–Roman War in the 60s CE.
Sirach, Wisdom of	A Jewish book in the wisdom tradition from c. 200–180 BCE, written by a teacher in Jerusalem by the name of Jesus son of Eleazar son of Sirach (Ben Sira). Includes an introduction by the grandson of Ben Sira, who translated the work from Hebrew to Greek. The book is also known as Ecclesiasticus.
Solomon	One of the Hebrew Bible's most learned figures, son of David and ruler of the united kingdom of Israel and Judah in his own right. Little is known about the historical Solomon of the tenth century BCE. In later times several literary works were written that used his name: Proverbs and the Song of Songs in the Hebrew Bible; the Wisdom of Solomon, one of the apocryphal or deuterocanonical books; the *Psalms of Solomon*, which contains expressions of the hope that the Messiah will be a political liberator; and the *Testament of Solomon*, which presents Solomon as an exorcist.
Tacitus	A Roman senator and historian, died c. 118 CE. Best known for his history of the Roman Empire up to 70 CE.
Talmud	An extensive compilation of expositions of Jewish law. The Talmud is composed of the Mishnah and of commentary on the Mishnah, known as the Gemara. It is extant in two versions with different temporal and geographical origins: the Jerusalem Talmud, which reached its final form in c. 400 CE in Galilee; and the Babylonian Talmud, which in its main outlines was compiled in c. 500 CE by Jews living in what is now Iraq.

targum	A translation of the Hebrew Bible into the Aramaic vernacular. The need for targums arose when Hebrew was no longer widely spoken by Jews. The targums are closely associated with liturgy and teaching in synagogues, and some targums exhibit very free and interpretive renderings of the original Hebrew.
Tarsus	A major city of trade and scholarship in Cilicia, in what is now Turkey. A credible report in the book of Acts mentions Tarsus as the birthplace of Paul.
Testament (New; Old)	A word of Latin origin corresponding to the Greek word for 'covenant' or 'contract'. A number of covenants between God and the people of Israel are mentioned in the Hebrew Bible. According to Paul, God had concluded a new covenant with humanity through Jesus' death and resurrection (1 Cor. 11.25; 2 Cor. 3.6). It was only later that the 'New Testament' began to be used as a term for the writings that were thought to have been written by the apostles or their disciples, and, by analogy, the Holy Scriptures of Judaism came to be known as the 'Old Testament' among Christians. In modern scholarship, the writings that are sacred to both Jews and Christians are often referred to as 'the Hebrew Bible' instead.
Theodosius I	Roman emperor 379–395 CE. The last to rule over the entire Roman Empire. Introduced Christianity as the state religion.
Thomas, Gospel of	A collection of individual sayings attributed to Jesus. The text was originally composed in Greek, most likely in the mid-second century CE. Parts of the Greek version have been recovered, but a more complete text is represented by the Coptic translation, and revision, that was found at Nag Hammadi. Although the *Gospel of Thomas* displays certain gnostic tendencies it is not an expression of outright Gnosticism.
Tiberius Alexander	Roman procurator of Judah *c.* 46–48 CE.
Torah	The Pentateuch, or five books of Moses, is called the Torah in Hebrew, literally meaning 'instruction'. But the term Torah can also have a wider meaning that includes authoritative oral traditions. Thus the rabbis make a distinction between the Written Torah and the Oral Torah. The Torah is often referred to as 'the Law', in part because the Septuagint uses a Greek word meaning just that to translate the Hebrew term. The same Greek term is also used throughout the New Testament.
Tosefta	An Aramaic word meaning 'addition'. The Tosefta is a supplement, of sorts, to the Mishnah, containing similar traditions of legal interpretation.

Vespasian	Roman emperor 69–79 CE. After leading the Roman forces for the greater part of the Jewish–Roman War, he proclaimed himself emperor. His son Titus brought the siege of Jerusalem to an end, finally capturing the city.
Vitellius (Lucis Vitellius)	Roman legate of Syria 36–37 CE. His actions contributed to Pontius Pilate being removed from office. He was the father of the better-known Vitellius, who was Roman emperor in 69 CE.

INDEX

Hebrew Bible
Genesis
  1 236
  1.28 161
  2.2 18
  2.24 126
  5.21-32 235
  6.1-5 31
  9.4 221
  10.4 236
  14.17-20 56
  14.18-20 237
  17–18 89
  19.1-11 52
  29–30 159
  49.1-28 109
  49.24 92
Exodus
  8.19 143
  11.19 29
  12.8-9 40
  12.46 207
  16.22-23 153
  19 236
  19.9-25 38
  19–24 34, 30
  20 148
  20.5 30
  20.7 151
  20.8 18
  20.8-11 152
  20.12 164
  20.13 150
  20.14 150
  21.17 164
  21.24 152
  22.10-11 126, 151
  22.22-23 159
  29.38-42 38
  29.40 39
  29.43-46 38
  31.14 153
  33.22 77
  34.14 30
  34.21 153
  35.2 153
  35.2-3 153
Leviticus
  1–7 38
  3.1 40
  4.3 54
  11 29, 165, 166
  12 36, 39, 160
  13 32, 163
  13.45-46 131
  13–14 236
  14 37
  15 36, 37, 166
  15.13 23
  15.18 35, 161
  15.19 35
  15.19-24 36
  17.2 221
  17.8-9 221
  17.10-16 221
  17–18 221
  18.6-18 158
  18.6-29 221
  18.16 94
  19.9 148
  19.9-18 148
  19.12 151
  19.18 125, 148
  20.21 94
  23.7 195
  24.5-9 38
  24.16 201

Numbers
    5.11-31 126
    11.16 200
    12 91
    15.32-36 153
    19 36
    19.11-22 187
    19.14 163
    19.14-22 37
    28–29 38
Deuteronomy
    4.19 53
    6.4-5 125, 147
    6.4-9 148
    6.6 148
    6.9 148
    10.12 148
    16.16 186
    18.15 56
    18.15-18 55
    18.18 173
    22.13-21 160
    23.21-22 151
    24.1 158
    24.1-3 126
    24.1-4 158
    24.4 158
    25.5-6 94
    32.8 51
Joshua
    5.14 52
Judges
    11.29-40 95
1 Samuel
    8.7 117
    12.12 117
    16 6
    16.14-23 141
    18.10-11 141
    19.9-10 141
    21 154
    21.1-9 154
    24.6 54
2 Samuel
    2.4 183
    5.1-3 183
    5.6-7 183
    7.13b-14 54
    12.1-12 120

1 Kings
    1.32-40, 44 189
    17.8-24 172
    19.16 103
    19.20 104
2 Kings
    1.8 89
    1.12 172
    2 89
    2.8 172
    7.11-16 182
    15.5 131
1 Chronicles
    1.7 236
2 Chronicles
    26.21 131
Esther
    2.9 95
    5.3 6, 95
    7.2 95
Psalms
    2.1 56
    2.7 7, 54
    8.3-4 53
    22 206
    22.1 207
    22.2 71
    22.7 206
    22.8 206
    22.18 206
    22.23-32 207
    22.27 207
    29 51
    31.6 71
    47.7-8 118
    77.20 77
    82 51
    86.8 30
    86.15 32
    89.27 54
    89.30 54
    93 117
    97 117
    99 117
    105.15 54
    110 181
    110.1 181
    110.4 56, 237
    113–118 189

   116.5 32
   118 188, 189
   118.25 188
   118.26 189
   146.7-8 55
Proverbs
   7 160
   31.10-31 228
Ecclesiastes
   5.5 151
   8.2 151
Isaiah
   1.24 92
   2.2-3 217
   5.1-7 120, 178
   6.5 52
   6.9-10 178
   9.7 54
   10.17 92
   10.33-34 91
   11 54, 55
   14.9-11 42
   14.13-15 178
   20.1-6 192
   26.19 144
   29.13 164
   29.18 144
   30.27-28 92
   33.22 117
   33.23-24 144
   35.5 144
   35.6 144
   40.3 87, 88, 96
   42.1 178
   42.6 217
   42.7 18, 144
   42.18 144
   43.10 118
   43.16 77
   44.1-2 21, 178
   45.6 144
   49.3 178
   49.6 178, 217
   50.6 206
   52.7 117, 179
   52.13-53.12 178
   53 197
   56.7 191
   61.1 55, 144, 178, 179, 183
   61.6 183
   66.18-21 217
Jeremiah
   7.11 191
   7.34 99
   19.10 192
   21.12 92
   23.5 54
   33.14-17 182
Ezekiel
   15.1-8 120
   40–48 192
Daniel
   4.35 114
   7 56, 58
   7.2-12 174
   7.8 233
   7.10 51
   7.13 80
   7.13-14 57, 92 174
   7.16 52
   7.25 233
   8.10 114
   8.16 52
   9.27 193
   10 52
   10.8-9 52
   10.13 52, 174
   10.21 174
   11.7 114
   11.13 114
   11.31 193
   12.1 174
   12.2-3 122
   12.11 193
Joel
   2.28-29 92
Zephaniah
   3.15 117
Zechariah
   4.14 55
   9 54
   9.9 188
   11.12 199
   12.10 207
   13.4 89
   13.7 198
   14.9 217
   14.16-19 217
   14.21 191

Malachi
  3.1 87
  4.1 92
  4.1-3 93
  4.5 89, 93, 96

Apocrypha or Deutero-Canonical Books
Tobit
  3.17 52
  4.15 149
  5.4 52
Sirach (Ben Sira)
  9.3-8 160
  23.9 126
  23.9-11 151
  25.13-24 157
  25.25-26 157
  26.7 157
  38.1-15 133
  38.15 132
  48.10 89, 109
  50.11-21 39
1 Maccabees
  1.41-58 193
  2.39-41 153
  4.36 189
  13.51 189
2 Maccabees
  6.18-7.41 197, 198
  10.7 189

New Testament
Matthew
  1.16 8
  2.1-18 72
  2.13-23 6
  3.3 88
  3.4 89
  3.5 89
  3.7 91
  3.7-10 73
  3.9 92
  3.10 91
  3.11-12 92, 93
  3.14-15 86
  3.16 172
  4.1-11 71, 73
  4.12 86
  4.13 22
  5–7 71, 72, 124
  5.3 178
  5.3-12 70, 123
  5.9 100
  5.17 149
  5.17-18 150
  5.20 150
  5.21-22 150
  5.23 191
  5.27-28 150
  5.31-32 150, 158
  5.32 69, 74, 75, 157
  5.33-37 126, 151
  5.38-39 152
  5.39-44 125
  5.44 148, 149
  5.45 125
  5.48 124
  6.9-13 70, 115
  6.12 32, 124
  6.19 123
  6.24 123
  6.25-34 123
  7.12 122, 149
  8.5-13 73
  8.11 103, 116, 119
  8.11-12 73
  8.19-20 123
  8.20 173, 174, 176
  8.21-22 78
  8.22 104
  8.28-34 142
  9.9 16
  9.9-10 70
  9.27 8
  9.29 162
  10 72, 73
  10.2-4 108
  10.6 119
  10.23 173
  10.35 230
  10.37 10
  10.39 123
  11.2 86
  11.2-3 177
  11.2-6 104
  11.3 92, 173
  11.4-5 55, 56

11.4-6 144
11.7-11 73
11.8 89
11.14 89
11.16-19 94
11.18 102
11.18-19 88, 94
11.19 102, 121
11.20-24 121, 178
11.46 177
12.1-8 154
12.9-14 154
12.11-12 156
12.23 181
12.24 44
12.27 141
12.28 143
12.38-42 136
13 72
13.24-30 120
13.32 120
13.33 106, 120
13.43 195
13.44 120
13.47-50 24
13.49 52
13.55 11
13.58 71
14.1-12 95
14.4 94
15.1-20 164
15.11 165
15.20 166
15.21-28 119
15.22 181
15.24 119
15.28 137
16.1-4 136
16.13 176
16.17-19 213
16.18 238
16.28 194
17.20 137
18 72
18.10 52
18.12-13 73
19.3-9 157
19.7 69
19.8-9 158

19.9 74
19.10 75
19.12 160
19.28 108, 195, 197
19.30 17, 122
20.16 122
20.30-31 181
21.4-5 188
21.9 188
21.21-22 137
21.31 107, 121
21.43 225
21.45 44
22.2-14 121
22.10 121
22.21 64
22.32 20
22.40 149
23.2-3 44
23.5 148
23.12 122
23.13 44
23.21 32
24–25 72
24.42-44 73
24.43 116
24.44 176
25.1-12 120
25.46 195
26.6 188
26.15 199
26.26-29 196
26.57 200
26.57-59 200
26.57-68 43
26.64 170
27.1 200
27.3-10 199
27.19 203
27.24 200
27.24-25 203
27.28-31 205
27.39 206
27.41-43 206
27.46 71
27.53 2
27.55 2
27.57 105
28.1-15 214

28.2-3 52
28.10 19, 213
28.16 213
28.16-20 213
Mark
  1.1 170, 235
  1.3 88
  1.4-5 90
  1.4 90
  1.5 101
  1.6 89, 97, 102
  1.7 87, 92
  1.9 86
  1.10-11 86
  1.10 172
  1.11 6, 77, 170
  1.14-15 117
  1.14 86
  1.15 116
  1.16-18 24
  1.16-20 104
  1.19-20 24
  1.21 18 25
  1.21-28 32
  1.21-34 105
  1.22 118
  1.23 139
  1.24 141, 170
  1.25 139
  1.26 139
  1.27 139
  1.28 32-34, 136
  1.28 101
  1.29-31 160
  1.29 24
  1.30-31 21
  1.31 106
  1.34 170
  1.40-45 32, 163
  1.41 139
  1.44 163, 191
  2.1 22
  2.1-12 132, 145
  2.4 23
  2.5 137, 178
  2.10 176
  2.14 16, 104
  2.14-15 70
  2.15-16 102

  2.15-17 121
  2.18 88, 102, 104, 107
  2.18-19 121
  2.23-28 153
  2.25-26 32
  2.26 154
  2.28 176
  3.11 170
  3.12 170
  3.14 108
  3.16 238
  3.1-6 154, 155, 156
  3.4-5 155
  3.6 44, 123
  3.16-19 108
  3.21 143
  3.22 44, 118, 135, 143
  3.31-35 32
  4.1 101
  4.4-9 18
  4.11 178
  4.26-29 120
  4.30-32 120
  5.1-20 78, 131, 142
  5.5 131, 140
  5.7 139, 141
  5.8 139
  5.11-13 136
  5.19 136
  5.22 18
  5.23 162
  5.25-26 133
  5.27-29 133
  5.30 135
  5.34 137
  5.35-40 163
  5.35-43 140
  5.36 137
  5.41 9, 139
  6.1-5 18
  6.2-4 85
  6.3 9, 11, 106
  6.5 71, 85
  6.6 136
  6.7-13 107
  6.17-29 95
  6.18 94
  6.20 95
  6.29 86

6.30-44 25
6.32-44 101
6.34-44 77
6.45-52 77, 136
7 164, 166
7.1-23 163
7.2 5, 107
7.3-4 163
7.5 118, 164
7.6-8 164
7.9-13 164
7.15 165, 166
7.18-23 165
7.19 165
7.24-30 119, 191
7.32-35 135
7.32-36 71
7.33 162
7.34 139
8.1-10 25
8.11-12 44, 136
8.15 123
8.22-25 140
8.22-26 71, 162
8.27-29 170
8.30 170
8.31 170, 171, 176, 211
8.31-33 208
8.35 123
8.38 176
8.38-9.1 176
9.1 113, 114, 226
9.7 77
9.9 173
9.20-29 139
9.22 140
9.23-24 137
9.25 139
9.29 138
9.31 171, 176, 211
9.35 122
9.43 123
10.2 44, 157
10.2-9 158
10.2-12 157
10.2-19 159
10.6-9 126
10.11-12 69, 74
10.17-22 106, 123

10.17-27 32
10.23-25 123
10.28-31 32, 123
10.31 122
10.32-33 176, 211
10.33-34 171
10.35 196
10.42-44 32
10.45 173
10.46 131
10.47-48 136, 181
10.47 8
10.52 137
11.8 188
11.9-10 189
11.11 190
11.12-14 78, 136
11.20-24, 136
11.12 187
11.15-17 30, 33, 190
11.18 118
11.22-24 137
11.25 124
11.27–12.12 44
11.30-33 94
12.1–9 178
12.13–7 44
12.25 160
12.26 31
12.28-31 147
12.29-31 125
12.32 149
12.35-37 8, 181
12.35 33, 35
12.42-44 159
13 32
13.1 33, 192
13.2 33
13.7-8 116
13.14-20 116
13.8 53
13.14-19 193
13.14 193
13.24-27 114, 174
13.26 53
13.26-27 57
13.27 176
13.31 44
14.2 195

14.3 188
14.7 8
14.10-11 198
14.12-17 195
14.17 195
14.18-21 81
14.22-24 197
14.22-25 196
14.25 117, 196
14.27 198
14.34-36 198
14.43 198
14.43-45 198
14.47 198
14.49 35
14.50 188, 198, 207
14.53-55 200
14.53-65 43, 200
14.54 198
14.57-58 192
14.58 100, 116, 192, 201
14.61 170
14.61-64 201
14.62 176, 194
14.65 205, 206
14.66-72 198
14.70-71 105
15.1 200
15.6-15 204
15.7 203
15.10 203
15.15 205
15.16-20 205
15.26 180, 202
15.27 203
15.29 192, 206
15.34 71
15.40-41 106, 187, 196
15.40 47, 106
15.40 207
15.42 209
16.1 106
16.1-8 214
16.7 213, 214
16.14-15 44
14.30 199
Luke
  1.5-25 38
  1.9 38

1.15 88
1.17 89
1.19 52
1.80 88
2.8-20 72
2.22-24 39
2.41-45 187
2.41-52 135
2.46-47 171
2.49 7
2.52 171
3.4 88
3.7-8 91
3.7-9 73
3.9 91
3.10-11 90
3.11 172
3.13-14 16
3.16-17 92
3.16-18 93
3.19 94
3.19-20 95
3.21 86
3.23 8, 11
4.1-13 71, 73
4.16 18
4.16-21 19
4.18-19 183
5.19 23
5.27 16
5.27-29 70
5.30 16
6 71
6.1-5 154
6.6-11 154
6.14-16 108
6.15 17
6.20 178
6.20-21 123
6.20-23 70, 123
6.21 16
6.27 148, 149
6.27-30 125
6.31 122, 149
6.35 125
6.36 124
7.1-10 73, 119
7.5 25
7.9 137

7.18-19 177
7.18-23 104
7.19 92, 173
7.22-23 55, 144, 177
7.24-28 73
7.31-35 94
7.34 121
7.36-50 44, 106
7.37-39 121
7.50 137
8.1-3 106
8.26-39 142
9.57-58 123
9.58 173, 174, 176
9.59-62 10
10 73
10.1-12 107
10.13-15 121, 178
10.18 143
10.25-37 16, 32
10.30-37 17
11.1 86, 107
11.2-4 70, 115
11.4 32, 124
11.16 136
11.17-20 143
11.19 141
11.20 121
11.29-32 136
11.37-54 44
12.8 173
12.22-32 123
12.33 123
12.39 116
12.39-40 73
12.40 176
13.10-17 19, 132, 154, 155
13.16 22
13.19 120
13.21 106
13.28-29 73
13.29 103, 116, 119, 226
13.29-30 196
13.30 122
13.31 123
13.32 14
14.1-24 44
14.1-6 154, 156
14.11 122

14.16-24 121
14.25-26 10
15.2 121
15.4-7 73
15.8 106
16.13 123
16.17 150
16.18 69, 75, 157
17.2 17
17.6 137
17.11 131
17.19 137
17.33 123
18.14 122
18.38-39 181
19.37 188
20.32 41
22.15-20 196
22.20 49
22.30 18, 108, 195, 197
22.43 32
22.50-52 138
22.52 198
22.66 200
22.68 170
23.4 203
23.6-12 200, 205
23.46 71, 207
23.55-24.12 214
24.16 37, 213
24.17 186
24.20-21 186
24.21 211
24.25-27 186
24.34 213
24.36-49 213, 215
24.42 25
24.48-49 213
24.50-52 214
John
 1.23 35, 88
 1.26-27 93
 1.28 87
 1.29 36, 195
 1.32-33 172
 1.32-34 86
 1.35 86
 1.35-39 86
 1.35-42 101

1.42 238
1.44 105
1.45 8
1.45-46 7
1.51 173
2.1-11 77
2.11 136
2.13-22 190
2.16 191
2.18-22 192
3.16 79
3.22 86
3.22-26 101
3.23 87
3.25-26 86
3.28 87
3.30 87
4.1-3 86, 101
4.9 16
4.52 21
5.2-3 105
5.2-7 134
5.14 132
6.59 25
6.67 108
6.70-71 81
7.22-23 152, 154
7.40-41 56
9.2 132
9.6 135, 162
9.8 131
9.14-16 152, 154
10.34 2
10.38 136
11.4 42, 136
11.39 140
11.47-48 118
11.49-51 98
11.50 202
12 188
12.1 187
12.1-8 106
12.12-13 188
12.12-19 188
12.13 189
13.1-2 195
13.3 171
13.5 195
13.26 166

13.27 81
13.38 199
15.12 148
18.2-3 198
18.10 198
18.12 200
18.12-18 198
18.12-24 200
18.13 14
18.14 202
18.24 200
18.28 195
18.29-31 202
18.36 100, 226
18.38 203
19.2-5 205
19.14 195
19.18 203
19.19 202
19.23-34 206
19.30 207
19.36 195
19.36-37 207
19.38 105
19.39-40 204
20.1-2 214
20.6-7 214
20.14 213
20.17 213
20.19-23 214
20.21-23 213
20.25 206
20.30-31 1
21.1-14 25
21.1-19 213
21.4 213
21.15-19 213
21.20-23 226
21.24 105
Acts of the Apostles
1.9-11 214
1.13 108
1.16 198
1.17-19 199
1.18 199
2.1-13 215
2.14-40 216
2.43 215
2.44 215

2.46-47 215
2.46-3.1 35
3.1 131
3.1-16 215
3.11 35
3.11-26 216
3.22-23 56
4.1 41
4.8-12 215
4.11-22 216
5.12-16 215
5.17 41
5.17-42 216
5.30-32 216
5.37 118
6.1-6 216
6.8-8.1 216
7.37 56
7.56 80
8.4-8 216
8.14-17 215
8.26-39 216
8.30-35 186
8.38 90
9.1-2 218
9.1-9 218
9.3-4 213
10.43 186
12 233
13.15 18
13.22-23 8
13.25 93
15.5 42, 220
15.13-21 215
15.19-20 221
15.36 221
16.14 220
16.14-15 40, 227
16.16-18 142
17.1-3 219
17.2-3 186
17.4 220
18.2 223
18.18-20 227
18.26 228
19.1-7 87
19.4 87
19.11-12 142
21.27-36 37

21.38 99
21.39 8, 218
22.3 218
22.6-7 213
22.6-11 218
23.6-7 41
23.8 41
26.9-18 218
26.13-14 213
Romans
  1.3 6, 8
  1.3-4 180
  1.4 6
  1.18-32 221
  6 219
  9.5 222
  13.1-2 229
  13.6-7 229
  14.17 226
  15.26 224
  16.1-2 228
  16.3-4 227
  16.7 228
1 Corinthians
  1.14-16 90
  2.2 199
  5.1-5 158
  5.7 197
  7 223
  7.8-9 230
  7.10-11 67, 69, 74, 157
  7.12-16 223
  7.15 80
  7.25 79
  7.29-34 230
  8.5 30
  8–10 221
  9.14 67
  9.20-21 222
  10.32 224
  11.2-16 228
  11.5 228
  11.10 51
  11.17-34 220
  11.23-25 67, 196
  11.23-26 196
  11.25 241
  14 223
  14.33-34 228

14.33-35 228
15.4 213, 214
15.5 108, 213
15.5-8 213
15.7 214
15.8 214
15.35 170
16.1-4 224
16.19 227
16.21 20
2 Corinthians
  3.6 241
  6.15 233
  8–9 224
Galatians
  1.13-14 218
  1.14 42, 222
  1.15-16 213, 218
  1.16 219
  1.18-19 224
  2.1-10 221
  2.9, 12 215
  2.10 224
  2.12 221
  2.21 222
  3.10-11 222
  3.22-23 222
  4.21-5.1 222
  4.22-30 49
Ephesians
  5.21-6.9 229
Philippians
  1.1 227
  3.5-6 218
Colossians
  2.22 164
  3.18-4.1 229
  4.15 227
1 Thessalonians
  1.9-10 222
  2.15 199
  4.14-15 217
  4.15 226
  4.16-17 41
  5.2-4 116
1 Timothy
  2 228
  2.11-12 228
  2.15 230
  3.1-7 227

Titus
  1.9 227
  2.1-10 229
Hebrews
  6.20 56
  7.14 181
  9.15-22 49
James
  1.17 159
  2.14-26 222
1 Peter
  2.10 225
  2.12 225, 229
  2.18-3.7 229
2 Peter
  3.3-4 226
  3.8-9 226
  3.10 116
Jude
  14-15 31
Revelation
  1 214
  2.1 52
  2.8 52
  2.12 52
  2.18 52
  2.20-23 228
  3.3 116
  7.13-17 52
  16.15 116

Dead Sea Scrolls
1QS Community Rule
  3.19-23 49
  3.4-9 91
  6.2-8 48
  8.1 110
  8.12-16 88
  9.11 55
  11.8 51
  11.10-11 50
1QSa Rule of the Congregation
  2.8-9 51
  2.11-22 55
1QH Hodayot/Thanksgiving Psalms
  8.29-30 50
  12.31-33 124
1QM War Scroll
  1.4-5 53

2.1-2 110
5.1 55, 110
4Q159 Ordinances 110
4Q174 Florilegium 182
    frag. 1-2 at 2-3 192
4Q246 Apocryphon of Daniel 182
    ii 1 54
4Q252 Commentary on Genesis A 182
4QSD 4Q265 Miscellaneous Rules
    fragment 6 4-8 156
D Damascus Document
CD (Medieval manuscripts of the
    Damascus Document)
    2.14-16 49
    3.12-17 50
    4.21-5.1 159
    7.20-21 55
    10.19 153
    10.22-23 154
    11.2 153
    11.13-17 156
    13.17 157
    15.1-5 152
    16.14-15 164
    [MS B] 19.5-6 50
    [MS B] 20.33-34 50
4Q266 Damascus Document fragment
    9 iii 157
4Q270 Damascus Document fragment
    7 159
4Q285 Sefer ha-Milhamah/Rule of
    War 55
4QMMT Miqsat Ma'aseh ha-Torah/
    Letter on Works 161
    C 21 50
4Q521 Messianic Apocalypse 144, 179
11Q11 Apocryphal Psalms 139
11Q13 Melchizedek 92, 179

Josephus
Antiquities of the Jews
    4.213 148
    4.304 40
    8.46-48 141
    13.171-173 40
    13.257 236
    14.403 12
    15.374 192
    17.41-43 98

17.217 187
17.271-285 183
17.289-296 13
17.306-308 16
18.12-22 40
18.14 41
18.17 41
18.18-22 45
18.23 118
18.27 15
18.55-59 14
18.60-62 14, 204
18.63-64 65, 199
18.85-89 204
18.95 204
18.93-94 14
18.117 89, 90
18.136 236
20.102-103 202
20.200 65
20.200-201 202
20.219 33
Against Apion
    2.102-105 35
    2.164-166 117
    2.165 40
    2.282 220
Life of Josephus
    10–11 40, 88
    191 43
The Jewish War
    1.88 194
    1.110 43
    1.112 43
    1.414 13
    2.118-119 40
    2.119 49
    2.119-161 45
    2.119-166 40
    2.135 152
    2.159 98
    2.161 159
    2.162 43
    2.165 41
    2.169-74 14
    2.175-77 14
    2.197 38
    2.409-410 38
    3.42 18

3.351-354 98
3.400-408 98
3.517-519 18
4.456 21
4.508 183
6.289-300 76
6.290 187
6.297-298 76
6.300-301 98
6.300-309 202
7.45 220
17.42 42

Miscellaneous Roman, Early Jewish and Christian Literature
Justin Martyr, 1 Apology
  65.3-4 197
  67.5 197
Didache
  9–10 197
Gospel of Thomas
  53 64
  86 173
  100.2 64
Infancy Gospel of Thomas
  2.1 135
  3.1-3 135
Pliny the Elder, Natural History
  53 45
Ignatius, Letter to the Smyrnaeans
  13.2 228

Philo
De decalogo
  82–95 152
Hypothetica
  7.6 149
Quod omnis probus liber sit
  75–91 45
  84 151
  87 49
De specialibus legibus
  2.1-38 152
  3.9 160
Legatio ad Gaium 30
  28 203

Pseudepigrapha
1 (Ethiopic) Enoch
  46.1-3 175
  48.6 175
  52.4 175
  89.73 193
  90.28-36 192
4 Ezra
  7.28-35 175
  13.1-13 175
  13.25-52 175
Jubilees
  1.15-18 192
  5.12 151
  23.21 193
  23.9-12 126
  23.26-29 126
  50.12-13 153
Psalms of Solomon
  17 55
  17.21-22 182
  17.26 110
  17.28 110, 119
  17.31 119
  17.32 182
  17.44 110
  17–18 182
Testament of Benjamin
  9.2 192
Testament of Issachar
  3.5-6 160
Testament of Levi
  16.1 193

Rabbinic Literature
Mishnah tractate Gittin
  9.10 158
Mishnah tractate Pesahim
  5.5 40
Mishnah tractate Rosh Hashanah
  2.5 157
Mishnah tractate Sanhedrin
  1.6 200
Mishnah tractate Yoma
  7.4 38
Babylonian Talmud tractate Shabbat
  31a 149
Tosefta tractate Sanhedrin
  11.7 203
Tosefta tractate Shabbat
  2.7 157
  9.22 155
  15.14-15 157
  15.15 157

www.ingramcontent.com/pod-product-compliance
Ingram Content Group UK Ltd.
Pitfield, Milton Keynes, MK11 3LW, UK
UKHW020912201125
465223UK00004B/416